The
NAPA & SONOMA
Book
A Complete Guide

Courtesy Sonoma County Convention & Visitors Bureau

THE
NAPA & SONOMA
BOOK

A Complete Guide

THIRD EDITION

TIM FISH and PEG MELNIK
With Chris Alderman and Jean Saylor Doppenberg

Berkshire House Publishers
Lee, Massachusetts

On the Cover and Frontispiece:
Front Cover: *Mustard vines in California's Wine Country,* © Brenda Tharp/F-Stock, Inc.
Frontispiece: *Wine Country,* Courtesy Sonoma County Convention & Visitors Bureau
Back Cover: *Gourmet pizza in Calistoga,* © 1996 Louisa Preston; *The blessing of the fleet in Bodega Bay,* © Thomas Hallstein/Outsight; *The Raford House Bed & Breakfast in Sonoma,* © 1996 Louisa Preston.

The Napa & Sonoma Book: A Complete Guide
Copyright © 1992, 1995, 1996 by Berkshire House Publishers
Cover and interior photographs © 1992, 1995, 1996 by Chris Alderman and other credited sources

Library of Congress Cataloging-in-Publication Data
Fish, Timothy, 1959-
    The Napa & Sonoma book: a complete guide / Timothy Fish and Peg Melnik,
  with Chris Alderman and Jean Saylor Doppenberg. — 3rd ed.
      p.   cm. — (The great destinations series. ISSN 1056-7968)
    Includes bibliographical references and index.
    ISBN: 0-936399-82-1
    1. Napa County (Calif.) — Guidebooks. 2. Sonoma County (Calif.) —
  Guidebooks. I. Melnik, Peg. II. Title. III. Series.
  F868.N2F57 1996   96-31084
  917.94'18—dc20   CIP

ISBN: 0-936399-82-1
ISSN: 1056-7968 (series)

Editors: Mary Grace Butler and Sarah Novak. Managing Editor: Philip Rich. Original design for Great Destinations™ series: Janice Lindstrom. Cover design: Jane McWhorter. Map revisions and new maps by Ron Toelke Associates. Production services by Ripinsky & Company.

Berkshire House books are available at substantial discounts for bulk purchases by corporations and other organizations for promotions and premiums. Special personalized editions can also be produced in large quantities. For more information, contact:

Berkshire House Publishers
480 Pleasant St., Suite 5, Lee, MA 01238
800-321-8526

Manufactured in the United States of America
10 9 8 7 6 5 4 3

No complimentary meals or lodgings were accepted by the authors and reviewers in gathering information for this work.

The GREAT DESTINATIONS™ Series

The Berkshire Book: A Complete Guide
The Santa Fe & Taos Book: A Complete Guide
The Napa & Sonoma Book: A Complete Guide
The Chesapeake Bay Book: A Complete Guide
The Coast of Maine Book: A Complete Guide
The Adirondack Book: A Complete Guide
The Aspen Book: A Complete Guide
The Charleston, Savannah & Coastal Islands Book:
  A Complete Guide
The Gulf Coast of Florida Book: A Complete Guide
The Central Coast of California Book : A Complete Guide
The Newport & Narragansett Bay Book: A Complete Guide
The Hamptons Book: A Complete Guide
Wineries of the Eastern States

The Great Destinations™ series features regions in the United States rich in natural beauty and culture. Each Great Destinations™ guidebook reviews an extensive selection of lodgings, restaurants, cultural events, historic sites, shops, and recreational opportunities, and outlines the region's natural and social history. Written by resident authors, the guides are a resource for visitor and resident alike. The books feature maps, photographs, directions to and around the region, lists of helpful phone numbers and addresses, and indexes.

Contents

CHAPTER ONE
Wine Country Chronicles
HISTORY
1

CHAPTER TWO
On The Road
TRANSPORTATION
14

CHAPTER THREE
The Keys to Your Room
LODGING
25

CHAPTER FOUR
La Dolce Vita
CULTURE
72

CHAPTER FIVE
Bon Appetit!
RESTAURANTS & FOOD PURVEYORS
107

CHAPTER SIX
On the Vine
WINERIES
165

CHAPTER SEVEN
On the Run
RECREATION
233

CHAPTER EIGHT
For the Sport of It
SHOPPING
275

CHAPTER NINE
Just the Facts, Ma'am
INFORMATION
294

Acknowledgments

The fingerprints of many people are all over this book. Particular thanks to Chris Alderman, our chief photographer, who for our first edition also wrote the *Recreation* chapter, a blueprint that served us well for future editions. Thanks likewise to Jean Saylor Doppenberg, who wrote the *Lodging* and *Transportation* chapters for the first edition, which proved invaluable for both updates. Another source of comfort was our fact-checker Chris Kent, who also helped research the *Shopping* chapter and was a key reviewer of restaurants and lodgings. Thanks also to Ron Toelke Associates for our fine maps.

Where would we be without our team of restaurant and lodging reviewers? Researchers included Chris and Theresa Coursey, Tom and Nita Chorneau, Loren and Jean Doppenberg, Maureen and John Geary, Paul Goff, Diane Holt, Chris Kent, Michele D. McFarland, Diane Peterson and Chris Smith, Barbara and Mario Santi, Randi Rossman and Rick Thomas, Annie Wells and John Malinowski, Betsy Wing, and Jon Bashor.

Numerous organizations proved to be great resources. The Napa County Historical Society and Sonoma County Museum supplied many of our priceless historic photographs. The chambers of commerce of Calistoga, St. Helena, and Napa as well as the Sonoma County Convention and Visitors Bureau and the Sonoma Valley Visitors Bureau provided detailed and valuable information.

Finally, particular thanks to Jean Rousseau, Philip Rich, Mary Grace Butler, and Sarah Novak at Berkshire House for pulling it all together.

We invite Wine Country travelers with comments about this guidebook to contact us directly at our e-mail address: FishTim1@aol.com.

Introduction

Eight million people a year vacation in Napa and Sonoma counties, so you may feel lost in the pack at times. It doesn't have to be that way. Our goal, as we put together the third edition of *The Napa and Sonoma Book*, was to become your personal travel planner. It was quite a challenge to improve a book that has already been called the best Wine Country guide by *The New York Times*, *The Los Angeles Times*, *San Francisco Focus* magazine, *The Orange County Register*, and *The California Grapevine*. But we gave it a shot and believe you'll be pleased with the results.

One thing has not changed since the first edition, of course. Napa and Sonoma counties are remarkable places. After a few days of sampling the cabernet sauvignons, zinfandels, and chardonnays, you may never go home. But as you read this book you'll see that there's far more to Napa and Sonoma than wine.

We are continually amazed at the beauty of this place. Merely driving to work remains a treat. There is a sense of mystery and strength in the surrounding mountains. The vineyards and fields take on a vibrant yellow in the spring as the wild mustard arrives with the fog and rain. In the summer, the vines grow bushy and green, weighted down with grapes, and in the fall they take on the delicate reds and yellows of autumn leaves. The hills rolling to the coast assume a shimmering green in the spring, reminding us unmistakably of Ireland. With its cliffs and pounding surf, the coastline is dramatic and jagged. It rivals even the famed Big Sur to the south.

With this Great Outdoors comes a whirl of recreational activities, everything from tennis to tide pooling. For those who prefer pampering to a strenuous hike among redwoods, Napa and Sonoma will indulge. Health spas soothe the body and soul. The restaurants of Wine Country insist that you can be healthy and luxurious at the same time, marrying the best of local meats and produce with just the right wine. The inns and bed & breakfasts appeal to every style, from easy country pleasure to posh extravagance.

How can you possibly know where to begin? That's where we come in. We've created a book to guide you through Wine Country with a minimum of fuss and a maximum of pleasure. We wish you a congenial and happy stay. Read on and enjoy.

Tim Fish and Peg Melnik
Santa Rosa, California

THE WAY THIS BOOK WORKS

This book is divided into nine chapters. Entries within each chapter are first divided into "Napa County" and "Sonoma County," and then each county is broken down geographically, according to the names of towns, moving generally from south to north.

Some entries include specific information, telephone numbers, addresses, business hours and the like, organized for easy reference in blocks in the left-hand column. All information was checked as close to the publication date as possible. Even so, since details can change without warning, it is always wise to call ahead.

For the same reason we have routinely avoided listing specific prices, indicating instead a range. Lodging price codes are based on a per-room rate, double occupancy during summer months. Off-season rates are often cheaper. Restaurant price ratings indicate the cost of an individual meal including appetizer, entrée, and dessert but not cocktails, wine, tax, or tip.

Price Codes

	Lodging	*Dining*
Inexpensive	Up to $75	Up to $10
Moderate	$75 to $125	$10 to $22
Expensive	$125 to $175	$22 to $35
Very Expensive	$175 or more	$35 or more

Credit cards are abbreviated as follows:

AE — American Express	DC — Diner's Club
CB — Carte Blanche	MC — Master Card
D — Discover Card	V — Visa

TOWNS IN NAPA AND SONOMA COUNTIES

Napa and Sonoma counties, you'll discover, resist being broken down into neat geographic areas. Easier to categorize is Napa Valley, with its strip of small towns and villages beginning in the south with the population center, the city of Napa. North from there is Yountville, a popular tourist mecca with shops and restaurants. The vineyard villages of Oakville and Rutherford come next, followed by St. Helena with its lovely downtown storefronts. Finally, at the county's warm northern end is the resort town of Calistoga. Sonoma

County is larger and more varied. Sonoma Valley, narrow and somehow separate, is home to the historical city of Sonoma and to the vineyard communities of Kenwood and Glen Ellen. In south-central Sonoma County is the river town of Petaluma, bordered on the north by the village of Cotati, and the ever-growing bedroom community of Rohnert Park. Santa Rosa is Sonoma County's largest city as well as its business and cultural hub. To the north, surrounded by vineyards, is the quiet community of Healdsburg. "West County," as locals call it, has a personality of its own. Its wild terrain makes it part "rugged individualist," but its popularity as an immigration spot for San Francisco's counter-culturalists during the 1960s makes it part "earth child," as well.

TOWN POPULATIONS

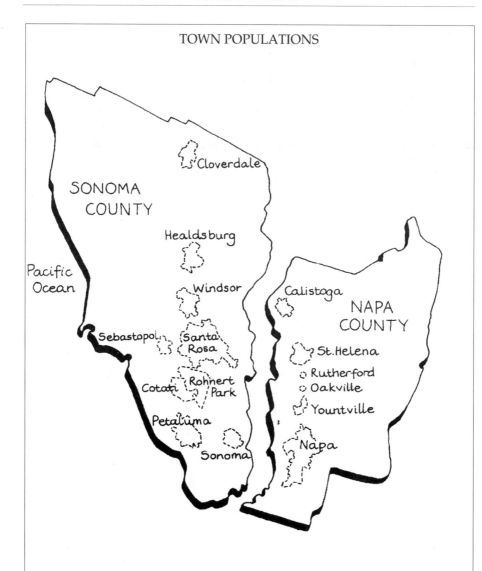

Napa County (118,200)

Calistoga (4,720)
Napa (66,300)
Oakville (209)
Rutherford (369)
St. Helena (5,600)
Yountville (3,520)

Sonoma County (420,586)

Cotati (5,484)
Healdsburg (9,799)
Petaluma (47,066)
Rohnert Park (39,019)
Santa Rosa (124,913)
Sebastopol (7,501)
Sonoma (8,696)
Windsor (17,342)

The
NAPA & SONOMA
Book
A Complete Guide

CHAPTER ONE
Wine Country Chronicles
HISTORY

History repeats itself; that's the one thing that's wrong with history.

— Clarence Darrow

Loggers topple a giant redwood tree near Guerneville, circa 1880.

Courtesy Sonoma County Museum

Why was it back in school that the worst, most monotonous teachers taught history? It didn't take long before all those dates and wars and proclamations made your brain glaze over like an Easter ham. Well, that history won't repeat itself here. It helps, of course, that Napa and Sonoma counties have a lively past, busy with fascinating people and places — and yes, dates and wars and proclamations, too. From the thunderous tremors that raised the land out of a prehistoric sea to the chic winery life of today, Napa and Sonoma counties have been twins, not identical but fraternal. They share similar origins but have grown into distinctly different siblings.

NATURAL HISTORY

A vast inland sea once spanned Napa and Sonoma counties, the salt water over the millennia nourishing the soil. The Mayacamas Mountains, as well as coastal and other mountain ranges, attest to the land's violent origins. Continental plates have fought for elbow room here for millions of years, col-

Powerful geysers and the occasional earthquake are the remnants of Northern California's volcanic era.

Courtesy Sonoma County Museum

liding and complaining, creating a tectonic furnace of magma and spewing forth volcanoes and towering mountain spines that now divide and surround the two counties.

The rolling hills of the Carneros mark the southern borders, where Napa and Sonoma counties meet the San Pablo Bay. Between them looms the Mayacamas range with the peaks of Mt. Veeder and Diamond Mountain. Low coastal hills border Sonoma on the west and the Blue Ridge shoulders Napa on the east. On the northern edge begins a vast stairstep of ranges that lead to the California border and beyond.

At 4,344 feet, Mount St. Helena is the area's tallest remnant of the volcanic era. Today, magma still simmers below the hills, producing the area's powerful geysers and Calistoga's soothing mineral water. Another vivid reminder occurs on occasion: earthquakes. The San Andreas fault runs up the center of Bodega Head on the coast and the more timid Rodger's Creek fault sits beneath Santa Rosa and Healdsburg.

When the ancient sea receded, it left bays and lagoons that became fertile valleys. The Napa and Russian rivers formed and for eons roamed back and forth over the face of the Napa and Santa Rosa plains, mixing the soil and volcanic ash. Napa Valley, five miles wide and 40 miles long, lies east of the Mayacamas. The land to the west was more vast, with dozens of smaller valleys: Sonoma the largest and most temperate, the parched Alexander and Dry Creek valleys to the north, and near the ocean the lush Russian River Valley, where redwoods the width of two-car garages began to grow. All the while the Pacific continued to pound western Sonoma, even today eroding its jagged coastline.

It's hard to imagine land more made-to-order for wine. The soil is rich with minerals from ancient oceans and volcanic ash, and the rocky nature of the land creates excellent drainage. Cool air masses from the Pacific meet the dry desert air from the east, creating a unique climate. Fog chills the mornings, then burns off as the days turn ideally warm, and as the sun sets the crisp air returns. And perhaps most important — rain. Typically, Napa and Sonoma counties are drenched from December through April, then things dry up until November. In all, a perfect spot for wine.

As humans were entering stage right, Napa and Sonoma counties already pulsed with life. Cougars, lynx, rattlesnakes, wolves, elk, and deer roamed along with the mightiest of all, the grizzly bear. Hawks, buzzards, eagles, and loons glided above the hillsides. Sturgeon and salmon swarmed in the rivers, and along the coast, whales, otters, and sea lions prospered and the Great White Shark lurked. Many have survived the arrival of man, though in reduced numbers. Others were not so lucky.

SOCIAL HISTORY

FIRST INHABITANTS

Brave the occasionally harrowing California freeway system and you'll inevitably see this bumper sticker: "California Native." How natives moan about newcomers. It's rather silly, of course, since people are such a recent addition to Northern California — 5,000 years, in the big scheme of things, is hardly enough time to unpack.

The earliest "newcomers" crossed the land bridge that once connected Asia and Alaska and wandered south. The first known inhabitants were the Pomo and Miwok tribes in Sonoma, and the Wappo who lived in Napa Valley and eastern Sonoma County. It was a plentiful place and allowed an unhurried way of life, the men hunting and women gathering berries, mussels, and other food. They gathered near the streams when salmon returned but were careful because the grizzly bear had a taste for salmon as well. Communities thrived. Most were small, but some villages had populations of 1,000 or more. Coastal Miwok used shells as money, and Pomo women achieved great expertise as basket makers. Pomo men lived away from their wives in communal lodges, which also served as ceremonial sweat houses as well as impromptu schools for boys. These early inhabitants gave special names to this land of theirs, names that remain today. Not that historians particularly agree on what the words mean. *Mayacamas* is a Spanish adaptation of an American Indian word that meant "howl of the mountain lion." *Napa*, depending on which story you believe, is Wappo for "grizzly bear" or "fish" or "bountiful place." *Petaluma*, a city in southern Sonoma County, may be Pomo for "flat back" or Miwok for "behind the hill" — both referring to the Sonoma Mountains and the flat

Baskets were a specialty of the women of the Pomo tribe. A 1905 photograph shows weaving technique; an exhibit of baskets is at the Sonoma County Museum.

Chris Alderman   Courtesy California Indian Library Collection

Petaluma plain. *Cotati,* another Sonoma County city, sounds poetic but its possible Pomo meaning is anything but romantic: "punch in the face." One name that didn't stick was *Shabakai* or "long snake" — that's what natives called the Russian River.

The first Europeans arrivals were heavily outnumbered. As many as 12,000 Wappo lived between Napa and Clear Lake to the north, and 8,000 Pomo prospered in what are now Sonoma, Lake, and Mendocino counties. That would quickly change.

Sonoma County was the first to be explored by the white man and, as explorers often seem to do, they stumbled onto it by accident. Lt. Francisco de Bodega y Cuadra was piloting his Spanish ship the *Sonora* along the coast in search of San Francisco Bay. Startled Indians paddled out in canoes to greet the *Sonora,* presenting the crew with elaborate feather and shell offerings. Rough seas and a damaged skiff prevented Bodega y Cuadra and crew from actually coming ashore but Bodega's name stuck somehow — Bodega Bay. The first expedition actually to land in Sonoma County came the following year when a small party of Spanish set out from their military outpost, or *presidio,* in San Francisco. Crossing the bay, they entered the mouth of the Petaluma River with the crazy notion that it ended up in Tomales Bay and the vast Pacific. (Always looking for shortcuts, those explorers.) It didn't, of course, so Lt. Fernando Quiros and his crew explored the Petaluma plain instead.

Russians and not the Spanish, however, were the first to establish an outpost in the area. By the early 1800s, the Russian-American Company, a private entity supported largely by imperial Russia, was expanding south after the Alaskan fur trade began to play out. In 1809, Ivan Kuskov and crew landed in Bodega Bay and scouted the area. They returned in 1812 and established a colony they called Rumiantsev. Exploring the coastline further, Kuskov selected a blustery bluff a few miles to the north and established Fort Ross the following year. The fort became the hub of Russian activity and Rumiantsev their major port. Though a prime location for fur trade, Fort Ross was not the most habitable place. Even today the bluffs overlooking the Pacific are fogged-in much of the year and the wind and dampness can be severe. One early visitor wrote: "It is so easy to catch cold here that even those inhabitants of Ross who were born here are sick almost every year." Later, ranches were established inland where the climate was more moderate, and the Russians grew much-needed grain and produce for their Alaskan settlements. The slaughter of sea otters, meanwhile, was ruthless and devastating. By 1821, the annual catch had dropped from hundreds to 32.

THIS LAND IS WHOSE LAND?

The Spanish weren't keen on the Russians hanging around just to the north. They were determined that their *presidio* in San Francisco would be the dominant force in the area. Even when Mexico declared independence from Spain in 1822, that didn't lessen the importance of the land north of San Francisco. California had been explored and established largely through the mission system, which began in 1769 as a way to civilize the "heathen" natives and convert them to Catholicism. It was also a way to establish a Spanish presence and, if the mission was successful, add greatly to the wealth and power of the church.

In 1823, Father Jose Altimira, an ambitious young priest at San Francisco's Mission Dolores, became convinced that a new mission was needed in the northern territory. Church authorities, cautiously considering their waning influence with the new Mexican government, balked, so Altimira turned to Don Luis Arguello, Mexican governor of California. Arguello saw an opportunity to thwart the Russians and approved the idea. Altimira set out that year with a party of 14 soldiers to explore the land north of the bay, from Petaluma to Napa to Suisun. According to legend, he marked his path by sowing mustard seed, which today blooms mint yellow every spring. Altimira was most impressed by Sonoma Valley, with its mild climate and tall trees.

On July 7, 1823, with a makeshift redwood cross, Altimira blessed the mission site in what is now the city of Sonoma, and the San Francisco Solano Mission was established. It was California's last mission and the only one estab-

Mission San Francisco Solano, as it may have appeared in the late 1820s.

lished under Mexican rule. In the early years, the mission was a great success and, despite having the reputation of being a harsh taskmaster, Altimira converted more than 700 Indians. In the fall of 1826, Indian laborers had just brought in a bountiful harvest when they staged a violent uprising. The mission was partially burned and Father Altimira fled for his life. He was replaced, the mission rebuilt, and in 1834 the mission was at the height of its prosperity when the Mexican Congress secularized the mission system and returned the acquired wealth to the people. It was the beginning of a new era.

Lt. Mariano Guadelupe Vallejo was an enterprising 28-year-old officer given the opportunity of a lifetime. The Mexican government sent him to Sonoma to replace the padres and also to establish a presidio and thereby thwart Russian expansion. Vallejo's ambitions were far greater than even that; he soon became one of the most powerful and wealthy men in California. As commandant general, Vallejo ruled the territory north of San Francisco and eventually set aside more than 100,000 acres for himself. He laid out the town of Sonoma around an eight-acre plaza — the largest in California — and for himself built the imposing Petaluma Adobe in 1836. It would be the largest adobe structure in Northern California and the first crop-producing rancho in the area.

It was Vallejo who pushed for the settlement of Napa and Sonoma counties. He found an ally in frontiersmen like George Yount. Others had been exploring Napa Valley since 1831, but Yount was the first with the notion of settlement. Befriending the already powerful Vallejo, Yount requested a land grant. Vallejo consented, but only after Yount converted to Catholicism and became a naturalized Mexican citizen. (Zoning laws were *really* tough then.) Yount never became an upstanding Catholic but he did establish the 11,814-acre Rancho Caymus in 1836, now the Yountville area of the central Napa County. About that same time, Vallejo was giving Sonoma land grants to family members, who established the rancho predecessors of Santa Rosa, Kenwood, and Healdsburg. Mexican influence continued to expand, particularly after 1839, when the Russians, having wiped out the otter population, gave up and sold Fort Ross.

Otters weren't the only inhabitants facing annihilation. Indian uprisings were not uncommon. Yount's house in Napa Valley was half-home, half-fortress. Vallejo occasionally led campaigns against rebellious Indians, but perhaps the most devastating blow came in 1837 when a Mexican corporal inadvertently brought smallpox to Sonoma Valley. The white man's disease all but wiped out Sonoma County's Indian population.

BEAR FLAG REVOLT

A sketch of the original Bear Flag.

Throughout the 1830s and early 1840s, American settlers streamed into California, lured by stories of free land. Mexican rule, however, denied Americans land ownership and this led to confrontations. Tensions peaked in 1846 when rumors spread that Mexico was about to order all Americans out of California. At dawn on June 14, 30 armed horsemen from Sacramento and Napa valleys rode into Sonoma. So began the Bear Flag Revolt, 25 eventful days when Sonoma was the capital of the independent Republic of California. Though significant, it was a revolution of almost comic proportions. Few soldiers still guarded the Sonoma outpost when the riders arrived, and the insurrectionists captured Sonoma without a single shot. Vallejo was roused from his bed and tied to a chair. One story has it that Vallejo tried sly negotiations with the rebels, freely offering rebel leaders his brandy and getting them drunk. Whether that's truth or folklore, the rebels prevailed. By noon, William Ide was elected leader of the new republic and a makeshift flag was hoisted to the top of a pole in the plaza. Saddle maker Ben Dewel crafted this flag for the new government, using a grizzly bear as the chief symbol. (Some said, however, it looked like a prized pig, not a bear.) The Bear Flag Republic had a short reign. In July, an American navy vessel captured the Mexican stronghold of Monterey and claimed California for itself. The Bear Flag boys immediately threw in with the Americans and four years later, in 1850, California became a state. The Bear Flag was eventually adopted as the state flag, in 1911.

The 1840s and 1850s were formative years for Napa and Sonoma counties. The Gold Rush of 1848 sent Americans by the thousands into the Sierras. Once powerful Sonoma almost became a ghost town, as residents left to pan gold and San Francisco achieved new significance. Other towns were born of miner commerce, such as the river ports of Napa and Petaluma.

A FIRST GLASS OF WINE

During this time, California's wine industry was conceived. Oats and wheat had been the primary crops of Sonoma and Napa counties, and sheep and cattle were also dominant. Vallejo and Yount grew the crude mission grapes brought north by the priests for sacramental wine, but it wasn't until 1856, when a Hungarian aristocrat named Agoston Haraszthy arrived in Sonoma, that the idea of a wine industry first took root. Haraszthy had attempted vineyards in San Diego and San Mateo and immediately recognized potential in the soil and climate of Sonoma and Napa valleys. Purchasing land and a winery northeast of the Plaza, Haraszthy established Buena Vista, "Beautiful View."

By 1858, Haraszthy had already surpassed Vallejo's accomplishments as a winemaker and even inspired a German apprentice named Charles Krug, who founded Napa Valley's first winery in 1861. That same year, convinced that the mission grape wasn't the only variety that would thrive in California, Haraszthy toured the wine regions of Europe and returned with cuttings from 300 classic varieties. It was his experimentations with these grapes that brought Haraszthy fame and earned him the title "Father of the California Wine Industry." Wineries began to spring up throughout Napa and Sonoma counties, the beginnings of wine dynasties such as Beringer and Inglenook that still live today.

The later part of the century was a boom period. Between 1850 and 1860, Napa county's population grew from 400 to almost 5,000. By 1869, Sonoma county's residents numbered 19,000. Petaluma, its largest city, was on its way to becoming the egg capital of the world. The burgeoning city of Santa Rosa had snatched the county seat from Sonoma in 1854, and with the completion of

The Beringer Brothers Winery in the late 1800s.

Courtesy Napa County Historical Society

the San Francisco and North Pacific train line in 1870, its destiny as the North Bay's largest city was established. It was the era of the highwaymen, as the legendary Black Bart and others robbed stage coaches around the North Bay. It was also an era of genius. Calling the area a "chosen spot," horticulturist Luther Burbank created varieties of fruit trees that brought the curious from around the country. And it was a time of pleasure. The resort town of Calistoga, founded by California's first millionaire, Sam Brannan, had become a vacation mecca. It was a time of creativity — Robert Louis Stevenson was inspired by a stay in Napa Valley and called its wine "bottled poetry."

The wine industry was small but growing in the late 1800s, though it shared the land with other important crops: hops, timber, and apples in Sonoma and wheat in Napa. Wine making and drinking in those days was anything but the chic activity it is today. Wine was sold almost exclusively in bulk, and often wasn't even blended until it reached its selling point. It was sold from barrels in saloons and stores with customers usually bringing their own containers. Gustave Niebaum of Inglenook and the old Fountaingrove Winery in Santa Rosa were among the first to bottle their own wine. Niebaum was also the first to use vintage dates on his wine and to promote "Napa Valley" on his labels.

Winemaking received two blows late in the century: the depression of the 1870s and phylloxera. The wine industry somehow weathered the economic hard times, though people like Haraszthy were not so lucky. His winery failed and business setbacks forced him to pursue dealings in Central America, where he met his death. Accounts say he was devoured by an alligator while crossing a Nicaraguan river. As for phylloxera, it attacked the vineyards of Sonoma and Napa counties with equal fervor.

Phylloxera, a microscopic voracious aphid that infests vine roots, first appeared in Europe in the 1860s, devastating the vineyards of Chateau Margaux, Chateau Lafitte, and others. Only by grafting their vines to American root stock were the Europeans able to save their classic wines. While the European wine industry recovered, California wine began to receive its first world notice. Sonoma County — not Napa — had been the undisputed capital of California wine, but fate and phylloxera would change all that. Phylloxera surfaced first in Sonoma Valley in 1875, and it slowly spread north to the Russian River. By 1889, Sonoma County's vineyards were in ruin when the French invited American wines to compete in the World's Fair. Napa Valley's wines scored well, raising Napa from obscurity to fame. Although phylloxera later came to Napa, the crown had been snatched. Growers tried everything to kill the bug, from chemicals to flooding their fields, but nothing worked. Eventually most were forced to pull out their vines. Some planted again, using resistant stock. Others gave up and planted fruit trees.

Not long after that, just after the turn of the century, famed writer Jack London began buying property in Glen Ellen. Saying he was tired of cities and people, he retired to the mountain retreat he called "Beauty Ranch," becoming the first of a long line of celebrities drawn to life in Wine Country.

Author Jack London in Glen Ellen, where his beloved Beauty Ranch is now an 800-acre state historic park.

Courtesy Jack London Library

A COMPLAINT FROM MOTHER NATURE

A new century brought new tragedy. Downtown Calistoga was leveled by a fire in 1901, and on April 18, 1906, what became known as the San Francisco Earthquake was equally as devastating in Sonoma County, particularly in Santa Rosa. Built on the loose foundation between two creek beds, Santa Rosa shimmied like gelatin, laying waste to the downtown and killing 100 people. (It didn't help that the brick buildings were poorly constructed.) Three large downtown hotels, one reporter wrote, "fell as if constructed of playing cards." It would be years before Calistoga and Santa Rosa recovered. San Fran-

---

Fruit of the Vine — Who's on First

Spanish missionaries are usually credited with bringing the first wine grapes to Sonoma and Napa, but that might not really be the case. Russian colonists at Fort Ross apparently imported vines from Peru as early as 1817, predating the Spanish by a good seven years. But the padres made up for it in volume. Father Jose Altimira, founder of Mission San Francisco Solano in Sonoma, planted 1,000 vines of mission grape, a rather coarse variety brought north from Mexico for sacramental wine.

Napa's first vineyard was planted in 1838 by Napa's first settler, George Yount. He brought mission vines east from Sonoma and made wine for his own use. It didn't take long before the entrepreneurial spirit set in, and Gen. Mariano Vallejo of Sonoma was the first to succumb. Vallejo became California's first commercial winemaker in 1841, eventually planting 70,000 vines. His wine sold under the name Lachryma Montis or "Tears of the Mountain," and became the toast of San Francisco. The winery was hardly a chic shop; his cellar, press, and sales outlet were housed in an army barracks. As for a tasting room . . .

The 1906 San Francisco earthquake was equally disastrous in Santa Rosa.

Courtesy Sonoma County Museum

cisco, of course, was destroyed, but a fact not often reported was the impact that event had on the California wine business. Many of the wineries stored their wine in the cooler climate of San Francisco and the quake destroyed almost two-thirds of the state's wine supply. The castlelike wineries of Napa County — Greystone Cellars, Beringer, Inglenook, and the others that harked back to the grandeur of Bordeaux — were spared the earthquake. But looming even more dangerously on the horizon was something called Prohibition.

Prohibition had been a growing movement in the United States since the turn of the century and, by 1917, a majority of states had outlawed alcohol. The United States Congress cinched it with the Volstead Act and, on January 1, 1920, Prohibition began. In Sonoma County alone, it left three million useless gallons of wine aging in vats. Sebastiani in Sonoma, Beaulieu in Rutherford, and a handful of others survived by making religious wine and medicinal spirits. Most wineries closed, almost 200 alone in Sonoma County and more than 120 in Napa Valley. By the time Prohibition was repealed in 1933, the Great Depression was on, followed by World War II. Recovery took time.

In 1937, the opening of a single bridge would forever change Sonoma County. It wasn't just any bridge, mind you, but the Golden Gate, spanning the mouth of the San Francisco Bay. Sonoma County became a thoroughfare in California's major north-south corridor, the Redwood Highway. And Sonoma County became its own destination — for example, the Russian River area, already a popular resort spot for San Franciscans, boomed.

After World War II, the vineyards of Europe were once again devastated and with the flow from Europe cut off, America turned to its own wine. The end of the war began the slow rebirth of the wine industry, and Napa and Sonoma began prospering in the 1950s and 1960s. By the early 1970s, a small tourist industry began forming around the wineries. Tourists were drawn to free wine tastings; restaurants and hotels began to appear. When corporations began eyeing the family-owned wineries, there was no question that Napa and Sonoma were ripe with potential *and profit*. Inglenook was the first to go corporate when United Vintners bought it in 1964; Beaulieu and others followed. In Napa Valley, new wineries began opening; some were small operations called "boutiques" in industry lingo, others more dramatic such as Sterling, a towering white villa perched on a hill south of Calistoga. Brash young winemakers such as Robert Mondavi promoted California wine like no one had in the past. By the 1970s, even the French, who so often had turned up their noses at California wine, saw California's potential, particularly for sparkling wine. Moet-Hennessy was the first to arrive, building Domaine Chandon in Yountville in 1975. Others were to follow.

Sonoma and Napa counties also became a favorite location of filmmakers. Alfred Hitchcock immortalized Bodega Bay in *The Birds*; thousands stop each year for a photo of one of Sonoma County's most recognizable landmarks, the Bodega School. Later, wine life at its most ruthless was portrayed in "Falcon Crest," which used Spring Mountain Vineyards in St. Helena as a backdrop.

Wine Country's greatest achievement and the final turning point for Napa and Sonoma came in the summer of 1976. At the now infamous Paris tasting (see p. 13) French wine experts for the first time picked several California wines over the classic wines of Bordeaux and Burgundy in a blind tasting. History was made, and Napa and Sonoma counties' prominence in the world of wine was set.

Today, Napa and Sonoma counties continue to grow, much to the chagrin of long-standing residents. More than eight million tourists arrive each year, drawn increasingly by wine, landscape, and climate. Santa Rosa is a small but blossoming metropolis of suburbs. Highway 29, the main road through Napa Valley, pulses with activity. How different it is from the days of grizzly bears and Wappo, yet Napa and Sonoma remain strikingly beautiful places.

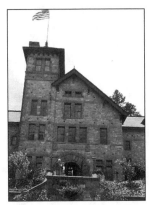

Historic Greystone Cellars, once home to Christian Brothers, is now the home of the Culinary Institute of America's west coast campus.

Tim Fish

Three renowned Americans meet in Santa Rosa in 1915: Thomas Edison, Luther Burbank, and Henry Ford.

Courtesy Sonoma County Museum

Upstaging the French

California and French wine lovers have a long-standing love-hate relationship — California loves French wine and France hates California's. We exaggerate, but only somewhat. California winemakers have always aspired to the quality and reputation of Bordeaux and Burgundy wines, while French enthusiasts ignored California. That is, until May 24, 1976.

It began with British wine merchant Stephen Spurrier, who had a taste for California wine but had a difficult time convincing his English and European customers. Spurrier hit upon the idea of staging a blind tasting of California and French wine, using the nine greatest palates of France. It was unheard of. California had beaten French wines in past tastings, but the judges were always American, and what did they know.

Judges knew they were sampling both French and American wines, though the bottles were masked. As the tasting progressed, the tasters began to point out the wines they believed were Californian and their comments about them grew increasingly patronizing. When the sacks were removed, the judges were mortified: the wines they thought classic bordeaux or burgundy were in reality Californian. Six of the 11 highest rated wines, in fact, were from California, almost entirely from Napa. The 1973 Stag's Leap cabernet beat 1970 vintages of Chateau Mouton-Rothschild and Chateau Haut-Brion, and a 1973 Chateau Montelena bested Burgundy's finest whites. France contested the findings, of course, but it was too late. California, particularly Napa, earned its place on the international wine map.

CHAPTER TWO

On the Road

TRANSPORTATION

Gridlock is still a rarity in Wine Country but it pays to know your way around. Hwys. 101 and 29, the main thoroughfares through Napa and Sonoma counties, are always hectic, especially on weekends. Of course, back when gridlock was an overturned ox cart and three gawking bystanders, Napa and Sonoma counties were easy places to get around. Not that the terrain doesn't conspire against smooth travel — any approach requires a minor mountain expedition.

Perhaps that's why the earliest explorers came by way of water in the late 1700s. The Sonoma coast was the area's first highway marker. And as sailing ships from around the globe made for the New World, the Napa and Petaluma rivers, which connect to San Francisco Bay, allowed early settlers a fast way inland.

Courtesy Sonoma County Museum

The opening of the Golden Gate Bridge in 1937 made Napa and Sonoma counties easily accessible to San Francisco.

By the mid-1800s, trails from the central valley would take travelers along Clear Lake to Bodega Bay, as well as south and east along the bay to Benicia. Carts and stagecoaches brought folks along primitive roads, stirring dust in the summer and churning mud in the winter.

By the 1860s, steamships were chugging up and down Napa and Petaluma rivers, but soon railroads steamed into the scene with names like "Southern Pacific" and "San Francisco North Pacific," and they connected the towns of the two budding counties to the East Bay.

The automobile changed everything, for better or for worse. Of course Sonoma County remained somewhat innocently isolated from San Francisco — it's a long loop around that Bay — until the big day in May 1937. That's when the Golden Gate Bridge opened a speedier route north, and Sonoma and Napa counties became one of *the* travel destinations for San Francisco, and for the world.

GETTING TO NAPA & SONOMA

BY CAR

Although planes and trains will bring you to the threshold of Wine Country, the vast landscapes and the romance of the region are best appreciated by automobile. There's no substitute for the convenience of having your own wheels so you can explore at your own pace. "Explore" is the operative word when traveling by car through this region. Your wanderings may be rewarded when you "discover" an off-the-road, up-and-coming winery or stumble upon a roadside diner with heavenly home cooking.

From the north: Travelers from the north can reach Wine Country via two major roadways — Hwy. 101 or I-5.

Hwy. 101 brings visitors into the heart of Sonoma County. One of the back roads not to be missed, especially if your destination is Napa Valley, is Hwy. 128 East, just north of Geyserville. To reach central Sonoma County, stay on Hwy. 101 southbound.

Travelers using I-5 must first connect with I-505, then can choose either scenic or fast routes. For scenery, exit at Hwy. 128 in Winters. Follow it west through the beautiful Howell Mountains, catching a panoramic view of Napa Valley. In a hurry? Connect with I-80 West, then take the Hwy. 12 exit, which leads to the cities of Napa and Sonoma.

From the south: Like visitors from the north, drivers arriving from southern California can choose between Hwy. 101 or I-5.

Traveling Hwy. 101 brings you through the heart of San Francisco. Stay alert — 101 empties onto the streets of the city and can be a bit confusing. Continue across the spectacular Golden Gate Bridge, and through the hills of Marin County. To reach central Sonoma County, continue north on 101. To reach the city of Sonoma or Napa Valley, exit to Hwy. 37 in Novato and connect with Hwy. 121.

If speed is a concern, and you want to avoid San Francisco, try I-5. First connect with I-580 and continue into downtown Oakland and connect with eastbound I-80. Exit on Hwy. 12 which leads to the cities of Napa and Sonoma.

NAPA & SONOMA ACCESS

Approximate mileage and times by car between towns and cities:

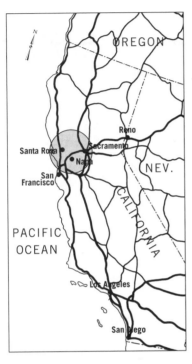

Napa County	Time	Miles
Napa (the city) to:		
Eureka	4 hrs.	255
Los Angeles	8 hrs.	439
Oakland	$3/4$ hr.	46
Reno	$3 1/2$ hrs.	200
Sacramento	1 hr.	61
San Francisco	1 hr.	56
San Diego	11 hrs.	600

Sonoma County	Time	Miles
Santa Rosa to:		
Eureka	4 hrs.	219
Los Angeles	8 hrs.	431
Oakland	1 hr.	60
Reno	4 hrs.	229
Sacramento	2 hrs.	97
San Francisco	1 hr.	56
San Diego	11 hrs.	600

Napa (the city) to:	Time	Miles
Calistoga	$1/2$ hr.	25
St. Helena	15 min.	18
Rutherford	10 min.	11
Sonoma	15 min.	12
Santa Rosa	$3/4$ hr.	36
Yountville	10 min.	8

Santa Rosa to:	Time	Miles
Bodega Bay	$3/4$ hr.	22
Geyserville	25 min.	21
Healdsburg	15 min.	15
Jenner	$3/4$ hr.	32
Petaluma	20 min.	16

WITHIN WINE COUNTRY

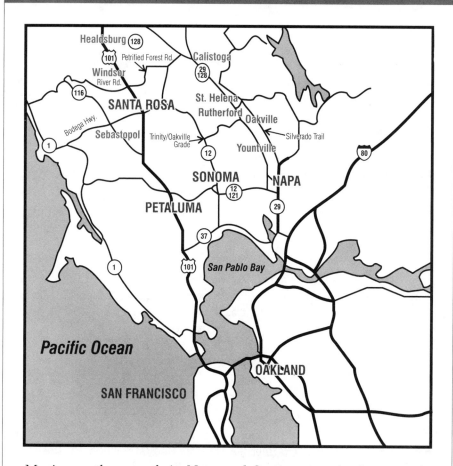

Moving north or south in Napa and Sonoma counties is easy going. Hwy. 29, Napa Valley's Main Street, cuts a long and straight path from the San Pablo Bay north to Lake County. Most of Napa's wineries are along this two-lane road so traffic can back up. Silverado Trail to the east is a quieter two-lane, though it has its share of wineries as well. In Sonoma County, Hwy. 101 will take you north and south at interstate speeds. Moving between Napa and Sonoma generally takes more patience. Hwy. 12 offers the smoothest path, although it has its own winding hills. The Oakville Grade/Trinity Road is a rollercoaster around Mt. Veeder that offers some of the best views of both counties. Petrified Forest and Spring Mountain roads scale the northern Mayacamas Mountains and, at the top, merge with Calistoga Road from Santa Rosa. Low gear on these roads is a good idea. Weather is *never* a problem. It rarely snows in Wine Country and when it does it melts quickly, even in the highest elevations.

From the east: Wine Country is an easy jaunt from Sacramento or Reno. From I-80, connect with Hwy. 12. Take it west to Napa and then onto Sonoma Valley.

BY BUS

G reyhound bus service to Sonoma and Napa counties is very limited. It is also possible to ride Greyhound to San Francisco, then make connections on Golden Gate Transit to reach Wine Country (see "Getting Around Napa & Sonoma" in this chapter). A travel agent will have the most up-to-date information on Greyhound schedules and connections.

Greyhound in San Francisco: 415-495-1569
Golden Gate Transit (for travel between San Francisco and Sonoma County) 415-332-6600 or 707-544-1323; one-way fare from San Francisco to Santa Rosa in late 1994 was $4.50.

BY TRAIN

A mtrak's westbound *California Zephyr* and north-to-south *Coastal Starlight* trains drop off Napa County-bound passengers in the city of Martinez, about 40 miles south of Napa. Amtrak has continuing ground transportation that delivers passengers directly to Napa, but not Sonoma.

For Amtrak information and reservations, call 800-872-7245. It is advisable to consult a travel agent for assistance in booking Amtrak.

BY AIR

A ir travelers bound for Wine Country can arrive and depart from one of three major airports handling numerous domestic and international airlines.

San Francisco International (SFO), Oakland International (OAK), and Sacramento Metropolitan (SMF) are all within easy driving distance of Napa and Sonoma counties. United Airlines' Express service operates commuter/connecting flights daily between SFO and Sonoma County Airport. Currently, there are no commuter services or connecting flights in or out of the Napa airport.

If you're piloting your own small plane or arriving by chartered plane, wing directly into Sonoma County Airport northwest of Santa Rosa or into Napa County Airport, six miles south of the town of Napa. Several private charter services are based at both county airports, primarily offering sightseeing flights but also providing for-hire transportation to and from Bay Area airports and beyond.

United Express: 800-241-6522 for information and reservations.

FROM THE AIRPORTS

Rental Car

The transportation of choice for most visitors. Rental companies are usually helpful in plotting routes and will often supply drivers with basic maps to reach their destinations. In Sonoma County, an automobile is almost a necessity, and although wineries are more centrally located in Napa Valley, a car is handy. Traffic is common on Saturday and Sunday and during peak summer months, so an ambitious itinerary can be cut short by the weekend tourist crush. A word of advice: if you can, visit Napa Valley and the city of Sonoma on weekdays, when traffic is lighter.

(Distances below are approximate; travel times depend upon traffic conditions and time of day. Refer to "Getting to Napa & Sonoma: By Car" and the Napa & Sonoma access map in this chapter for further details.)

From San Francisco International Airport: Take Hwy. 101 northbound and into San Francisco. The highway empties onto the streets, so watch the signs. Continue through the city and across the Golden Gate Bridge. For central Sonoma County, continue north on 101. To reach the town of Sonoma or to continue eastward to Napa Valley, take Hwy. 37 in Novato and connect with Hwy. 121.

     Miles: 72 to Santa Rosa; 82 to Napa
     Time: 90 minutes

From Oakland International Airport: To reach Napa County directly, take I-80 north through Oakland, continue north, then follow the signs for Vallejo and Sacramento. Cross the Carquinez Bridge into Vallejo, and connect with Hwy. 29 northbound to Napa.

     Miles: 46
     Time: 1 hour

Until Hwy. 101 was built, Redwood Highway ambled through the heart of Santa Rosa.

Courtesy Sonoma County Museum

To reach Sonoma County, take I-80 north to Oakland, connect with I-580, and cross the Richmond–San Rafael Bridge. Connect with Hwy. 101 North in Marin County and continue north to Sonoma County.

>   Miles: 82
>   Time: 75 minutes

From Sacramento Metropolitan Airport: Take I-5 South and connect with the I-80 West bypass, and follow the signs to San Francisco. Take Hwy. 12 to Napa, continuing west to the cities of Sonoma and Santa Rosa.

>   Miles: 61 miles to Napa; 97 miles to Santa Rosa
>   Time: 90 minutes to Napa; 2 to 2 $^1/_2$ hours to Santa Rosa

Airport Shuttle

Reasonably priced express shuttle buses and vans operate to and from the San Francisco and Oakland airports. These comfortable vehicles operate from 16 to 20 hours a day, seven days a week. Shuttles depart from airports about every 60 minutes to two hours, depending on the operator, and deliver passengers to selected drop-off points in Wine Country, such as the Flamingo Hotel in Santa Rosa.

One-way fares (cash only) range from $15 to $25, depending on the operator, the drop-off point, and any excess luggage requirements. Children usually ride free or at half-fare. Reservations are not usually required, but on weekends and in peak seasons, buses fill up and you may be forced to stand in the aisle. Schedules fluctuate, so it's smart to reserve shuttle services in advance. (Some operators suspend service on major holidays; others offer a limited number of trips on holidays and weekends.)

Airport Express: SFO to Santa Rosa, 707-837-8700
Evans Airport Service: SFO to Napa, 707-255-1559, 707-944-2025
Sonoma Airporter: SFO to the town of Sonoma, 707-938-4246
Santa Rosa Airporter: SFO and OAK to Santa Rosa, 707-545-8015

GETTING AROUND NAPA & SONOMA

BY RENTAL CAR

Most Wine Country visitors will rent a vacation car at the metro airports but rentals are also available in Napa and Sonoma counties. Local information and reservation numbers are listed below and reservations up to a week in advance are recommended.

Per-day charges may vary significantly between the big names and the bargain-basement agencies based in Wine Country. Renting a mid-size vehicle, for example, can range from $34.95 daily with unlimited mileage (Budget Rent-A-Car in Santa Rosa) to $49 daily, unlimited mileage (Hertz in Napa). Most companies allow 100 to 150 free miles daily, or up to 1,000 free miles weekly. (All prices quoted are current in late 1994.)

Napa County

Budget Rent-A-Car: 707-224-7845
Enterprise Rent-A-Car: 707-253-8000
Hertz: 707-226-2037 or 800-654-3131
Rent A Wreck: 707-257-1911 or 707-963-3681

Sonoma County

Santa Rosa

Bay Area Auto Rental: 707-575-1600
Budget Rent-A-Car: 707-545-8013
Encore Rent-A-Car: 707-579-4833
Enterprise Rent-A-Car: 707-586-4170

Sonoma County Airport

Avis: 707-571-0465
Hertz: 707-528-0834
Thrifty: 707-573-0131

BY BUS

Public bus service is available through *Sonoma County Transit* and *Napa Valley Transit*. This method of travel could be indispensable for the Wine Country visitor on a tight budget. One drawback: bus stops, which can be few and far between, are usually not close to wineries and other tourist attractions.

One-way fares average between $1 and $2.50 and weekend service is limited. If buses will be your primary form of transportation, it may be essential to gather together the most current timetables and route maps, which are updated frequently. *Golden Gate Transit, Sonoma County Transit,* and *Napa County Rideline* will mail detailed maps and up-to-the-minute schedules at your request. The cities of Santa Rosa, Napa, Healdsburg, and Petaluma also offer bus service within those city boundaries.

Napa County

Napa Valley Transit: Travels mainly along Hwy. 29 between Calistoga and Vallejo, with bus and ferry connections to and from San Francisco, 800-696-6443

The V.I.N.E.: Napa city bus, 707-255-7631

Intercity Van-Go: Limited service between most Napa Valley towns, 707-963-4222 or 707-252-2600

Sonoma County

Sonoma County Transit: (for travel within Sonoma County) 707-576-RIDE

Santa Rosa Transit: (city bus) 707-543-3333

Petaluma Transit: (city bus) 707-778-4460

Healdsburg In-City Transit: (city bus) 707-431-3309

BY TRAIN

The *Napa Valley Wine Train*, with luxurious Pullman dining cars, travels the 36 miles round trip between the towns of Napa and St. Helena. It is actually a gourmet restaurant on rails and not a true form of transportation. There are no stops along the line. (See Chapter Five, *Restaurants & Food Purveyors*.)

BY LIMOUSINE

The ultimate in personal transportation is the limousine, and for many visitors to Wine Country, chauffeured travel goes hand-in-hand with wine tasting. For others, the pricey three-hour ride to the Sonoma Coast can be a romantic and unforgettable luxury.

Limousines tour Wine Country in style.

Both Napa Valley and Sonoma County have an abundance of professional limousine services that will map out wine-tasting itineraries for the novice or deliver connoisseurs to wineries of their choosing. Most also offer day-long, fixed-rate touring packages with extras, such as gourmet picnic lunches or evening dining, included in the price. Per-hour rates range from $30 on weekdays to $60 on weekends, not including taxes, driver gratuities, parking fees, or bridge tolls. A three- or four-hour minimum is standard, and complimentary champagne is often served. Reservations are required at least two or three days in advance, and as much as a week in advance during peak vacationing months. Some recommend booking at least a month ahead of time. (Prices quoted are current at mid-1994.)

For your added safety, the limousine service you engage should be both licensed and insured. Ask your hotel concierge to recommend a service or talk to your travel agent. Listed below are some of Wine Country's most popular limousine services. Companies may be based in one county, but they frequently take passengers all over Wine Country and beyond.

Napa County

Antique Tours: 707-226-9227
Chardonnay Limousine: 707-944-1194
Crown Limousine: 707-226-9500
Evans Inc.: 707-255-1557
Limousine Service of the Valley: 707-226-2106

Sonoma County

A Perfect Experience Limousine: 707-585-1320
Advantage Limousine: 707-762-1724
All Occasions Limousine: 707-584-0701
A Dream Limousine: 707-545-4442, 415-952-6810
Style and Comfort Limousine: 707-579-0433
Lon's Limo Scene: 707-539-5466
North Bay Limousine: 707-578-4777

BY TAXI

When buses are too inconvenient and limousines too expensive, call for an old standby: the taxicab. The companies below are on duty 24 hours a day, seven days a week. Per-mile fares average $2.

Napa County

Yellow Cab: 707-226-3731
Napa Valley Cab: 707-257-6444

Sonoma County

Bill's Taxi Service, Guerneville: 707-869-2177
Sonoma Valley Cab: 707-996-6733
George's Taxi Yellow Cab, Santa Rosa: 707-546-3322 or 707-544-4444

NEIGHBORS ALL AROUND

TO THE SOUTH

The striking countryside and tony hamlets of Marin County are directly south. In San Rafael, just east of Hwy. 101, don't miss the dramatic Marin Civic Center, one of the last buildings designed by Frank Lloyd Wright. If you're not in a hurry, consider trekking north or south on Hwy. 1, the winding two-lane that hugs the rugged coastline. It will take you by Muir Woods, home to some of the tallest redwoods north of the Bay, and also to the majestic Mount Tamalpais. Drive to its 3,000-foot summit for a spectacular view of San Francisco (clear weather permitting, that is). Point Reyes Lighthouse is also worth a stop along Hwy. 1, as well as the many oyster farms near Marshall.

Farther south is one of the most intriguing, romantic, and ethnically diverse cities in America: San Francisco. It's just a one-hour drive from Wine Country. Ride a cable car, snack on scrumptious dim sum in Chinatown, gorge on culture and shopping, or just admire the view. See Chapter 4, _Culture_, for more suggestions. Across the Bay is Oakland and the ever-eclectic Berkeley, both stops worth making.

TO THE EAST

While motoring your way to Sacramento along I-80, your thoughts may turn to . . . onions. The aroma of onions and other commercially grown produce fills the air in fertile Sacramento Valley, where fruits and vegetables are tended in endless flat fields. The city of Sacramento, the state capital and once a major hub for rail and river transportation, is proud of its historic center, Old Town, a faithful recreation of the city's original town center with a multitude of shops, restaurants, and museums.

TO THE NORTH

Not to be outdone by Napa and Sonoma, Mendocino County is also a major player in the game of fine wine, with several premium wineries along Hwy. 101 and in beautiful Anderson Valley. The coastal hamlet of Mendocino, one of Hollywood's favorite movie locations, is also a treasure trove for shoppers. Its art galleries, antiques shops, and fine dining, and its New England-like atmosphere, make it a popular second destination for Wine Country visitors.

CHAPTER THREE
The Keys to Your Room
LODGING

In the late 1970s, only 50 bed & breakfast inns were operating in California; today there are 800-plus and more open for business every year. One of the largest concentrations of B&Bs in the state is in Wine Country, and many are housed in structures rich in history. The morning meal has evolved from the standard "light continental" fare to a breakfast that is often a gourmet delight, including creative egg entrées, quiche, sausages, waffles or pancakes, oven-fresh breads with homemade jams, fresh fruit, and champagne.

Chris Alderman

The grounds of Madrona Manor invite romantic strolls.

The list of amenities at finer inns goes on: private balconies and decks, pools and saunas, evening wine tastings, home-baked chocolate chip cookies, etc. Private baths are not only standard these days, but many are equipped with whirlpool tubs for two.

If you're more at ease staying at a familiar motel chain or if the budget is your first consideration, Wine Country offers many delightful options. Many of these are listed in the motel section included at the end of this chapter.

Don't expect a B&B to be less expensive than a conventional hotel or motel. Unlike its budget-wise British cousin, the Wine Country B&B is an intimate, serene, and often pricey luxury accommodation and almost always worth it. Keep in mind that over time, policies, amenities, and even furnishings may change at some inns, as will the complimentary goodies.

NAPA AND SONOMA LODGING NOTES

Referral Services: Many of these services will arrange accommodations in both Napa Valley and Sonoma County. Some can also make reservations for balloon rides, visits to spas, and wine tours.

> *Accommodation Referral:* 707-942-5900
> *B&B Style:* 800-995-8884
> *Wine Country Inns of Sonoma County:* 707-433-4667
> *Wine Country Reservations:* 707-257-7757 or 707-944-1222

Minimum Stay: A majority of inns and B&Bs require a two-night minimum on weekends; a three-night minimum is the norm on holiday weekends. (Virtually all inns and B&Bs are open year-round in Wine Country.)

Reservations/Cancellations: Make reservations at popular inns and hotels several weeks in advance, as most fill up on weekends even in the off-season. A deposit by credit card for the first night is usually required. Expect a charge for last-minute cancellations.

Restrictions: Smoking is not permitted inside most inns, and pets are prohibited almost unanimously. As a general rule, children under 12 are discouraged, but some inns welcome kids and infants. In-room telephones and televisions are not usually furnished at B&Bs; likewise, room service is limited. Always ask about restrictions before booking.

Rates: High season for Wine Country innkeepers is generally from April to October; off-season runs November to March. Many inns, however, make no distinction between the seasons and may charge the same rate year-round. At those that do recognize off-season, expect to pay 20% to 30% less. Likewise, mid-week rates may be significantly less than weekend rates.

The following price codes are based on per-room, double-occupancy, high-season weekend rates at B&Bs and the better lodgings.

> Inexpensive: Up to $75
> Moderate: $75 to $125
> Expensive: $125 to $175
> Very Expensive: Over $175

Coastal Rentals: Few places in Northern California are more wild and beautiful than the rugged Sonoma Coast. Fortunately, there are scores of rental properties. Most are privately owned homes with equipped kitchens, etc. Many have full ocean views. Bed linens, towels, and maid service may or may not be provided. There is usually a two-night minimum and fees vary greatly, depending on the number of occupants, the location of the home, the amenities, and the season.

Listed below are property management companies that arrange home and condo rentals on the Sonoma Coast.

Vacation Rentals USA 707-875-4000
Don Berard Associates: 707-884-3211
Beach Rentals: 707-884-4235

LODGING IN NAPA COUNTY

Napa

ARBOR GUEST HOUSE
Innkeepers: Rosemary & Bruce Logan.
707-252-8144.
1436 G St., Napa, CA 94559.
Lincoln Ave. exit E. off Hwy. 29, R. on Jefferson, R. on G St.
Price: Moderate to Expensive.
Credit Cards: MC, V.
Handicap Access: Yes.

Built in 1906, this white Victorian is reminiscent of grandmother's Midwestern farmhouse, done in antiques and flowered wallpaper and curtains. In the heart of a residential area near downtown, the inn is a quiet haven with a lovely backyard and garden. There are five guest rooms in the main house and carriage house, all restored by the Logans. (Bruce is an architect.) A two-person whirlpool tub near the fireplace makes the Winter Haven room popular, and Rose's Bower, the top floor of the carriage house, is requested often. The Logans are attentive innkeepers, quick with recommendations for dinner and sightseeing. Breakfast is excellent, often featuring thick French toast, chicken sausage, and fresh fruit.

A quiet moment by the fire at the Beazley House.

Chris Alderman

BEAZLEY HOUSE
Innkeepers: Jim & Carol
  Beazley.
707-257-1649.
1910 1st St., Napa, CA
  94559.
1st St. exit E. off Hwy. 29
  near Jefferson St.
Price: Moderate to Expen-
  sive.
Credit Cards: MC, V.

One of Napa's first B&Bs, this wood-shingled circa-1902 mansion has six charming and cozy rooms. Even more desirable is the carriage house, built in 1983, with fireplaces and two-person spa standard in each of its five rooms. The main house is a beauty; the dining and common rooms have coved ceilings and oak floors with mahogany inlays. The Sherry Room is pleasantly done in blue wallpaper and rich cherry wood, but if you're sensitive to street noise, request a room in the carriage house. The garden is a peaceful refuge with an old-fashioned swing. The Beazleys offer a warm welcome at breakfast and Carol — a former nurse — concocts healthy but tasty fare served buffet style.

BLUE VIOLET MANSION
Innkeepers: Bob & Kathy
  Morris.
707-253-2583.
443 Brown St., Napa, CA
  94559.
1st St. exit E. off Hwy. 29,
  R. on Jefferson, L. on
  Oak, R. on Brown.
Price: Moderate to Very
  Expensive.
Credit Cards: AE, D, DC,
  MC, V.

This graceful Queen Anne Victorian, built in 1886, is one of the newest B&B additions to Old Town Napa. On one lush acre, with a garden gazebo and vine-covered deck, the inn is delightfully restored. Antiques and art work decorate each of the 14 rooms; at least eight have gas fireplaces and eight have whirlpool tubs. Two rooms also open onto the front balcony. A full breakfast is served and private candlelight dinners can be arranged.

BROOKSIDE VINEYARD
Innkeepers: Tom & Susan
  Ridley.
707-944-1661.
3194 Redwood Rd., Napa,
  CA 94558.
Off Hwy. 29, 2 1/2 mi. W. on
  Redwood Rd.
Price: Moderate.
Credit Cards: None.
Special Features: Pool.

Not just a B&B, Brookside is a working vineyard and Christmas tree farm. During grape harvest season, guests are welcome to help out. Built in the 1950s, the Mission-style inn is set along a lush creek, a romantic setting for the three guest rooms furnished in Laura Ashley prints. The Britannia room has a fireplace, sauna, and private patio. Furnishings are a blend of family treasures and antiques. Breakfast is served buffet style in a gazebo that overlooks the creek.

CANDLELIGHT INN
Innkeepers: Joe & Carol
  Farace.
707-257-3717.
1045 Easum Dr., Napa, CA
  94558.
1st St. exit W. off Hwy. 29
  to Easum Dr.

This 1929 English Tudor-style mansion is in the heart of suburbia but the one-acre grounds along Napa Creek are beautifully parklike. There are three romantic suites, all with two-person whirlpool baths, balconies or decks, and fireplaces. One has a cathedral ceiling and a stained-glass

Price: Expensive.
Credit Cards: AE, D, MC, V.
Handicap Access: Yes.
Special Features: Pool.

CHURCHILL MANOR
Innkeepers: Joanna
Guidotti & Brian Jensen.
707-253-7733.
485 Brown St., Napa, CA
94559.
1st St. exit E. off Hwy. 29,
R. on Jefferson, L. on Oak
St.
Price: Moderate to Expensive.
Credit Cards: AE, D, MC, V.
Handicap Access: Limited.

**COUNTRY GARDEN
INN**
Innkeepers: Lisa & George
Smith.
707-255-1197.
1815 Silverado Trail, Napa,
CA 94558.
Imola Ave. exit E. off Hwy.
29, 1 1/2 mi. N. on Silverado Trail.
Price: Moderate to Expensive.
Credit Cards: MC, V.

CROSS ROADS INN
Innkeeper: Nancy Scott.
707-944-0646.
6380 Silverado Trail, Napa,
CA 94558.
Off Silverado Trail, S. of
Yountville Cross Rd.
Price: Very Expensive.
Credit Cards: MC, V.

window. Breakfast is served overlooking the lovely gardens that surround the house.

From the moment you spy Churchill Manor, you know it's special. The inn, now a National Historic Landmark, was built in 1889 on a lush acre, and has the Greek Revival columns, wraparound verandahs, and grand parlors of days gone by. The 10 guest rooms are on the second and third floors of this graceful mansion, and all have private baths and queen- or king-size beds. Handpainted Delft tiles, 24-carat gold trim, and an antique beaded opera gown are among the rich details in the rooms. A generous buffet-style breakfast is served in the marble-tiled solarium, where wine and cheese are offered in the evening.

A little bit of England is hidden away on 1 1/2 acres along Silverado Trail. Built as a coach house in the 1850s, Country Garden Inn is run by British-bred Lisa Villiers Smith and husband George, charming innkeepers. Secluded in a glen of trees and flowers along the Napa River, the inn has 9 rooms and one cottage with a fireplace and deck. Rooms have a refined Old World atmosphere, with English and Irish pine antiques. The Rose House includes three rooms, each with four-poster beds, fireplaces, whirlpools, and a balcony overlooking the shaded rose garden with its lily pond and fountain. The buffet breakfast includes champagne and the likes of French toast, scones, and other British treats. Guests sensitive to traffic noise — minimal in this case — should request a room secluded from Silverado Trail.

Stunning valley views are just one of the attractions at Cross Roads Inn. The three-story chalet on 23 mountainous acres is surrounded by oak trees, wildflowers, and hiking trails. The common room has a wall of windows and an unusual circular fireplace that rises 20 feet. The four guest rooms, some with whirlpools, are named after Beatrix Potter characters, and each is in a separate

Special Features: View, exercise equipment.

ELM HOUSE INN
Managers: Christopher & Christine Green.
707-255-1831.
800 California Blvd., Napa, CA 94559.
1st St. exit E. off Hwy. 29 to California Blvd.
Price: Moderate to Expensive.
Credit Cards: AE, MC, V.
Handicap Access: Yes.
Special Features: Whirlpool.

HENNESSEY HOUSE
Innkeepers: Lauriann Delay & Andrea Lamar.
707-226-3774.
1727 Main St., Napa, CA 94559.
Lincoln Ave. exit E. off Hwy. 29, R. on Main St.

wing of the house. All have private baths and decks. Scott's stylish breakfasts are served in your room — a nice touch.

Sheltered by three huge, historic elm trees, this wood-shingled inn is modern but done in the style of an old European village. There are Italian marble fireplaces in many of its 16 rooms (all with private baths) and each has a TV, phone, and stocked refrigerator. There's also a honeymoon suite with high ceilings, chandelier, and a private whirlpool. The inn's elevator also makes it accessible to wheelchairs. A breakfast buffet is served in the courtyard when weather permits. On a busy intersection.

This home on the National Register of Historic Places is a stunning example of a perfectly restored 1889 Eastlake-style Queen Anne. The main house has six rooms, all appointed with antiques and private baths. Larger and more luxurious are

Hennessey House, a beautifully restored Queen Anne, is listed on the National Register of Historic Places.

Chris Alderman

Price: Moderate to Expensive.
Credit Cards: MC, V.
Special Features: Sauna.

INN AT NAPA VALLEY
Manager: Reynaldo
Zertuche.
707-253-9540 or
800-433-4600.
1075 California Blvd.,
Napa, CA 94559.
1st St. exit E. off Hwy. 29
to California Blvd.
Price: Moderate to Very
Expensive.
Credit Cards: AE, D, DC,
MC, V.
Handicap Access: Yes.
Special Features: Indoor
and outdoor pools,
sauna, whirlpool, and
restaurant.

The courtyard of the Inn at Napa Valley.

JOHN MUIR INN
Manager: Joan Shelsta.
707-257-7220.
1998 Trower Ave., Napa,
CA 94558.
Hwy. 29 at Trower Ave.

the four carriage house rooms, each equipped with two-person whirlpool tubs. The Bridle Suite is done in masculine tones and has a fireplace and skylight. A full breakfast is served in the dining room, where the restored handpainted and stamped tin ceiling is the focal point. The neighborhood is urban but quiet.

All 205 rooms in this hotel are two-room suites with French country furnishings and are equipped for light cooking with mini-refrigerators, coffee makers, and microwave ovens. In addition, all rooms have wet bars, phones, and TVs. Daily complimentary full breakfast is cooked to order, and two hours of complimentary cocktails are served each evening. Outside there's a pond with swans and ducks, and a tropical atrium with a skylight for dining. This is an elegant business-class hotel — part of the Crown Sterling Suites chain — that's also ideal for leisure travelers.

Chris Alderman

A 60-room, better-than-average motel on the north side of Napa for easy access to up-valley wineries and restaurants. Built in 1986, the inn was redecorated in 1993. The spacious rooms are tastefully furnished, and many have wet bars and kitch-

Price: Inexpensive to
  Expensive.
Credit Cards: AE, D, DC,
  MC, V.
Handicap Access: Yes.
Special Features: Pool,
  whirlpool.

enettes and many overlook the garden courtyard.
There are also a handful of suites equipped with
whirlpool baths. Continental breakfast is included.

LA BELLE EPOQUE
Innkeepers: Claudia &
  Merlin Wedepohl.
707-257-2161.
1386 Calistoga Ave., Napa,
  CA 94559.
1st St. exit E. off Hwy. 29,
  N. on Jefferson St. to Cal-
  istoga Ave.
Price: Moderate to Expen-
  sive.
Credit Cards: AE, D, MC,
  V.

The stained glass windows and fine Victorian
furniture at this seven-room inn will transport
you to another time and place. Built in 1893, this
gingerbread beauty is near downtown and the residential area is still a little funky. Family heirloom
antiques and collectibles are scattered throughout
the guest rooms and the common parlor. All rooms
have private baths and three have fireplaces. Breakfast is served in the dining room or sun porch.
There's also a remodeled wine cellar and tasting
room, open every afternoon for guests to try complimentary Napa Valley wines.

*The guest rooms of La Residence Country Inn are lushly
appointed.*

Courtesy La Residence Country Inn

**LA RESIDENCE
  COUNTRY INN**
Innkeepers: Craig Claussen
  & David Jackson.
707-253-0337.
4066 St. Helena Hwy.
  (Hwy. 29), Napa, CA
  94558.
Price: Inexpensive to
  Expensive.
Credit Cards: AE, D, MC,
  V.

Built in 1870 by a New Orleans riverboat pilot
who arrived in San Francisco during the Gold
Rush, this Gothic Revival inn still has the flavor of
the Old South with its plantation shutters and parklike setting. Eleven of the inn's 20 rooms are in
Cabernet Hall, a modern building styled after a
French country barn. Between the two buildings is
a garden with a pool and white gazebo. Nineteenth-
century antiques and chandeliers decorate the

Handicap Access: Yes.
Special Features: Pool,
  whirlpool.

rooms, many of which have fireplaces. The pace is slow and easy, with lots of porches and decks and a jogging and bicycling trail. A full breakfast is served in the dining room, where guests dine privately at small tables near a fireplace.

**MARRIOTT NAPA
  VALLEY**
Manager: Dan Zerbonia.
707-253-7433 or
  800-228-9290.
3425 Solano Ave., Napa,
  CA 94558.
Hwy. 29 at Redwood Rd.
Price: Expensive to Very
  Expensive.
Credit Cards: AE, CB, D,
  DC, MC, V.
Handicap Access: Yes.
Special Features: Pool,
  whirlpool, tennis courts,
  restaurant.

With 191 rooms and suites, the Marriott is one of the largest inns in the valley. Nicer than a motel, it's not quite a hotel either, but it is comfortably appointed and has the usual services you would expect from a chain hotel. On the north edge of the city, it is convenient to most of the valley.

THE NAPA INN
Innkeepers: Ann & Denny
  Mahoney.
707-257-1444.
1137 Warren St., Napa, CA
  94559.
1st St. exit E. off Hwy. 29 to
  Warren St.
Price: Moderate to Expensive.
Credit Cards: MC, V.

Music plays a starring role at this unique Victorian-era inn. The parlor is filled with antique instruments, from a player piano to an accordion, violin, and music box. Upstairs, the finest of the five guest rooms is the Grand Suite. Encompassing the entire third floor of the house, it has a sitting and dressing area, and boasts a private balcony as well. Painted a warm blue, this 1899 Queen Anne is in a tree-lined historic neighborhood near downtown. A full breakfast is served in the dining room.

THE OLD WORLD INN
Innkeeper: Diane Dumaine.
707-257-0112.
1301 Jefferson St., Napa.
1st St. exit E. off Hwy. 29,
  L. on Jefferson.
Price: Moderate to Expensive.
Credit Cards: AE, D, MC,
  V.
Special Features:
  Whirlpool.

One of the most beautifully appointed B&Bs in the valley, Old World Inn is a charming 1906 Victorian. The interior is impeccably designed, done in tastefully dramatic pastels, draped fabric, and ruffles. The dining and common rooms on the first floor have gorgeous redwood woodwork and polished wood floors, and each of the eight guest rooms are individually decorated; most have claw-foot tubs. The Stockholm Room has a whirlpool bath and the Garden Room has a skylight for stargazing from bed. The breakfast buffet includes

Old World Inn, a 1906 Victorian, has been lovingly restored.

Chris Alderman

the likes of pineapple muffins, fresh fruit, and frittatas, and guests dine privately at small tables in the dining room. On a busy street, the inn is surprisingly quiet.

SILVERADO COUNTRY CLUB
Manager: Kirk Candland.
707-257-0200.
1600 Atlas Peak Rd., Napa, CA 94558.
Silverado Trail at Atlas Peak Rd., 1 mi. NE. of Napa.
Price: Expensive to Very Expensive.
Credit Cards: AE, CB, D, DC, MC, V.
Special Features: Two 18-hole golf courses, 8 pools, tennis, restaurant, room service.

Golf is king at Silverado. Its two courses are considered the best in Napa Valley. With more than 1,000 regular members, the area is constantly bustling with activity. The main house, an imposing mansion built just after the Civil War, was remodeled in 1992.

Today there are 280 rooms scattered over the 1,220-acre estate, ranging in size from studios to three-bedroom suites. The units are individually owned by members, but rented out like hotel rooms. (The Oak Creek East area is the most secluded; the Clubhouse side is convenient to the tennis courts and golf courses.) All rooms are comfortably furnished to feel like home, and the kitchenettes have just about everything you need for light cooking. The concierge staff is perhaps the best in the valley.

STAHLECKER HOUSE
Innkeepers: Ron & Ethel Stahlecker.
707-257-1588.
1042 Easum Dr., Napa, CA 94558.
1st St. exit W. off Hwy. 29 to Easum Dr.

This 1948 ranch-style house seems more like a home than a B&B, but it has appealing guest rooms with canopy beds, antique furniture, and private baths. One is newly equipped with a whirlpool spa, fireplace, and private patio. Relax on the immense sun deck surrounded by gardens and oak and laurel trees, or read in the living room.

Price: Moderate to Very
Expensive.
Credit Cards: AE, MC, V.

The hosts serve a gourmet candlelight breakfast in the dining room and complimentary beverages around the clock.

Yountville

BORDEAUX HOUSE
Innkeeper: Jean Lunney.
707-944-2855.
6600 Washington St.,
Yountville, CA 94599.
Off Hwy. 29 at Washington St.
Price: Moderate to Expensive.
Credit Cards: MC, V.

Six of the seven guest rooms in this inn have fireplaces, most have balconies or patios, and all have private baths. The inn is a distinctive red brick and the design is modern. The furnishings are done in Italian contemporary style. Continental breakfast is served in the common room. It's close to all of Yountville's shops and restaurants.

BURGUNDY HOUSE
Manager: Deanna Roque.
707-944-0889.
6711 Washington St.,
Yountville, CA 94599.
Washington St. exit off Hwy. 29, L. $^1/_2$ mi.
Price: Moderate.
Credit Cards: MC, V.
Handicap Access: No.

A brandy distillery built in 1891, this charming two-story structure is now a five-room inn. Antique furniture and period pieces are at home amidst the 22-inch-thick walls of rugged fieldstone and river rock masonry. A decanter of Napa Valley wine helps visitors settle in, and a full breakfast is served in the garden or inside. All rooms have private baths and one has a fireplace.

MAISON FLEURIE
Manager: Roger Rasbill.
707-944-2056.
6529 Yount St., Yountville, CA 94599.
1 block E. of Washington St.
Price: Moderate to Very Expensive.
Credit Cards: AE, MC, V.
Special Features: Pool, whirlpool.

Blessed with a colorful past — it was a bordello and a speakeasy — this 13-room inn was recently known as Magnolia Hotel but became Maison Fleurie in 1994. Encompassing three red brick, vine-covered buildings built in 1873, it is styled after a French country inn, although it's right in the heart of Yountville. Six rooms have fireplaces. The pool and whirlpool offer relaxation in a private setting. A full breakfast is served family-style in the fireside dining room.

**NAPA VALLEY LODGE,
BEST WESTERN**
Manager: Erika Cimpher.
707-944-2468.
Hwy. 29 at Madison St.,
Yountville, CA 94599.
Price: Moderate to Expensive.

This delightful lodge has 55 well-appointed and spacious rooms and suites decorated with wicker and tropical plants and postcard views of the valley. It is styled as a Spanish hacienda with a red-tile roof and balconies. The pool and whirlpool spa are in a pleasant courtyard. In-room coffee makers and cooler/refrigerators are provided, and

Credit Cards: AE, D, DC, MC, V.
Handicap Access: Yes.
Special Features: Pool, whirlpool, sauna, and exercise room.

NAPA VALLEY RAILWAY INN
Manager: Vickie Gillis.
707-944-2000.
6503 Washington St., Yountville, CA 94599.
Off Hwy. 29 to Washington St.
Price: Moderate.
Credit Cards: MC, V.
Handicap Access: Yes.

Chris Alderman

OAK KNOLL INN
Innkeepers: Barbara Passino & John Kuhlmann.
707-255-2200.
2200 E. Oak Knoll Ave., Napa, CA 94558.
3 mi. S. of Yountville, Oak Knoll Ave. to Big Ranch Rd., L., then R. $^4/_{10}$ mi.
Price: Very Expensive.
Credit Cards: MC, V.
Special Features: Pool, whirlpool.

a continental buffet breakfast is served. This is a restful location surrounded by ripening grapes in the vineyards, and it's an easy walk to Yountville's shops.

Take a step back to the time that railroads reigned — stay in one of nine turn-of-the-century railroad cars (three cabooses and six rail cars) thoroughly refurbished into luxurious suites. Period furniture and decor help guests relive the past glory of rail travel. A brass bed, sitting room with a love seat, and a full bath complete each room. Next door is the shopping mecca Vintage 1870.

The guest rooms at Oak Knoll Inn offer dramatic French windows, fieldstone walls, and vaulted ceilings.

Oak Knoll Inn is a treasure, perhaps our favorite B&B in Napa Valley. It's intimate, with only four guest suites, but the rooms are roomy and luxurious, with tall French windows, rustic fieldstone walls, and vaulted ceilings. The rooms have king-size brass beds, Italian marble fireplaces, private baths, and sitting areas with overstuffed chairs and sofas. Surrounded by gardens and 600 acres of chardonnay vineyards, it is well off the bustle of Hwy. 29, and the setting is peaceful and the view magnificent. The innkeepers are also gracious and unstuffy.

The phrase "gourmet breakfast" is used loosely at many B&Bs, but not here — Barbara Passino creates truly magnificent breakfasts, including poached eggs in puff pastry and an indulgence called a chocolate taco stuffed with fresh sorbet. Breakfast is served in the dining room or on the verandah near your room. There's also quite a spread set out at the nightly wine and cheese hour.

OLEANDER HOUSE BED & BREAKFAST INN
Innkeepers: John & Louise Packard.
800-788-0357.
7433 St. Helena Hwy. (Hwy. 29), Yountville, CA 94599.
Price: Moderate to Expensive.
Credit Cards: AE, MC, V.
Special Features: Whirlpool.

A contemporary two-story house with four guest rooms decorated in Laura Ashley fabrics, this is a comfortable base for a Wine Country stay. The high-ceilinged rooms have private baths, antiques, and queen-size brass or four-poster beds. They also have private balconies, wood-burning fireplaces, and spectacular views of the valley. Breakfast is served at a large table where guests get to know each other, and the menu often includes baked pancakes, a fluffy crêpe-like creation. Mustards Grill, one of Napa Valley's premier restaurants, is just a few steps away (see Chapter Five, *Restaurants*). The innkeepers are quite gracious. Traffic noise is a drawback.

A tiny canal with fountains laces the grounds of the Vintage Inn.

Chris Alderman

VINTAGE INN
Manager: Nancy Lockmann.
707-944-1112.
6541 Washington St., Yountville, CA 94599.
Washington St. exit off Hwy. 29.
Price: Expensive to Very Expensive.

This is an exceptional inn designed with villa-style units clustered around a common waterway. The 80 spacious and beautifully decorated rooms have oversized beds, whirlpool spa tubs, ceiling fans, in-room coffee makers and refrigerators, private verandahs and wood-burning fireplaces. Second-story rooms cost a little more but have vaulted ceilings and the views are worth it.

Credit Cards: AE, CB, D,
DC, MC, V.
Handicap Access: Yes.
Special Features: Pool,
whirlpool, tennis; chil-
dren welcome.

THE WEBBER PLACE
Innkeeper: Diane
Bartholomew.
707-944-8384.
6610 Webber, Yountville,
CA 94599.
Just off Washington St.
Price: Inexpensive to Mod-
erate.
Credit Cards: AE, MC, V.

Smoking or non-smoking rooms are available, as is room service. California bubbly is served with the continental breakfast. The Vintage 1870 shopping complex is next door.

In the section of town called "Old Yountville," this red farmhouse with a white picket fence was built in 1850 and now has four comfy guest rooms and a refreshingly unpretentious atmosphere. After awakening in iron and brass beds with classic antique quilts, guests enjoy breakfast complete with biscuits. Two rooms have private baths with old-fashioned tubs. The Verandah Suite, the largest room, has a feather bed, private entrance, and verandah with hammock. Plans are in the works for a pool. The inn is within walking distance to all of Yountville's attractions.

Rutherford

AUBERGE DU SOLEIL
Manager: George Goeggel.
707-963-1211.
180 Rutherford Hill Rd.,
Rutherford, CA 94573.
Hwy. 29 to Hwy. 128 to Silverado Trail to Ruther-
ford Hill Rd.
Price: Very Expensive.
Credit Cards: AE, D, MC,
V.
Handicap Access: Yes.
Special Features: Restau-
rant, pool, whirlpool,
tennis courts with staff
pro, golf privileges; children welcome.

Auberge du Soleil is Napa Valley's most luxurious experience. Fifty rooms and suites are nestled in olive trees on a remote 33-acre hillside. The style is distinctly southern France, with deep-set windows and wood shutters and doors. Each room or suite has a terrace and private entrance; most have spectacular views of the valley. All furnishings are leather and terra cotta tiling is used generously throughout on floors and countertops, helping to keep rooms cool during Napa Valley's toasty summer days. The rooms range from standard bedroom and bath to deluxe suites with fireplaces and whirlpool baths. Fresh flowers, terrycloth robes, wet bars, and refrigerators are standard in all rooms. Take in the sculpture garden set along a half-mile path. The restaurant is not to be missed (see Chapter Five, *Restaurants*).

RANCHO CAYMUS INN

Innkeeper: Otto Komes.
707-963-1777.
1140 Rutherford Rd.,
  Rutherford.
From Hwy. 29, E. on
  Rutherford Rd.
Price: Moderate to Very
  Expensive.
Credit Cards: MC, V.

This romantic hacienda may recall the film *Like Water For Chocolate* (rose petals are optional). The stucco inn with a red-tile roof is built around a serene courtyard garden and it's clear an artist's hand was involved in the design. The original owner, sculptor Mary Tilden Morton, created an inn distinguished by stained glass windows, hand-hewn beams, hand-thrown stoneware, and tooled wooden lamps. Ecuadorian and Guadalajaran craftsmen made the colorful furnishings. Most of the 26 rooms have private balconies and adobe beehive fireplaces, and four suites have whirlpools. A generous continental breakfast is served in the dining room by the fireplace or in the courtyard. The staff is obliging.

St. Helena

AMBROSE BIERCE HOUSE

Innkeeper: Jane Gibson.
707-963-3003.
1515 Main St., St. Helena,
  CA 94574.
On Main St. (Hwy. 29) bet.
  Madrona & Adams Sts.
Price: Moderate to Expensive.
Credit Cards: None.

This lovely 1872 Victorian was home to renowned writer and curmudgeon philosopher Ambrose Bierce (*The Devil's Dictionary*), before he vanished in Mexico in 1913 (detailed in the 1989 film *Old Gringo*). The mystique of his life and work surrounds guests in distinctive air-conditioned suites decorated with antiques, queen-size brass beds, and armoires. Guests in street-front rooms may be bothered by traffic along Main Street.

CHESTELSON HOUSE

Innkeeper: Jackie Sweet.
707-963-2238.
1417 Kearney St., St.
  Helena, CA 94574.
2 blocks off Main St. near
  Adams St.
Price: Moderate to Expensive.
Credit Cards: MC, V.

The sun-soaked porch at this 1904 Victorian cottage offers relaxation after a day of shopping and wine tasting. The four guest rooms are spacious, unfussy, and filled with light, and all have private baths and queen beds. The room dubbed "Shadow" — the names are taken from verses by Robert Louis Stevenson — has a two-person whirlpool tub and private entrance. The innkeeper is a former caterer and her delicious breakfasts are served family-style. The location is a quiet residential neighborhood a few steps from St. Helena's Main Street.

CINNAMON BEAR INN

Innkeeper: Cathy Raneri.
707-963-4653.
1407 Kearney St., St.
  Helena, CA 94574.
2 blocks off Main St. near
  Adams St.

Once the home of St. Helena's mayor, this converted B&B is where innkeeper Jenkins raised her three children. The inn's warm atmosphere is apparent the moment you walk in the door. Lace curtains and multicolored quilts add to the comfortable feel of the guest suites, which all have

Price: Moderate to Expensive.
Credit Cards: AE, MC, V.

queen beds and private baths, as well as the stuffed teddy bears that lend the inn its name. (The bear motif is not as saccharine as it might sound; the bears are kept to a subtle but sweet minimum.) The wraparound porch with its peeled willow furniture is great for reading. The inn is on a quiet street a few blocks off Main Street.

EL BONITA MOTEL
Managers: Philippe &
   Pierette Therene.
707-963-3216.
195 Main St., St. Helena,
   CA 94574.
Price: Inexpensive to
   Expensive.
Credit Cards: AE, MC, V.
Special Features: Pool,
   whirlpool, sauna.

Don't let "motel" fool you. The 1950s meet the 1990s at El Bonita, a chic Art Deco, pastel-hued classic. It's also Napa's best bargain. Built in 1953, the motel was renovated and newly landscaped in 1992. With a new wing of deluxe rooms, El Bonita now has 41 units, all cheerfully appointed; a few have kitchens and whirlpool baths. The garden and lawn spans 2 1/2 acres, all sheltered from busy Hwy. 29. Trees and hedges also help cushion the steady hum of traffic.

FOREST MANOR
Innkeeper: Corlene &
   Harold Lambeth.
707-965-3538.
415 Cold Springs Rd.,
   Angwin, CA 94508.
Silverado Trail to Deer Park
   Rd., to Las Posadas Rd.
   to Cold Springs Rd.
Price: Moderate to Very
   Expensive.
Credit Cards: MC, V.
Special Features: Pool,
   whirlpool, tennis, game
   room.

At this secluded 20-acre English Tudor estate, now a country inn with a honeymoon suite among its three guest rooms, there are vineyards and forest trails to explore. The three-story manor is furnished in English antiques and Persian rugs, and has vaulted ceilings, fireplaces, and verandahs. The rooms have private baths, refrigerators, coffee makers, down comforters, and oversized beds. The Canterbury Suite is elegant and roomy, with a fireplace and private entrance. Somerset Suite has a whirlpool bath. A full breakfast — quiche, fresh fruit, and the like — is served in your room, or in the dining room or verandah if you feel social. About five miles from Hwy. 29, this friendly inn is a romantic getaway from the bustle of Napa Valley.

GLASS MOUNTAIN INN
Innkeepers: Diane & Jerry
   Payton.
707-963-3512.
3100 Silverado Trail, St.
   Helena, CA 94574.
Price: Very Expensive.
Credit Cards: MC, V.
Handicap Access: No.

This distinctive wood-shingle Victorian is nestled in a shady hillside. The stone dining room, in fact, opens into a cave. Diane and Jerry Payton, who also own Zinfandel Inn, have run this inn since 1994. There are three rooms. The Private Reserve room is at the bottom of the inn's tower and it includes a king size mahogany four-poster bed, a hand-carved oak fireplace, whirlpool, and private deck. High in the tower is the Vintage

Lady, equipped with a queen-size iron bed, fireplace, and nine-foot Roman soaking tub. The smallest room is the Victorian Princess, which offers a queen iron bed, claw-foot tub, and a private deck with a hot tub.

The Harvest Inn recalls an Old English manor house.

Chris Alderman

HARVEST INN
Manager: Jeff Perry.
707-963-9463 or
 800-950-8466.
1 Main St., St. Helena, CA
 94574.
On Hwy. 29 S. of St.
 Helena.
Price: Moderate to Very
 Expensive.
Credit Cards: AE, D, DC,
 MC, V.
Special Features: Two
 pools, whirlpools.

There's a bit of Old England in Napa Valley — the Harvest Inn, a stately English Tudor-style lodge built from the bricks and cobblestones of old San Francisco homes. Most of the 54 guest rooms have king-size beds, brick fireplaces, wet bars, and refrigerators, and all are furnished with antiques and reproductions. Several suites also have whirlpool tubs. The lush landscaping also helps to create the aura of another time and place. The inn's Harvest Centre has a wine bar and dance floor, and a complimentary continental breakfast is served in the dining hall. Overlooking a 14-acre working vineyard, the inn is within strolling distance of many wineries.

HOTEL ST. HELENA
Manager: Athena Ateshian.
707-963-4388.
309 Main St., St. Helena,
 CA 94574.
Price: Moderate to Expen-
 sive.
Credit Cards: AE, CB, D,
 DC, MC, V.

In the thick of St. Helena's shopping and dining, this 18-room hotel on the town's Main Street is richly furnished with antiques. Its turn-of-the-century charm makes it especially homey. There's a wine bar, and continental breakfast is served every morning. Some baths are shared.

INK HOUSE BED &
 BREAKFAST
Innkeepers: Diane & David
 Horkheimer

A glass-enclosed, rooftop observatory with a 360-degree view of vineyards distinguishes this yellow 1884 Italianate Victorian listed on the

707-963-3890.
1575 St. Helena Hwy.
(Hwy. 29), St. Helena,
CA 94574.
1 mi. N. of Rutherford at
White Hall Ln.
Price: Expensive.
Credit Cards: MC, V.

National Register of Historic Places. Each of the seven second-story guest rooms has a vineyard view, and period furnishings and private baths. Just for fun, take a lesson on the antique pump organ in the parlor. A full gourmet breakfast is served. This is an exceptional location and setting. While it's right on Hwy. 29 the inn is remarkably quiet. The innkeepers couldn't be friendlier.

MEADOWOOD RESORT
Manager: Jorg Lippuner.
707-963-3646.
900 Meadowood Ln., St.
Helena, CA 94574.
E. of St. Helena to Silverado
Trail, to Howell Mtn. Rd.
to Meadowood Ln.
Price: Very Expensive.
Credit Cards: AE, DC, MC,
V.
Handicap Access: Yes.
Special Features: Croquet,
restaurants, golf, pool,
tennis; children welcome.

Meadowood never falters in its interpretation of luxury. Reminiscent of New England's turn-of-the-century cottages, the lodges are scattered around a gorgeous wooded 250-acre property, and are tiered with gabled windows and porches, all trimmed in white. The staff pamper with style and a soothing sense of privacy prevails.

Most of the resort's 70 rooms and suites have cathedral ceilings, skylights, ceiling fans, and air conditioning. Rooms range in size from one-room studios with fireplaces to one-bedroom suites with sitting rooms. Each room has a private deck with a view of pine trees or gardens, and a queen- or king-size bed with a goosedown comforter. Additionally, terrycloth robes, wet bars, refrigerators, coffee makers, toasters, and television are standard in all rooms.

Breakfast is not included in the tariff; a continental repast can be delivered to your door or full feast is available at the Grill. Better still, try a light breakfast by the pool, surrounded by lush lawns and trees. At night, a walk to the Restaurant, Meadowood's premiere dining room, makes for a cozy evening (see Chapter Five, *Restaurants*). Meadowood also has one of the finest health facilities in the valley, with aerobic and exercise rooms and a full spa (see Chapter Seven, *Recreation*).

**OLIVER HOUSE
COUNTRY INN**
Innkeepers: Richard &
Clara Oliver.
707-963-4089.
2970 Silverado Trail N., St.
Helena, CA 94574.
3/4 mi. N. of Deer Park Rd.
on Silverado Trail.
Price: Moderate to Very
Expensive.
Credit Cards: AE, MC, V.

If typical Victorian architecture isn't your cup of tea, visit Switzerland instead. Tucked away on four acres outside St. Helena, this small chalet-style inn is a slice of Old Europe on Silverado Trail. Four guest rooms (three with French doors) are appointed with antiques (a 120-year-old Scottish brass bed, for example, and an armoire born in Salzburg the same year as Mozart); two rooms have wood-burning fireplaces. The top floor suite has an open-beam ceiling and a balcony. All rooms have private baths and three rooms have private entrances. The inn serves a full breakfast.

ROSE GARDEN INN
Innkeepers: Joanne & Tom
   Contreras.
707-963-4417.
1277 St. Helena Hwy. S.
   (Hwy. 29), St. Helena,
   CA 94574.
S. of St. Helena on Hwy. 29
   just N. of Zinfandel Ln.
Price: Moderate.
Credit Cards: None.

Once a ranch foreman's home, this comfy inn is located on three acres surrounded by vineyards, and now houses three spacious and comfortable guest rooms with queen-size iron beds and private baths. The shade of its century-old trees invites reading and relaxing.

SHADY OAKS
   COUNTRY INN
Innkeepers: Lisa Wild-
   Runnells & John
   Runnells.
707-963-1190.
399 Zinfandel Ln., St.
   Helena, CA 94574.
2 mi. S. of St. Helena, E. on
   Zinfandel Ln.
Price: Expensive.
Credit Cards: None.
Handicap Access: Yes.

Oak and walnut trees surround this friendly country inn with four guest rooms, all furnished with antiques and private baths. The main house, built in the 1920s, has two pleasant rooms. Built in the 1880s, the old stone winery has two more luxurious rooms, one with a vineyard view from a private deck, the other with a distinct stone interior. A full champagne breakfast — eggs benedict or Belgian waffles the norm — is served in your room or the dining room and garden patio.

VINEYARD COUNTRY
   INN
Innkeepers: Gene & Ida
   Lubberstedt.
707-963-1000.
201 Main St., St. Helena,
   CA 94574.
Price: Expensive.
Credit Cards: AE, MC, V.
Special Features: Pool,
   whirlpool.
Handicap Access: Yes.

This lovely new inn takes its inspiration from a French country village. Surrounding a central court, the buildings are crowned with steeply pitched roofs and intricate brick chimneys. There are 21 elegant suites, with exposed beam ceilings, red brick fireplaces, king or queen beds, and wet bars with refrigerator. Many have balconies with vineyard views. For breakfast, small tables are grouped around a large dining room fireplace. The inn is along busy Hwy. 29 but the rooms are relatively quiet.

WHITE SULPHUR
   SPRINGS RESORT
Innkeepers: Buzz & Betty
   Foote.
707-963-8588.
3100 White Sulphur
   Springs Rd., St. Helena,
   CA 94574.

Established in 1852, White Sulphur Springs was California's first resort. A rustic, Old World retreat in a canyon above St. Helena, it is set in 330 acres of redwood, fir, and madrone and has hiking trails and waterfalls. The resort has eight cottages and two small lodges, with a total of 28 rooms, some with shared baths. The large cottages have

W. on Spring St. from Hwy.
  29.
Price: Inexpensive to Moderate.
Credit Cards: MC, V.
Special Features: Spa treatments, mineral pool,
  whirlpool.
Handicap Access: No.

WINE COUNTRY INN
Innkeeper: Jim Smith.
707-963-7077.
1152 Lodi Ln., St. Helena,
  CA 94574.
Hwy. 29 N. of St. Helena, E.
  on Lodi Ln.
Price: Moderate to Expen-
  sive.
Credit Cards: MC, V.
Special Features: Pool,
  whirlpool.

ZINFANDEL INN
Innkeepers: Diane & Jerry
  Payton.
707-963-3512.
800 Zinfandel Ln., St.
  Helena, CA 94574.
1 mi. S. of St. Helena on Hwy.
  29, E. on Zinfandel Ln.
Price: Moderate to Expen-
  sive.
Credit Cards: MC, V.
Handicap Access: No.

Calistoga

**BRANNAN COTTAGE
  INN**
Innkeeper: Peter Bach.
707-942-4200.
109 Wappo Ave., Calistoga,
  CA 94515.
Just off Hwy. 29 near
  Brannan St.
Price: Moderate to
  Expensive.
Credit Cards: MC, V.
Handicap Access: Limited.

kitchenettes, and the sleeping cottages and private rooms have kitchen privileges. Continental breakfast is served daily. The sulphur spring that gave the resort its name more than a century ago still flows out of the mountain and into an outdoor soaking pool at a temperature maintained between 85 and 92 degrees. (For details on spa treatments, see Chapter Seven, *Recreation*.)

This 24-room guest house is modern but a tall stone tower gives it an Old World feel. All rooms have private baths and are furnished with antiques; many have alcove beds and balconies or decks with lush views. Four rooms have private hot tubs. Fireplaces are standard in most rooms but are inoperable from mid-April to mid-October. A buffet-style breakfast is served daily.

A striking example of an English Tudor, this is a luxury getaway planted in the heart of Wine Country. A fountain and an arched doorway crowned with fieldstone greet you. The dining room has an oak floor with beautiful inlays. There are three guest rooms, all named after grape varieties. The Chardonnay Suite may be the most elegant with its stone fireplace, king-size bed in a bay window, and private entrance. The Zinfandel Room has stained glass accents, a private deck, and whirlpool tub.

Built around 1860 by Calistoga founder Sam Brannan, this inn is listed on the National Register of Historic Places, and is the only guest house constructed for Brannan's Hot Springs Resort that still stands on its original site. Not surprisingly, it's also the oldest building in town. Restoration got under way in the 1980s; reconstruction of the gingerbread gable was based on enlarged vintage photographs.

Today, an eclectic collection of furnishings, including plush and comfortable antiques, furnish

BRANNAN COTTAGE INN

the six guest rooms. All have private baths, private entrances, and air conditioning. A generous breakfast may be served in the courtyard under lemon trees. The house is surrounded by gardens, so guests can always find a private, quiet spot to read and relax, and the sunny courtyard beckons after a day of "spa-ing."

BRANNAN'S LOFT
Innkeeper: Suzi Pestoni.
707-963-2181.
1436 Lincoln Ave.,
   Calistoga, CA 94515.
On Hwy. 29 downtown.
Price: Moderate to
   Expensive.
Credit Cards: MC, V.
Handicap Access: No.

Above the Cinnabar Restaurant in a historic building on the main business thoroughfare, this inn has four units with a private bath, color TV, modern kitchenettes, oak furnishings, and ceiling fans. One unit is a 600-square-foot suite and the two rooms have private balconies.

CALISTOGA INN
Innkeeper: Rose Dunsford.
707-942-4101.
1250 Lincoln Ave.,
   Calistoga, CA 94515.
On Hwy. 29 near Cedar St.
Price: Inexpensive.
Credit Cards: AE, MC, V.
Special Features: On-site
   brewery, beer garden,
   and restaurant.

Wine isn't the only beverage in this neck of the woods. A brewery, Napa Valley Brewing Co. (see Chapter Five, *Restaurants*), makes its home in the old water tower next to Calistoga Inn. This turn-of-the-century hotel is charming but the 18 guest rooms are basic. Double beds are standard and baths are shared. A light continental breakfast is served. The inn, about a block from the main highway, is within walking distance to spas and dining.

CHRISTOPHER'S INN
Innkeepers: Christopher &
   Adele Layton.
707-942-5755.

One of Napa Valley's newest B&Bs, this stylish inn has 13 rooms, all with private baths. Its rich antiques and Laura Ashley wallpaper and curtains evoke an English country inn. An architect by

1010 Foothill Blvd. (Hwy.
29), Calistoga, CA 94515.
On Hwy. 29 just S. of
Lincoln Ave.
Price: Moderate to Expen-
sive.
Credit Cards: AE, MC, V.
Handicap Access: Limited.

trade, Christopher Layton renovated three old
summer cottages. The grounds are impeccably
tended, bright with color and shaded by tall trees;
one room has a private garden patio and another
has a porch shaded by star jasmine. A modest continental breakfast is delivered to your room. Plans
are in the works for nine more rooms. Location is a
drawback; Hwy. 29 can be noisy but most rooms
are well off the road.

CULVER'S COUNTRY INN
Innkeepers: Meg & Tony
Wheatley.
707-942-4535.
1805 Foothill Blvd.,
Calistoga, CA 94515.
On Hwy. 128 N. of Lincoln
Ave.
Price: Moderate.
Credit Cards: None.
Special Features: Pool,
whirlpool, indoor sauna.

A registered historical landmark, circa 1875, this
special inn operated by British-born hosts has
six guest rooms decorated with Victorian furniture,
and all have private baths. The inn, set on a shady
hillside, is an easy walk to Calistoga's main-street dining and shopping. A full breakfast is served. The inn
is also air conditioned, a plus during Calistoga's
toasty summers.

THE ELMS
Innkeepers: Stephen &
Karla Wyle.
707-942-9476.
1300 Cedar St., Calistoga,
CA 94515.
Just N. of Lincoln Ave. on
Cedar.
Price: Moderate to Expen-
sive.
Credit Cards: MC, V.

This grand three-story French Victorian is in a
quiet residential neighborhood not far from
downtown. Time seemingly stands still inside this
grand dame with towering windows and a formal
parlor. The rooms, all with private baths, are beautifully done in European antiques. There is also a
cottage for a more private getaway.

FOOTHILL HOUSE
Innkeepers: Doris & Gus
Beckert.
707-942-6933.
3037 Foothill Blvd.,
Calistoga, CA 94515.
On Hwy. 128 N. of Petrified
Forest Rd.
Price: Moderate to Very
Expensive.
Credit Cards: AE, D, MC,
V.

This cozy inn is a find. Shaded by tall trees and
set amid gardens lush with herbs, vegetables,
and flowers, this modest turn-of-the-century farmhouse is a soothing getaway. Foothill House offers
two elegant suites and a private cottage. All have
private baths (two with whirlpool tubs), private
patio door entrances, refrigerators, and wood-burning stove or fireplace. Antiques furnish the rooms,
including queen or king-size four-poster beds.

The cottage, called Quail's Roost, is accented in
whitewashed pine and is equipped with a kitchenette and a two-person whirlpool that looks out to

Chris Alderman

Foothill House is a soothing getaway set in shady trees and flower gardens.

a waterfall. Doris and Gus Beckert pamper guests with a generous gourmet breakfast delivered to your room that includes fresh fruit and croissants and such treats as a rich cheese and potato casserole. Afternoon wine and cheese in the sun room is an extravagant spread.

HIDEAWAY COTTAGES
Manager: Ole Yearian.
707-942-4108.
1412 Fairway, Calistoga, CA 94515.
Just off Lincoln Ave.
Price: Inexpensive to Moderate.
Credit Cards: AE, MC, V.
Handicap Access: Yes.
Special Features: Pool.

These 17 units are comfy but utilitarian. Air conditioning and televisions are standard and most have kitchenettes. Adjacent to Dr. Wilkinson's Hot Springs Resort, the cottages are set amid tall mature trees on a quiet residential street close to Lincoln Avenue restaurants and shops.

LA CHAUMIERE
Innkeeper: Gary Venturi.
800-942-5139.
1301 Cedar St., Calistoga, CA 94515.
Just N. of Lincoln Ave. on Cedar.
Price: Expensive.
Credit Cards: AE, MC, V.

This is an intimate and homey bungalow in a peaceful residential area not far from downtown. The main house has two guest rooms; one has a private deck and each have private baths. The inn's jewel is out back: a private cabin under a giant redwood tree. Built in 1932, it has a private deck and a fireplace made from petrified wood. The grounds are lovingly tended. Be prepared for a hearty breakfast.

LARKMEAD COUNTRY INN
Innkeeper: Tim Garbarino.
707-942-5360.

Built on land once owned by flamboyant San Francisco heiress Lillie Coit in the late 1880s, this inn was originally part of Larkmead Winery,

1103 Larkmead Ln.,
   Calistoga, CA 94515.
S. of Calistoga off Hwy. 29
   at Larkmead Ln.
Price: Moderate.
Credit Cards: None.
Handicap Access: Yes.

MOUNT VIEW HOTEL
Manager: Billy Martin.
707-942-6877.
1457 Lincoln Ave.,
   Calistoga, CA 94515.
Price: Moderate to Very
   Expensive.
Credit Cards: AE, MC, V.
Special Features: Pool,
   whirlpool, restaurant.

THE PINK MANSION
Innkeepers: Toppa Epps
   & Leslie Sakai.
707-942-0558.
1415 Foothill Blvd.,
   Calistoga, CA 94515.
On Foothill Blvd. (Hwy.
   128) near Hwy. 29.
Price: Moderate to Expen-
   sive.
Credit Cards: MC, V.
Special Features: Indoor
   pool, whirlpool.

**QUAIL MOUNTAIN BED
   & BREAKFAST**
Innkeepers: Don & Alma
   Swiers.
707-942-0316.
4455 N. St. Helena Hwy.
   (Hwy. 29), Calistoga, CA
   94515.
W. of Hwy. 29 at Scott Way
   near Dunaweal Ln.

as was Larkmead-Kornell Champagne Cellars next door. It is set in the heart of a vineyard and was built by an Italian-Swiss family before Prohibition. The Palladian-style architecture is unique to the area. The main part of the house is upstairs, the better to oversee work in the vineyards and catch afternoon breezes. Four guest rooms, all with private baths, are along a hallway in one wing of the house. The king-size bed in the Chardonnay Room was made from two brass beds salvaged from a Paris hotel. Persian rugs, wicker, and colorful fabrics add to the homey feel.

Restored in Art Deco style and on the National Register of Historic Places, this elegant lodge was originally a European-style hotel built in 1917. There are 34 units, including nine luxurious suites furnished in Deco period pieces. It's in the heart of Calistoga shopping and dining, with major spas just steps away. Just off the lobby is one of the valley's best restaurants, Catahoula, where California meets Louisiana (see Chapter Five, *Restaurants*).

Postcard views of Napa Valley and lush forests await visitors who stay at this 1875 Victorian. The home's pink exterior will catch your attention, while the flowers, rare plants, and exotic palms will hold your interest. All five guest rooms have private baths and queen-size beds. (The Angel Room also has a treasured family collection of angels; the Forest Room is decorated in green.) Innkeeper Seyfried was once a professional chef, so expect a unique full breakfast each morning. Wine and cheese cap off the afternoon. Three acres of landscaped gardens surround the estate.

Off the beaten track and 300 feet above the din of valley traffic, Quail Mountain B&B sits on 26 acres of forested mountain. It is a secluded, romantic retreat with three guest rooms. The style is contemporary; lots of floor-to-ceiling glass, skylights, and a solarium will have you believing you're lodging in an elegant tree house, and the white wicker furniture adds to the illusion.

King-size beds, and private decks and baths

Price: Moderate.
Credit Cards: MC, V.
Special Features: Pool.

round out the room amenities. (The Fern Room is the most popular, with a sitting area, oak floor, and outdoor-inspired mural.) Complimentary wine and full breakfast featuring fruit from the inn's orchards is served in the solarium, by the pool, or on the front deck.

Poolside at Scott Courtyard.

Chris Alderman

SCOTT COURTYARD
Innkeepers: Lauren & Joe
   Scott.
707-942-0948.
1443 2nd St., Calistoga, CA
   94515.
From Lincoln Ave., N. on
   Washington, E. on 2nd.
Price: Moderate to Expen-
   sive.
Credit Cards: AE, MC, V.
Special Features: Pool,
   whirlpool.

If you've slept in enough Victorian inns to last a lifetime, then this B&B is a refreshing change of pace. In four buildings that center around a beautiful and quiet garden courtyard, the inn has six suites, all decorated tastefully and unpretentiously. The Rose Suite is cozy with hardwood floors and a private porch. All the suites have queen-size beds, and private entrances and baths. The Scotts are avid readers, so there's always a good book around. A breakfast buffet is served in the common room warmed by a stone fireplace or in the courtyard by the pool. Check out the aviary. This inn is near downtown but quiet, and the hospitality is first-rate.

SILVER ROSE INN
Innkeepers: J-Paul, Sally, &
   Derrick Dumont.
707-942-9581.

Perched on a rocky outcropping and surrounded by ancient oak trees, this unique retreat has sweeping views of upper Napa Valley and Mount St. Helena. The main house is a spacious contem-

351 Rosedale Rd., Calistoga,
CA 94515.
Just off Silverado Trail, S. of
Hwy. 29.
Price: Moderate to Very
Expensive.
Credit Cards: AE, D, MC, V.
Special Features: Pool,
whirlpool, spa treatments,
exercise room, tennis.

porary inn with nine rooms; each has a distinct personality. The intimate Turn-of-the-Century Room is decorated with antique dolls. The Oriental Room has Asian rugs, rattan furniture, shoji screens, and a Japanese lacquered headboard; there's also a cathedral ceiling, whirlpool bath, and gorgeous vineyard views. The Garden Room has white wicker furniture, a two-person whirlpool, fireplace, and private deck. Silver Rose expanded recently, adding a new 11-room building called the Inn of the Vineyard.

Guests gather in the evening for wine and cheese around a large stone fireplace. Breakfast is served in the dining room, on the red stone deck near the rose garden and gazebo, or in your room. Breakfast is a hearty continental affair and includes Sally's luscious baked goods such as a delightful Hawaiian Bread. The Dumonts are superb hosts.

WINE WAY INN
Innkeepers: Cecile & Moye
Stephens.
800-572-0679.
1019 Foothill Blvd. (Hwy.
29), Calistoga, CA 94515.
Hwy. 29 just S. of Lincoln
Ave.
Price: Moderate.
Credit Cards: AE, MC, V.
Handicap Access: No.

"Like staying with friends" is the apt motto of this quaint California bungalow. The Stephens, who bought the inn in 1990, are warm hosts and Cecile's breakfasts are among the best in the valley, with menus that include frittatas with homemade salsa and a sticky sweet "bubble bread." All six guest rooms are modest in size, have private baths, and are nicely done with antiques and handmade quilts. The multi-level deck out back offers a spectacular view of the Palisades. The only negative — it's near a busy intersection so traffic noise is an issue.

Calistoga Spa Lodging

Many spas offer lodging/spa treatment discount packages. For complete spa treatment information, see Chapter Seven, *Recreation.*

Calistoga Spa Hot Springs (Manager: Michael Barrett; 707-942-6269; 1006 Washington Ave.) Price: Inexpensive to Moderate. MC, V. Relaxed and unpretentious, this inn has the amenities of a resort but at budget prices. All 57 family-oriented units have kitchenettes, air conditioning, TVs, and telephones. Features include weight and aerobics rooms, four outdoor mineral pools. Children welcome.

Calistoga Village Inn & Spa (Manager: Paul Schreiner; 707-942-0991; 1880 Lincoln Ave.) Price: Inexpensive to Expensive. AE, D, DC, MC, V. This inn has been everything from a motel to a Moonie camp. Rooms, freshly redecorated, are pleasant but modestly appointed. Some suites have whirlpool

Mineral pools at Calistoga Spa Hot Springs.

Peter Hickey/Courtesy Calistoga Chamber of Commerce

tubs. Two outdoor mineral pools offer an expansive view of the mountains. There is an inside mineral whirlpool, sauna, and steam room.

Dr. Wilkinson's Hot Springs (Manager: Mark Wilkinson; 707-942-4102; 1507 Lincoln Ave.) Price: Inexpensive to Moderate. AE, MC, V. This spa has 42 spacious and functional motellike rooms, many with kitchenettes. There are two outdoor mineral pools plus an indoor mineral whirlpool. Shopping and dining is within walking distance.

Golden Haven Hot Springs and Resort (Manager: Lea Kendall; 707-942-6793; 1713 Lake St.) Price: Inexpensive to Moderate. AE, MC, V. Amid towering oak trees and immaculate gardens, this 30-room spa offers many rooms with kitchenettes and all with refrigerators. Rooms with whirlpools, saunas, or waterbeds are also available.

Indian Springs Spa and Resort (Manager: John Hultgren; 707-942-4913; 1712 Lincoln Ave.) Price: Moderate to Expensive. MC, V. Seventeen whitewashed bungalow-style cottages overlook 16 acres of palm trees and views of Mount St. Helena. Gorgeous Olympic-size mineral pool. An easy walk to downtown shopping and dining.

Nance's Hot Springs (Managers: Sara Wright & Debbie Hughes; 707-942-6211; 1614 Lincoln Ave.) Price: Inexpensive. AE, MC, V. A no-frills family-run motel. Rooms include kitchenettes. Indoor mineral pool.

Pine Street Inn & Eurospa (Manager: Lori Baker; 707-942-6829; 1202 Pine St.) Price: Moderate. MC, V. Each of the 12 rooms at this older inn and spa are decorated in a different theme. Rooms have private baths. There is an outdoor mineral pool and whirlpool. Close to downtown yet away from the main street bustle.

Roman Spa (Manager: Gil Duarty; 707-942-4441; 1300 Washington St.) Price: Moderate to Expensive. AE, MC, V. Lushly landscaped grounds surround this older 60-room motellike resort. Most units have kitchenettes. There is an outdoor mineral pool and whirlpool, plus a large indoor whirlpool and sauna.

LODGING IN SONOMA COUNTY

Sonoma Valley

BELTANE RANCH
Manager: Rosemary Wood.
707-996-6501.
11775 Sonoma Hwy. (Hwy. 12), Glen Ellen, CA 95442.
On Hwy. 12 bet. Kenwood & Glen Ellen.
Price: Moderate.
Credit Cards: None.
Handicap Access: No.
Special Features: Tennis, hiking.

This former bunkhouse was built in 1882 and has been everything from a brothel to a turkey farm, but now it's a quiet and unpretentious B&B. A stylish porch and verandah were added to the house years ago, and there is an elaborate gingerbread railing. There are five guest rooms, each with a private entrance and bath. One room has a wood-burning stove. A full breakfast is served in the wood-paneled dining room. The ranch is also a working vineyard.

EL DORADO HOTEL
Manager: Jana Trout.
707-996-3030 or 800-289-3031.
405 1st St. W., Sonoma, CA 95476.
On the downtown Plaza.
Price: Moderate to Expensive
Credit Cards: AE, MC, V.
Handicap Access: Yes.
Special Features: Restaurant, pool.

The El Dorado is a special hotel. Restored to their original elegance, the 27 rooms all have private baths. French windows and terraces offer views of the hotel's Spanish courtyard or the historic Plaza. Breakfast is included in the tariff, as is a complimentary bottle of wine. The lobby restaurant Piatti serves regional Italian cuisine (see Chapter Five, *Restaurants*).

GAIGE HOUSE INN
707-935-0237.
13540 Arnold Dr., Glen Ellen, CA 95442.
Off Hwy. 12 on Arnold Dr. to Glen Ellen.
Price: Moderate to Very Expensive.
Credit Cards: AE, D, MC, V.
Special Features: Pool.

This inn is an Italian Gothic Victorian built in the 1880s and recently restored with nine pleasant guest rooms, all with private baths and air conditioning; three have private entrances and two have fireplaces. The best is the Gaige Suite, which has a canopied king-size bed, an oversized whirlpool tub, and a private balcony with a grand view. Full breakfast is served. It's in an ideal location for wine touring and Sonoma dining.

Glenelly Inn's verandahs command brilliant views of the surrounding gardens.

Courtesy Glenelly Inn

GLENELLY INN
Innkeepers: Kristi & Ingrid
 Hallamore.
707-996-6720.
5131 Warm Springs Rd.,
 Glen Ellen, CA 95442.
Off Hwy. 12 at Arnold Dr.,
 R. $^1/_3$ mi. on Warm
 Springs Rd.
Price: Moderate to Expen-
 sive.
Credit Cards: MC, V.
Special Features:
 Whirlpool.

Originally established in 1916 as a railroad inn, this French colonial has grand verandahs on both floors and six rooms, with two garden suites nearby. All rooms have stylish country furnishings, queen-size beds with goosedown comforters, and clawfoot tubs with showers. One room holds a personal collection of hats; the Vallejo Suite features mementos of local figure of note, Gen. Mariano Vallejo. All rooms open to the verandah or garden in this quiet, wooded setting with nearby wineries and restaurants. A generous buffet breakfast is served near the stone fireplace in the dining room. Hospitality is best when Kristi is on duty.

HIDDEN OAK
Innkeeper: Catherine
 Cotchett.
707-996-9863.
214 E. Napa St., Sonoma,
 CA 95476.
1 block E. of the Plaza.
Price: Moderate to Expen-
 sive.
Credit Cards: AE, D.

Park your car and put on your walking shoes. Everything you desire for a relaxing visit to Sonoma is just a stroll away from this homey inn a block off the Plaza. The house is a Craftsman bungalow built in 1913; the four guest rooms all have private baths, and a new suite will be available in 1995. A full breakfast and afternoon refreshments are served daily.

**KENWOOD INN AND
 SPA**
Innkeeper: Terrence
 Grimm.
707-833-1293.

This intimate resort looks like a small Tuscan village in a grove of oak trees. The inn includes 12 lush and large rooms, each with a fireplace and a pleasant view. At the heart of the compound is the pool and gardens, where a spa facility was

10400 Sonoma Hwy. (Hwy. 12), Kenwood, CA 95452
1 mi. S. of Kenwood.
Price: Very Expensive.
Credit Cards: AE, MC, V.
Special Features: Pool, spa treatments.

added in 1994. Treatments include massage, aromatherapy, and facials, all available on the terrace when weather permits. A full country breakfast is included and there is also a lunch menu offered poolside.

MAGLIULO'S PENSIONE
Innkeeper: Lori Magliulo.
707-996-1031.
691 Broadway, Sonoma, CA 95476.
2 blocks S. of the Plaza on Broadway.
Price: Moderate.
Credit Cards: D, MC, V.
Handicap Access: Yes.
Special Features: Restaurant.

Fresh flowers, antique quilts, ceiling fans, and an outdoor cabana add warmth to your stay. There are five guest rooms, two with private baths; the remaining three rooms share bath facilities. Continental breakfast is served daily in the dining room. The pensione is within easy walking distance of historic Sonoma Plaza.

SONOMA HOTEL
Innkeepers: Dorene & John Musilli.
707-996-2996.
110 W. Spain St., Sonoma, CA 95476.
On the downtown Plaza.
Price: Moderate.
Credit Cards: AE, CB, DC, MC, V.
Special Features: Restaurant.

Many of the 17 rooms in this hotel share bath facilities, but each room is sumptuously appointed with antiques, old oak, and stained glass. The best is the Bear Flag Room, with a glorious antique mahogany bedroom suite. Complimentary continental breakfast is served. The location is ideal, with downtown Sonoma at your feet.

SONOMA MISSION INN AND SPA
Manager: Jack Burkam.
707-938-9000.
18140 Sonoma Hwy. (Hwy. 12), Boyes Hot Springs, CA 95416.
Just N. of Sonoma.
Price: Very Expensive.
Credit Cards: AE, DC, MC, V.
Handicap Access: Yes.
Special Features: Spa treatments, tennis, pool, exercise rooms, restaurants.

Native Indians considered this spot a sacred healing ground; by the turn of the century it had become a getaway for well-heeled San Franciscans who came to Boyes Hot Springs Hotel to "take the waters." The resort, now the Sonoma Mission Inn and Spa, has been a destination ever since.

The Sonoma Mission Inn is Sonoma County at its most luxurious, from the impressive Mission-style façade to its health spa pamper palace. The rich and famous who have stayed there include Sylvester Stallone, Billy Crystal, and Tom Cruise. The 170 rooms and suites, while not lavish, are done in pastel hues and appointed with plantation shutters and ceiling fans. Many offers views of the inn's shady grounds and a few have fireplaces.

The sophisticated symmetry of a spa interior at the Sonoma Mission Inn and Spa.

Courtesy Sonoma Mission Inn

The main building dates to 1927 and has been expanded and renovated over the years. A world-class spa was opened in 1981 and numerous accommodation/spa packages are available. In 1993, after years of research, the inn found a new source of mineral water, a 135-degree artesian well 1,100 feet below the surface. Now the inn's whirlpools and two outdoor pools are naturally warmed by this soothing aqua (see "Spas" in Chapter Seven, *Recreation*, for more details).

The eight-acre grounds also include two restaurants: the Grille, a winning albeit expensive dining room, and the Café, an adequate eatery for breakfast and lunch (see Chapter Five, *Restaurants*). If there's a drawback to the Sonoma Mission Inn, it is location. While it is convenient to wineries and historic sites of Sonoma Valley, it's located along a hectic and well-developed thoroughfare. The grounds, however, remain peaceful.

SONOMA VALLEY INN, BEST WESTERN
Manager: Aaron Krug.
707-938-9200.
550 2nd St. W., Sonoma, CA 95476.
1 block W. from the Plaza off Hwy. 12.
Price: Moderate to Expensive.
Credit Cards: AE, CB, D, DC, MC, V.
Handicap Access: Yes.
Special Features: Pool, whirlpool.

An "intimate motel" may be the best way to describe this exceptional lodge just a block from Sonoma Plaza. Rooms and furnishings are well above average for a motel — most are equipped with kitchenettes, wet bars, whirlpools, or fireplaces. All rooms open onto a lovely courtyard. It's ideal for families visiting the valley. Complimentary continental breakfast is included. Special golf packages are also available.

SPARROW'S NEST INN
Innkeepers: Thomas &
Kathleen Anderson.
707-996-3750.
424 Denmark St., Sonoma,
CA 95476.
Price: Moderate.
Credit Cards: AE, D, MC, V.

This charming cottage is set in a flower garden on the edge of the city of Sonoma. The 500-sq.-ft. doll house is an English-style cottage with a queen-size bed and Laura Ashley bedding, a living room with hideabed, kitchenette, air conditioning, and cable TV with VCR. A continental breakfast is included.

THISTLE DEW INN
Innkeeper: Larry Barnett.
707-938-2909.
117 W. Spain St., Sonoma,
CA 95476.
$1/2$ block off the town Plaza.
Price: Moderate to Expen-
sive.
Credit Cards: AE, MC, V.
Handicap Access: Yes.
Special Features: Whirlpool.

This inn is decorated throughout with vintage Mission furniture. Each of the six guest rooms (two in the main house and four in the adjacent cottage) has a private bath, air conditioning, and ceiling fans. Four rooms have private entrances. One room opens to a deck, three rooms have gas fireplaces, and three are equipped with a large whirlpool tub. A full gourmet breakfast is served in the dining room or on the deck. This is a charming inn, reasonably priced and in an excellent location for strolling to all of Sonoma's finest.

TROJAN HORSE INN
Innkeepers: John & Doris
Leonard.
800-899-1925.
19455 Sonoma Hwy. (Hwy.
12), Sonoma, CA 95476.
Near Spain St.
Price: Moderate to
Expensive.
Credit Cards: AE, MC, V.
Handicap Access: Yes.
Special Features:
Whirlpool.

This turn-of-the-century B&B inn was originally the home of one of Sonoma's pioneer families. The six guest rooms, all with private baths, are lavishly furnished with antiques and modern conveniences. The Grape Arbor room has a whirlpool bath. The inn is close to restaurants, wine tasting, and shopping. On the down side, there is busy daytime traffic along Hwy. 12; request rooms away the street.

**VICTORIAN GARDEN
INN**
Innkeeper: Donna Lewis.
800-543-5339.
316 E. Napa St., Sonoma,
CA 95476.
2 blocks W. of the Plaza.
Price: Moderate to Expen-
sive.
Credit Cards: AE, MC, V.
Special Features: Pool, spa.

This 1870 Greek Revival farmhouse has a wrap-around porch furnished with comfy wicker. The garden is a peaceful treasure. The four guest rooms, one in the main house and the rest in a century-old water tower, have private baths and are elegantly decorated with Victorian furniture. Woodcutter's Cottage is a private retreat with a fireplace, clawfoot tub, and garden view. Breakfast is served in the dining room, on the patio, or in your room. Wine is served in the evening by the parlor hearth.

VINEYARD INN
Innkeeper: Lee Kjos.
707-938-2350.
23000 Arnold Dr., Sonoma,
  CA 94931.
S. of Sonoma at junction of
  Hwys. 12 & 121.
Price: Inexpensive to
  Expensive.
Credit Cards: AE, MC, V.
Handicap Access: Yes.

This California Mission-style establishment was once a popular stopover for motorists traveling between San Rafael and Sacramento. Today it is thoroughly remodeled and lavishly redecorated, but still reminiscent of those 1950s-era side-of-the-highway motels. The 12 bungalows are furnished with queen- or twin-size beds; there are also two-room suites with wet bars and refrigerators. Continental breakfast is served. Perhaps the most striking feature of this inn is its gardens, created by a landscape designer for Disneyland. Be warned: it's on a busy intersection.

Rohnert Park

RED LION HOTEL
Manager: Joe Topper.
707-584-5466.
Red Lion Dr., Rohnert Park,
  CA 94928.
Just off Hwy. 101 at Golf
  Course Dr. exit.
Price: Moderate to Very
  Expensive.
Credit Cards: AE, MC, V.
Handicap Access: Yes.
Special Features: Restau-
  rant, lounges, pool,
  whirlpool, exercise room.

A Mission-style hotel surrounded by two 18-hole golf courses, the Red Lion is popular primarily for its conference and banquet facilities. Leisure travelers will also appreciate its full-service hotel amenities. There are 246 rooms, including six suites. The rooms are decorated with standard hotel furnishings, the suites with French country-inspired furniture. If you're looking for an intimate getaway, steer clear of this sprawling hotel.

Santa Rosa

DOUBLETREE HOTEL
Manager: Dave Lawrence.
707-523-7555.
3555 Round Barn Blvd.,
  Santa Rosa, CA 95403.
Off Hwy. 101 at Old Red-
  wood Hwy. exit, E. on
  Fountaingrove Pkwy.
Price: Moderate to Expen-
  sive.
Credit Cards: AE, D, MC,
  V.
Handicap Access: Yes.
Special Features: Pool,
  restaurant, lounge.

Looking for a nice hotel in Santa Rosa? This is the best bet. Doubletree has luxurious accommodations on a hillside overlooking the city with easy access to Hwy. 101. There are 246 spacious, above-average guest rooms and suites scattered over several acres. The hotel caters to business travelers; all rooms have telephone-equipped desks. There are full hotel services, but the Harvest Grill is merely adequate. Ask for a room with a view when making your reservation.

FLAMINGO RESORT HOTEL
Manager: Floriann Bynum.
707-545-8530 or
   800-848-8300.
2777 4th St., Santa Rosa, CA
   95405.
Farmers Ln. at 4th St.
Price: Inexpensive to
   Expensive.
Credit Cards: AE, CB, DC,
   MC, V.
Handicap Access: Yes.
Special Features: Pool,
   whirlpool, tennis, fitness
   center, restaurant.

French country furnishings and lush landscaping make this resort hotel friendly and comfortable. Sonoma Valley's premium wineries are just minutes east on Hwy. 12. Guests have access to an adjacent fitness center, and specialty shops and excellent restaurants are just blocks away on Farmers Lane. Popular with both business travelers and tourists; continuous shuttle bus service is provided to and from San Francisco International Airport.

FOUNTAINGROVE INN
Manager: William Carson.
707-578-6101.
101 Fountaingrove Pkwy.,
   Santa Rosa, 95403.
Off Hwy. 101 at Old Red-
   wood Hwy. exit.
Price: Inexpensive to
   Expensive.
Credit Cards: AE, CB, D,
   DC, MC, V.
Handicap Access: Yes.
Special Features: Pool,
   whirlpool, restaurant.

The redwood and stone exterior of this luxury hotel is modern but blends harmoniously with the landscape, and the deliberately low sweep of the architecture affords an unobstructed view of the Round Barn historical landmark just up the hill. The rooms are elegantly simple and decorated with tasteful furnishings. Continental breakfast is included in the tariff, and standard hotel services are available. Equus Restaurant has improved somewhat but we still can't recommend it (see Chapter Five, *Restaurants*).

THE GABLES
Innkeepers: Michael & Judy
   Ogne.
707-585-7777.
4257 Petaluma Hill Rd.,
   Santa Rosa, CA 95404.
Rohnert Park Express-
   way E. exit off Hwy.
   101 to Petaluma Hill
   Rd.
Price: Moderate to
   Expensive.
Credit Cards: AE, D, MC,
   V.

The 15 gables above unique keyhole-shaped windows lend their name to this 1877 High Victorian Gothic Revival inn with a mahogany staircase and Italian marble fireplaces. The five spacious guest rooms have private baths with clawfoot tubs and the adjacent cottage is furnished with a kitchenette, wood stove, and two-person whirlpool tub. Full gourmet breakfast and afternoon snacks are included.

HOTEL LA ROSE
Manager: Debbie
   Neumann.
707-579-3200.
308 Wilson St., Santa Rosa,
   CA 95404.

Built in 1907, this sturdy stone classic is in historic Railroad Square, an eclectic urban area busy with bohemian coffee houses, nightclubs, and a few street folks. Reconstructed in 1985, the hotel has 49 rooms with English country interiors, pri-

Downtown exit off Hwy. 101, W. on 3rd St., N. on Wilson St.
Price: Moderate.
Credit Cards: AE, MC, V.
Special Features: Restaurant.

vate baths, and televisions. Twenty rooms have patios or balconies overlooking a courtyard garden. A continental breakfast buffet is included. Josef's Restaurant is recommended.

MELITTA STATION INN
Innkeepers: Diane Crandon & Vic Amstadter.
800-504-3099.
5850 Melitta Rd., Santa Rosa, CA 95409.
5 mi. E. of downtown on Hwy. 12, 1 mi. S. on Melitta Rd.
Price: Inexpensive to Moderate.
Credit Cards: AE, MC, V.

At the north end of the Valley of the Moon (and just minutes from Santa Rosa dining), this home was once a busy railroad station, general store, and post office. Today it's a warm inn with six guest rooms furnished with antiques and collectibles. Five rooms have private bath. An ample breakfast is served by the wood-burning stove in the large sitting room or on the balcony.

PYGMALION HOUSE
Innkeeper: Caroline Berry.
707-526-3407.
331 Orange St., Santa Rosa, CA 95407.
Downtown exit off Hwy. 101 to 3rd St., to Wilson St., 1 block on Laurel St. to Orange St.
Price: Inexpensive.
Credit Cards: MC, V.

A restored Queen Anne Victorian home near the historic Railroad Square district, Pygmalion House is a five-room inn serving hearty full breakfasts and complimentary afternoon refreshments. It's near shopping and dining in Railroad Square and at Santa Rosa Plaza, the downtown mall. All rooms have private baths with showers and/or clawfoot tubs.

One of Vintners Inn's Provençal-inspired guest rooms.

Chris Alderman

VINTNERS INN
Manager: Cindy Duffy.
707-575-7350.

Surrounded by a 45-acre vineyard planted in sauvignon blanc wine grapes, Vintners Inn is one of Sonoma County's finest establishments. It's

4350 Barnes Rd., Santa
  Rosa, CA 95403.
W. on River Rd. off Hwy.
  101.
Price: Moderate to Very
  Expensive.
Credit Cards: AE, DC, MC,
  V.
Handicap Access: Yes.
Special Features:
  Whirlpool, restaurant.

a European-style hotel with an Old World atmosphere, from its French country decor to the central plaza with a fountain. The 44 guest rooms are separated into three buildings that ring the courtyard.

Climbing the staircase in each building is akin to going upstairs to bedrooms in a friendly farmhouse. Many of the oversized rooms in this Provençal-influenced inn have fireplaces, beamed ceilings, and pine furniture, some dating back to the turn of the century. All rooms have telephones, TVs, and large tub/shower combination baths. Ground floor rooms have patios; second floor suites have balconies with vineyard or courtyard views. Deluxe suites have sitting areas, wet bars, and refrigerators. Continental breakfast is included in the tariff; room service is also available. The inn is convenient to both Sonoma and Napa Valley wineries. Next door is the superb John Ash & Co. restaurant (see Chapter Five, *Restaurants*).

Healdsburg

*Peace and quiet
are specialties of the
Belle de Jour Inn.*

Chris Alderman

BELLE DE JOUR INN
Innkeepers: Tom & Brenda
  Hearn.
707-431-9777.
16276 Healdsburg Ave.,
  Healdsburg, CA 95448.
1 mi. N. of Dry Creek Rd.
  on Healdsburg Ave.
Price: Expensive to Very
  Expensive.
Credit Cards: D, MC, V.

Perhaps the most private and peaceful bed and breakfast inn in Healdsburg, Belle de Jour is set on a tranquil six-acre hilltop with spectacular views of rolling hills and distant mountains. The Italianate main farmhouse, built around 1873, is where the innkeepers live and prepare scrumptious breakfasts.

The five guest suites, all decorated with French country-inspired furniture and sun-dried linens, are set behind the main house. Two of the rooms have private patios and whirlpool tubs for two. The Terrace Room has an intimate whirlpool tub with views of the unspoiled countryside. The Caretaker's Suite has a king-size canopy bed and French doors leading to a trellised deck. There is also a large suite in the loft of the barn, and it's equipped with a whirlpool tub and gas fireplace. The Hearns' 1923 antique touring car is available for personally escorted wine-tasting tours capped by a gourmet lunch. Belle de Jour Inn is elegance and hospitality at its finest.

CAMELLIA INN
Innkeepers: Ray & Del
  Lewand.
707-433-8182.
211 North St., Healdsburg,
  CA 95448.
2 blocks E. of Healdsburg
  Ave. on North St.
Price: Moderate to
  Expensive.
Credit Cards: MC, V.
Special Features: Pool.

This 1869 Italianate Victorian home entered the turn of the century as Healdsburg's first hospital. It is now a magnificent inn with nine guest rooms, and still has many of its original and unique architectural details, including the twin marble fireplaces in the double parlor. The rooms have private baths and are furnished with antiques and accented with chandeliers and Oriental rugs. On a quiet residential street just two blocks from the Plaza, the inn is named for the 50-some varieties of camellias that grace its gardens. A full breakfast buffet is served in the dining room, dominated by a mahogany fireplace mantel. Very friendly innkeepers.

**DRY CREEK INN, BEST
  WESTERN**
Manager: Aaron Krug.
707-433-0300.
198 Dry Creek Rd.,
  Healdsburg, CA 95448.
Off Hwy. 101 at Dry Creek
  Rd. exit.
Price: Inexpensive.
Credit Cards: AE, CB, DC,
  MC, V.
Handicap Access: Yes.
Special Features: Pool,
  whirlpool, exercise room.

This motel is distinguished by its outstanding location for wine touring. There is fairly standard motel decor throughout, but a spectacular view of Dry Creek Valley is the payoff in many rooms. Rooms are equipped with refrigerators and coffee makers and a continental breakfast is included — great for families. It's well situated for a day of wine tasting followed by dining downtown on the Plaza; the down side — the inn fronts busy Hwy. 101.

FRAMPTON HOUSE
Innkeeper: Paula Bogle.
707-433-5084.
489 Powell Ave.,
  Healdsburg, CA 95448.
⁴/₁₀ mi. S. of Dry Creek Rd.,
  ¹/₂ mi. E. of Healdsburg
  Ave.

Just three guest rooms, all with private baths, offer the right balance of service and privacy in this stately Victorian inn. Two rooms are upstairs; the third is in an adjacent cottage with private deck. French windows and skylights are among the amenities. Flowers abound in the large yard

Price: Inexpensive to
  Moderate.
Credit Cards: MC, V.
Special Features: Pool,
  sauna.

shaded by a tall palm and magnolia tree. A generous breakfast is served in the sun room.

**GEORGE ALEXANDER
  HOUSE**
Innkeepers: Christian &
  Phyllis Baldenhofer.
800-310-1358.
423 Matheson St., Healds-
  burg, CA 95448.
4 blocks E. of Healdsburg
  Ave.
Price: Moderate to Expen-
  sive.
Credit Cards: MC, V.

This 1905 Victorian has a small tower and distinct
quatrefoil and stained-glass windows. There are
four rooms in this lovely inn, each with private bath,
a down comforter, and gorgeous wallpaper and custom-made furnishings. The Mr. and Mrs. George
Alexander room has a fireplace and bay window,
while the Back Porch has a private entrance with
deck, wood-burning stove, and whirlpool tub for
two. The Baldenhofers pride themselves on breakfast, with a menu that includes the likes of lemon
ricotta pancakes with sautéed apples.

GRAPE LEAF INN
Innkeepers: Karen & Terry
  Sweet.
707-433-8140.
539 Johnson St., Healds-
  burg, CA 95448.
2 blocks E. of Healdsburg
  Ave. near Piper St.
Price: Moderate.
Credit Cards: D, MC, V.

The seven elegant guest rooms in this 1900
Queen Anne Victorian are lushly furnished
with iron beds, armoires, and warm oak accents,
and are all named after grape varietals. The five
rooms all have skylights and tubs for two; the
Chardonnay Suite is the most luxurious, with
stained-glass windows and cedar walls. The quiet
porch is perfect for unwinding after a day of wine
touring. A full country breakfast is served in the
dining room. On Saturday nights, guest vintners
occasionally arrive with wine for private tastings.
Within walking distance is Healdsburg's historic
downtown Plaza.

HAYDON STREET INN
Innkeeper: JoAnne Claus.
707-433-5228.
321 Haydon St., Healds-
  burg, CA 95448.
Off Hwy. 101 at Central
  Healdsburg exit, N. to
  Matheson St., E. to Fitch
  St., S. to Haydon St.
Price: Moderate to Expen-
  sive.
Credit Cards: MC, V.

In a quiet residential area and surrounded by
trees, this Queen Anne Victorian inn has six
charming guest rooms with hardwood floors,
antiques, and down comforters; two rooms share a
bath. More romantic are the two cottage rooms,
both with large whirlpool tubs. The Victorian
Room has a queen-size wicker bed and the Pine
Room has a lovely four-poster bed covered in
white linens. A generous breakfast buffet is served
in the dining room. The inn is a short walk to
Healdsburg's Plaza.

HEALDSBURG INN ON THE PLAZA

Innkeeper: Genny Jenkins.
707-433-6991.
110 Matheson St., Healdsburg, CA 95448.
Matheson St. off Healdsburg Ave.
Price: Expensive.
Credit Cards: D, MC, V.
Special Features: Art gallery.

Right on Healdsburg's delightful downtown Plaza, this 10-room inn welcomes guests through the main floor art gallery. Four rooms (most have fireplaces) overlook the Plaza with its bevy of shops, restaurants, and tasting rooms. The solarium and roof garden is the common area where guests take breakfast and afternoon refreshments. In-room TVs and phones are available on request. All rooms have private baths, some with old-fashioned tubs. Luxurious.

MADRONA MANOR

Innkeepers: John & Carol Muir.
707-433-4231.
1001 Westside Rd., Healdsburg, CA 95448.
From Hwy. 101, Central Healdsburg exit, W. 1 mi.
Price: Expensive to Very Expensive.
Credit Cards: AE, CB, D, DC, MC, V.
Handicap Access: Yes.
Special Features: Pool, restaurant.

This country inn and restaurant is the grande dame of Sonoma County. The three-story Victorian was built in 1881 and with its mansard roof, expansive porch, and surrounding lush gardens, it is a majestic sight amid a glade of trees. Large and ornate antiques decorate most of the mansion's formal guest rooms. Some of the 18 fireplaces are graced with delicate handpainted borders, and eight of the rooms have balconies or decks. All rooms are air conditioned and include private baths.

Three outlying buildings house six other rooms and three suites. In the carriage house, ask for Suite 400, which has a fireplace and whirlpool tub. For seclusion, try the Garden Suite, with a fireplace, rattan furniture, and private deck. Well off the main road, a stay at Madrona Manor is guaranteed to be unhurried, a throwback to the slower pace of the home's Victorian heyday. Full breakfast is included in the tariff. The restaurant is also first-rate (see Chapter Five, *Restaurants*).

Geyserville

CAMPBELL RANCH INN

Innkeepers: Mary Jane & Jerry Campbell.
707-857-3476.
1475 Canyon Road, Geyserville, CA 95441.
Hwy. 101 Canyon Road exit, 1 1/2 mi. W.
Price: Moderate to Expensive.
Credit Cards: MC, V.
Special Features: Pool, tennis court.

This ranch-style home sits atop a quiet hill with vistas of vineyards and mountains. Although the furnishings in the five guest rooms are more traditional than antique, all rooms have king-size beds, fresh flower accents, and private baths. The cottage has a fireplace and private deck. Guests can gather in the living room, with a high sloping ceiling and a fireplace. Baked goodies are a specialty and a full breakfast is served in the dining room or on the brick terrace.

HOPE-MERRILL HOUSE
Innkeeper: Rosalie Hope.
707-857-3356.
21253 Geyserville Ave.,
   Geyserville, CA 95441.
Off Hwy. 101 at Geyserville
   exit, 1 mi. N.
Price: Moderate.
Credit Cards: AE, MC, V.
Handicap Access: Limited.

A stagecoach stop in the 1870s and now an enchanting inn, Hope-Merrill House is listed on the Sonoma County Landmarks Register. Aficionados of architectural details will enjoy the historical significance of the structure: a striking example of 19th-century Eastlake-Stick style, the home was built entirely of redwood. Notice the authentic Victorian hand-screened wallpaper. Its seven rooms all have private baths; two have whirlpool tubs. A superb and generous breakfast is served in the dining room. The innkeeper also runs the less formal Hope Bosworth House across the street.

West County

APPLEWOOD
Innkeepers: Jim Caron &
   Darryl Notter.
707-869-9093.
13555 Hwy. 116,
   Guerneville, CA 95446.
$1/4$ mi. S. of Guerneville on
   Hwy. 116.
Price: Moderate to Very
   Expensive.
Credit Cards: AE, MC, V.
Handicap Access: Yes.
Special Features: Pool,
   whirlpool.

This Mission-style inn — hidden in a stand of redwoods — is one of Sonoma County's finest. It's romantic and formal yet familiar, like a wealthy grandmother's house. The site was originally an apple orchard and now harbors a circa-1922 mansion with nine rooms and a matching house, added in 1995, with seven rooms.

No stuffy Victorian-era museum furnishings here — the rooms have been decorated to feel like a private home, blending antiques with contemporary pieces and family heirlooms. Rich fabrics drape windows and upholstered furniture, and beds are dressed in fine pastel linens. All rooms have private baths, TVs, and phones. The new rooms have private decks, fireplaces, whirlpool tubs; a few have refrigerators.

The common area is centered around a huge double-sided stone fireplace. Breakfast is served in the solarium with wicker furniture and a redwood view, or in the formal dining room with arched ceilings. The kitchen, once reserved for breakfast, now offers dinner Thursday to Sunday. A single four-course prix-fixe meal is served at one seating each night and the food is superb (see Chapter Five, *Restaurants*).

BODEGA BAY LODGE
Manager: Jerry Schahfer.
707-875-3525.
Hwy. 1, Bodega Bay, CA
   94923.
Price: Moderate to Very
   Expensive.

Luxurious and more intimate than a standard Best Western hotel, this wood-shingled seaside lodge is sheltered from coastal winds but close enough for the sound of the surf. All rooms have ocean or bay views and private balconies, and many feature fireplaces, vaulted ceilings, spa baths,

---

Credit Cards: AE, CB, D, DC, MC, V.
Handicap Access: Yes.
Special Features: Restaurant, exercise room, whirlpool, sauna, pool.

refrigerators, wet bars, and coffee makers. Even the pool and whirlpool offer a breathtaking view.

THE FARMHOUSE INN
Innkeeper: Rebecca Smith.
707-887-3300.
7871 River Road, Forestville, CA 95436.
9 mi. W. of Hwy. 101 on River Rd.
Price: Moderate to Expensive.
Credit Cards: AE, MC, V.
Handicap Access: Yes.
Special Features: Pool.

Colorful is one way to describe this inn's history. "Bizarre" is the word Rebecca Smith prefers. Built as a farmhouse in 1878, it later became a horse ranch and a roadhouse lodge before gaining a questionable reputation as a bath house. In 1990, Smith took over, remodeling the house down to its studs and transforming a row of farmhand housing into six lovely guest rooms and two suites. The English country cottage decor is plush and each room has a private entrance and a ceramic tile whirlpool tub. Most of the rooms have fireplaces and private saunas.

The interior of the main house sets a distinct New England tone, with a long Shaker-style dining room where a rich breakfast feast is spread out. Dinners are also offered Thursday through Sunday (see Chapter Five, *Restaurants*). The din of daytime traffic on River Road may jangle some nerves; ask for a rear cottage. Exceptionally friendly innkeeper and staff. Be forewarned: the inn was for sale in late 1996.

GRAVENSTEIN INN
Innkeepers: Kathleen & Frank Mayhew.
707-829-0493.
3160 Hicks Rd., Sebastopol, CA 95472.
3 1/2 mi. N. of Sebastopol on Hwy. 116, L. on Graton Rd., R. on Hicks Rd.
Price: Moderate.
Credit Cards: MC, V.
Special Features: Pool.

On six sloping acres amid a Gravenstein apple orchard, this delightful three-story inn was built in 1872. It has four guest rooms, two with a shared bath. The Bavarian Suite is the most luxurious with a fireplace, private bath, and summer porch. A continental breakfast is served in the dining room, in the wisteria arbor, or in your room. The location is quiet and the atmosphere unhurried, with fine restaurants in Santa Rosa and Sebastopol only minutes away.

HOLIDAY INN
Manager: Hamish Scott Knight.
707-875-2217.
521 Hwy. 1, Bodega Bay, CA 94923.
Price: Moderate to Very Expensive.
Credit Cards: AE, D, MC, V.
Handicap Access: Yes.
Special Features: Whirlpool.

Part of a chain, yes, but a fine lodging nonetheless, with 45 nicely appointed rooms and suites with balconies offering lovely views of the bay and ocean. A few rooms have fireplaces, whirlpool tubs, saunas, and vaulted ceilings. It lacks a pool but it remains a wise choice for families. Breakfast is not included in the tariff.

On a hill overlooking a quiet village, The Inn at Occidental is delightfully off the beaten path.

Courtesy Inn at Occidental

INN AT OCCIDENTAL
Innkeeper: Jack Bullard.
707-874-1047.
3657 Church St., Occidental, CA 95465.
1 block off Bohemian Hwy.
Price: Moderate to Very Expensive.
Credit Cards: MC, V.
Handicap Access: Limited.

Perched on a hill overlooking the quiet village of Occidental, this comfortable three-story Victorian inn is a jewel, one of Wine Country's best. It is well off the beaten path and delightfully so. Guarded by fruit trees and a lush courtyard garden with a fountain, the inn was built in 1877 and was long known as Heart's Desire Inn.

The eight rooms have private baths and are sumptuously furnished with antiques Jack Bullard has collected over the years. The color palette of each room is designed around a specific collectible. The Leaf Umbrella room has a queen-size pine canopy bed; the walls are stenciled to match a watercolor of pink roses, and the room features a cherished collection of umbrella glass. The Tiffany Room features a collection of Tiffany silver, as well as a four-poster mahogany bed, fireplace, and private deck.

Bullard is an exceptional host, offering wine, cheese, and homemade cookies by the living room hearth each evening. A superb gourmet breakfast is served in the dining room, the verandah, the courtyard, or in your room.

INN AT THE TIDES
Manager: Carlo Galazzo.
707-875-2751.
800 Hwy. 1, Bodega Bay, CA 94923.
Price: Moderate to Very Expensive.
Credit Cards: AE, D, MC, V.
Handicap Access: Yes.

Six coastal acres with natural landscaping surround this inn, which is actually 12 separate lodges scattered over a hillside. The 86 guest rooms are agreeably designed, and most rooms have tiled fireplaces and bay or ocean views, with refrigerators, coffee makers, and a hideabed. One of Sonoma County's popular winemaker dinner series is organized here monthly during the spring

The Inn at the Tides
B O D E G A   B A Y

Special Features:
  Indoor/outdoor pool,
  whirlpool, sauna,
  restaurant.

— if interested, inquire when making your reservations. Continental breakfast is served across Hwy. 1 at the Tides.

JENNER INN
Manager: Jenny Carroll.
707-865-2377.
10400 Hwy. 1, Jenner, CA 95450.
Price: Inexpensive to Very Expensive.
Credit Cards: AE, MC, V.
Handicap Access: Limited.
Special Features: Restaurant.

Thirteen rooms, suites, and cottages make up this cozy inn in the quiet coastal village of Jenner. The units all have private baths and entrances and most are decorated with antiques and quilts. Four have access to a hot tub and several have fireplaces and kitchenettes. The Rosewater Cottage is on the water and has a king-size bed and stone fireplace. A buffet breakfast is included. The innkeeper also manages several private vacation rental homes.

RAFORD HOUSE INN
Innkeepers: Jack & Carole Vore.
800-887-9503.
10630 Wohler Rd., Healdsburg, CA 95448.
River Rd. W. to Wohler Rd., N. 1/4 mi.
Price: Moderate to Very Expensive.
Credit Cards: AE, D, MC, V.
Handicap Access: No.

Conveniently near many of Sonoma County's premium wineries, Raford House is an attractive inn with a wide porch. Sitting on a verdant hillside where its century-old windows overlook the tending and harvesting of hundreds of acres of premium vineyards, it is one of Sonoma County's oldest Victorian homes and a favorite of visitors searching for authentic Wine Country atmosphere. Two of the seven guest rooms have fireplaces and five have private baths. The two rooms that share a bath are in a separate wing and are often combined as a two-bedroom suite. Each room is decorated in a dominant color; the Blue Room is furnished with a four-poster bed and armoire. Stately palm trees stand as sentinels on the front lawn.

RIDENHOUR RANCH HOUSE INN
Innkeepers: Diane & Fritz Rechberger.

Within walking distance of Korbel Champagne Cellars, this circa-1906 inn is built of redwood and has eight guest rooms, each with a private bath. The rooms are decorated with English and

707-887-1033.
12850 River Rd.,
   Guerneville, CA 95446.
12 mi. W. of Hwy. 101. on
   River Rd.
Price: Moderate to
   Expensive.
Credit Cards: AE, MC, V.
Special Features: Hot tub.

American antiques and some have forest or rose garden views. Hawthorn Cottage has a fireplace and cozy window seat. Fritz Rechberger, trained as a chef in Europe, creates masterly breakfasts and guests can also arrange for dinner (requested in advance).

RIVER'S END
Manager: Wolfgang
   Gramatzki.
707-865-2484 or 869-3252.
11051 Hwy. 1, Jenner, CA
   95450.
Price: Moderate to
   Expensive.
Credit Cards: MC, V.
Handicap Access: Limited.
Special Features:
   Restaurant.

The view is spectacular from this modest resort on the edge of a sheer cliff overlooking the Russian River and the Pacific Ocean. The resort includes a small house, four cabins, and three rooms below the restaurant. All are simply appointed and have private baths. Most are wood-paneled and have decks for ocean gazing. Wolfgang Gramatzki is also a talented chef (for details on River's End Restaurant, see Chapter Five, *Restaurants*).

SANTA NELLA HOUSE
Innkeepers: Alan & Joyce
   Ferrington.
707-869-9488.
12130 Hwy. 116,
   Guerneville, CA 95446.
3 mi. SE. of Guerneville.
Price: Moderate.
Credit Cards: AE, MC, V.

Nestled in a quiet redwood forest, this inn is an 1870 Victorian with a grand wraparound verandah. There are four guest rooms, all with private baths and furnished with functional antiques and queen-size beds. All have wood-burning fireplaces. A full country-style breakfast — eggs benedict is a house specialty — is served in the kitchen by the wood-burning stove. The parlor/ music room is a favorite gathering place.

SEA RANCH LODGE
Innkeeper: Marianne
   Harder.
707-785-2371 or
   800-732-7262.
60 Sea Walk Dr., Sea Ranch,
   CA 95497.
29 mi. N. of Jenner on Coast
   Hwy. 1.
Price: Expensive.
Credit Cards: AE, MC, V.
Special Features:
   Restaurant.

On bluffs above the Pacific Ocean, this lodge has one of the best vistas in Wine Country. All but one of the 20 rooms face the sea, and cozy window seats offer front-row viewing for spectacular sunsets. The location is remote, but if you're in need of a peaceful getaway, this is it. Outside, the weathered wood recalls New England and the interior feels like a rustic cabin, with knotty pine, cathedral ceilings, and quilted bedspreads. Some rooms have fireplaces and hot tubs. Three caveats: walls are thin, locate your room's flashlight immediately since lighting is poor outside at night, and bring a sweater because fog keeps it cool even in summer. The restaurant is adequate but pricey —

but oh that view. Hiking trails are well marked along the bluffs and tennis and golf at hand (see Chapter Seven, *Recreation*).

TIMBERHILL RANCH
Innkeepers: Barbara Farrell, Tarran McDaid, Michael Riordan, & Frank Watson.
707-847-3258.
35755 Hauser Bridge Rd., Cazadero, CA 95421.
Hwy. 1 N. of Jenner to Meyers Grade Rd., to Hauser Bridge Rd.
Price: Very Expensive.
Credit Cards: AE, D, MC, V.
Handicap Access: Yes.
Special Features: Pool, tennis court, restaurant.

Seclusion is one reason so many seek out the Sonoma Coast, and West County doesn't get any more secluded than Timber Hill, a magnificent getaway that blends country comfort with luxury. High on Hauser Ridge, nearly a two-hour drive from Santa Rosa, the 80-acre resort is made up of 15 rustic but elegantly appointed cedar cottages, as well as a main lodge and dining hall.

The cottages, each with a deck overlooking trees and hills, are very private and magnificently furnished with overstuffed chairs, handmade quilts, fresh flowers, fireplaces, and mini-bars and refrigerators stocked with refreshments. Breakfast is delivered to your doorstep, and chef Bob Peterson creates winning menus for lunch and dinner, served in the casual dining hall with a high-beamed ceiling and huge stone fireplace. The view is soothing from the 40-foot heated pool and a whirlpool, and hiking trails weave in and out of the adjacent 6,000 acres of wilderness.

MOTELS

Napa Valley

Best Western Napa Inn (707-257-1930; 100 Soscol Ave., Napa) Price: Expensive to Very Expensive. AE, CB, D, DC, MC, V. 68 rooms, some wheelchair-accessible. Heated pool and spa, restaurant, loft suites available.

Chablis Lodge (707-257-1944; 3360 Solano Ave., Napa) Price: Expensive to Very Expensive. AE, MC, V. Basic 34-unit motel; some units have wet bars, refrigerators, private spas, or whirlpools. Includes continental breakfast.

Comfort Inn (707-942-9400; 1865 Lincoln Ave., Calistoga) Price: Moderate to Expensive. AE, CB, D, DC, MC, V. 54 rooms; swimming pool, whirlpool, sauna, continental breakfast.

Silverado Motel (707-253-0892; 500 Silverado Trail, Napa) Price: Inexpensive. AE, MC, V. 15 rooms recently remodeled, some with kitchenettes.

Sonoma County

Best Western Garden Inn (707-546-4031; 1500 Santa Rosa Ave., Santa Rosa) Price: Inexpensive to Moderate. AE, D, DC, MC, V. Two pools, coffee shop; 78 rooms. Wheelchair-accessible and non-smoking rooms. Guest laundry. Nicely landscaped.

Best Western Hillside Inn (707-546-9353; 2901 4th St., Santa Rosa) Price: Inexpensive. AE, D, DC, MC, V. Tree-surrounded setting with 35 units, pool, sauna, restaurant, and lounge. Suites and kitchenettes available.

Bodega Harbor Inn (707-875-3594; Bodega Ave. at Hwy. 1, Bodega Bay) Price: Inexpensive to Very Expensive. MC, V. 14 rooms, 2 suites, cottages, and homes, some with ocean views, decks, hot tubs, fireplaces, and kitchens.

Days Inn (707-573-9000; 175 Railroad St., Santa Rosa) Price: Inexpensive to Moderate. AE, CB, D, DC, MC, V. 130 rooms and suites. Swimming pool, spa, non-smoking rooms, café, lounge, room service. Handicap-accessible. Close to downtown and Railroad Square. The Airporter, an airport shuttle service to and from San Francisco and Oakland airports, is based here.

El Pueblo Motel (707-996-3651; 896 W. Napa St., Sonoma) Price: Inexpensive. AE, MC, V. 38-room motel with pool. Restaurants nearby. On a busy intersection.

Fairview Motel (707-433-5548; 74 Healdsburg Ave., Healdsburg) Price: Inexpensive. AE, D, MC, V. Pool, whirlpool, complimentary coffee. Restaurants nearby.

Los Robles Lodge (707-545-6330; 1975 Cleveland Ave., Santa Rosa) Price: Inexpensive to Moderate. AE, CB, D, DC, MC, V. Hot tub, pool, restaurant; 105 rooms.

Salt Point Lodge (707-847-3234; 23255 Hwy. 1, Jenner) Price: Inexpensive to Expensive. MC, V. Just 16 rooms. Restaurant and lounge, hot tub, sauna, sun deck, some ocean-view rooms. Seaside state park and marine reserve nearby.

Timber Cove Inn (707-847-3231; 21780 N. Coast Hwy. 1, Jenner; 25 mi. N. of Bodega Bay on Hwy. 1) Price: Expensive. AE, MC, V. Charming but funky, with a breathtaking location perched on a rocky cliff overlooking the ocean. Many of the 50 rooms have ocean views, and some have fireplaces and private hot tubs. Restaurant and lounge. Two-night minimum on weekends.

Vineyard Valley Inn (707-433-0101; 178 Dry Creek Rd., Healdsburg) Price: Inexpensive to Moderate. AE, MC, V. A new and stylishly pleasant motel close to wineries. There are 23 rooms plus two suites with refrigerators and whirlpool tubs. Indoor whirlpool and sauna and exercise room. Continental breakfast included.

A Word to the Wise

We are confident that as of press time, all of the establishments recommended in this chapter, as elsewhere in the book, meet the standards a reasonable traveler would set for comfort, interest, and convenience. Inevitably, there are "off" days in the best of hotels or B&Bs, and while we hope you'll never encounter one of these, we cannot guarantee that you won't. If it happens to you, we hope you can go with the flow, keep a sense of humor and perspective, and push on with the pleasure of anticipation of your next Napa or Sonoma destination. If you have any particular experiences to report, we would welcome the opportunity to hear from you about it, either by letter or e-mail (see the e-mail address in the Introduction to this book).

CHAPTER FOUR

La Dolce Vita
CULTURE

Wine Country culture is more blue jeans than black tie and tails, but that doesn't mean we don't appreciate the finer things. Nearby San Francisco, of course, is a world-class city and while Napa and Sonoma counties can't compete with its museums, opera, and ballet, Wine Country is more than just wineries, food, and scenic views.

Wine Country's literary heritage dates back to writer Robert Lewis Stevenson, who brought a touch of civilization to St. Helena in the 1880s.

Chris Alderman

The Hess Collection features the work of internationally known artists.

Later, Jack London, author of *The Call of the Wild*, retired to Glen Ellen and became a gentleman farmer. Carefully preserved historical sites, such as Sonoma's Mission San Francisco Solano, built in 1825, are reminders that we have long honored our culture.

Music, as it always seems to, helped lead the way. The Santa Rosa Symphony was the first to be organized in 1927, followed a few years later by the Napa Valley Symphony. As the communities began to grow after World War II, and with the renewal of the wine industry in the 1960s, Napa and Sonoma's cultural landscape began to flourish as well.

Artists weary of the city and drawn to the beauty of Wine Country began moving north, making Napa and Sonoma the popular artistic havens they are today. Art galleries appeared and wineries began to display art in their tasting rooms. The first theater companies formed in the early 1970s, and theaters have proliferated in Sonoma County to become a dominant force in the local arts. Wineries have played a special role in this cultural expansion, promoting the arts as one of life's necessities as well as the perfect accompaniment to wine.

The following pages will give you some idea of the arts and entertainment possibilities in Napa and Sonoma. The best place to find current happenings are the entertainment pages of the *Napa Register* and Santa Rosa's *Press Democrat*. The **Arts Councils** of both counties are also good sources of information. For Napa, phone 707-257-2117 and for Sonoma, phone 707-579-2787.

ARCHITECTURE

The 1892 Richie Block Building, with its unique latticework and stained-glass detailing, dominates Main Street in downtown St. Helena.

Chris Alderman

While Napa and Sonoma may not have the strong architectural traditions found in the East and Midwest, Wine Country has its own grand style. Plain and practical dried brick buildings called adobes ruled until the first buildings in a European style were built in the 1860s, and many of those — particularly in Sonoma County — were lost in the earthquake of 1906. Architectural gems remain, however, and newer ones have been added.

The most obvious treasures are the castlelike wineries of Napa Valley. Most notable is **Beringer's** stately, German-style mansion called Rhine House, built in the late 1800s. Nearby is the Gothic fortress of **Greystone Cellars** built in 1889. It was once the winery for Christian Brothers, but is now home to the Culinary Institute of America. Inglenook's grand chateau was built in 1887. In Sonoma, **Hop Kiln Winery** along the Russian River is inside a towering hop kiln built in 1880. The building with three tall spires was used to dry beer hops, back when the area was a center for growing that commodity. **Korbel Champagne Cellars** is an ivy-covered brick beauty with a brandy tower.

There are also newer winery wonders. Most striking is the white hilltop villa south of Calistoga of **Sterling Vineyards**. Nearby is the postmodern temple to wine and art, *Clos Pegase,* designed by Princeton architect Michael Graves. Across Napa Valley is the distinctive shake-roofed *Rutherford Hill Winery,* which recalls an early Wine Country barn. The chateaux of *Domaine Carneros* near Napa and *Jordan* in Sonoma's Alexander Valley are extravagant reminders of France. Open since 1991, the high-tech *Codorniu Napa* is spectacularly understated. Built into the side of a Carneros hillside and nearly impossible to make out from the road, it recalls a buried temple. *Opus One* winery, a joint venture between Robert Mondavi and France's Chateau Mouton-Rothschild, is another extravagant temple, designed by the firm that created San Francisco's Transamerica Pyramid.

The oldest city in the area, Sonoma, also has many of the oldest buildings, including adobes like the simple but majestic *Mission San Francisco Solano.* Surrounding the Sonoma Plaza are a number of historic buildings, including the fading but still regal *Sebastiani Theatre,* built in 1933.

The cities of Napa and Petaluma offer walking tours of downtown Victorian neighborhoods. (Check at visitor centers for maps.) Napa's tour includes the *Napa Opera House,* 1018 Main St., an Italianate beauty built in 1879, now being refurbished. There's also the *First Presbyterian Church* at the corner of 3rd and Randolph streets, a Victorian Gothic built in 1874. Walking tour maps are available at the **Napa Valley Conference and Visitors Bureau** (1310 Napa Town Center, Napa, 707-226-7459).

A thriving river port in the 1870s, Petaluma has retained many of its beautiful homes and the downtown is beautifully preserved — the city amazingly was spared during the 1906 quake. Browse along Petaluma Boulevard and Kentucky Street, taking in the antique shops and admiring the classic architecture. Drive through the Victorian neighborhoods and check out the majestic Queen Anne styling of the old Gilger house at 111 6th St., or the intricately ornate Spanish Colonial at 47 6th St. Pick up a copy of "The Streets of Petaluma" at the **Petaluma Area Chamber of Commerce** (799 Baywood Dr., Petaluma; 707-762-2785).

Many of Santa Rosa's great buildings were lost in the 1906 earthquake, though *McDonald Avenue* on the west edge of downtown has survived. Alfred Hitchcock filmed *Shadow of a Doubt* in Santa Rosa. Downtown has changed considerably since then, but the McDonald Avenue residential area, shown extensively in the film, remains the city's architectural prize. Just west of downtown is a lovely neighborhood of large homes, wide streets, and tall trees. The centerpiece is *Mableton* at 1015 McDonald. Built in 1878, it was inspired by the plantation homes of Mississippi.

CINEMA

Although few of Napa's or Sonoma's grand old movie houses still stand — blame it on urban renewal or earthquakes — movie-going remains an ardent

One of the few grand old movie houses still standing.

Tim Fish

passion. *The Wine Country Film Festival,* a month-long celebration of the latest foreign and art films, is small but respected. *The Sonoma Film Institute,* staged in a classroom at Sonoma State University but open to the public, is low on atmosphere but high on quality. Finally, Sonoma and Napa are home to many top-name stars, and the two counties' landscapes are cinema stars in their own right — both are favorite locations for Hollywood feature films and commercials.

Two movie theaters of particular interest are in Healdsburg and St. Helena:

The Raven Film Center (707-433-5448; 115 North St., Healdsburg) The main Raven theater is easily the finest movie house in Wine Country. The downtown Healdsburg theater, which seats 600, was meticulously restored a few years back by Don Hyde and partners. The projection and sound equipment is state-of-the-art and the theater is roomy, as a movie house should be. In late 1994, Hyde added four smaller theaters at the rear of the original. The cinemas show first-runs, art movies, and revivals of classics. Hyde even brings in live music on occasion.

Liberty Theatre (707-963-3946; 1340 Main St., St. Helena) A charming theater in downtown St. Helena showing first-run films, though as you might expect for a small town, a few weeks after release. Mostly American fare, though occasional art and foreign films come for a stay.

Additional movie theaters are listed below.

Napa County

Cinedome (707-257-7700; 1175 West St., Napa) Modern eight-theater complex showing first-runs in downtown.

Uptown Cinemas (707-224-7977; 1350 3rd St., Napa) A downtown four-plex showing first-runs and discount double-feature second runs.

Sonoma County

Airport Cinema 8 (707-522-0330; 409 Aviation Blvd., Santa Rosa) Opened in 1995, this eight-screen cinema is one of the best in Wine Country.

Coddingtown Cinemas (707-544 1970; 1630 Range Ave., Santa Rosa) A four-theater complex showing first-runs.

Empire Cinemas (707-584-0123; Redwood Drive, Rohnert Park) Four theaters showing first-run films.

Lakeside 5 Cinemas (707-538-7469; Summerfield Rd., Santa Rosa) First-run American and foreign films. A former skating rink and it feels like it.

Pacific's Petaluma Cinema (707-769-0700; 1363 N. McDowell Blvd., Petaluma) So much room and style, you forget it's a multi-plex. Eight theaters, two quite large and with state-of-the-art equipment. Eight more screens in the works.

Sebastiani Theatre (707-996-2020; 476 1st St. E., Sonoma) A delightful old theater in dire need of refurbishing. Shows late first-run films.

Sebastopol Cinemas (707-829-3456; McKinley St. & Petaluma Ave., Sebastopol) Open since fall 1994, this five-theater cinema is inside a refurbished brandy distillery. Shows first-run films.

Sonoma Cinemas (707-935-1234; Hwy. 12 & Siesta Way, Boyes Hot Springs) This four-plex theater, open since summer 1994, shows first-run movies.

United Artists Cinema 5 (707-528-7200; 547 Mendocino Ave., Santa Rosa) Compact little multi-plex hidden away in downtown. Don't blink or you'll drive right past. First-run films.

United Artists Cinema 6 (707-528-8770; 620 3rd St., Santa Rosa) Ditto Cinema 5.

Film Festivities

Sonoma Film Institute (707-664-2606; Sonoma State University, Darwin Theater, Rohnert Park) If you can overlook the classroom atmosphere, the Institute is a great place to catch classics and art films. Whether you prefer the Marx Brothers in *Duck Soup* or the latest Kurosawa, the Friday and Saturday night double-features are a great bargain at $4.

Wine Country Film Festival (707-935-2536; 12000 Henno Rd., Glen Ellen) This annual July and August event is a fast-paced potpourri of movie screenings, workshops, and parties. The events spread throughout Napa and Sonoma counties. Some of the movies that made their debut at WCFF include *sex, lies, and videotape* and *When Harry Met Sally*. Stars are usually on hand to schmooze, including Gregory Peck, Nicolas Cage, and Dennis Hopper. Caution: the films are excellent, but the festival has a reputation for organizational problems.

Seeing Stars

Hollywood seems enamored with Wine Country, Sonoma County in particular. Look closely, and you'll recognize more than a few famous movie and TV sites. The most famous is perhaps the old Bodega School in Bodega, immortalized by Alfred Hitchcock in *The Birds*. It's just off Bodega Highway, a few miles inland from Bodega Bay. Another familiar spot is downtown Petaluma, used for the cruising scenes in *American Graffiti*. TV fans, of course, will recognize Spring Mountain Winery in St. Helena as the backdrop for *Falcon Crest*.

More than a few celebrities call Napa and Sonoma home, at least part time. "Peanuts" creator Charles Schulz is Santa Rosa's most famous denizen. Robin Williams owns a mountain-top ranch between Napa and Sonoma counties. The late Raymond "Perry Mason" Burr was a well-known Healdsburg resident. Other high-profiles include comedian-vintner Tommy Smothers, musician-actor Tom Waits, and Jon Provost, known to millions as Timmy on the old "Lassie" TV show. And film star Winona Rider was raised in Petaluma.

GALLERIES

Whether your thing is abstract expressionism or dolphins jumping through rainbows, there's an art gallery for you somewhere in Napa and Sonoma counties. A new gallery seems to open every weekend. The hills of Northern California shelter some of the finest artists in the country.

Each of the galleries has its own specialty. Some galleries are cooperatives, owned and operated by local artists. Others specialize in ceramics or offer paintings and prints of nationally known artists. Vineyards and seascapes, of course, are the dominant themes.

Napa County

CLOS PEGASE WINERY
707-942-4981.
1060 Dunaweal Lane,
  Calistoga.
Open: 10:30–4:30 daily,
  tours 11 & 2 daily.
Fee: None.

This winery is a work of art in itself. Designed by the award-winning architect Michael Graves, it looks like a postmodern Babylonian temple. A commanding edifice of tall pillars and archways, done in bold hues of cream and terra cotta, Clos Pegase is an eye-catcher.

The lawn and courtyard serve as a sculpture garden. That collection includes Richard Serra's provocative "Twins," a minimalist masterpiece. The regular winery tour offers a glimpse of owner Jan Shrem's impressive art collection, including 17th- and

The imposing entrance of Clos Pegase, designed by noted architect Michael Graves.

Courtesy Clos Pegase

18th-century French statuary artfully displayed in the winery's massive underground cave. Also, a casual browse through the visitor center reveals more treasures.

THE HESS COLLECTION
707-255-1144.
4411 Redwood Rd., Napa.
Open: 10–4 daily.
Fee: None.

If there's a gallery in Wine Country that deserves the title museum, it's the Hess Collection. Swiss entrepreneur Donald Hess transformed the old Mont La Salle Winery into a ultra-modern showcase for his two great passions: art and wine. Built on the rugged slopes of Mt. Veeder, the Hess Collection opened to the public in 1989.

The entrance opens onto a dramatic three-story staircase. The 130-piece collection spans the upper two floors and features the works of internationally know artists such as Francis Bacon, Robert Motherwell, and Frank Stella. A mix of paintings and sculptures, the works are provocative and often haunting, though humor plays a role, too.

I. WOLK GALLERY
707-963-8800.
235 Main St., St. Helena.
Open: 10–5:30 Weds.–Mon.
Fee: None.

A second floor walk-up above downtown St. Helena, this is an excellent gallery with serious intentions about art, specializing in contemporary paintings, photography, and crafts by emerging American artists. "Contemporary" does not necessarily read "abstract," since the emphasis is on realist imagery. Exhibitions feature single artists but a wide range of artists is shown continuously.

JESSEL GALLERY
707-257-2350.

Jessel is the essence of what Northern California galleries are all about. The art is not particularly

1019 Atlas Peak Rd., Napa.
Open: 9:30–5:30 daily.
Fee: None.

challenging but lovely nonetheless and the atmosphere is laid-back, almost meditative. If you're
weary of the bustle of Hwy. 29, Napa's main drag,
make a detour to this delightful gallery. Jessel, an
artist who prefers just one name, opened the
gallery in 1987 and offerings include gorgeous pastels and watercolors, as well
as jewelry and ceramics.

Sonoma County

**CALIFORNIA MUSEUM
OF ART**
707-527-0297.
Luther Burbank Center for
the Arts, Mark West
Springs Rd., Santa Rosa.
Open: 11–4 Weds.–Sun.
Fee: None.

A museum only in name, the gallery-sized California Museum of Art has nonetheless become
one of Sonoma County's most important art
spaces. It earns the name "museum" in the way it
displays art. The emphasis is not on money, but
artists — Sonoma artists in particular. The art may
be for sale, but this isn't a showroom. Paintings
don't fight for space with postcards, T-shirts, and
earrings. And rather than displaying whatever art
is handy for quick showings, exhibits pride themselves on quality and linger
six to eight weeks. Occasionally the work of a single artist is featured, though
usually two people or groups share the space.

PRESS HOUSE GALLERY
800-938-1266.
Buena Vista Winery, 18000
Old Winery Rd., Sonoma.
Open: 10:30–4:30 daily.
Fee: None.

The artist-in-residence program at Buena Vista
is one of Wine Country's best art ideas. The loft
of the historic Press House tasting room becomes a
gallery and working studio for a different Bay Area
artist each month. Visitors taste wine and watch
the creative process in action. The artists, most
often working in pastels, oils, and watercolors,
welcome questions and friendly discussion.

**ZIMBABWE SHONA
SCULPTURE**
707-938-2200.
452 1st St. E., Sonoma.
Open: 10–6 daily.
Fee: None.

If you think African art is just masks and primitive carvings, think again. The Shona tribe in
Zimbabwe, known as "the people of the mist,"
carve extraordinary stone sculptures. They believe
that each stone hides a unique spirit and the sculptor's task is to remove what has been hiding the
spirit. The sculptures — which depict gods, peo-
ple, and animals — reveal both vivid talent and primitive charm. A second
Shona gallery is in Village Outlets, 3111 N. St. Helena Hwy. (Hwy. 29), St.
Helena.

OTHER GALLERIES

Napa County

Canard Fine Art (707-944-0131; 6550 Washington St., Yountville) Wildlife, flowers, and pleasant landscapes. Mostly limited edition prints.

Codorniu Napa (707-224-1668; 1345 Henry Rd., Napa) This winery is an architectural work of art; built into a hillside, it looks like a lost tomb. A single artist is displayed for two months and the quality is superb.

Evans Ceramics Gallery (707-942-0453; 1419 Lincoln Ave., Calistoga) A small factory outlet for decorative ceramics.

The Gallery on Main Street (707-963-3350; 1359 Main St., St. Helena) Paintings and prints by Northern California artists; vineyards and other landscapes.

Images Fine Art (707-944-0404; 6540 Washington St., Yountville) Specializes in limited edition prints. Art meets interior decoration.

Lee Youngman Galleries (707-942-0585; 1316 Lincoln Ave., Calistoga) Southwest art from nationally known artists; oils, watercolors; metal and wood sculptures.

Mumm Napa Valley (800-999-3801; 8445 Silverado Trail, Napa) The long hallways of this winery are devoted to art and it's a lovely space. Revolving shows are featured and Ansel Adams' "Story of a Winery" is on permanent display.

Patricia Sweetow Gallery (707-224-2577; 1144 Main St., Napa) A first-rate gallery featuring California and Northwest artists. No simple vineyard pastels here. Great stuff with serious intent.

Raku Ceramics Collection (707-944-9424; 6540 Washington St., Yountville) Raku is a distinctive Japanese style of ceramics that creates a rustlike glaze. Some beautiful pieces here.

RASberry's Art Glass Gallery (707-944-9211; 6540 Washington St., Yountville) A gift shop disguising itself as a gallery. You may consider these garish creations art. We don't.

Robert Mondavi Winery (707-226-1395; 7801 Hwy. 29, Oakville) One of the first wineries to show art; rotating shows on display in the Vineyard Room.

Washington Square Gallery (707-944-0606; 6795 Washington St., Yountville) Specializes in limited edition prints, easy landscapes, etc.

Sonoma County

Arts Guild of Sonoma (707-996-3115; 140 E. Napa St., Sonoma) A cooperative of Sonoma County artists, displaying a potpourri of artists, from colorful vineyard landscapes to playful ceramic figures.

Bodega Landmark Studio (707-876-3477; 17255 Bodega Hwy., Bodega) West county artists a specialty; oils, watercolors, ceramics.

Le Haye Art Center (707-996-9665; 148 E. Napa St., Sonoma) A historic foundry that has been converted into six artist studios. See art in action.

Ren Brown Collection (707-875-2922; 1781 Hwy. 1, Bodega Bay) Modern Japanese prints are the focus of this gallery.

Santa Rosa Junior College Gallery (707-527-4298; 1501 Mendocino Ave., Santa Rosa) Group shows by faculty and students.

Snoopy's Gallery (707-546-3385; 1667 W. Steele Ln., Santa Rosa) More of a museum and gift shop than a gallery, but it's worth checking out if you're a "Peanuts" fan. Creator Charles Schulz is a local and many of his originals are on display.

Sonoma State University Gallery (707-664-2295; E. Cotati Ave., Rohnert Park) Traveling exhibits of nationally known painters and sculptors, as well as student and faculty group shows.

On the Trail of Art

ARTrails (707-579-ARTS) A Sonoma County tradition every October. For two weekends, dozens of artists open their studios to the public. It's rare chance to see artists in their natural habitat, not to mention an opportunity for a bargain since there's no art gallery middleman. Sponsored by the Cultural Arts Council of Sonoma County; handy tour maps are available.

Napa Valley Artists' Open Studio Weekends (707-257-2117) Similar to ARTrails — dozens of artists open their studios to the public during the last two weekends in October. Tour maps available through the Napa County Arts Council for a nominal fee.

Ray and Judy Watten hard at work during the annual ARTrails.

Courtesy Cultural Arts Council of
Sonoma County

HISTORIC PLACES

The Bale Grist Mill was built in 1846.

Chris Alderman

Napa County

BALE GRIST MILL
707-942-4575.
3369 Hwy. 29, 3 mi. N. of
   St. Helena.
Open: 10–5 daily.
Fee: $2 adults, $1 children.
Gift shop.

Just think, if wheat had caught on in Napa Valley, you might be cruising Hwy. 29 in search of the perfect loaf of bread. When settlers first began arriving in Napa in the 1830s and '40s, wheat, corn, and wild oats — not grapes — were the crops of choice. Mills, of course, were a necessity, not only as places to grind grain into meal and flour, but also as social centers for the community. Edward Turner Bale's grist mill, built in 1846, was one of three in Napa and the only one that survives.

If traffic or the glitz of wineries gets on your nerves, take an hour for a quiet getaway at the Bale Grist Mill State Historic Park. It seems miles and generations away.

The mill is at the end of a short path, a refreshing walk through dense woods and across a lively brook. The first thing you'll notice is the 36-foot-high wooden waterwheel, rolling at a leisurely pace, water trickling down its curved steps. Inside the three-story wood mill house, a woman in a bonnet and period dress greets visitors. She might even offer you a slice of dense bread, made on-site with grain from the mill. The miller may actually crank up the giant millstones and grind flour.

The mill has a colorful past. Its builder, Dr. E.T. Bale, had a reputation as a rogue and scoundrel. He was fond of the bottle and refused to pay his debts. Jailed on a number of occasions, he was publicly whipped and once nearly lynched for shooting a relative of the important Gen. Mariano Vallejo. Finally, Bale settled down and built the mill. It became the gathering spot for the north valley, where friends could exchange gossip and even stage dances. In those days, a miller was a leading citizen in the community and his counsel in business matters was highly respected.

With the coming of new technology at the turn of the century, the mill fell into neglect. It was restored by the Native Sons of the Golden West in 1925 and then again in 1967. It became a state historic park in 1974.

Sonoma County

Fort Ross, built by the Russians in 1813, sits on a windy bluff north of Bodega Bay.

Courtesy Sonoma County Convention & Visitors Bureau

FORT ROSS
707-847-3286.
12 mi. N. of Jenner on Hwy. 1.
Open: 10–4:30 daily.
Fee: $6 per car.
Picnic area, gift shop, camping.

A quick history quiz. Who were Sonoma's first settlers (besides the Indians, of course)? If you said the Spanish, you're wrong. It was actually the Russians who established Fort Ross, predating the Sonoma Mission by 11 years.

The Russian-American Trading Company, a firm controlled largely by the Imperial Russia government, came to California to escape the cruel winters of Alaska and to hunt for valuable sea otters. They landed south in Bodega Bay, which they called "Rumiantsev," and explored to the north. On a windy bluff overlooking the Pacific, they built their fort and community, now the centerpiece of Fort Ross State Historic Park.

Under the Russians, the fort thrived for 30 years as a major trading center for trappers and explorers. The Spanish and, later, Mexican settlement of Napa and Sonoma was established largely to thwart the Russian presence at Fort Ross. By 1830, the sea otter population was decimated and Fort Ross fell into decline. The Russians sold Fort Ross in 1839. It's certainly off the beaten path, miles from the nearest winery, but history buffs won't want to miss it and the drive along Hwy. 1 is spectacular.

One structure built by the Russians still stands: the Commandant's House. The two blockhouses, the stockade, and the Russian Orthodox Chapel have been carefully rebuilt. The visitor center and museum offer a look at the fort's past, as well as a peek at Russian and Indian artifacts.

LUTHER BURBANK HOME AND GARDEN
707-524-5445.
Corner of Santa Rosa & Sonoma Aves. in Santa Rosa.
Open: Apr.–Oct. 10–4 Weds.–Sun.; garden 8–7 summer, 8–5 winter.
Fee: Docent-led house tour $2 for adults, free to children under 12; no fee for garden.
Gift shop.

Plant genius Luther Burbank remains Santa Rosa's favorite son. Sixty-five years after his death, buildings and businesses bear his name. At the turn of the century his fame was international. Burbank arrived from his native Massachusetts in 1877. In a letter home he wrote — and Santa Rosans love to quote this — "I firmly believe . . . this is the chosen spot of all this earth as far as nature is concerned."

From his Santa Rosa garden, Burbank developed more than 800 new strains of fruits, flowers, vegetables, and grasses. Burbank, along with other geniuses like George Washington Carver, transformed plant breeding into a modern science. So great was Burbank's fame that by 1900, 150 people a day came to see the man and his garden. Among his visitors one day in 1915 were Thomas Edison, Henry Ford, and Harvey Firestone.

The house was built in about 1870 and is rather small, a modified Greek Revival cottage. Burbank lived there from 1884 to 1906, when the earthquake damaged the house and Burbank moved. When Burbank died in 1926, his wife Elizabeth returned to the cottage. The property was designated a National Historic Landmark in 1964, and upon Elizabeth's death in 1977, the house and garden became city property.

The half-hour tour of the house is full of facts and artifacts and includes a glimpse inside one of Burbank's original greenhouses. The garden, as you might expect, abounds in Burbank creations, particularly the Paradox Walnut Tree and the Burbank Rose.

MISSION SAN FRANCISCO SOLANO
707-938-1519.
Corner of Spain St. & 1st St. E., Sonoma Plaza, Sonoma.
Open: 10–5 daily.
Fee: $2 for adults, $1 children 6–12; admission also good toward entry

This is where European settlement really began. Sure, technically, the Russians established the first outpost at Fort Ross, but the true origins of Napa and Sonoma lie at Sonoma's Mission San Francisco Solano. The white adobe mission with a red-tile roof is probably the most popular historic attraction in Wine Country.

To appreciate its significance, it helps to understand the history of California's mission system.

Mission San Francisco Solano was the birthplace of Sonoma and Napa counties.

Courtesy Sonoma Valley Visitors Bureau

to Petaluma Adobe & Vallejo House; other historic sites are also along the Plaza.

The Spanish government and Catholic Church began establishing California missions in 1769, both as a way of converting "heathen" Indians and claiming land for Spain. There were already 20 missions when the young and ambitious Father Jose Altimira received permission from the Mexican governor of California to establish a new one north of the San Francisco Bay. On July 4, 1823, Altimira celebrated Mass with a makeshift redwood cross and blessed the site.

The Sonoma Mission was the last to be established, and the mission system was dissolved in 1833. It became a center of religion and culture under Gen. Mariano Vallejo's rule, but it was sold by the church in 1881. Used variously as a blacksmith shop and hay barn, the mission was nearly lost until the state intervened in 1906; restoration began three years later.

Today, only the long, low building to the east of the present chapel is original, although the current chapel was only built a few years later, in 1841. Displays explain how adobe buildings are constructed and how the mission was restored. The chapel is decorated with 14 stations of the cross, authentic relics of the mission period. The chapel decor is also patterned after mission interiors of the period, highly stylized primitive renderings by Christianized Indians.

PETALUMA ADOBE
707-762-4871.
3325 Adobe Rd., 3 mi. E. of Petaluma.
Open: 10–5 daily.
Fee: $2 for adults, $1 children 6–12; admission also good toward entry

Once the heart of Gen. Mariano Vallejo's sprawling 100-square-mile rancho, the Petaluma Adobe is the area's most meticulously restored adobe. The commanding two-story house was built in 1836 and has three-feet-thick mud walls and a redwood verandah all around.

Authentic is the key word here. The rooms are

to Mission San Francisco
Solano & Vallejo House.
Picnic tables.

furnished to the period, and goats and chickens roam the outdoor corridors. Outdoor displays include working replicas of a forge and a large oven for baking bread.

The tour is self-guided; the museum details the history of the adobe and how it was restored.

**GENERAL VALLEJO
  HOME**
707-938-1519.
W. Spain St., ¹/₂ mi. W. of
  Sonoma Plaza, Sonoma.
Open: 10–5 daily.
Fee: $2 adults, $1 children
  6–12; admission also
  good toward entry to
  Mission San Francisco
  Solano & Petaluma
  Adobe.
Picnic tables.

Gen. Mariano Vallejo may have been the most powerful man in Northern California in the 1850s, but he had a sense of poetry about him when he named his house *Lachryma Montis*. Latin for "Tears of the Mountain," the name was derived from a mountain spring on the property.

Vallejo was born in Monterey in 1807; his father was a Spanish soldier. Following his father into military service, Vallejo was commander of the presidio, the Spanish fort and settlement in San Francisco, when he was sent north in 1834. He commanded the northern frontier for 14 years and was largely responsible for encouraging the settlement of both Sonoma and Napa counties.

Vallejo's home, finished in 1852, reflects his embrace of the American culture. Instead of an adobe house, he built a two-story Gothic Victorian. The house was prefabricated, designed and built on the East Coast, and shipped around the Horn. Vallejo and his family lived in the house for 35 years; the state bought the property in 1933.

The house and grounds are gorgeous, a quiet stop if you need relief from the bustle of Sonoma Plaza. The long driveway is flanked by tall cottonwood trees and the gardens and vineyards are carefully tended. The self-guided tour begins in a large warehouse, where displays detail Vallejo's life and the history of the house. One detraction: instead of tasteful ropes in the doorways guarding the rooms as in most historic homes, ugly white metal bars and cages have been installed to protect the considerable collection of artifacts and personal effects on display.

**JACK LONDON STATE
  HISTORIC PARK**
707-938-5216.
2400 London Ranch Rd.,
  Glen Ellen.
Open: Park open 8 to sun-
  set daily; house open
  10–5 daily.
Fee: $5 per car.
Picnic tables, barbecue pits,
  hiking, horseback riding.

"When I first came here, tired of cities and people," Jack London wrote of Glen Ellen, "I settled down on 130 acres of the most beautiful land to be found in California." The writer famed for *The Call of the Wild* and other adventure stories called his home in the Sonoma Mountains "Beauty Ranch."

Today his ranch is in the heart of Wine Country's most beautiful state park, now a vast 880 acres of

The ruins of Jack London's Wolf House.

Courtesy Napa County Historical Society

woodlands, fields, and hiking trails. The Wolf House is perhaps the park's most prominent feature. The massive castlelike stone building was four stories tall; it was the culmination of Jack and Charmian London's dreams. On the night of Aug. 22, 1913, only days before they were to move in, Wolf House mysteriously burned. The ruins remain today, although it requires a hike to see it. London died in 1916, reminding many of words he once said: "The proper function of man is to live, not exist. I shall not waste my days in trying to prolong them. I shall use my time."

London's grave along the half-mile trail to Wolf House is another popular stop. You can also visit London's ranch house, his stone barn, and pig palace. The House of Happy Walls, built by Charmian after London's death, serves as a museum, displaying an 18,000-volume library, original furnishings, memorabilia, and the Londons' collection of South Pacific artifacts.

LIBRARIES

Wine Country has two distinguished libraries: the *Napa Valley Wine Library* and the *Sonoma County Wine Library*. Both are exceptional resources.

The Napa Wine Library is inside St. Helena Public Library (707-963-5244; 1492 Library Lane). It has a vast collection, including more than 6,000 books, tapes, etc., detailing everything from the art of winemaking to the history of Napa wine to the current community of wineries throughout the valley.

The Sonoma County Wine Library occupies a small wing inside the Healdsburg branch of the Sonoma County Public Library (707-433-3772; 139 Piper St.). Its collection is similar but somewhat smaller, though no less impressive. The library also subscribes to nearly 75 wine magazines and newsletters.

MUSEUMS

Napa County

Sharpsteen Museum's model of early Calistoga life.

Chris Alderman

SHARPSTEEN MUSEUM
707-942-5911.
1311 Washington St.,
  Calistoga.
Open: Noon–4, winter;
  10–4, summer.
Fee: None.

If you want a quick lesson in early Napa life, this quaint museum is the place to go. Ben and Bernice Sharpsteen created the museum almost as a hobby after Ben retired as a producer for Walt Disney and the couple moved to Calistoga. Before long, it became a community project and today it is run by volunteers.

The first section of this museum is devoted to the Sharpsteens themselves and, frankly, it's rather dull. But the miniature model of early Calistoga that follows is delightful. The town was founded in 1859 as a resort by the flamboyant Sam Brannan. Brannan was a man of many firsts: California's first newspaper publisher, banker, and land developer. He built the first railroad and telegraph. He was also California's first millionaire. His elegant Hot Springs Resort was a gathering place for California's rich and famous, and his vision of Calistoga as a haven of healing waters and relaxation still lives today. Only one tiny Victorian cottage remains from Brannan's resort; it was moved in 1977 and is attached to the museum. Step inside the wonderfully ornate cottage and you'll step back into the 1860s.

The museum also details a great deal of Northern California history. One display, a Napa Valley timeline, is particularly intriguing, dating back to the first explorers and the Sonoma Mission through the turn of the century. There are also lessons about the early stagecoach days — a restored coach is on display — the first railroad, Robert Louis Stevenson's days in Napa, and more.

There are enough old photos, newspapers, and artifacts to keep any history buff happy.

SILVERADO MUSEUM
707-963-3757.
1490 Library Ln., St. Helena.
Open: Noon–4 daily, closed Mon.
Fee: Free.

Writer Robert Louis Stevenson was taken by Napa Valley. In 1880, the author of *Dr. Jekyll and Mr. Hyde* and *Treasure Island* honeymooned with his wife in a cabin near the old Silverado Mine. He wrote about the area in "The Silverado Squatters." He called Napa's wine "bottled poetry" and Mount St. Helena was the inspiration for Spyglass Hill in *Treasure Island*. Although Stevenson spent only a few months in Napa Valley, he has been accepted as an adopted son.

Part of the St. Helena Library Center, the museum has a feeling of a small chapel. Founded in 1969, on the 75th anniversary of Stevenson's death, Silverado is more a library than a museum. It contains more than 8,000 artifacts, including dozens of paintings and photographs, as well as original Stevenson letters and manuscripts. There are also hundreds of books and first printings.

Sonoma County

RIPLEY'S MEMORIAL MUSEUM
707-524-5233.
492 Sonoma Ave., Santa Rosa.
Open: 10–4 Weds.–Sun., Mar.–Oct.
Fee: $1.50 adults, $.75 youths & seniors.

Robert L. Ripley — Believe It Or Not — was born in Santa Rosa, and if you have a taste for tacky, this is the place for you. It's one of 13 museums devoted to Ripley, who for 30 years was the world's authority on the exotic and unusual, as immortalized in his newspaper feature "Ripley's Believe It Or Not."

The museum is almost worth the $1.50 admission for its sheer absurdity. By far the most interesting thing about the museum is the building itself: The Church Built From One Tree. A single tree from the massive redwoods along the Russian River supplied the wood for this 1873 church. It's a noble little red chapel in a quiet neighborhood, a church that Ripley himself attended as a youth.

Few Santa Rosans even remember that Ripley was born in the city. He was still a student at Santa Rosa High School when he sold his first cartoon to *Life* magazine for $8. A budding sports illustrator for the old *New York Globe*, he created his first "Believe It or Not" cartoon in 1918. Before he died in 1959, he scoured the world for the weird.

The museum includes an unintentionally comical video on Ripley and introduces you to some of his odd friends. There's the man who drives six inch nails into his nose. ("In fact, he claims it cleared up his sinus condition!") Or there's the man who can smoke through his eye. The exhibits are all rather

One of Ripley's famous "Believe It or Not" features.

Courtesy Ripley Entertainment Inc.

wacky and sometimes lame: a few Ripley originals, a life-sized wax figure of Ripley, a battered suitcase plastered with travel stickers, a stuffed Siamese calf, among others.

SONOMA COUNTY MUSEUM
707-579-1500.
425 7th St., Santa Rosa.
Open: 11–4 Weds.–Sun.
Fee: $2 adults, $1 students & seniors.
Gift shop.

The Sonoma County Museum building, a classic post office from early in the century, was saved from an insidious fate: progress. When the building was slated for demolition, preservationists prevailed and it was moved to its present site in 1979. Now on the National Register of Historic places, the structure is beautifully restored. A mix of Spanish and Roman influences, it is considered one of the few remaining examples of classic Federal-style architecture in California. Inside the two-story stucco building are marble floors and rich oak paneling — no better place for a museum. Lobby displays detail the history of the building and its laborious move two blocks north. The main exhibit room offers rotating displays keyed to Sonoma history.

OTHER MUSEUMS

Napa County

Napa Firefighters Museum (707-259-0609; 1201 Main St., Napa) Antique firefighting equipment on display. Open weekends only.

Napa County Historical Society Museum (707-224-1739; 1219 1st St., Napa) A small collection of Indian artifacts, pioneer tools, etc., used largely for research.

Napa Valley Museum (707-963-7411; 473 Main St., St. Helena) Rotating exhibits plus displays of artifacts and crafts. Plans for a new museum underway.

Veterans Museum (707-944-4918; California Veteran's Home, Yountville) This fine Spanish Revival complex is home to a collection of military memorabilia.

Sonoma County

Healdsburg Museum (707-431-3325; 221 Matheson St.) Devoted to early Healdsburg history, including Indian artifacts and 5,000 photographs.

Native American Art Museum (707-527-4479; 1501 Mendocino Ave., Santa Rosa Junior College) Artifacts and current works by Native American artisans.

Petaluma Historical Museum and Library (707-778-4398; 20 4th St.) Devoted to early Petaluma history. Inside a classic Carnegie Library.

MUSIC

Napa County

NAPA VALLEY SYMPHONY
707-226-6872.
Lincoln Theater, California Veteran's Home, Yountville.
Season: Oct.–Apr.; pops concerts June & Dec.
Tickets: $8–$16.

The young Asher Raboy is the conductor for this symphony that dates to 1933 when Luigi Catalano first gathered a cadre of amateur and professional musicians. Today there are more than 75 musicians from Napa Valley and the Bay Area in the orchestra.

Each of the season's five concerts feature guest artists performing the great music of the classical repertoire. Past soloists have included pianist Philippe Bianconi and violinist Robert McDuffie.

Each summer since 1969, the lovely Robert Mondavi Winery has played host to the symphony's Wine Country Pops, a warm and delightful June evening.

Asher Raboy, conductor of the Napa Valley Symphony.

Courtesy Napa Valley Symphony

Sonoma County

BAROQUE SINFONIA
707-546-4504.
Burbank Center for the
  Arts, 50 Mark West
  Springs Rd., Santa Rosa.
Season: Oct.–Apr.
Tickets: $6–8.

If you're a CPA who finds artistic solace in playing the oboe, then Baroque Sinfonia is the place for you. This chamber orchestra is a more leisurely paced version of the Santa Rosa Symphony (see below). The 40 musicians are all volunteers and are led by 73-year-old maestro Eugene Shepherd. They play for sheer pleasure and it shows. Don't expect perfection, but the concerts are user-friendly. Their "Sing-Along *Messiah*" in December is a community favorite.

**SANTA ROSA
  SYMPHONY**
707-546-8742.
Burbank Center for the
  Arts, 50 Mark West
  Springs Rd., Santa Rosa.
Season: Oct.–May.
Tickets: $9.50–$25.

A new conductor means a new direction for this symphony. In the 1995-96 season, Jeffrey Kahane succeeded Corrick Brown, who led the symphony for the better part of its existence (it dates from 1927). Musicians — all of respectable talent — come from around the Bay Area. Some are semi-professionals with day jobs; others keep busy roaming from one orchestra to another. Guests of emerging musical reputation are featured in each concert. Recent soloists have included guitarist David Tanenbaum and British pianist Ian Hobson.

Burbank Center for the Arts, a former church, is a large hall of about 1,500 seats. Acoustics aren't what they might be, but the symphony strives to overcome the limitations. The symphony's Redwood Summer Music Festival is one of the highlights of Sonoma County's musical year.

OTHER MUSIC

Napa County

Dixieland Jazz Society (707-226-8114) These Dixieland jazz lovers stage various concerts throughout Napa Valley all year long.

Domaine Chandon Music Series (707-944-2280; just off Hwy. 29, Yountville) From the elegant voice of Jane Olivor to the classics of the Modern Mandolin Quartet, concerts on the lawn at this sparkling wine facility are given throughout the summer.

Napa Jazz and Art Festival (707-257-0322; Veteran's Park, downtown Napa) A day-long showcase of jazz in July. Also plenty of food, wine, and art.

Napa Valley Music Festival (707-252-4813; Napa Exposition Center, Napa) A three-day festival of acoustic music that features Bay Area and national acts.

Robert Mondavi Summer Music Festival (707-963-9611; 7801 Hwy. 29, Oakville) A tradition since 1969, these June through August concerts on the lush lawns of Mondavi's winery bring in top names in popular music: Tony Bennett, David Benoit, and the Preservation Hall Jazz Band.

Sonoma County

Cotati Jazz Festival (707-584-2222; downtown Cotati) Jazz lovers hop between nightclubs listening to the best jazz musicians the Bay Area has to offer.

Cotati Accordion Festival (707-664-0444; La Plaza Park, downtown Cotati) Those crazy accordion players gather to play "Lady of Spain" every August.

Healdsburg Plaza Sunday Concert Series (707-433-6935; downtown Healdsburg) From May through September, an eclectic array of music livens Sunday afternoons on this lovely plaza.

Petaluma Summer Music Festival (707-763-8920) Cinnabar Theater's annual ode to music and musical theater. Concerts and performances are staged throughout Petaluma during this August series.

Redwood Summer Music Festival (707-546-8742) Annual outdoor concert series by the Santa Rosa Symphony. Picnickers spend a carefree evening in various outdoor locales listening to Mozart, Gershwin, Copland, and the like.

Rodney Strong Music Series (707-433-0919; 11455 Old Redwood Hwy., Healdsburg) A summer-long series of concerts on this winery's lawn.

Russian River Jazz Festival (707-869-3940; Johnson Beach, Guerneville) Jazz along the lazy Russian River has made this the most popular music festival in Wine Country. For two days every September, music lovers sun on the beach or listen from floating inner tubes. The line-up of jazz greats has recently included Larry Carlton, Grover Washington, Jr., David Benoit, and Etta James.

Courtesy Russian River Jazz Festival

Santa Rosa Dixie Jazz Festival (707-539-3494; Red Lion Hotel, Rohnert Park) Sonoma County swarms with Dixie jazz nuts for one weekend every August. A BIG event, bringing in bands from around the world. Don't ask them to play "When the Saints Go Marching In."

Sonoma County Folk Festival (707-546-3600; Burbank Center for the Arts, 50 Mark West Springs Rd., Santa Rosa) A three-day festival of acoustic music that features Bay Area and national acts such as Joan Baez and John Prine.

NIGHTLIFE

If you're cruising for a good time in Napa Valley at night, you'll discover quickly that things are rather sleepy. It's the nature of the beast. Napa is largely a haven for visitors seeking quiet and relaxation. Tourists, on the other hand, have less of an impact on Sonoma, which has its own large population to entertain. There's plenty to do after 10pm, particularly in Santa Rosa. The Friday edition of Santa Rosa's *Press Democrat* is a good source for what's happening.

Napa County

O'Sullivan's Oasis (707-224-7427; 359 1st St., Napa) is a popular pub with some locals. It's not in the greatest neighborhood, but there is dancing and live music on weekends. *Marlowe's* (707-224-2700; 1637 Imola Ave., Napa) has live music, DJ dancing, karaoke, and a game room. *Downtown Joe's* (707-258-2337; 902 Main St., Napa) is a great spot with live music and it brews its own beer. *Compadres* (707-944-2406; 6539 Washington Ave., Yountville) is a Mexican restaurant with a lively bar atmosphere and outdoor patio. Avoid the food. *Showley's at Miramonte* (707-963-1200; 1327 Railroad Ave., St. Helena) is a restaurant that often has jazz trios on weekends. *Catahoula Saloon* (707-942-2275; 1457 Lincoln Ave., Calistoga) is a stylish watering hole before or after dinner. On a warm evening, try the beer garden at *Calistoga Inn* (707-942-4101; 1250 Lincoln Ave., Calistoga). They brew their own and it's great stuff.

Sonoma County

Sonoma County's club scene is thriving. Live music can be found some-where every night, and DJs seem to be spinning discs in a corner of every bar.

Santa Rosa is the center of Sonoma County's nightlife, although the outly-ing areas have a number of fine night spots. Sonoma County's premier stage is *Burbank Center for the Arts* (707-546-3600; 50 Mark West Springs Rd., Santa Rosa). Once a sprawling church complex, the center's main stage is the largest hall in the area, seating about 1,500 in cushioned pews. Recent headliners have included k.d. lang, Bob Newhart, Tori Amos, Bonnie Raitt, and B.B. King.

Santa Rosa's hotels are another good source for late-night fun. Try *The Flamingo* (707-545-8530; 4th St. & Farmers Ln.) and *Equus Lounge of Fountain Grove Inn* (707-578-6101; 101 Fountain Grove Pkwy.) In the Red Lion Hotel just south of Santa Rosa, *Club Maxi* (707-584-5466; 1 Red Lion Dr., Rohnert Park) is a hot locale for older singles. There are happening brewpubs in Santa Rosa; both *Third Street Aleworks* (707-523-3060; 610 Third St., Santa Rosa) and *Santa Rosa Brewing Co.* (707-544-4677; 458 B St.) regularly offer live music. Brits rule at *The Old Vic* (707-571-7555; 731 4th St.), a dark and casual pub offering a fine selection of British beers and live music most nights. Check out the second floor of *The Cantina* (707-523-3663; 500 4th St., Santa Rosa) if you like to dance to DJs playing 1970s tunes and modern R&B. The crowd is young. For comedy, check out *Sweetriver Saloon* (707-526-0400; Coddingtown Center, just off Hwy. 101, Santa Rosa) on Friday and Saturday nights.

Like Napa Valley, Sonoma Valley is quiet at night. *Murphy's Irish Pub* (707-935-0660; 464 1st St. E.) is small but cozy and it offers a great selection of imported ales. A different crowd entirely hangs out at *Little Switzerland* (707-938-9990; Grove & Riverside, Sonoma). This place is a kick! Polka is king at Little Switzerland, a club and restaurant that dates from 1906. The crowd is older, largely serious polka dancers, but they don't care if you show up for a kitsch thrill and make a fool of yourself on the dance floor. The place is delightfully tacky, with plastic flowers and Swiss Alps murals and faded red-and-white checkered tablecloths. There's also a beer garden, of course.

Petaluma has one of Sonoma County's most active scenes. *Phoenix Theatre* (707-762-3565; 201 Washington St., Petaluma) is an old movie theater that doubles occasionally as a concert hall. It brings in some cutting-edge music: Metallica, Primus, and Red Hot Chili Peppers. *Mystic Theater and Music Hall* (707-765-2121; 21 Petaluma Blvd. N., Petaluma) is another former movie house that discovered live music. Recent acts have included Van Morrison and Leo Kottke. Next door is *McNear's* (707-765-2121; 23 Petaluma Blvd. N., Petaluma), a comfortable gathering spot with video games, pool tables, and live music on weekends. It's also one of the few places that serves food late.

West County has another popular stop for the Texas Two-Step, *Marty's Top O' the Hill* (707-823-5987; 8050 Bodega Ave., Sebastopol). Local bands help country boys and gals dance the night away. It's a lively place, not rowdy, and the long-neck beers are ice cold. *The Powerhouse Brewing Company* (707-829-9171; 268 Petaluma Ave., Sebastopol) is a cozy night spot with a schedule of eclectic music. One of the hot tickets in Sonoma County is the Johnny Otis Show. Otis, a member of the Rock and Roll Hall of Fame, closed his cabaret in 1995 and now performs in clubs around the Bay Area. Wherever he performs, Otis is worth checking out. *Jasper O'Farrell's* (707-823-1389; 6957 Sebastopol Ave., Sebastopol) is another pub that makes you feel at home. There's live music almost every night and it's a potpourri: jazz, bluegrass, folk, rock. Darts are also a serious passion. In Healdsburg, *Molly Malone's* (707-431-1856; 245 Healdsburg Ave.) offers an array of solid local bands and it's a good place to sip a cold one. *Bear Republic Brewing Co.* (707-433-BEER; 345 Healdsburg Ave., Healdsburg) may be Healdsburg's hottest night spot, featuring live music and some excellent hand-crafted beers.

THEATER

Theater is just taking root in Napa County. There are just a few community theaters and outdoor Shakespeare festivals. Sonoma, on the other hand, boasts a long tradition of theater. It has one professional company and several highly regarded semi-professional groups. There is also a vastly successful summer stock repertory series that brings in top college talent from around the country every year. As one local director said of the Sonoma drama scene: "I think there are more people who *do* theater than *see* theater."

Sonoma County

CINNABAR THEATER
707-763-8920.

Opera is a scary prospect for a lot of people. Perhaps it's the elitist air that surrounds it, the

3333 Petaluma Blvd. N.,
Petaluma.
Season: Year round.
Tickets: Various.

assumption that it's only for the wealthy and educated. Or perhaps singing in a foreign language
turns people off. Whatever the reason, Marvin
Klebe came to Petaluma in the early 1970s to
change that notion. From that began Sonoma
County's most eclectic and dynamic theater. "Our
main goals are to explore opera as an immediate
and human experience to an audience that is not necessarily highbrow,"
Cinnabar's Elly Lichenstein commented.

Klebe, a powerful baritone, bought the old Cinnabar School on the northern
outskirts of Petaluma and set about transforming it into a studio theater.
(Luckily, he's also a master carpenter.) Soon, others — musicians, dancers,
actors, technicians — got involved and Cinnabar became a small, thriving performing arts center.

Ann Woodhead, a professor at nearby Sonoma State University, stages
avant-garde dance pieces in the theater, and First Stage Company and Western
Union Theatre Company are two drama troupes that call Cinnabar home. Nina
Shuman, the theater's musical director and conductor, has a taste for the offbeat and has gathered a core of devoted chamber musicians.

The heart of the place is Cinnabar Opera Theater. There's not a more intriguing theater company north of San Francisco. No, you won't find a tenor from
San Francisco Opera on stage, but you will see the finest singers hovering on
"the outskirts" of Bay Area opera fame. Productions have run the gamut from
The Magic Flute to musical chestnuts such as *Fiddler on the Roof.*

**THE FIRST STAGE
COMPANY**
707-763-8920.
Cinnabar Theater, 3333
Petaluma Blvd. N.,
Petaluma.
Season: Sept.–June.
Tickets: $8–$12.

After working with nearly every theater company in Sonoma County, actor-director
Michael Fontaine started his own in 1992. He
prefers the lesser-known works of Shaw and Ibsen
to the contemporary dramas and comedies other
studio theaters favor. Winning productions have
included Shaw's *Candida* and *Mrs. Warren's Profes-
sion*. First Stage also tinkers with political satire
such as Dario Fo's *We Won't Pay, We Won't Pay* and
musical revues in the vein of *Tomfoolery*, an ode to the works of Tom Lehrer.
An excellent company and a fine addition to Cinnabar's fold.

MAIN STREET THEATRE
707-823-0177
104 N. Main St., Sebastopol.
Season: Year round.
Tickets: $10.

Sebastopol's only theater company, Main Street
is a dynamic troupe performing in one of
Sonoma County's best intimate spaces. Main Street
rose from the ashes of Nova Theater, which was
originally a downtown drug store. Production values are modest but acting is generally excellent.
Artistic director Jim de Priest has genuine flair and

Much Ado About Nothing *at Sebastopol Summer Shakespeare by Main Street Theatre.*

Courtesy Main Street Theatre

he prefers lesser classics to contemporary plays. Recent successes include *The Importance of Being Earnest* and *Suddenly Last Summer.* Main Street is also responsible for Sebastopol Summer Shakespeare every August in Ives Park.

PACIFIC ALLIANCE STAGE COMPANY
707-584-1700.
Spreckels Performing Arts Center, 5409 Snyder Ln., Rohnert Park.
Season: Sept.–May.
Tickets: $8–$16.

Pacific Alliance is the county's first professional Actor's Equity company and it brought mixed reactions in the local theater community. While most seemed to like the idea that Sonoma was coming up in the theater world, we suspect they were worried the competition could make them look bad. And yet — maybe they could land a role and earn that Equity card.

Pacific Alliance certainly upped the ante, and except for a handful of subpar shows, it has lived up to the highest expectations. A recent production of *A Walk in the Woods* was an excellent example. It helps, of course, that the company has the backing of Spreckels Center, which in turn is backed by the city of Rohnert Park. Artistic Director Michael Grice continues to bring superior talents from around the Bay Area. A few talented local "amateurs" are also earning that all-important card.

While acting is approaching the level of San Francisco, production values reveal a limited budget. Spreckels is also experimenting with a few offbeat productions in its small studio. It's all very refreshing.

SONOMA VALLEY SHAKESPEARE FESTIVAL
707-575-3854.
Gundlach-Bundschu Winery, 2000 Denmark St., Sonoma.

Looking for a pleasant evening after a busy day of touring? This is it. Pack a picnic, take a blanket, dress casually, and enjoy fine outdoor theater. The hillside above the winery makes for a natural amphitheater and the festival's all-purpose stage

Season: June–Sept.
Tickets: Season pass $55,
    single ticket $17.

becomes anything from ancient Rome to the Wild West.

Three or more plays are performed in repertory throughout the summer and consistency is a problem. *The Merry Wives of Windsor*, for example, was delightful, but *A Midsummer Night's Dream* was an amateurish dud. If Shakespeare is not your cup, feareth not. Artistic director Carl Hamilton lowers his brow with charming fare like that randy musical *A Funny Thing Happened on the Way to the Forum.*

**SUMMER REPERTORY
THEATER**
707-527-4342.
1501 Mendocino Ave.,
    Santa Rosa.
Season: June–Aug.
Tickets: Season tickets
    $25–$50, single tickets
    $7–$12.

No one has a bigger local following than SRT. Every summer the Santa Rosa Junior College organizes this three-ring circus of theater, bringing in talented student actors and technical people from around the country. Opening six major productions in four weeks and performing them in a repertory format packs a year's experience into two months.

Some summers are better than others, of course. It all depends on the show and the talent pool, but SRT is always worth a try. The play selection is generally rather safe, but SRT has proven its mettle with every genre: comedy, musical, or drama. Recent highlights have included sparkling productions of *Evita* and *Little Shop of Horrors,* and an electrifying adaptation of Arthur Miller's drama *The Crucible.*

SRT's production values are the highest in the area. Sets are always dynamic, on par with many professional theaters. It's also significant that SRT is one of the few local companies performing in the summer, and thus a perfect choice for tourists looking for a pleasurable evening on the town.

Lend Me a Tenor *at Santa Rosa's Summer Repertory Theater.*

Courtesy Summer Repertory Theater

OTHER THEATER

There are more than a dozen other theater companies in Napa and Sonoma. Many are community theaters. We include a selection of the best.

Napa County

The fledgling *Napa Valley Shakespeare Festival* (707-963-5057; Charles Krug Winery, 2800 Main St., St. Helena) performs the Bard on the lush lawn of a historic winery. *Dreamweavers* (707-255-5483; 101 S. Coombs St., Napa) is a community theater performing favorites such as *Arsenic and Old Lace*. *Magical Moonshine Theater* (707-257-8007; Yountville) is an internationally known puppet theater that doesn't have a regular Napa performance space. Look for them locally when they're not away on tour — charming and great for the family.

Sonoma County

Santa Rosa Players (707-544-7827; 709 Davis St., Santa Rosa) is an institution and it has its good runs and bad, but just when you're ready to write them off, they delight you. Not to be outdone by SRJC, *Sonoma State University* (707-664-2353; Rohnert Park) also has a talented theater department and SSU's new performing arts center has the county's best stage for theater. *Sonoma Vintage Theatre* (707-939-1369) has been performing Shakespeare al fresco at various Sonoma Valley wineries since 1981.

SEASONAL EVENTS

If there's one thing they know how to do in Wine Country, it's throw a party. If you live in or are visiting Napa or Sonoma counties and find that you have an open weekend in the summer, then maybe there's something wrong with you. There are enough festivals and fairs to keep you busy all year. We list here some of the most popular seasonal attractions. The agricultural products of the Napa and Sonoma region shine forth at the many county fairs. Wine, of course, is the centerpiece of many festivals; we've included those in a separate section that follows.

Bodega Bay Fisherman's Festival (707-875-3422) A decades-old tradition for this coast town made famous by Alfred Hitchcock's *The Birds*. This mid-April celebration includes bathtub races, harbor tours, kite flying, a golf tournament, and a boat parade. The high point of the weekend is the annual blessing of the fleet.

Calistoga Beer & Sausage Festival (707-942-6333; Napa County Fairgrounds, Calistoga) Napa Valley's way of celebrating Oktoberfest. On tap in early

October are some of the best beers brewed by area micro-breweries, not to mention tasty tidbits from the region's sausage specialists. Fee.

Celebrate Sonoma (707-546-3600; Burbank Center for the Arts, Santa Rosa) A little bit of everything: arts and crafts, food, dance, live music, and clowns. Much of the fun is outdoors in this annual mid-June weekend.

Gravenstein Apple Fair (707-829-4728; Ragle Ranch Park, Sebastopol) Sebastopol was once the apple capital of the world and today specializes in the distinctive Gravenstein variety. There's a potpourri at this August event: arts and crafts, music, hay rides, storytelling, and, of course, apple treats of all kinds. Fee.

Health & Harmony Festival (707-575-9355; Sonoma County Fairgrounds, Santa Rosa) An only-in-California type of event. A celebration of food, music, and "lifestyle," this annual June fair includes everything from puppet theater to psychic palm readers. Fee.

Hometown Harvest Festival (707-963-5706; downtown St. Helena) A rich Napa tradition, celebrating the end of the growing season and the summer's bountiful harvest. One weekend in late October, there's scads of food, arts and crafts, music, and even a parade.

Hot Air Balloon Classic (707-838-5151; Airport Business Center, N. of Santa Rosa) Easily the most visually striking event of the year. For two days in June, 60 colorful balloons take to the skies of Sonoma and race with the wind. Balloon races begin at 5:30am (that's when the wind is best). Fee.

Comedian Tommy Smothers takes part in the annual Kenwood Pillow Fights.

Courtesy Kenwood Pillow Fights

Kenwood Pillow Fights & Fourth of July Celebration (707-833-2440; Kenwood) The best excuse we know to have a pillow fight astride a greased pole over a mud pit. So silly it's addicting. A favorite with local celebrities like Tommy Smothers. There's also a parade, live music, and fireworks.

Napa County Fair (707-942-5111; fairgrounds, Calistoga) The usual down-home fun, but with a twist of chic Napa style, with social gatherings and wine tastings. The usual rides, animals, produce and music, plus wine, wine, wine. Every July. Fee.

Napa Town and Country Fair (707-253-4900; Napa Exposition Center, Napa) The usual: livestock, food and wine tasting, arts and crafts displays, a carnival, and entertainment. Every August. Fee.

Old Adobe Fiesta (707-762-4871; 3325 Adobe Rd., Petaluma) History comes alive every August with period costumes and craft demonstrations at this historic adobe, one of Sonoma County's oldest homesteads.

Petaluma Butter & Eggs Day (707-769-0429; downtown Petaluma) A celebration of this south county town's early reputation as "The Egg Basket of the World." Poultry, milk, and eggs remain a strong presence in Sonoma. One Sunday every April the town celebrates with a parade, music, and food.

Sebastopol Apple Blossom Festival (707-823-3032; downtown Sebastopol) When the apple trees are in striking form in April, you won't find a more beautiful place than Sebastopol. Apples rule, of course. Eat apple fritters, cobbler, pies. Plus music, games, and arts and crafts.

Swing through the air at the Sonoma County Fair.

Courtesy Sonoma County Convention & Visitors Bureau

Sonoma County Fair (707-545-4200; fairgrounds, Santa Rosa) Sonoma County practically shuts down for two weeks every July, as thousands pour in from the countryside for food, music, rides, blue-ribbon animals, and produce. You can even bet on horse races. Fee.

Yountville Days Festival (707-944-0904; downtown Yountville) Celebrate the history of Napa Valley's first settlement. This September event includes a parade, music, food.

WINE EVENTS

The Napa Valley Wine Auction raises money for charity.

Courtesy Napa Valley Vintners Association

We're still waiting to see this sign along a Napa or Sonoma road: "Garage Sale & Wine Tasting." Wine events are everywhere and all the time in Napa and Sonoma. There's also considerable appeal to sampling and comparing all sorts of wine in one sitting. Most of the following events are staged outside.

Napa Valley Wine Auction (707-963-5246; Meadowood Resort, St. Helena) *The* chic wine outing. This three-day June event is busy with extravagant parties, dances, and dinners. Auction tickets cost a fortune but are in high demand. All the big names of the Napa wine industry and otherwise attend, and the auction raises millions for local charities.

Patrick O'Dell of Turnbull Wine Cellars was the No. 1 bidder at the 1994 Napa Valley Wine Auction.

Courtesy Napa Valley Vintners Association

Napa Valley Wine Festival (707-253-5111; Napa Exposition Center, Napa) The November wine tasting, dinner, and auction raises money for a local charity and marks the end of the wine season. Fee.

Russian River Barrel Tasting (707-433-6782; countryside surrounding Healdsburg) Always the first event of the wine season, and helps lift wine lovers out of the winter doldrums. Besides, everyone loves a sneak preview of wine that hasn't been bottled yet. Best of all — it's free.

Russian River Wine Festival (707-433-6935; Healdsburg Plaza) The wines of 30 wineries in one place. One Sunday every May, the fest also includes delights from local restaurants, arts and crafts, and live music. Fee.

Salute to the Arts (707-938-1133; Sonoma Plaza) A showcase for local artists, writers, restaurants, and wineries. Roam the beautiful historic square and browse the many booths. Fee for wine and food.

Sonoma County Harvest Fair (707-545-4200; fairgrounds, Santa Rosa) This event could easily be listed with the regular seasonal offerings, but the wine tasting is *the* most important in Sonoma County. The fair brings in top wine experts from around the country. Then local wine buffs gather to compare their taste buds to the judges'. Great fun. There's also plenty of food and the annual grape stomping contest is a crazy attraction. Fee.

Sonoma County Showcase and Wine Auction (707-586-3795; various locations) A bit less chi-chi than its Napa counterpart, but remains quite the elegant affair. The gala weekend includes tastings, parties, and the auction itself. The event is usually sold out weeks in advance, despite steep ticket prices.

Sonoma County Wine & Food Series (707-576-0162) A long-time favorite with locals. Gatherings at different wineries throughout the summer feature a

The Sonoma County Harvest Fair is one of Wine Country's most popular events.

Courtesy Sonoma County Harvest Fair

The Sonoma Valley Harvest Wine Auction prefers irreverence to high culture.

"I told you we were overdressed..."

SONOMA VALLEY HARVEST WINE AUCTION & BBQ DINNER

SEPTEMBER 4 & 5, 1993 • SONOMA MISSION INN & SPA

Ron Zak Photography

particular varietal, chardonnay for example. Wine is paired with food from local restaurants and live music is also included. Fee.

Sonoma Valley Harvest Wine Auction (707-935-0803; various locations) A casual and fun weekend affair that includes winery parties, a main auction, and even a golf tournament. Every September.

Napa Wine and Crafts Fair (707-257-0322; downtown Napa) A busy event that draws wine as well as arts and crafts buffs from around the county. Every September. Tasting fee.

NEIGHBORS

With San Francisco so close, it's impossible to talk of culture without mentioning what that world-class city has to offer.

Museums are one of the most popular excuses for the pleasant hour's drive south. Best known is *The Exploratorium* (415-561-0360; 3601 Lyon St.), a magnetic place for families because of its hands-on science displays. Likewise, *The California Academy of Sciences* (415-750-7145; Golden Gate Park) is a popular spot for kids and families. Art museums include the cutting edge *San Francisco Museum of Modern Art* (415-357-4000; 151 3rd St.), *The De Young Memorial Museum* (415-750-3600; Golden Gate Park), and the graceful *Palace of the Legion of Honor* (415-750-3600; Lincoln Park), which specializes in Rodin sculpture.

The performing arts are still another of San Francisco's many lures. *The San Francisco Ballet* (415-703-9400; War Memorial Opera House) is one of the best in the country. *The San Francisco Symphony* (415-864-6000-5400; Davies Symphony Hall) is gaining a national reputation as well, and the *San Francisco Opera* (415-

864-3330; War Memorial Opera House) is one of the Bay Area's great artistic traditions. And while San Francisco is hardly Broadway, the theater district around Union Square is a happening place. *The American Conservatory Theater* (415-749-2228; 345 Mason St.) is the city's most respected, and small off-Broadway style theaters abound.

As for nightlife, San Francisco's South of Market district is the place to be seen, a former industrial area with nightclubs on almost every corner. Hot clubs in the city at this writing include Paradise Lounge, Slim's Elbo Room, Crash Palace, and the Palladium. You might be home in time to see the sun rise.

CHAPTER FIVE

Bon Appetit!

RESTAURANTS & FOOD PURVEYORS

If wine is "bottled poetry," as novelist Robert Louis Stevenson wrote, then superb dining in Wine Country is its culinary equivalent. As wineries have encroached on the farmland of Napa and Sonoma counties, gourmet restaurants have overtaken the burger joints. The urban sprawl of fine dining hasn't upset the natives and certainly not the tourists. Today, Wine Country is widely known as a delicious place.

The Press Democrat/Mark Aronoff

Jan Birnbaum, chef-owner of Catahoula Restaurant & Saloon.

There are more restaurants than ever that are worth a visit, running the gamut from palatial chateaux to storefront bistros, along with ethnic eateries offering Mexican, Chinese, and Thai fare. There is more to dining out than just the food, of course. We consider atmosphere, for one. Did the restaurant set the tone for the meal to come? Was it warm, interesting, or unique? Most of all, did it work? Service was also key; after all, you *are* on vacation and deserve to be pampered. We were most interested in knowing how well the servers knew the menu and could make intelligent comments about particular dishes.

Each restaurant is given a price code, signifying the cost of a single meal including appetizer, entrée, and dessert, but not cocktails, wine, tax, or tip. Reviews are organized first by county, then by city or region, then alphabetically. Food purveyors are grouped alphabetically by type, then name of establishment. Every restaurant appears in the general index, too.

Dining Price Code:

Inexpensive: Up to $10
Moderate: $10 to $22

Expensive: $22 to $35
Very Expensive: $35 or more

Credit Cards:

AE — American Express
CB — Carte Blanche
D — Discover

DC — Diner's Club
MC — Master Card
V — Visa

NAPA COUNTY RESTAURANTS

Napa

Bistro Don Giovanni is one of Napa Valley's best destinations.

Chris Alderman

BISTRO DON GIOVANNI
707-224-3300.
4110 St. Helena Way.
    (Hwy. 29), Napa.
Price: Moderate to
    Expensive.
Credit Cards: AE, D, MC, V.
Cuisine: Italian.
Serving: L, D.
Reservations: Recom-
    mended.
Special Features: Outdoor
    dining.
Handicap Access: Yes.

The seduction begins the moment you enter Bistro Don Giovanni. The setting is romantic, a high-ceilinged room done in warm tones, white linen, and modern art, with vineyard views through tall windows. The perfume from the open kitchen makes you anxious to get down to business: eating. And what fine business it is. Bistro Don Giovanni has usurped Tra Vigne and Piatti as the best Italian dining in the valley.

Donna and Giovanni Scala were the founding chefs of Piatti before opening this restaurant in 1993 in the former Table 29. With roots in the country cooking of Italy and France, the food is delightfully straightforward. The menu includes the requisite salads, pasta, and risotto, as well as pizza from a white-tiled oven. Salads are first-rate, particularly a beet and spinach salad with golden beets, crumbled English Stilton, and sherry vinaigrette.

Entrées to recommend include thin and tender ravioli filled with basil, parmesan, and ricotta, impressively paired with an understated lemon cream sauce. Try the risotto of the day, particularly grilled chicken with roasted sweet peppers and saffron, a potpourri of textures and flavors. Bravissimo the filet of salmon, seared in a pan for a thin crust to protect its moist and flaky heart. It's served with buttermilk mashed potatoes that may cause plate warfare.

Desserts include sensuously intense sorbets and a well-executed berry crème brûlée. The wine list is mostly Napa and Italian and it's rather pricey. Service is attentive. Don't miss this place.

NAPA VALLEY WINE TRAIN
800-427-4124.
1275 McKinstry St., Napa.
Price: Very Expensive.
Credit Cards: AE, CB, D, DC, MC, V.
Cuisine: California.
Serving: SB, L, D.
Reservations: Required.
Special Features: Train ride through heart of Napa Valley.

This is one of the biggest disappointments in Wine Country. The train itself is a gloriously restored vintage beauty and the trip through Napa Valley is a charming and scenic adventure. But oh the price! A dinner excursion tops $150, and the food is adequate at best. A safer bet is riding the deli lunch car; the fare is $24 and the al a carte menu has prices ranging from $5 to $14.

The train traverses 21 miles of track from Napa to St. Helena and back again in three hours. As you dine, you glide past world-famous vineyards and wineries. Some locals feel the Wine Train is too "Disneyland," and there is an element of that in the canned commentary that continually crackles "Ahead to your left . . ." through the train's speakers. The train may begin making stops along the way if plans proceed, but staying on board is not a bad proposition, considering the polished mahogany and brass, the velvet swag curtains, etched glass, and white table linens set with bone china.

Except for the deli car, meals are prix fixe. Lunch offers poached salmon and angel hair pasta with shrimp and scallops. A typical dinner appetizer includes a pleasant salmon pate served with a rubbery chicken and red pepper galantine. The second course is a plate of crisp young lettuce often topped with an indistinct hazelnut-sherry vinaigrette. A sorbet course is an excellent diversion, with lovely renditions of kiwi, white peach, or strawberry fruit ices served in a liqueur glass.

Diners typically select from one of four entrées. If you like poached Pacific salmon, avoid the menu's waterlogged offering. Somewhat better is an agreeable rack of lamb, roasted with fragrant herbed mustard breading. Dessert is equally uninspired. A California fruit tart is a sweet experience, with a crisp crust and apricot sauce, but the chocolate swirl cheesecake is too gelatinous. The wine list is solid, with a variety available by the glass. Service is genuine but lacks the polish of restaurants in this price range.

ROYAL OAK AT SILVERADO COUNTRY CLUB
707-257-0200.
1600 Atlas Peak Rd., Napa.
Price: Very Expensive.
Credit Cards: AE, DC, MC, V.
Cuisine: American.
Serving: D.
Reservations: Recommended.
Handicap Access: No.

If you don't mind the country club atmosphere, this is the traditional place to go in Napa Valley for thick steaks and chops. The valley's oldest resort (see Chapter Three, *Lodging*) the heart of Silverado is a venerable 1870s mansion built by Gen. John Miller.

Like the menu, the Royal Oak recalls an earlier era, with its dimly lit dining room accented with rustic wood beams, heavy tables and chairs, and gleaming copper cookware. The aroma of steaks roasting on a mesquite grill whets your appetite. Service, however, lacks panache.

Appetizers include a generous and tasty caesar salad prepared at your table. The spicy duck cilantro quesadilla is nicely flaky yet shy on duck. The seafood sampler, which includes fresh oysters and clams, is a refreshing overture. Steak options include an impeccably grilled New York sirloin, juicy and tender and seasoned with crushed peppercorns. Another treat is the grilled duck breast, winningly accented with an agile black peppercorn butter sauce.

Desserts are a disappointment and include a lifeless chocolate linzertorte with pear and lemon sorbet too frosty from the freezer. Royal Oak has an extensive but expensive wine list and mysteriously absent is a menu of wines by the glass. There is a modest selection but you must ask. Pleasantly included with the tariff is an after-dinner drink — a cart of 36 cordials is brought to your table.

Yountville

BRIX
707-944-2749.
7377 St. Helena Hwy. (Hwy. 29), Yountville.
Price: Expensive.
Credit Cards: AE, DC, MC, V.
Cuisine: California-Asian.
Serving: L, D.
Reservations: Recommended.
Handicap Access: Yes.

When a menu blends Asia and California with as much bravado as Brix, our interest is piqued. Unfortunately the kitchen can't quite follow through, so dinner is an exercise in disappointment. Still, chef Tod Michael Kawachi's concept shows great promise and we predict Brix will join the ranks of Napa Valley's best.

Opening in the summer of 1996, Brix quickly established itself as one of Wine Country's most elegant restaurants. Its peaked wood ceiling and warm earthy tones recall a private club. The view is gorgeous: an organic garden, a vineyard, and the rugged Mayacamas Mountains. Lovely sunsets are staged nightly. Service is so skilled that it's almost inconspicuous, and the wine list is fairly priced, with a fine selection of modestly priced bottles as well as wine-by-the-glass.

Starters range from the simple — baby greens with sesame citrus dressing —

to the exotic. Crunchy seafood cigares with a sweet 'n sour pineapple chili sauce is a tepid variation on egg rolls. Inside is a bland and mushy paste surrounded by an overly hard wonton-like crust. The prosciutto, pear, and baby green tower salad with peppered goat cheese is brilliant, however. Entrées, which sound so wondrous on the menu, are surprisingly bland. The potato-crusted halibut with asparagus, fennel jus, and truffle oil is pleasant but flavorless. Dessert is a high note, particularly a luscious selection of sorbets that often includes plum-sake, blackberry, and honeydew.

NAPA VALLEY GRILLE
707-944-8686.
Washington Square, 6795
  Washington St.,
  Yountville.
Price: Expensive.
Credit Cards: AE, MC, V.
Cuisine: California.
Serving: SB, L, D.
Reservations: Recom-
  mended.
Special Features: Outdoor
  dining.
Handicap Access: Yes.

This restaurant may be part of a small chain but we appreciated its unpretentious tone and varied menu. In the touristy Washington Square shopping complex, Napa Valley Grille is a fine choice for a quick lunch while browsing, or for a more luxurious dinner. The café is done in warm colors and quartz bulbs dangle over each table. The kitchen is open and its energy flows through the dining room. By contrast, service can be sluggish. The wine list is not voluminous but is nicely done, with a fine offering of wines by the glass.

The menu is large and offers a bit of everything, a stretch many kitchens can't handle. Chef Bob Hurley, whose resume includes Domaine Chandon and Masa's in San Francisco, pulls it off with aplomb. Starters include a rich and smooth roasted polenta, a generous timbale infused with cambozola and herbs. The smoked salmon appetizer is appealing, yet its delicate flavors are nearly lost against the intense sun-dried tomato tapenade that joins it.

Main courses include a large selection of pastas. Fish, fowl, and meat are roasted over a wood fire, lending a strong smoky oak flavor to everything. The filet mignon is moist and tender and served with marvelous bacon scallion mashed potatoes. Less successful is the grilled swordfish steak inundated with a banana curry sauce that belongs on a dessert.

THE DINER
707-944-2626.
6476 Washington St.,
  Yountville.
Closed: Mon.
Price: Moderate.
Credit Cards: No.
Cuisine: American,
  Mexican.
Serving: B, L, D.

Take a detour, travel back to the '50s via The Diner, a good place for breakfast, lunch, or a full-blown dinner. The menu is eclectic, a mix of Mexican and diner food: burgers, sandwiches, and soda fountain fare — great for kids, as you might imagine. Service is quick and friendly and there's a modestly priced wine list as well as import beers.

The Diner *is* authentic — it was a Greyhound bus station and diner in the '50s. Booths wind their

A real honest-to-goodness 1950s diner, still going strong.

Chris Alderman

Reservations: Not accepted.
Handicap Access: Yes.

way around the restaurant, while the counter takes center stage. A large collection of brightly colored Fiesta ware is displayed over the soda fountain, along with vintage gadgets and a newfangled espresso machine.

Breakfast runs from standard huevos rancheros to German potato pancakes. Lunch and dinner offer burgers like the Paul Bunyan plate, a six-ounce deluxe beast. Soups are hearty and fresh, particularly the white bean with sun-dried tomatoes. Salads rely on simple but fresh greens and lavishly flavored home-made dressing.

Entrées include a delightful chicken breast picatta, *lightly* breaded and sautéed to perfection in lemon and garlic and served with grilled veggies. Vegetarians should look for the baked potato dinner, a cheap create-your-own meal built over a huge organic baked potato. What diner doesn't have great desserts? Try the cream cheese pound cake with fresh berries or finish with the buttermilk shake, a thick swirl dubbed liquid cheesecake. They leave the metal blender cup on your table for second helpings.

DOMAINE CHANDON
707-944-2892.
California Dr. at Hwy. 29, Yountville.
Closed: Mon. & Tues. D, Mon. & Tues. L in winter.
Price: Very Expensive.
Credit Cards: AE, D, DC, MC, V.
Cuisine: French, California.
Serving: L, D.

Hot new restaurants come and go, but after two decades, Domaine Chandon remains Napa Valley's consummate experience. Granted, it is not for every taste or pocketbook. Housed in a modern, curved concrete building with terrace views of the landscaped grounds, the restaurant is elegant but not pretentious. Servers in tuxedos dote over the table, often to distraction, but we don't mind being pampered.

As part of the Domaine Chandon winery, the emphasis is naturally on sparkling wine. Philippe

The terrace at Domaine Chandon.

Courtesy Domaine Chandon

Reservations: Required.
Special Features: Coat
requested at dinner; out-
door dining.
Handicap Access: Yes.

Jeanty has been Chef de Cuisine at Domaine Chandon since 1978. Trained at the Reims Culinary Academy in the heart of Champagne, he envisions food that complements sparkling wine while combining California innovation with the great traditions of French cooking.

The menu changes with the seasons. Appetizers range from an exquisite home smoked salmon tartare, flaky and lightly smoked and served with herb aïoli croutons. The roasted beet salad with feta cheese and citrus vinaigrette is nicely done but the beets taste pickled rather than roasted. Seafood dominates the entrée list, although meat eaters will find satisfaction in the roasted Paine Farm squab or venison tournedos. Not to be missed is the tuna pepper steak, slices of medium rare tuna with an exhilarating crust of whole grain mustard sauce. The fish is arranged around a sculpted mound of mashed potatoes. Our nominee for Best Entrée in Wine Country goes to the caramelized sea scallops, brawny medallions seared with a hint of onion and served with chanterelles and crispy onion rings in a wide bowl. Brilliant.

Dessert is an ungodly affair. Hot gooey chocolate cake is straightforward but dazzling nonetheless. Rich vanilla ice cream tops a fluffy puck of cake with a heart of rich and lavalike filling. The superb wine list covers America and France with a surprisingly low mark-up, particularly for Chandon bubbly, which sells at retail prices.

**FRANKIE, JOHNNIE &
LUIGI TOO**
707-944-0177.

If the prospect of a fancy (and expensive) restaurant scares you off, Frankie, Johnnie & Luigi Too is a good alternative. The atmosphere is polished

6772 Washington St.,
    Yountville.
Price: Moderate.
Credit Cards: AE, D, DC,
    MC, V.
Serving: L, D.
Reservations: Recom-
    mended.
Special Features: Outdoor
    dining.
Handicap Access: Yes.

but lacking in pretension, the food is hearty, the portions are generous, and the price is right. Kids are also welcome, too, with huge family-style dinners on the menu.

The sloping ceiling of the main dining room makes it cozy, a feeling further warmed by a giant painting of a plate of spaghetti. At lunch and on warm evenings, the two patios are busy. The menu is just what you'd expect: pizza, pasta, veal parmigiana, etc. The antipasti plate for two is particularly well done, with spicy salami, good quality provolone, and mozzarella and roasted peppers.

Entrées to recommend include a healthy and scrumptious primavera arrosto, al dente vegetables sautéed in a white wine and garlic sauce served over spaghetti. The fettuccine prawns portofino is less successful: while the rich cream sauce is serviceable the prawns are dry and chewy. For dessert, try the yummy chocolate-raspberry gelato. The wine list is a fine match for the menu — well priced and hearty — and service is excellent.

The French Laundry is housed in a romantic 1890s stone house.

Faith Echtermeyer

THE FRENCH LAUNDRY
707-944-2380.
6640 Washington St.,
    Yountville.
Closed: Sun.–Tues. L.
Prix fixe: $28 or $36 L; $52
    or $58 D.
Credit Cards: AE, M, V.
Serving: L, D.
Reservations: Required.
Special Features: Outdoor
    dining, garden.

It's a good thing "Bar and Brothel" didn't catch on, because a restaurant as romantic as the French Laundry needs a name to match. The grand stone house, built in the 1890s, was indeed a bar and brothel before becoming a French-style laundry. As a restaurant, it gained distinction under chef Sally Schmitt, but we never understood the fuss. Chef Thomas Keller bought the restaurant in 1994 and it is finally living up to its reputation.

Keller has an impressive resume, including a stint at Checkers in Los Angeles. You might call his cuisine "California labor-intensive." Every dish is an artistic feat, as well as a culinary joy. Four- or five-course meals are offered and portions are *not* as modest as they first appear. The kitchen's pace is unhurried although service is attentive. Allow at least two hours. The wine list is not the glorious bargain it once was, but it remains impressive, though wines by the glass are lacking.

Appetizers to recommend include a salmon smoked so gently it might be considered sushi. Superb. The butternut squash agnolotti is well done but a rich way to begin. Entrées include salmon steak Dijonnaise, a moist filet that marries well with the spicy mustard. Sautéed gulf prawns are equally luscious but the boneless rack of lamb is lacking. The cheese course includes an inventive and heavenly tête de moine with mission fig tart and an indulgent wedge of Maytag blue cheese paired with a roasted Bartlett pear. For desserts, consider the pink pearl apple pithiviers with tart apple ice cream and the chocolate truffle cake with a warm gooey heart.

Mustards Grill has a lively atmosphere and hearty bistro food.

Chris Alderman

MUSTARDS GRILL
707-944-2424.
7399 St. Helena Hwy.
  (Hwy. 29), Yountville.
Price: Moderate.
Credit Cards: CB, D, DC,
  MC, V.
Cuisine: California.
Serving: L, D.
Reservations: Recom-
  mended.

Highly hyped among Napa Valley's eateries, Mustards Grill lives up to its reputation. Opened in 1984, Mustards, one of the earliest players in Napa's burgeoning restaurant boom, is brought to you by the same folks who run Tra Vigne and San Francisco's hot Fog City Diner. Mustards' secret isn't a secret at all — hearty bistro food prepared with style, at a moderate price and in a lively atmosphere, dubbed by another writer as "truck-stop deluxe."

The open kitchen takes center stage, dominating an interior rich with dark wood, black and white tile, and broad open windows. The tables are close, but the din becomes so loud it lends an air of privacy. While servers seem harried, they are efficient and friendly.

Mustards' menu is varied, but it never spreads itself too thin. It's comfort food with flair. Chicken, duck, rabbit, ribs, and fish are grilled over wood. A must are the onion rings, a heaping pile that comes thinly sliced and highly seasoned. The homemade ketchup lacks zing, though. The caesar salad is also a creamy classic. The list of entrées is ever-evolving but a few favorites are constant. The baby back ribs will disappoint Southern barbecue fanatics but our mouths water sufficiently. The ribs are excellent quality but the sauce lacks panache. Chef Terry Lynch has a way with duck, emphasizing its savory gaminess rather than disguising it. Hamburgers, of course, are big and delicious.

The wine list is well focused and priced fairly. The wine by-the-glass selection is also first-rate. For dessert, try the Jack Daniels cake. Though rich and deadly, thankfully it carries nowhere near the kick of its namesake.

RISTORANTE PIATTI
707-944-2070.
6480 Washington St., Yountville.
Price: Moderate to Expensive.
Credit Cards: AE, MC, V.
Cuisine: Italian.
Serving: L, D.
Reservations: Recommended.
Special Features: Outdoor dining.
Handicap Access: Yes.

Piatti is not the brilliant experience it once was, but considering everything — food, atmosphere, wine list, price — Piatti is hard to beat. Like its sister restaurant in Sonoma, Piatti is styled as an Italian trattoria, with tile floors and braids of garlic. The atmosphere is electric — the hum of diners and the open kitchen pulses throughout the airy dining room. Piatti is rustic and elegant at the same time.

The menu offers the best of Tuscany: pasta, pizzas, and grilled meat and fish. The wood-burning pizza oven produces pies with crusts lighter than air and the toppings are always exceptional, from pesto to Parma prosciutto. Starters included a superlative house-cured salmon. Equally good is the calamari fritti, lightly battered squid fried and served with spicy aïoli sauce.

A popular dish is pescatore in rosso although we've never been impressed. It sounds intriguing — linguini with mussels, clams, calamari, fish, and shrimp — but the sauce is dull and the seafood portions skimpy. Chef Lorenzo Veronese has a way with traditional Italian roasted chicken and the grilled lamb loin with rosemary and orzo is also enticing.

Napa and Italian wines are available, with a hearty chianti and a few others served by the glass. Desserts range from gelato to a beautifully presented and tongue-numbing torta di formaggio e amaretto, an amaretto cheesecake with warm chocolate sauce. Service is competent but harried.

Auberge du Soleil is a page from Metropolitan Home magazine.

Tim Fish

Oakville/Rutherford

AUBERGE DU SOLEIL
707-963-1211.
180 Rutherford Hill Rd.,
  Rutherford.
Credit Cards: AE, D, MC,
  V.
Price: Very Expensive.
Serving: B, L, D.
Reservations: Required.
Special Features: View,
  outside dining.
Handicap Access: Yes.

If you want a postcard view of Napa Valley, a tapestry woven of vineyards, make a reservation at Auberge du Soleil. Make sure you slip in early enough to grab a table on the outside deck. While the food is praiseworthy, the check may cause a double take. You may find comparable food at better prices, but it won't come with a view this spectacular.

Auberge du Soleil or "Inn of the Sun" is Wine Country's most luxurious resort (see Chapter Three, *Lodging*). The restaurant, a page from *Metropolitan Home* magazine, suggests a villa in southern France, done in soft pastels and accented with rough-hewn wood, a large hearth, and bold arrangements of fresh flowers.

Menus change with the season, and while the kitchen offers its share of standards, chef Andrew Sutton is an adventuresome soul. Breakfast might begin with griddled cornbread or hickory-smoked trout scrambled eggs. Lunch might offer chilled salmon, a tasting plate of Middle Eastern specialties, or jerk-spiced shrimp.

A typical summer dinner menu offers roasted lobster sausage and pan-seared scallops, the latter a luscious undertaking ruined by clashing condiments: mango-citrus relish and black beans. Entrées include an outstanding hickory barbecued rack of lamb, with a subtle bourbon sauce. A real adventure is the spicy grilled rare ahi with Monterey squid, served in a pool of black garlic-ink sauce. Super.

Desserts are typically dramatic creations. A warm nectarine phyllo pillow is a monument of golden phyllo hiding a heart of naturally sweet fruit. The wine list is excellent though pricey, but a fine selection by the glass cushions the blow. Service, too, is impeccable but never overly attentive.

RUTHERFORD GRILL
707-963-1792.
St. Helena Hwy. (Hwy. 29)
    at Rutherford Crossroad,
    Rutherford.
Price: Moderate.
Credit Cards: AE, MC, V.
Cuisine: American.
Serving: L, D.
Reservations: Not accepted.
Handicap Access: Yes.

So you discovered a big burly cabernet sauvignon while wine tasting? What do you eat with it? California cuisine is not always cabernet friendly, so the arrival of Rutherford Grill in 1994 filled a Napa Valley niche — steak.

The prime rib and filet mignon may not be the best you've ever had, but the beef is tasty and tender and the portions are generous. Steaks are grilled over hard wood, along with baby back ribs and spit-roasted chicken. The wild mushroom meatloaf is a tantalizing take on the comfort food classic; two hefty slices of ground veal and beef are included, although the mushrooms were anything but wild. Appetizers include Maytag blue cheese potato chips, a less than impressive mound of plain chips topped and quickly saturated by warm cheese. Desserts include a homemade Oreo ice cream sandwich with chocolate sauce, a surprisingly light confection.

A modern façade along Hwy. 29, Rutherford Grill says "chain," and it is one of 30 similar eateries. The atmosphere is classy in a casual sort of way, with a decor that's steak-house-meets-diner. The open kitchen and table chatter generates a constant hum, yet the booths with overhead lights create a sense of intimacy. The patio is busy at lunch when hamburgers are popular. The wine list is narrow but well focused on Napa and the service is deft.

STARS OAKVILLE CAFÉ
707-944-8905.
7848 St. Helena Hwy.
    (Hwy. 29), Oakville.
Closed: Tues. & Weds.
Price: Expensive.
Credit Cards: D, DC, MC,
    V.
Cuisine: American-
    California.
Serving: L, D.
Reservations: Recom-
    mended.
Handicap Access: Yes.

A cook tosses garlic in hot olive oil and allows it to dance in the skillet. At Stars Oakville Café, the kitchen is center stage with three large picture windows showcasing dinner in progress. Jeremiah Tower, owner of the legendary Stars restaurant in San Francisco, brought his award-winning cuisine to Wine Country in late 1993. The food is hearty fare, similar to Stars although a touch more rustic. It's *also* not nearly as glorious. Locals have been turned off by the kitchen's inconsistency, so it was no surprise when chef Mark Franz — Tower's longtime collaborator — resigned in 1994.

The dining room, done in earth tones, is unpretentiously elegant. There's a patio for al fresco dining, as well as an herb and vegetable garden, lemon trees, and lavender. Bird lovers will enjoy the aviary.

The menu changes daily. Lunch offers the obligatory hamburgers as well as grilled sausage, pasta, and sandwiches. Dinner appetizers may include a gorgeous bouquet of local greens or duck liver on bruschetta crowned with salsa, a sumptuous combination. Entrées arrive from the wood-burning oven or mesquite grill. Consider the pan-roasted halibut and grilled lamb sirloin. The halibut comes with crispy polenta and green bean-radicchio salad. It's pleasing to the eye and plentiful, but lacks *oomph*. The lamb, succulent and medium rare, is served with roasted eggplant and marinated tomatoes.

The desserts are classic. The lemon pound cake, for example, gives new meaning to comfort food. Yum. The wine list is superb but expensive. Ditto the by-the-glass selection. Service is agile even on the busiest nights.

St. Helena

Brava Terrace has one of Napa Valley's best al fresco dining experiences.

Courtesy Brava Terrace

BRAVA TERRACE
707-963-9300.
3010 St. Helena Hwy.
(Hwy. 29), St. Helena.
Closed: Weds. in winter.
Price: Expensive.
Credit Cards: AE, D, DC, MC, V.
Cuisine: California.
Serving: L, D.
Reservations: Recommended.
Special Features: Outdoor dining.

The terrace, as the name suggests, is the place to be here. Surrounded by trees and illuminated at night by hundreds of white lights, the rear terrace of this restaurant offers one of Napa's best al fresco dining experiences. The food by chef-owner Fred Halpert doubles the pleasure. His menu matches the robustness of country French food to California's more delicate preferences. While the food may derive from southern France, the interior reflects the north. Styled as a French chalet, the Brava Terrace evokes an airy ski lodge with peaked ceiling, exposed wood beams, and stone fireplace.

Starters include an exceptional grilled portobello mushroom, a plate-sized delicacy browned but juicy inside, served with a walnut vinaigrette. The radicchio and arugula salad with sun-dried tomatoes and asiago cheese is a bold but successful fusion of flavors. A cold tomato-basil soup offers the fresh essence of a spring garden. Halpert's burgers are winning, and the daily pasta and risotto specials are a good bet. The grilled veal T-bone is worthy but not nearly as impressive as the garlic smashed potatoes that share its plate. The grilled pork chop is a monster, succulent inside but with a crisp crust rubbed with Mediterranean herbs.

Dessert includes an uninspired strawberry sorbet but the chocolate chip crème brûlée is a silky and decadent creation. Service is knowledgeable and attentive, and Halpert's wine list is one of the most fairly priced in the valley.

THE GRILL AT MEADOWOOD
707-963-3646.
900 Meadowood Ln., St. Helena.
Price: Moderate.
Credit Cards: AE, DC, MC, V.
Cuisine: California.
Serving: B, L.
Reservations: Recommended.
Special Features: Resort setting, outdoor dining.
Handicap Access: Yes.

Snare a table on the deck in warm weather and enjoy the view from this casual dining spot, a sibling to Meadowood's formal dining room (see following review). Breakfast and lunch are the focus, when guests of this resort take a break from the emerald lawns of the golf and croquet courses. Dinner, however, is served Friday and Saturday.

At breakfast, a buffet offers a standard spread of croissants, muffins, and fruit, with French toast and other specialties made to order. The lunch menu is light but not dull, with fare ranging from fruit plates and cheeseburgers to grilled pork chops. Appetizers include a succulent tiger shrimp salad with curried vinaigrette. The grilled chicken quesadilla is a charming version of the summer classic, but the grilled filet of salmon is unmoving.

PAIRS PARKSIDE CAFÉ
707-963-7566.
1420 Main St., St. Helena.
Closed: Tues.
Price: Moderate.
Credit Cards: AE, MC, V.
Cuisine: California.
Serving: L, D.
Reservations: Recommended.
Special Features: Wine bar.
Handicap Access: Yes.

With so many distinctive restaurants in St. Helena, Pairs is often overlooked and perhaps rightly so. Not to be too harsh; the café and the menu are both smartly done and prices are modest, but Pairs is a plain tree in a lush forest.

The decor is natty yet casual, with polished pine floors and walls painted a faux gold. Service is efficient but annoyingly harried. The name Pairs refers to the café's dedication to matching food and wine; some 20 wines, all available by the glass, are posted and menu items have recommended matches.

Brothers Craig and Keith Schauffel own the café and run the kitchen. Toothsome grilled flatbread served with various aïolis greets every table. Lunch includes salads and sandwiches, plus fish like Dijon mustard-crusted sea bass, a fluffy and immaculately browned filet manhandled by stout mustard.

Dinner appetizers include lemon fried calamari, crispy rings made harsh by bitter fennel and lemon chips. Entrées include honey toasted suckling pig, a juicy and satisfying cutlet served with pomegranate and apple chutney. Even better is the sage roasted salmon, a silken filet with a savory crust atop a hearty porcini, pumpkin, and white bean stew. For desserts, look for the warm apple crisp, a humble delight rich with cinnamon and served with vanilla ice cream.

PINOT BLANC
707-963-6191.
641 Main St. (Hwy. 29), St. Helena.
Price: Expensive.
Credit Cards: AE, MC, V.
Cuisine: California-Mediterranean.
Serving: L, D.
Reservations: Recommended.
Handicap Access: Yes.

Joachim Splichal, celebrity chef and owner of Los Angeles' famed Patina Restaurant, opened this bistro with considerable fanfare in the summer of 1996. Pinot Blanc will probably fair well, but it has a long way to go before it can compete with Terra, The French Laundry, Catahoula, and the valley's other top restaurants.

Considering it's a spin-off of a trendy L.A. eatery, Pinot Blanc has a surprisingly conservative atmosphere. With its dark wood wainscoting and compartmentalized dining areas separated by thick curtains, the room has the comfortable feeling of a private club. The wine list is excellent and the prices are the going rate, but the wine-by-the-glass selection is rather limited.

The menu offers an expansive list of warm and cold starters, but only a modest slate of entrees. The food is innovative yet hearty and the presentations unfussy. Starters include the likes of crispy sweetbread hash and corn pancakes with marinated salmon and crème fraîche. The potato scallop roll, a Splichal trademark, is superb, an invigorating collage of textures and flavors. However, the kitchen needs works on its risotto. A recent version with shiitake mushrooms, poached garlic, corn, and asparagus was a real letdown. The flavors were rich but lost in a gooey jumble, and the rice was beyond firm — it was *chewy*. Fish seems to be a forte, particularly the planked Atlantic salmon with shallot apple smoked bacon crust. A smoky char on the outside, moist and luscious on the inside, it is exceptional. It's always a challenge for us to find something interesting on Pinot Blanc's dessert menu. It consistently lacks either decadence *or* the simple fruitful pleasures of the season.

THE RESTAURANT AT MEADOWOOD
707-963-3646.
900 Meadowood Ln., St. Helena.
Price: Very Expensive.
Credit Cards: AE, DC, MC, V.
Cuisine: California, Country French.
Serving: SB, D.
Reservations: Recommended.

The restaurant at Meadowood, at the foot of Howell Mountain in St. Helena, is nestled in a bucolic, wooded setting. The restaurant draws almost exclusively guests of Meadowood Resort (see Chapter Three, *Lodging*) yet its reputation was rather lackluster until chef Roy Breiman, a youthful veteran of Provençal kitchens, upped the ante somewhat. (Breiman, unfortunately, left the restaurant in November 1996.)

The dining room boasts a cathedral ceiling with exposed beams and views of the plush grounds of

Special Features: Resort setting, outdoor dining.
Handicap Access: No.

Meadowood. The atmosphere is distinctly New England. Although the wine list offers Napa exclusively, it is impeccable, selected by John Thoreen, Meadowood's learned yet refreshingly down-to-earth wine pro. In addition to the regular menu, four prix-fixe dinners are offered, including a five-course vegetarian meal.

Entrées include a specialty Breiman calls Napa Valley tart, a creation of sautéed prawns and crispy bacon that bursts from the plate like a flower arrangement. Rich and contrasting flavors dance for your attention yet never clash. The baked squab makes a more simple statement. Too simple. Served with caramelized endives, wild mushrooms, and artichokes, it is tender yet undistinguished. For dessert, try the soufflé of the day — outstanding. Large fluffy concoctions, they defy gravity.

SHOWLEY'S AT MIRAMONTE
707-963-1200.
1327 Railroad Ave., St. Helena.
Closed: Mon.
Price: Expensive.
Credit Cards: AE, D, MC, V.
Cuisine: California.
Serving: L, D.
Reservations: Recommended.
Special Features: Outdoor dining.
Handicap Access: Yes.

L ike the classic country restaurants of Europe, Showley's has an elegant simplicity that is refreshing. For flamboyant decor and food, look elsewhere. Owner-chef Grant Showley accentuates fresh and unfettered flavors in palate-pleasing traditional dishes like veal sweetbreads and wild mushroom risotto. The building, once an Italian family restaurant, dates to 1860. The atmosphere has the warmth of a country inn and the brick courtyard is a choice locale for summer dining. The staff is among the best in Wine Country, professional yet friendly.

Starters include a trio of mushrooms sautéed in a red wine butter sauce and served over a puff pastry. The sauce is too weighty for our tastes but the mushrooms are impeccable, moist yet firm. The sauce is more successful with a roast monkfish fillet coated with chestnut flour. With the fluffy consistency of lobster, the monkfish is pleasing but not memorable. The wild boar cassoulet, inspired by the traditions of Provence, is magnificent. The boar, a cross between turkey and beef, is simmered until succulent with white beans and vegetables. For dessert, try the exquisite chocolate hoo-hoo, a Frank Lloyd Wright construction of chocolate mousse and pastry.

SPRING STREET RESTAURANT
707-963-5578.
1245 Spring St., St. Helena.
Price: Moderate.
Credit Cards: MC, V.
Cuisine: California.
Serving: B, L, D.

S pring Street is a homey stucco bungalow framed by two stately evergreen trees, trim hedges, and an ivy fence. You feel as though you're stopping at a neighbor's for dinner. The kitchen may be as inconsistent as your neighbor's, as pleasing as it is disappointing.

Service is efficient and the lunch and dinner

Reservations: Recom-
mended.
Special Features: Outdoor
dining, garden.
Handicap Access: Yes.

menus are large and varied, offering vegetarian choices as well as hearty meat dishes. The wine menu is small but boasts an excellent list by the glass and a fine line-up of beers. The best bet is lunch in the garden, savoring a sandwich like crunchy tuna, which combines curried tuna with almonds and chutney. The grilled polenta platter is an inspired lunch combination of polenta, pepper Jack cheese, marinated tomatoes, and basil.

Dinner appetizers are lackluster and include a roasted bulb of garlic overwhelmed by olive oil and a soggy artichoke with green chili remoulade. The caesar salad lacks zest, likewise the spinach and goat cheese salad. Entrées include a tame blackened red snapper and a seafood pasta with a tangy dillanise sauce and overcooked mussels, clams, and shrimp. A must for dessert is Spanish chocolate, a moist cake with a splash of rum.

TERRA
707-963-8931.
1345 Railroad Ave., St.
Helena.
Closed: Tues.
Price: Expensive.
Credit Cards: V.
Cuisine: California, Asian.
Serving: D.
Reservations: Required.
Special Features: In the historic Hatchery Building.

At Terra, East meets West and the restaurant's Asian influence leaves an indelible mark on California cuisine. Terra's chef, Hiroyoshi Sone, succeeds with daring entrées such as sea bass marinated in sake. The setting is the historic Hatchery Building, where high ceilings, tall arched windows, and stone walls are embellished with elegantly simple decor.

The duo behind Terra has an impressive resume. Sone led the kitchen at Wolfgang Puck's Spago in Los Angeles and his wife Lissa Doumani was a pastry chef.

Appetizers may include a remarkable lobster flan, a rich but not sweet lobster custard with a touch of curry, or a marvelously understated delicacy, steamed mussels in white wine. Favorite entrées include grilled salmon topped with Thai red curry sauce, an ingenious pairing. More hearty is a massive and tender veal chop with garlic mashed potatoes. The aforementioned sea bass is brilliant, broiled to a fluffy consistency then paired with shrimp dumplings in shiso broth.

The desserts are enticing and you can't miss with strawberries sautéed in a black pepper and cabernet sauvignon sauce and served in a towering martini glass. The Bartlett pear tart with ginger and cream is also a knockout. The wine list is superb with many selections in the $15 to $30 range. Wine by the glass, however, is sorely limited. The service at Terra is always attentive, gracious, and knowledgeable. Terra is a rare find indeed.

TRA VIGNE
707-963-4444.
1050 Charter Oak Ave.,
St. Helena.

One of Napa Valley's most popular restaurants, Tra Vigne is a sensory delight, from the fragrance of roasted garlic wafting through the court-

Tim Fish

Tra Vigne is, literally, among the vines.

Price: Expensive.
Credit Cards: D, DC, MC, V.
Cuisine: Italian, California.
Serving: L, D.
Reservations: Required.
Special Features: Outdoor dining.
Handicap Access: Yes.

yard, to the neo-Gothic atmosphere of the tall stone building, to the pool of herb-infused olive oil at your table. The food is generally cooked with a fiery passion. Most dishes linger on the palate (though a few muster only a mediocre rating). The odds are truly in your favor.

Chef Michael Chiarello has described the cuisine as "American food prepared with the heart, hands, and eyes of an Italian." Perhaps part of Chiarello's success is the freshness. Everything is made at the restaurant, including prosciutto, breads, pastas, cheeses, and gelato.

Tra Vigne, which means "among the vines," charms its guests with rows of grapevines just outside the courtyard. Inside, the decor is part Italian villa, part Hollywood, with gold stripes on the molding softened by earth tones. The restaurant swarms with beeper-clad waiters and the service is impeccable.

Appetizers include the oven-roasted polenta, bathed in balsamic vinegar, and the prosciutto di Parma, succulent Comice pears under a blanket of prosciutto — both are splendid. For entrées, pass on the ravioli di magro al burro, pasta filled with homemade ricotta, spinach, and red chard. Disappointingly bland. However, the petto di pollo al ferri, grilled lemon marinated chicken breast with mascarpone potatoes, is tangy and delicious. Bravo to the cavatappi con coniglio e funghi, corkscrew pasta with braised rabbit, pancetta, and wild mushrooms. Exceptional.

You'll fight over the budino di cioccolata e castagne, chocolate pudding and chestnuts with a tart cherry sauce, or the cannoli Siciliani, chocolate pastry with creamy ricotta inside. The wine list offers the finest of Napa and Italy; diners may also bring their own bottle (the corkage fee is modest and often waived entirely).

TRILOGY
707-963-5507.
1234 Main St., St. Helena.
Closed: Mon., Sat., & Sun.
L.
Credit Cards: MC, V.
Price: Expensive.
Cuisine: California, French.
Serving: L, D.
Reservations: Required.
Handicap Access: Yes.

Strip away the glitz, pare away the showy presentations and the chic crowd, and you're left with Trilogy. This storefront restaurant in St. Helena is understated, pleasantly unpretentious, and, most importantly, intimate. The focus is food and wine and chef-owner Diane Pariseau lavishes attention on each dish. She favors understatement over a deluge of cream, butter, or exotic spices, and restraint has its price; a bit more zeal would be nice at times. As for the wine list, it is exhaustive, among the best in Wine Country. The selection by the glass is adequate. The service is exceptional, aware but not bothersome.

The menu focuses on a handful of offerings, all fairly traditional — roasted duck breast, rack of lamb, and the like. Appetizers include pan-roasted rock shrimp with white beans, tomatoes, and baby artichokes, sensuously scented with rosemary and garlic. Splendid. Also recommended is the smoked trout on mascarpone rillettes with an endive and apple salad. Aside from too much turmeric, a chilled eggplant soup with curry makes for a delightfully unusual starter.

For entrées, there's a bit of magic in the pan-roasted veal loin, four lovely medallions served with sautéed spinach, asparagus, and a rich broth with sliced shiitake mushrooms. Another winner is the sautéed Pacific halibut, a moist and subtle fish married with a distinctive saffron aïoli. Desserts are spirited and include a luxurious and surprisingly airy chocolate chiffon cake with a mascarpone and caramel cream sauce and strawberries.

**WINE SPECTATOR
GREYSTONE
RESTAURANT**
707-967-1010.
2555 Main St. (Hwy. 29),
St. Helena.
Closed: Tues.
Price: Expensive.
Credit Cards: AE, CB, DC,
MC, V.
Cuisine: Mediterranean.
Serving: L, D.
Reservations:
Recommended.
Handicap Access: Yes.

You expect to be impressed by a restaurant affiliated with the Culinary Institute of America (CIA). Perhaps our expectations are too high, but we're always a little disappointed when we dine here.

The atmosphere is promising, if not downright dramatic. The restaurant is in the north wing of the recently restored Greystone Cellars, an historic Wine Country castle that was once known as Christian Brothers and is now home to the West Coast campus of the CIA. With stone walls and a towering ceiling, the room is cavernous and a bit noisy, but the decor is accented with bright colors and three open kitchen stations lend energy and warmth to the space.

The menu looks impressive, an ambitious selection from various Mediterranean countries, such as paella, pork kabobs, risotto, as well as grilled meat, fish, and fowl. Everything is competently done, but we expect more panache, perhaps a bit of brilliance from the CIA. The risotto changes regularly, but a recent version with black chanterelles, English peas, and prosciutto lacked focus and seemed a mishmash of flavors. The grilled oyster mushroom bruschetta, toasted bread topped with delicate slices of mushroom, is richly flavored but far too oily. Grilled tuna with Mediterranean toasted orzo salad and grilled spring onions is nicely done, and the Greystone paella, a traditional Spanish casserole with saffron rice, shrimp, mussels, chicken, and chorizo sausage, is worthy but has a lingering sweet tomato paste taste. Don't miss the marinated lamb sirloin served with fresh baked pita and Turkish salad. Light yet satisfying, it's a meal to eat with your fingers. Desserts follow a similar path: good but that's all.

For a restaurant named after Wine Spectator magazine, the wine list leaves room for improvement. The selection is surprisingly limited and the wine-by-the-glass offerings meagerly cover the many flavors of the menu.

Calistoga

ALL SEASONS CAFÉ
707-942-9111.
1400 Lincoln Ave., Calistoga.
Closed: Weds.
Price: Moderate.
Credit Cards: MC, V.
Cuisine: French, California.
Serving: SB, L, D.
Reservations: Recommended.
Handicap Access: Yes.

All Seasons Café reminds us of a Greenwich Village bistro. It has an imaginative menu matched with a modest but urbane setting. Ceiling fans spin slowly over stained glass lights, the floor is black and white tile, and through two walls of windows you can watch downtown Calistoga go by. The wine selection is fabulous. All Seasons, in fact, has a wine shop in back of the restaurant stocked with new and old vintages and all available at your table for a fair price.

All Seasons' menu is part wine steward as well, offering general matches with each course. Sauvignon blanc, zinfandel, and Rhone wines are suggested to go with pastas and pizzas, etc. Starters typically range from a plate of warm brie and roasted garlic to a local favorite of chilled Dungeness crab, the best of which is on par with lobster. Entrées run from simple pizzas to duckling with wild huckleberry sauce.

Soups are exceptional, particularly the cream of artichoke. Huge calzones are a lunch specialty, with infinitely agreeable interiors such as smoked Andouille sausage, mushrooms, and provolone cheese. Look for a masterpiece of a dish called chicken bastilla, shredded curry chicken with almonds, currants, and minted arugula pesto imprisoned in a golden phyllo crust. Fabulous. Service at All Seasons Café is professional and warm. After a meal, linger over a slab of "the pie of the day" or a glass of port.

BOSKOS RISTORANTE
707-942-9088.
1364 Lincoln Ave.,
Calistoga.

This Italian eatery moved across the street in 1994. The food is still basic and hearty and the price is right. With sawdust on the floor, the atmosphere is casual and perfect for families; you order

Price: Moderate.
Credit Cards: No.
Cuisine: Italian.
Serving: L, D.
Reservations: Not accepted.
Handicap Access: Yes.

at the counter and seat yourself. Lunch and dinner menus are the same, with a half-order pasta special available for lunch during the week. That's good because portions are generous. Pastas range from the basic spaghetti and meatballs to an enjoyable Palermo, fettucine with sautéed onions, sausage, and a creamy tomato sauce. There are also sandwiches, Italian sausage, capocollo, and the like, and pizza from a wood-burning stove. The beer and wine list is adequate.

CALISTOGA INN
707-942-4101.
1250 Lincoln Ave., Calistoga.
Price: Expensive.
Credit Cards: AE, MC, V.
Cuisine: California.
Serving: L, D.
Reservations: Recommended.
Special Features: Outdoor dining.
Handicap Access: Yes.

Calistoga Inn has two strengths. First, its soothing trellis-covered courtyard is shady and green, the perfect spot for lunch on a warm day. Second, the beer is superb — the Napa Valley Brewing Co. is right on the premises. The food, however, is merely serviceable.

The restaurant is inside a turn-of-the-century hotel. The main dining room has the elegance of a simple country inn, with dried flower arrangements and hardwood floors. Action shifts to the courtyard when weather allows. Service is attentive and the wine list is solid, but go for the beer.

Salads and sandwiches dominate the lunch. The dinner menu includes more than a dozen entrées, often a stretch. Appetizers include sweet and tangy Buffalo wings, a tasty plate although we don't prefer our wings so thickly breaded. Entrée specialties include sausage pan fry, a hearty potpourri of spicy Italian sausage, roasted potatoes, garlic, and tomatoes. The sausage is of excellent quality but the fry sorely lacks fresh vegetables. Chicken diablo is a pleasant boneless breast topped with a bland mustard breadcrumb crust and stuffed with mushrooms. The accompanying garlic mashed potatoes are pasty. Dessert includes a lackluster raspberry-apple crisp, with fruit that is less than fresh and a gummy crust.

CATAHOULA RESTAURANT & SALOON
707-942-BARK.
1457 Lincoln Ave., Calistoga.
Closed: Tues.
Price: Moderate to Expensive.
Credit Cards: MC, V.
Cuisine: Southern-inspired American.
Serving: L, D.
Reservations: Recommended.

Wine Country was long on oregano and tarragon and short on cayenne until Catahoula came along. Chef-owner Jan Birnbaum blends the refinement of California cuisine with the earthy flavors of his native Louisiana. The result is one of the most high-spirited eating adventures north of San Francisco.

Birnbaum was a protégé of Paul Prudhomme before making his name at New York's Quilted Giraffe and Campton Place in San Francisco. He opened Catahoula, named for the state dog of Louisiana, in 1994. The main dining room, which has

Special Features: Outdoor dining.
Handicap Access: Yes.

the panache of a big city restaurant and none of the pretension, is done in vivid green and buttermilk, and one wall is dominated by an abstract construction. Birnbaum and his brick oven are at center stage.

An appetizer not to be missed is the spicy rooster gumbo. It arrives in an oversized ceramic bowl; inside is a dark and rich brown broth alive with the luxurious textures of sausages, rice, and tender chicken. Its fire is light, not overpowering. Less inspired is the "oozing raclette" with cured sausage, a rich combination that's less greasy than it appears.

Main dishes include sassafras-encrusted lamb, a revelation of rare lamb sliced and fanned over a creamy red potato salsify pie. Marvelous. A pan-fried jalapeno pecan catfish is less seductive than it sounds. Breaded and crispy, it had a tender heart but lacked kick. Desserts are hearty and homey creations like apple molasses grunt, warm and crisp apples swimming in molasses and topped with a crunchy crust.

WAPPO BAR AND BISTRO
707-942-4712.
1226B Washington St., Calistoga.
Closed: Tues., Wed. D.
Price: Moderate to Expensive.
Credit Cards: AE, MC, V.
Cuisine: Eclectic.
Serving: L, D.
Reservations: Recommended.
Special Features: Outdoor dining.
Handicap Access: Yes.

This warm-blooded bistro is suited for adventurous souls, up for an eclectic trip around the culinary world. The imaginative and hearty fare is inspired by Latin America, the Mediterranean, and who knows where. The narrow dining room — with reddish-brown wainscoting and copper-covered tables and lights — blends European bistro with Southwestern warmth. If the weather is warm, the brick courtyard patio, covered with a grapevine arbor, is a must.

Owners Aaron Bauman and Michelle Mutrux opened in 1993 and they share kitchen duties. The menu finds an eccentric match in the wine list, which refreshingly downplays chardonnay and the like. Service is personable but sluggish. Lunch includes Thai sweet potato fries, a yummy creation made clumsy by thick breading but saved by an addictive coconut and peanut dipping sauce. Another unusual treat is pibil yucateco, corn cakes piled with tender and lightly spicy sirloin, black beans, and guacamole. The textures and flavors tango across your palate.

Soups include an imposing gazpacho, a chunky melange of chilled goodies. Main courses include seared sea bass with garam masala, a fresh and tangy jacket protecting a moist filet and invigoratingly paired with mint chutney and a lentil crepe. Bravo. The sea bass returns in the vatapa, an exotic Brazilian seafood stew that's ripe with prawns and coconut milk. Desserts explore the globe but even a homey blueberry cobbler is nicely done.

SONOMA COUNTY RESTAURANTS

Sonoma Valley

AMEDEO
707-996-3077.
14301 Arnold Dr., Glen Ellen.
Closed: Mon.
Price: Moderate to Expensive.
Credit Cards: AE, MC, V.
Cuisine: Italian.
Serving: D.
Reservations: Recommended.
Special Features: Outdoor dining.
Handicap Access: Yes.

A restaurant of many charms, Amedeo is a country-style Italian eatery inside a grist mill that dates from the 1800s. Cloistered amid tall trees and along a rambling creek, Amedeo is an appealing spot for lunch, particularly in the summer when the deck is open. On a cool winter evening, the restaurant takes on the cozy warmth of a rustic lodge, with dark wood and exposed beams. A few tables are reserved for romantic fireside dinners.

Atmosphere is one thing, but is the food any good? Yes. The menu is heavy on pasta, seafood, and veal. The caesar salad is nicely done, and the calamari fritti may be the best we've had, tender circles of succulent squid lightly breaded, fried, and served with an understated lemon-garlic butter sauce. Pastas to recommend include porcini pappardelle, wide and delicate ribbons of pasta in a creamy rich sauce with peas and mushrooms. Exquisite in its simplicity is the gulf prawns sauté, a plate of muscular prawns cooked to a moist crispness and sautéed in white wine and garlic.

Desserts include an adequate tiramisu and a hearty apple-cranberry concoction that tastes remarkably like mincemeat pie. The wine list is limited but has good selections from the surrounding vineyards. Service is attentive and knowledgeable.

BABETTE'S
707-939-8931.
464 1st St., E., Sonoma
Closed: Sun. & Mon., Wed. Nov.–June.

Like its cinematic namesake *Babette's Feast*, Babette's offers exquisite French food prepared with sublime passion. Snug at the end of a cobblestone courtyard off Sonoma Plaza, Babette's is lush

Prix Fixe: $45.
Credit Cards: MC, V.
Cuisine: French.
Serving: D.
Reservations: Required.
Special Features: Wine bar.
Handicap Access: Yes.

in a funky sort of way, the decor done in velvet and brocade. The adjacent wine bar is more bohemian, like a Parisian jazz club.

Chef Daniel Patterson, who owns the restaurant with wife Elizabeth Ramsey, worked at Domaine Chandon and Eastside Oyster Bar and Grill. He creates a seasonal menu that is *very* French but with a light touch. His presentation is artistic but not excessive.

Service is superb and knowledgeable about the menu and the restaurant has an ace wine list. Starters include a divine Sonoma foie gras sautéed with bing cherries (sometimes caramelized pears) and hazelnuts. A smoked salmon mousse with cucumber, basil, and curry vinaigrette is light and elegant but shy on curry.

Main courses include pan-roasted swordfish, a lightly crispy shell protecting a moist and flaky interior. It is served with various sauces, including a savory corn coulis and red pepper reduction. A bit of heaven is the roulade of pork and roasted peppers, a sumptuous combination served with creamy polenta and a luscious tomato and red wine sauce. For desserts, try the warm apple tart — the buttery crust is matched with almond ice cream and caramel sauce.

CAFÉ CITTI
707-833-2690.
9049 Sonoma Hwy.
   (Hwy. 12), Boyes Hot
   Springs.
Price: Moderate.
Credit Cards: MC, V.
Cuisine: Italian.
Serving: L, D.
Reservations: Not
   accepted.
Special Features: Outdoor
   dining, deli.

A trattoria in the strictest Italian sense — a casual atmosphere with hearty wine and yummy and inexpensive pasta — Café Citti is a pleasure. There's no menu, just a chalkboard on the wall. Customers order from the counter, cafeteria-style. Lunch includes sandwiches: sweet Italian sausage and the usual cold deli fare. Pasta is mix and match; choose penne, linguine, etc. and pair it with the sauce (marinara, bolognese, etc.) of choice. Other offerings include a zesty caesar salad and homemade focaccia. The traditional Italian herb-roasted chicken is hearty but we've had better.

**THE CAFÉ AT SONOMA
   MISSION INN**
707-938-9000.
18140 Sonoma Hwy. (Hwy.
   12), Boyes Hot Springs.
Price: Moderate.
Credit Cards: AE, DC, MC,
   V.
Cuisine: California.
Serving: SB, L, D.
Reservations: Recom-
   mended.

Looking for a nice breakfast or lunch spot? You could do worse than the Café. You could also do better. There is promise both in the atmosphere and the menu. The room is done in tasteful shades of green and white, with fans whirling from the tall ceilings and garlic braids and dried peppers hanging over the open kitchen. The breakfast menu allows indulgence as well as moderation, and lunch and dinner blends California and Italy.

A popular breakfast item are apple oat cakes with walnuts and crème fraîche. Ooo! The spa

Special Features: Spa menu of lighter dishes.
Handicap Access: Yes.

menu offers a reliable low-fat granola with fresh fruit, but the oat bran pancakes have the appeal of wet sawdust. At lunch, avoid the grilled chicken breast on focaccia. Smothered with grilled peppers, onions, tomatoes, and melted mozzarella, it tastes like a street-vendor hoagie.

The Press Democrat/Annie Wells

Della Santina's brings a touch of old Italy to Sonoma Plaza.

DELLA SANTINA'S
707-935-0576.
101 E. Napa St., Sonoma.
Price: Moderate.
Credit Cards: MC, V.
Cuisine: Italian.
Serving: L, D.
Reservations: Recommended.
Handicap Access: Yes.

Ah, the mighty aromas that escape from this petite café. Don't overlook this Italian trattoria on bustling Sonoma Plaza. The food is as authentic and unfussy as the best from Mama's kitchen. (And at a price that would make her smile.)

The Della Santina family opened shop in 1990 and the restaurant is an intimate no-frills room, with a handful of tables and the warm din of the kitchen mingling with Puccini and Verdi. Chicken roasts lazily on a spit in the window. The caesar salad here is a vibrant cut above the usual. Entrées include penne pasta with shiitake mushrooms in a creamy wine sauce that's robust but not ponderous. Pollo allo spiedo, a traditional Italian roast chicken, is the best in Wine Country. Infused with flowery herbs, it's tender and heavenly. For dessert, tiramisu is called for and Della Santina's dances on air.

THE FEED STORE
707-938-2122.
529 1st St. W., Sonoma.
Price: Moderate.
Credit Cards: MC, V.
Cuisine: American.
Serving: B, L.
Reservations: Not needed.
Special Features: Outdoor
  dining, bakery.
Handicap Access: Yes.

After a hard stint of winery hopping, deciding where to eat for lunch can be a chore. Feel like Mexican or a sandwich? That's when a place like the Feed Store Café & Bakery comes in handy. It serves a bit of this, a little of that, all of it appetizing but not fancy or extraordinary. The name comes from its location, a circa 1921 feed store. Like the menu, the decor is a little this, a little that: exposed pipes give the ceiling that industrial look; a "Don't Tread On Me" flag and other funky items hang on the walls.

A big draw is its bakery counter, where you'll see delectables like pumpkin cheesecake and zinfandel brownies. Fresh croissants and tasty omelet combinations are the highlight of breakfast. Stick with sandwiches and salads for lunch. Beer-battered onion rings are a good bet, and the quesadilla is reliable, not too greasy and topped with generous portions of salsa, sour cream, and guacamole. The curried chicken salad sandwich topped with crisp apple slices is yummy but burdened by too much sweet chutney.

Chris and Karen Bertrand of the Glen Ellen Inn.

The Press Democrat/Mark Aronoff

GLEN ELLEN INN
707 996-6409.
13670 Arnold Dr., Glen
  Ellen.
Closed: Mon., L. Sat. & Sun.

The Glen Ellen Inn is quaint: small-town, front-porch-swing kind of quaint. Yet somehow in this quiet corner of the world chef Chris Bertrand holds his own with Wine Country's finest. Bertrand and wife Karen own the restaurant in the

Price: Moderate to Expensive.
Credit Cards: MC, V.
Cuisine: California.
Reservations: Recommended.
Special Features: Outdoor dining.
Handicap Access: No.

charming cottage. Six tables keep the kitchen company in the main dining room, a cozy fit. There's also a covered patio outside for dining al fresco. Karen waits on many of the tables herself and the service is intimate but never smothering. The wine list specializes in the best Sonoma Valley wines with a smart list by the glass.

Bertrand was schooled at the Fifth Avenue Grill in Manhattan; he cooks with a French accent, depending on fresh, local ingredients. The menu is modest but packs in as much variety as a small kitchen can muster. Salads are exceptional. Fall brings a refreshing autumn salad, a mix of greens tossed with mint, fresh fruit, and sweet pecans. Delightful. A soothing carrot and ginger soup is a perfect balance of flavors. Entrées include grilled salmon and roasted rib-eye steak, both wonderfully realized. The salmon is bathed in a light but tangy lemon cream sauce and topped with a fresh tomato salsa. Exceptional. The rib-eye is a faux-beef Wellington, done to a light pink, wrapped in a rich pastry and topped with a morel mushroom sauce. One wickedly decadent dessert is the French vanilla ice cream rolled in toasted coconut and swimming in fresh caramel sauce. Ooo.

The Grille at Sonoma Mission Inn and Spa.

Chris Alderman

THE GRILLE AT SONOMA MISSION INN
707-938-9000.
18140 Sonoma Hwy. (Hwy. 12), Boyes Hot Springs.
Price: Very Expensive.

Sonoma Mission Inn is among Wine Country's most gracious resorts, drawing guests from around the country with its luxurious rooms, full spa, and easy proximity to Sonoma Valley wineries (see Chapter Three, *Lodging*). The Grille is a key

Credit Cards: AE, DC, MC, V.
Cuisine: California.
Serving: SB, L, D.
Reservations: Recommended.
Special Features: Outdoor dining, resort setting.
Handicap Access: Yes.

ingredient. Both the atmosphere and the menu are elegant yet not the least stuffy. The Grille is one of Sonoma County's most expensive restaurants. Is it worth it? Yes; though you man not encounter here the sheer panache displayed in other Wine Country restaurants, the food is winning and the presentation stunning. Service, too, is knowledgeable but not haughty.

The calming peach tones of its Spanish-California decor makes the Grille a tranquil dining spot, a casual yet elegant setting enhanced by a view of the gardens and pool. The Grille also has a superb wine list, mostly from California, and the selection of wines by the glass is much improved in recent years.

The menu is ever-evolving, although lighter spa cuisine, with calorie and fat content indicated, is always included. To begin, consider the bruschetta or the Dungeness crabcake, crispy brown on the outside with a tender and impeccably fresh heart. Salads include a delightfully understated caesar with bite-sized wafers of dried Jack. Entrées range from pasta and fish to duck and beef. The grilled Sonoma lamb loin is tender but less than memorable, yet the sautéed Alaskan salmon with a ragout of artichoke hearts and tomato is sumptuous. The dessert menu rewards both decadence and restraint. A strawberry rhubarb tart, served warm and with fresh ginger ice cream, is a mammoth undertaking, yet the real prize is the spa mocha soufflé, a custard cup of fluffy mousse with intense chocolate flavors but never cloyingly sweet.

THE GENERAL'S DAUGHTER

707-938-4004.
400 W. Spain St., Sonoma.
Price: Expensive.
Credit Cards: MC, V.
Cuisine: California.
Serving: SB, L, D.
Reservations: Recommended.
Special Features: Outdoor dining.
Handicap Access: Yes.

This 1883 farmhouse is a showplace. The kitchen can't quite live up to the decor's standards, but that could be forgiven if the menu was more modestly priced and the service was less lethargic. Suzanne Brangham renovated this once dilapidated pink house, which belonged to Gen. Mariano Vallejo's daughter Natalia, and opened the restaurant in 1994. The place is gorgeous, with lush landscaping, a wide porch, and a classic interior of hardwood floors, antiques, and lively murals. The bar is done in rich Honduran mahogany.

The lunch menu offers salads and sandwiches and dinner is traditionally Californian, with selections of fish, beef, and chicken. A standout appetizer is the buttermilk and cornmeal onion rings, which come as wispy curls piled high and topped with lemon-pepper aïoli. The kitchen tends to overcook fish and chicken. A grilled salmon filet can be dangerously parched, though it is livened by pairings like sage brown butter and lentil ragout. More satisfying is a dish like pork tenderloins, grilled yet succulent, with a lightly spicy sauce of roasted pepper, tequila, and cumin. For dessert, try the jumbled berry pie, a hefty deep dish stuffed with a luxurious mix of berries and topped with a perfect crust.

**KENWOOD RESTAU-
RANT AND BAR**
707-833-6326.
9900 Sonoma Hwy. (Hwy.
12), Kenwood.
Closed: Mon.
Price: Expensive.
Credit Cards: MC, V.
Cuisine: California.
Serving: L, D.
Reservations: Recom-
mended.
Special Features: Outdoor
dining.
Handicap Access: Yes.

This bistro, a California roadhouse turned upscale, is in the heart of the Valley of the Moon, one of the most beautiful spots in Wine Country. The patio offers marvelous views of Sugar Loaf Ridge, where vineyards rib the lower slopes. The charm of sipping wine made next door should not be underestimated, and Kenwood's wine list is a who's who of Sonoma Valley vintners.

The decor and chef Max Schacher's food are well matched — both paint a refined picture with subtle strokes. The dining rooms have steep wood ceilings and the rooms are done in muted tones brightened by colorful paintings. Likewise, Schacher believes in artistic presentation paired with a sense of understatement, with dishes that emphasize the quality of local duck or fish rather than exotic creations. We, frankly, would like more adventure. Also, the same menu is served lunch and dinner, which makes for a pricey lunch.

Appetizers range from a bland caesar salad to an inspired plate of portobello mushrooms baked with goat cheese. The crispy roast duck can be too crispy for our tastes, yet it's always tender. Truly memorable is the prawns with saffron Pernod sauce. Fragrant in their liqueur bath, the prawns are sautéed to crisp succulence and paired with a puff pastry and vegetables flawlessly steamed. Spectacular.

Desserts includes a luxurious tapioca that — thankfully — is nothing like Mom made, and a caramelized apple tart that's too much like candy and not enough like apples. Service is always attentive.

RISTORANTE PIATTI
707-996-2351.
405 1st St. W., Sonoma.
Price: Moderate to
Expensive.
Credit Cards: AE, MC, V.
Cuisine: Italian.
Serving: L, D.
Reservations: Recom-
mended.
Special Features: Outdoor
dining.
Handicap Access: Yes.

Like its twin in Napa Valley, this Piatti is a fun and festive Italian trattoria, with terra cotta floors and bright murals of tomatoes, asparagus, and braids of garlic. The patio is tranquil, removed from the busy Sonoma Plaza, while the main room hums with happy diners and the wonderful fragrance of the open kitchen envelopes the room like olive oil. Considering everything — solid food, warm atmosphere, price — Piatti is hard to top. Now *only* if it had crisp table service as well.

Chef Douglas Lane delivers the best of Tuscany: pasta, pizzas, and grilled meat and fish. Starters included a fine house-cured salmon and a rather dull oven-baked flatbread lined with Italian cheeses. A must is the bruschetta, a luscious pairing of ripe marinated tomatoes with grilled bread. Superb.

The wood-burning pizza oven produces pies with crisp and light crusts, particularly a margherita pizza with tantalizing fennel salami. Scholars of traditional Italian herb-roasted chicken pollo arrosto will not consider Piatti's a classic — for that try Della Santina's across the square — but it is appealing and served with flawlessly steamed carrots and green beans. If you prefer a little kick in your pasta, try penne all'Amatriciana, a dish livened with chili flakes, pancetta, and onions. A solid selection of Sonoma and Italy wines are available, with a hearty chianti and a few others served by the glass. Desserts range from gelato to a simple but spectacular torta de pesca, a warm peach cobbler that oozes fruit, not sugar.

ZINO'S
707-996-4466.
420 1st St. E., Sonoma.
Price: Moderate to
   Expensive.
Credit Cards: AE, MC, V.
Cuisine: Italian.
Serving: L, D.
Reservations: Accepted.
Special Features: Outdoor
   dining.
Handicap Access: Yes.

With names like Sebastiani and Rafanelli on so many local wine labels, it's no secret that an Italian community thrives in Sonoma. A steaming plate of pasta is one of the area's oldest and richest traditions. Though others have more style or a more dynamic menu, Zino's serves a helluva plate of spaghetti. It's traditional fare without any fuss.

With its brick walls, dark wood bar, and checkered tablecloths, Zino's is right out of New York's Little Italy. So is the service: waiters with Italian accents are efficient but amusingly impatient. The wine list is modest but the prices are fair and every wine is available by the glass.

Appetizers include a fine calamari, pounded thin, breaded, and delicately fried. Roasted garlic with brie on toast is a simple delight. A garlic head is sliced open and the garlic spreads over the cheese like decadent butter. Pastas are mix and match, with your choice of fettucine, linguine, angel hair, or penne served with a variety of sauces. The bolognese is the same hearty red meat sauce Italian grandmothers make. Even better is the ravioli, thick yet delicate shells filled with a fluffy combo of beef and spinach and topped with a marinara sauce of sweet tomatoes. Desserts are inconsistent. The chocolate mousse is delicious but the caramelized flan is often rubbery.

Santa Rosa

JOHN ASH & CO.
707-527-7687.
4330 Barnes Rd., Santa
   Rosa.
Closed: Sat.–Mon. L.
Price: Very Expensive.
Credit Cards: AE, MC, V.
Cuisine: California.

Before John Ash helped pioneer the notion that Northern California had a "cuisine," Wine Country was largely burger joints and Foster Freezes. *Food & Wine* magazine called Ash one of the 25 hot new chefs in America in 1991 and *Condé Nast Traveler* magazine named the restaurant one of the top 50 in America. Today, Ash has little to do

French windows look out on vineyards at John Ash & Co.

Chris Alderman

Serving: SB, L, D.
Reservations: Required.
Special Features: Outdoor
 dining.

with the daily operation of the restaurant. His protégé, Jeff Madura, lacks the brilliance of Ash but the restaurant remains a destination. Madura strives to make each entrée a masterpiece by tending to taste, texture, color, and design.

The lunch menu offers imaginative salads and sandwiches such as a grilled portobello mushroom club on focaccia. The dinner menu is ever-changing. For starters, grilled radicchio provides a brilliant array of tastes and textures — Italian bacon, goat cheese, mustard sauce, and beautiful greens. Crabcakes are succulently paired with a mild salsa.

Entrées include sautéed Maine sea scallops in a pool of coconut milk sauce atop tart apples, a delicate and successful pairing of contrasting tastes. Less appealing is poached salmon with black bean salsa and chipotle aïoli. The filet is moist but spiritless and the salsa was lacking. A loin of venison with a blackberry and wild mushroom sauce is visually stunning but the sauce overpowers the venison's delicate taste. More impressive is the grilled tenderloin of pork with a subtle raspberry sauce.

Desserts include a hearty apple jack tart and a rapturous peaches and cream, succulent fruit slices over a mold of thick cream with blackberry and raspberry sauce. The wine list is one of the best in Wine Country and the by-the-glass selection is excellent. The service staff is attentive but at these prices we expect more pampering. The setting is a bucolic site next to Vintners Inn (see Chapter Three, *Lodging*), with vineyard views through French windows. The restaurant, with its Southwest-inspired decor and cathedral ceiling, is stunning.

CAFÉ LOLO
707-576-7822.
620 5th St., Santa Rosa.
Closed: Sat. & Sun. L.

The 5th Street storefront has seen many incarnations, from the popular French bistro Matisse to the short-lived Fans restaurant, but Café Lolo is

Price: Moderate to Expensive.
Credit Cards: MC, V.
Cuisine: California.
Serving: L, D.
Reservations: Recommended.
Handicap Access: Yes.

the finest of the trio. Chef Michael Quigley's food is inventive and served with panache. Entrées are priced moderately and portions are generous, the antithesis of most California cuisine.

If we have any criticism, it's the dining room itself. The tables are too close together, creating an intrusive atmosphere. The decor is simple and elegant, although the crisp white linens and white walls with a touch of blue seem rather flat in Wine Country, where restaurateurs are increasingly more daring with decor.

Here the food is the main attraction. Starters include terrine of grilled eggplant, roasted peppers, and Laura Chenel goat cheese, as well as an phenomenal house-cured salmon on a jumbo corn pancake. The spiral of salmon sprouts from the plate like a gladiolus. Entrées include an appealing sautéed salmon on a bed of green lentils and a fine pan-roasted liberty duck doused in a port wine sauce. For dessert, try the house special chocolate kiss, a temptingly rich puck of chocolate in a puddle of raspberry sauce. The non-chocoholics won't be disappointed with the lemon and raspberry sorbet, adorned with a dollop of fresh fruit. The wine list is brief but well chosen, with an excellent selection by the glass.

Caffe Portofino is one of downtown Santa Rosa's busiest spots.

Chris Alderman

CAFFE PORTOFINO
707-523-1171.
535 4th St., Santa Rosa.
Closed: Sun.
Price: Expensive.
Credit Cards: AE, MC, V.
Cuisine: Italian.
Serving: L, D.

Caffe Portofino is one of the busiest night spots in downtown Santa Rosa, with a cozy din of drinkers gathering around the bar. The food is generally good but is no match for the atmosphere. The interior of the building, which dates from 1907, is rugged red brick, with handsome oak and a mirror behind the bar that gives the narrow restaurant the illusion of spaciousness. The menu is extensive

Reservations: Recom-
mended.
Special Features: Outdoor
dining.

— too extensive, really, with two dozen entrées of pasta, meat, fish, and poultry. The wine list is also far ranging, with a select list of wines by the glass.

Lunch offers sandwiches, from a decidedly un-Italian reuben to traditional Italian sausage with sautéed bell peppers, onions, and cheese. Dinner appetizers include antipasto portofino, a generous and tasty plate of smoked salmon and marinated calamari with a mustard caper sauce. Mozzarella di bufala and pomodoro is a dreadful rendition of the classic, however, pairing bland mozzarella with lifelessly hard tomato slices. Entrées include an admirable fettuccine portofino, pasta with small bites of pork tenderloin and mushrooms in a garlic sauce. A real disappointment is the tortellini con pesto, soggy pasta drowning in olive oil. Fish is often a good choice, particularly mahi mahi di Capri .

Dessert finds another suspiciously long list from which to choose. Two capable but uninspiring desserts include tiramisu, rum-soaked ladyfingers, and sorbetto di stagione, scoops of pear, lemon, and hazelnut sorbet. Service is good but forgetful at times, understandable given the Grand Central Station traffic on many nights.

EQUUS
707-578-6101.
101 Fountaingrove Pkwy.,
Santa Rosa.
Price: Expensive.
Credit Cards: AE, D, DC,
MC, V.
Cuisine: American, Conti-
nental.
Serving: SB, L, D.
Reservations: Recom-
mended.
Handicap Access: Yes.

Eating where the locals eat is a good idea if you're after hamburgers or ethnic food. But too often the masses favor mediocrity in fine dining. Such is the case with Equus, the restaurant of Fountaingrove Inn (see Chapter Three, *Lodging*). It consistently draws crowds at the expense of more worthy kitchens. Why? Don't ask us.

The dining room is generically ornate, the way so many hotel dining rooms are, with horses as the main design theme. A nice touch is the pianist working the center of the room, performing soothing versions of "Rhapsody in Blue" and the like. Service is efficient even on the busiest nights. The wine list is also a treat, a vast selection well priced.

New to the kitchen is chef Peter Coleman, who ups the ante but not sufficiently. His menu is too vast, offering 18 entrées, for example, suggesting that freshness is sorely lacking. An example is the roast duck appetizer; served cold and chewy, it recalls a Thanksgiving turkey drumstick ignored in the fridge. Caesar salads, on the other hand, are delectable, prepared fresh at your table.

For entrées, stick with the reliable rib-eye steak or filet mignon. The roasted Petaluma chicken is savory and tender, served with a creamy juniper berry glaze. Avoid adventures like the Pacific sea bass and clam bake, a lifeless filet drowning in a flat tomato sauce. Desserts are straight from the cooler (or freezer), and include a bourbon chocolate pecan pie served heartlessly cold.

LA GARE
707-528-4355.
208 Wilson St., Santa Rosa.
Closed: Mon.
Price: Moderate.
Credit Cards: AE, DC, MC, V.
Cuisine: French.
Serving: D.
Reservations: Recommended.
Handicap Access: Yes.

If it's adventure you seek, look elsewhere. If you like hearty old-style French fare at reasonable prices, then La Gare is a charming choice. A favorite of locals, La Gare ("the railway station") is an out-of-the-way restaurant tucked appropriately along Santa Rosa's historic Railroad Square. The dining room is softly lit and decorated with lace curtains and stained glass. The solid wine list offers California and French wines but incomprehensibly omits vintage dates — a sin in Wine Country.

La Gare specializes in dishes exorcised from trendier — and healthier — menus years ago. The offerings include Châteaubriand, veal, sweetbreads, thick and cheesy onion soup, frog legs, and escargot. Starters include an uninspiring pâté as well as a ho-hum dinner salad made with butter lettuce.

The filet of salmon with a lemon and white wine sauce is a La Gare specialty we have never liked. The pepper steak is from the old school: an exquisite slice of beef floundering in creamy white sauce. A crime against steak! Yet, the beef Wellington — a choice filet surrounded by rich pâté, spinach, and a flaky crust — is always outstanding. Rack of lamb and the duck a l'orange are also winning.

LISA HEMENWAY'S
707-526-5111.
714 Village Court, Montgomery Village, Santa Rosa.
Price: Expensive.
Cuisine: California.
Credit Cards: D, DC, MC, V.
Serving: SB, L, D.

Nestled in a courtyard of Montgomery Village shopping center is this cultivated eatery. Lisa Hemenway, a protégé of John Ash, is no longer the "new kid" but her restaurant has lost none of its appeal. In the summer, French doors welcome the warm air and open onto sidewalk tables shaded by a wisteria arbor. The interior is elegant with archways and terra cotta tiles. Paintings by local artists complete the mood. Hemenway's menu focuses on

Reservations: Recom-
   mended.
Special Features: Outdoor
   dining, wine bar.
Handicap Access: Yes.

imaginative combinations of fresh, local ingredients, downplaying fish to emphasize hearty dishes
of lamb, chicken, and veal.

Lunch does not translate "light" at Hemenway's,
with items that include a hearty but not sweet chutney burger and succulent grilled prawns with Thai
peanut sauce. Evening appetizers include fresh oysters, a luscious grilled
baguette with cambozola, and roasted garlic and soup specials such as sweetly
aromatic mulligatawny. A masterly entrée is pan-seared salmon lightly dusted
with garlic breadcrumbs and served on white beans and frisée marinated with
Dijon vinegar. Bucatini, a thick spaghetti, is deftly paired with summer vegetables and smoked chicken and served with a yeasty rich Red Tail Ale sauce.

Hemenway's wine list is priced reasonably, with a fine selection of half-bot-
tles and by-the-glass offerings. Imported and specialty domestic beers are a
specialty. Dessert offers hits but also misses, particularly a weakly realized
peach and blackberry cobbler that was nothing more than a bowl of warm pre-
serves topped by a sugar cookie. Service is knowledgeable but understaffing is
occasionally a problem.

MiXX has a stylish Art Deco interior.

Chris Alderman

MIXX
707-573-1344.
135 4th St., Santa Rosa.
Closed: L. Sat. & Sun.
Price: Expensive.
Credit Cards: AE, MC, V.
Cuisine: California.
Serving: L, D.
Reservations: Recom-
   mended.
Handicap Access: Yes.

Where do locals go for great food? Right here.
A cornerstone in historic Railroad Square,
MiXX is not a tourist destination, which pleases
locals to no end. The menu is creative, the wine is
reasonably priced, and the atmosphere is intimate
and elegant without being stuffy. Expanding into
the adjacent storefront in 1994, MiXX added elbow
room without sacrificing its Art Deco ambiance.
The main room is dominated by a magnificent oak
and mahogany bar.

Chef Dan Berman oversees the kitchen, leaving wife Kathleen to concentrate on desserts. The menu is divided between small plates and large, but the kitchen can enlarge small plates and vice versa. The Bermans take influences from around the culinary world: Cajun, Indian, Italian, and California. Salads include a delectable hearts of romaine that could be called caesar-light. Berman does imaginative things with fish, and the ravioli of the day is a house specialty. There is the occasional miss. The polenta with grilled portobello mushrooms and balsamic vinegar sauce makes a pleasant but unmoving combination. The grilled lamb with a sauce of sherry vinegar and black currants demands devotion, but the menu's true star is the Sonoma Liberty Duck, marinated in a glaze of honey and chili paste and grilled to perfection.

After dinner temptations often include a heavenly crème brûlée, one of the best we've tasted, as well as fresh sorbet that explodes fruit on your tongue.

Don't let the unassuming roadhouse of Willowside Cafe fool you. The food is among the best in Wine Country.

Chris Alderman

WILLOWSIDE CAFÉ
707-523-4814.
3535 Guerneville Rd., Santa
    Rosa.
Closed: Mon. & Tues.
Price: Moderate to Expen-
    sive.
Credit Cards: MC, V.
Cuisine: California.
Serving: D.
Reservations: Recom-
    mended.
Handicap Access: Yes.

Willowside Café, tucked inside a plain red roadhouse, doesn't make a hullabaloo with a big sign outside. It doesn't have to. It's busy with people seeking out its great California cuisine and urban brand of farmhouse funk. Copper-topped tables and eclectic silverware create an irreverent backdrop for a dining experience unmatched by more established restaurants in Wine Country. This isn't shocking when you consider the clever trio behind Willowside. Michael Hale managed Greens in San Francisco and Carol Hale still makes pastries for the Downtown Bakery and Creamery in Healdsburg. Chef Richard Allen worked at Chez Panisse, Domaine Chandon, and Jordon Winery.

The menu is limited and that's key to Allen's quality control. Nearly every dish is mastered with aplomb. A must-try is an appetizer called the Oregon blue cheese tart with red onion marmalade. The blue cheese is subtle, the crust is delicious and flaky, and the red onion marmalade looks like ribbon — a festive package. The Hawaiian escolar with grilled Vidalia onion vinaigrette and summer squash is superb. The Bodega Bay rabbit, served with chard and polenta, is masterly. A dish that needs to be tamed a bit is the roast pork tenderloin and lentil chili. The spicy dish begins to wear on you.

Carol's nectarine crisp is perfect after a rich dinner — not too heavy, not too sweet. Equally appealing is the plum brown butter tart and Babcock peaches poached in zinfandel. The wine list, affectionately selected, offers true bargains. Service was not Willowside's strong suit in the early months, but it's improving.

Healdsburg

BISTRO RALPH
707-433-1380.
Closed: L. Sat. & Sun.
109 Plaza St., Healdsburg.
Price: Expensive.
Credit Cards: MC, V.
Cuisine: French, California.
Serving: L, D.
Reservations: Recommended.
Special Features: Outdoor dining.
Handicap Access: Yes.

Bistro Ralph recalls a café on Manhattan's Upper West Side, a narrow and noisy space with a towering tin ceiling and chic but chilly minimalist industrial decor. It's not your typically cozy Wine Country café. The food by chef-owner Ralph Tingle is more fanciful that most bistros, inventive yet maddeningly inconsistent.

The lunch menu runs from a vigorous caesar salad to lamb burgers and grilled salmon. Dinner begins with Tingle's patented focaccia puffs, a tasty and unusual bread sprinkled with rock salt. Starters include corn fritters with smoked salmon, a refreshingly simple dish with immaculate fish. The warm goat cheese salad is light and winning, topped with a fetching balsamic vinaigrette. A grilled marinated chicken breast is a puzzle; cooked to near extinction, it is paired with invigorating sauces like a spicy sun-dried tomato pesto.

Desserts include an exquisite warm pear tart, a puff pastry deliciously marooned on a sea of caramellike sauce. Bistro Ralph has an efficient and modestly priced wine list. Service, a weakness in the bistro's opening months, has improved markedly.

MADRONA MANOR
707-433-4231.
1001 Westside Rd., Healdsburg.
Price: Expensive to Very Expensive.
Credit Cards: AE, D, DC, MC, V.

Although chef Todd Muir's dinner menu is often engaging, it would be a shame to approach this 1881 Victorian in the dark. Its mansard roof rising three stories, Madrona Manor is a majestic sight set in a quiet glade of gardens. Sunday brunch, served only in high season, is the best way to enjoy the surroundings. The dining

The lush grounds of Madrona Manor make it a Sunday brunch destination.

Courtesy Sonoma County Convention & Visitors Bureau

Cuisine: French, California.
Serving: SB, D.
Reservations: Recommended.
Special Features: Outdoor dining.
Handicap Access: Yes.

rooms, which seem too formal at night, take on a more gentle elegance as the sun warms through tall windows. Whether you choose brunch or dinner, you'll feel pampered. Service is alert and Madrona Manor has one of the best wine cellars around, with a fine selection of half bottles.

Muir trained at Chez Panisse and after many years at Madrona Manor, his passions ebb and flow; his food is brilliant at times, adequate at others. Muir takes Sunday brunch seriously. It begins with a glass of bubbly, followed by a round of freshly baked breads and cheeses. Entrées include a delightful eggs benedict with a champagne hollandaise sauce.

Muir maintains a modest dinner menu, lavishing attention on a handful of entrées. Starters include chicken shui mai, a delicately flavored Asian-style dumpling stuffed with pork and chicken. Understatement becomes boredom with a dish like petrale sole, medallions of salmon mousse wrapped in delicate white fish. It is a magnificent sight but even the wine sauce couldn't revive the washed-out flavors. Better is the tender breast of young chicken, spiked with truffles and served with a luxurious foie gras sauce. Desserts include a brilliant blueberry soufflé, an airy plateau served with vanilla sauce.

SOUTHSIDE SALOON
707-433-4466.
106 Matheson St., Healdsburg.
Price: Moderate to Expensive.
Credit Cards: AE, MC, V.
Cuisine: California.
Serving: L, D.

Southside is a roll of the dice. Sometimes the food is exceptional, sometimes it's merely so-so. Chef Charles Saunders opened this restaurant on Healdsburg Plaza in 1994 but is no longer affiliated with it day-to-day, so the future of the eatery is a question mark.

The menu is high on imaginative yet comforting food, à la hamburgers, baby back ribs, smoked

Reservations:
   Recommended.
Handicap Access: Yes.

pork chops, hearty soups, and Dungeness crab sandwiches. Southside is an airy hall with large booths. The atmosphere and service are equally casual and the food and wine prices reasonable. Children are welcome; the menu includes fries and hot dogs, etc.

Oysters start off the menu and they are not always as fresh as they could be. Served on the half shell, oysters come with exotic sides like apple cider mignonette. Soups include a savory salmon soup with chunky veggies and a hint of mint. A refreshing twist is the caesar salad served with breaded and fried calamari rings. Entrées include roast garlic and rosemary chicken, so moist and luscious it slides off the bone, served with indulgent garlic smashed potatoes. The grilled salmon with a ragout of lentils and mushrooms is a sound rendition but not particularly inspiring.

Geyserville

The café at Chateau Souverain is an elegant room with a view.

Chris Alderman

CHATEAU SOUVERAIN
707-433-3174.
400 Souverain Ln.,
   Independence Ln. exit
   off Hwy. 101,
   Geyserville.
Closed: Mon.–Thurs.
Price: Expensive.
Credit Cards: AE, MC, V.
Cuisine: California.
Serving: L, D.
Reservations: Recom-
   mended.

From the tall French windows of Chateau Souverain, you can spy the graceful hills of Alexander Valley, a view homeowners dream about. The restaurant's interior is nearly as stunning, a romantic setting with towering cathedral ceilings and a massive fireplace. The food is appealing, though chef Martin Courtman lacks the brilliance of Gary Danko, who brought the restaurant fame before leaving for the Ritz-Carlton in San Francisco. A hefty cut in prices in 1993, however, nearly makes up for it.

Special Features: Outdoor dining.
Handicap Access: Yes.

The wine list is limited to Chateau Souverain's own, a sound list of reds and whites with pricing that's fair by restaurant standards. Service is also vastly improved from the old regime, which seemed to promote an aloof attitude. Lunch is perhaps your best bet, since the menu is similar to dinner and the view is better.

Starters include a fine salad of local greens topped with a slice of cheddar and a soothing vinaigrette. The scallop and salmon terrine, a creamy pâté-like slice with sorrel sauce, is beautiful with its colorful chunks of fish, but the flavors never congeal. Entrées include a superb Cornish hen, deboned and with a smoky bacon glaze, served with warm spinach and couscous. The lamb ragout in merlot sauce is a comfort-food delight, tender chunks of meat in a savory wine and sage sauce with pappardelle noodles and fresh vegetables. The grilled filet of sea bass with chardonnay curry butter was delicious but restrained, although the potato gratin side dish is masterly. Desserts include a silky crème brûlée studded with ginger and a flourless chocolate decadence cake that is short on decadence.

Sonoma West County

The solarium dining room at Applewood

APPLEWOOD
707-869-9093.
13555 Hwy. 116, Guerneville.
Closed: Mon.–Weds.
Price: Expensive.
Credit Cards: AE, D, MC, V.
Cuisine: Eclectic.
Serving: D.

A stand of redwoods harbors this Mission-style country mansion built in 1922 (see Chapter Three, Lodging). The kitchen, once reserved for guests, is now open to the public. Innkeepers Darryl Notter and Jim Caron share kitchen duties and prepare a single four-course prix-fixe dinner for one seating each night. Notter describes the food as "a step above home cooking." And a lengthy step it is,

Reservations: Required.
Handicap Access: Yes.

too. The food is hearty, stylish but without fussy presentation.

Applewood has two small dining rooms, one formal, with an arched ceiling and near the kitchen, the other in a solarium with a stone fireplace and wicker furniture. Menus include orange-glazed pork loin with tomato-basil fritters, and beef tenderloin with dried figs, apricots, and prunes in a brandy cream sauce. A specialty is a nicely done Tuscan roast chicken with a risotto of pancetta and mustard greens. It's usually paired with a sumptuous Italian-style wild mushroom soup with vermouth. Salads are glorious creations culled from local farms. Desserts include an impressive Tuscan cream cake, a surprisingly light but rich layered indulgence.

BAY VIEW RESTAURANT AT THE INN AT THE TIDES
707-875-2751.
800 Hwy. 1, Bodega Bay.
Closed: Mon. & Tues.
Price: Expensive.
Credit Cards: AE, MC, V.
Cuisine: Seafood, California.
Serving: D.
Reservations: Recommended.
Handicap Access: Yes.

If the hectic hum of The Tides or Lucas Wharf is too much and if you seek something more than basic fish, then the Bay View Room might be an alternative. While the food is simply on par with those two popular restaurants, the presentation has more flair and the view is more impressive. If that's important, you might not mind the added cost.

The decor is elegantly simple with an open-beam cathedral ceiling and Scandinavian furnishings. Servers, wearing black ties and tuxedo shirts, are efficient. The wine list is superbly selected with a credible list by the glass. The menu is dominated by local seafood. Appetizers include sweet Hog Island oysters and broiled jumbo shrimp, four juicy prawns on a bed of polenta and black beans with fiery chili pepper sauce. Soup or salad comes with dinner; soups are unfussy but luscious and salads are thick with exotic Sonoma greens.

Main courses include a luxurious bouillabaisse de Marseilles, a saffron-laced stew brimming with fresh clams, prawns, mussels, even a tiny lobster tail. It arrives still in the skillet and is ladled over crusty bread. Another winner is grilled lamb chops, hearty and elegantly served with a garlic, clove, and wild mushroom glaze. Desserts include a winning torta prieta, a flourless hazelnut chocolate cake with a raspberry and chocolate sauce.

BREAKERS CAFÉ
707-875-2513.
1400 Hwy. 1, Bodega Bay.
Price: Moderate to Expensive.
Credit Cards: MC, V.
Cuisine: Seafood.

This unassuming eatery overlooking Bodega Bay harbor has many fans but we don't understand the fuss. There are far better choices along Hwy. 1 for seaside seafood. Situated in a small complex of shops, the café's atmosphere is pleasant enough, particularly in the sunroom.

Serving: B, L, D.
Reservations: Accepted.
Special Features: Harbor
    view.
Handicap Access: Yes.

Service is laid-back and the wine list is similarly easygoing, with a short slate of local vino. The kitchen is active from breakfast through dinner — always a stretch — and likewise the menu attempts too much. Dinner offerings range from burgers and steaks to jambalaya and pasta.

Consistency is a problem. Crab corn cakes succulent and crisp one trip are rendered mushy (by the microwave?) the next. Pastas are seldom memorable. The mariners' pasta is chewy fettucine with a marinara sauce that tastes suspiciously canned. Dinner salads are a treat, served with feta cheese and a minty vinaigrette. The lunch menu's shrimp and crab sandwich — served open face and either hot or cold — has appeal.

THE FARMHOUSE INN
707-887-3300.
7871 River Rd., Forestville.
Closed: Mon.–Weds.
Price: Expensive.
Credit Cards: AE, MC, V.
Cuisine: California.
Serving: D.
Reservations: Required.
Special Features: Outdoor
    dining.

No longer content with just breakfast, this B&B — a wood-frame country beauty circa 1878 — is serving dinner to guests and locals alike (see Chapter Three, *Lodging*). The atmosphere is informal and the decor reveals owner Rebecca Smith's New England heritage. For a dining room that seats only 22, service is not the least intrusive. The menu offers a surprisingly varied menu of fish, pasta, fowl, and beef, all done with considerable finesse and a modest sense of adventure.

Appetizers include an onion and herb soup that is so overpowering it is like biting into an onion. Better is the roasted garlic and onion tart, flaky and light with distinct but not overwhelming flavors. Entrées include a tender grilled duck breast with an ambrosial sauté of mango, bacon, and brandy. Rather than overdress fish, the kitchen emphasizes a filet's unique character; a velvety Chilean sea bass is served with an engaging sweet pepper, scallion, and orange sauté. Desserts include chocolate pecan pie, a seductive mousse filling topped with a pecan crust. The Farmhouse has a small but fairly priced list of wines devoted to surrounding vineyards. Be forewarned: the inn was for sale in late 1996.

LUCAS WHARF
707-875-3522.
595 Hwy. 1, Bodega Bay.
Price: Moderate to Expen-
    sive.
Credit Cards: MC, V.
Cuisine: Seafood.
Serving: L, D.
Reservations: Accepted
    Mon.–Thurs. only.
Special Features: Harbor
    view.

Ask a group of locals the best place to eat seafood on the Sonoma Coast and you're liable to start an argument. The coast is not nearly as populated with restaurants as, say, Cape Cod — there are just a handful. We find ourselves at Lucas Wharf more often than not. Built on piers over Bodega Bay harbor, it's cozy and romantic, with a fireplace and cathedral ceiling. From your table you'll see great sunsets and fishing boats unloading the catch of the day.

Lucas Wharf is on Bodega Bay harbor.

Chris Alderman

Choose what's fresh off the boat and you won't go wrong, particularly salmon when it's in season (May through September) and Dungeness crab (November to June). At Lucas Wharf, we prefer the salmon poached, not grilled, which is too often dry and flaky. The seafood pasta is delectable, with fettuccine and a rich cream sauce studded with fish, mussels, and clams. A favorite comfort food is the fisherman's stew, a brothy concoction of fish, mussels, clams, and bay shrimp, but the chef is too careful with the herbs and spices. Desserts are appealing, particularly a smooth and tangy chocolate mint cheesecake.

The wine list and by-the-glass selection has improved but remains too limited. Lucas Wharf is popular with locals and tourists alike, so be prepared to wait for a table on weekends. Want something more low-key? At Lucas Wharf's carry-out counter next door, munch fish and chips and have a cold beer at the picnic tables.

RIVER'S END
707-865-2484.
11051 Hwy. 1, Jenner.
Closed: Dec. & Jan.
Credit Cards: MC, V.
Cuisine: Eclectic.
Price: Expensive.
Serving: L, D.
Reservations: Recommended.
Special Features: Ocean view.

River's End has the best view in Wine Country. Auberge du Soleil in Napa Valley offers keen competition, but the vista from River's End is spectacular. It's set on the edge of a bluff where the Russian River meets the Pacific. Sea lions sun on the beach below and Goat Rock is a towering monument amid the waves.

Chef Wolfgang Gramatzki's menu is nearly as impressive as the view, combining elements of German, Asian, French, and California cuisine. Appetizers include a seviche of octopus, scallops, and shrimp that offers your tongue a wonderfully exotic experience. Standards such as beef Wellington share the menu with baby pheasant and bahmie goreng, a delicious Indonesian plate of chicken, shrimp, scallops, and beef satés. Seafood, of course, is fresh, including the beefy oysters from nearby Hog Island. Specialties include coconut fried shrimp, succulent beauties surrounded by crunchy breading sweetened by orange rum sauce. Less successful is something called gravlox pizza, a puff pastry unceremoniously topped with lox, sour cream, and watery bay shrimp.

Dessert includes Gramatzki's uniquely decadent chocolate mousse and a fluffy cold hazelnut soufflé. The wine list concentrates on Sonoma County and foreign selections, with a limited number by the glass. Service can be lethargic.

THE TIDES WHARF
707-875-3652.
835 Hwy. 1, Bodega Bay.
Price: Moderate to Expensive.
Credit Cards: AE, MC, V.
Cuisine: Seafood.
Serving: B, L, D.
Reservations: Recommended.
Special Features: Harbor view.

The Tides was immortalized by Alfred Hitchcock in *The Birds*, but you'll never recognize it. The original restaurant, which was attacked by vengeful gulls in a major scene, is long gone and a new eatery is in its place. But the unpretentious attitude remains, making it the favorite of locals. The atmosphere is rather ordinary, but out the dining room's broad windows the harbor goes about its busy business and the sunsets are stunning.

The "catch of the day" is a rather voluminous list: red snapper, swordfish, ling cod, and Pacific oysters. Native salmon, in season May through September, is a good choice, likewise Dungeness crab, in season November to June. A favorite is the poached salmon with a simple hollandaise sauce, and the crab cioppino, a zesty Italian stew, is a knockout. The wine list is hefty, but if you love red wine you'll go thirsty. For casual eats, try the snack bar out back, which serves fish and chips and monstrous and succulent fried oysters.

FOOD PURVEYORS

A chic restaurant isn't the only place to feast. From Mexican eateries that burn your tongue to old family delicatessens, with lingering irresistible smells of smoked meats and cheese, Napa and Sonoma have specialty food shops aplenty.

BAKERIES

Napa County

The Model Bakery (707-963-8192; 1357 Main St., St. Helena) Everything here is baked in a big brick oven. Sweet or sour baguettes are stacked like kindling

Craig Ponsford bakes prize-winning breads at Artisan Bakers.

Courtesy Artisan Bakers

in tall wicker baskets, and scones, muffins, and croissants compete for shelf space. Behind the counter are burly loaves of rye, powdered white on top.

Napa Valley Ovens (707-942-0777;1353 Lincoln Ave.) Chef Fred Halpert of Brava Terrace restaurant runs this cozy yet chic bakery, specializing in tasty breakfast goodies as well as foccacia, mini-pizzas, and restaurant-class desserts.

Sugar House Bakery (707-963-3424; 587 St. Helena Hwy., St. Helena) A St. Helena tradition that dates from 1971, specializing in Swiss-style goodies like farmhouse bread.

The Yountville Pastry Shop (707-944-2138; Vintage 1870) Hidden away in the rear courtyard of a popular shopping complex, this shop offers tortes, muffins, and danishes, all available for the nibbling on an outside deck.

Sonoma County

Artisan Bakers (707-939-1765; 750 W. Napa St., Sonoma) Some of the finest bread in Wine Country is made right here. Stop in the bakery yourself or look for loaves in markets around Sonoma County. In 1996, during the baking equivalent of the Olympics, Craig Ponsford of Artisan achieved the impossible: he baked a better baguette than the French.

Brother Juniper's Bakery (707-542-6546; 463 Sebastopol Ave., Santa Rosa) The bread here is nationally recognized, thanks to a series of bestsellers. Try the three pepper Cajun bread.

Goodies are an art form at the Downtown Bakery and Creamery.

Chris Alderman

Café Des Croissants (Three Santa Rosa locations: 1226 4th St., 2444 Lomitas Ave., 1791 Marlow Rd.) A good place for breakfast-in-a-bag; whether you prefer a classic or a croissant stuffed with chocolate, these shops make some of Wine Country's best.

Downtown Bakery and Creamery (707-431-2719; 308A Center St., Healdsburg) Fabulous desserts but it doesn't look like much as you walk in. What's the secret? The Chez Panisse connection. Owners Kathleen Stewart and Lindsey and Therese Shere are veterans of that famed Berkeley kitchen. Lindsey, in fact, is still pastry chef there. Tortes and cakes are ungodly, likewise the sticky buns, the monster fig newtons, and blueberry scones. No seating, but the downtown plaza is across the street.

The Grateful Bagel (404 Mendocino Ave., Santa Rosa; 300 S. Main St., Sebastopol) Locals flock here for — yes — great bagels in California. They're light yet chewy, as good as you'll find east of Queens.

Mom's Apple Pie (707-823-8330; 4550 Gravenstein Hwy. N., Sebastopol) This roadhouse makes fat pies better than most moms, served in tin pans or by the slice. The coconut cream is to die for. The fried chicken is good, too.

Sonoma Valley Bagel Co. (2310 Mendocino Ave. and 515 Hahman Dr., Santa Rosa) Fine bagels and gourmet coffee.

BURGERS, ETC.

Big Daddy's (707-942-9503; 1522 Lincoln Ave., Calistoga) Not much more than a drive-in, but the hamburgers are killer. Eat one outside under the red awning and watch the gliders land.

Rob's Rib Shack (707-938-8520; 18709 Arnold Dr., Sonoma) This funky roadhouse (note the little pig lights) has been discovered. The succulent baby back ribs — $12.95 for a full slab — have a sweet and spicy sauce. Live music and barbecue oysters on Sundays.

The Spot (707-963-2844; 587 St. Helena Hwy., St. Helena) The atmosphere is pure neon and it's a favorite with locals and tourists alike. Great for kids, with a menu of pizza, French fries, and fried chicken. Burgers are the best bet and sample the soda fountain goodies.

COFFEE HOUSES

Napa County

Napa Valley Coffee Roasting Co. (948 Main St., Napa and 1400 Oak Ave., St. Helena) The premier coffee house in the county now has two outlets. The classic old façade in downtown Napa is a popular hang-out. Bags of raw greenish beans are open in the back. The St. Helena shop is larger and sunnier with outdoor seating. To go with the brew, there are treats galore.

San Marco Espresso Co. (707-942-4671; 1336 Lincoln Ave., Calistoga) This recently expanded café still makes an uncompromising cup of coffee, plus fruit and milkshakes are now offered.

Sonoma County

A'Roma in Santa Rosa's Railroad Square.

Chris Alderman

A'Roma Roasters (707-576-7765; 95 5th St., Santa Rosa) Facing historic Railroad Square, A'Roma is a touch bohemian, with exposed rafters, a copper counter top, and a coffee bean roaster as a centerpiece. Lots of tables and you'll roll your eyes over goodies like blackberry pie.

Catz (707-829-6600; 6761 Sebastopol Ave., Sebastopol) This funky café is like the tea room of a Victorian train station. There's also an outdoor patio.

The Coffee Garden (707-996-6645; 415 1st St. W., Sonoma) This café looks plain enough but it's in an adobe built in the 1830s. The main draw is the lovely garden patio.

Healdsburg Coffee Co. (707-431-7941; 312 Center St., Healdsburg) Inside a historic storefront on the downtown plaza, this is a pleasant spot to savor a cup and scone or cookie.

Wolf Coffee Co. (614 4th St. and 1810 Mendocino Ave. in Santa Rosa) Maybe the best cup of coffee in Sonoma County. The 4th Street shop is a classy downtown affair with marble counters. The Mendocino shop is a popular take-out in the Santa Rosa Junior College area.

DELI & GOURMET SHOPS

Napa County

Cantinetta Tra Vigne (707-963-8888; 1050 Charter Oak Ave., St. Helena) This classic stone building may be the best lunch in Napa Valley. The menu is limited but superbly done. Breakfast offers sinful brioche sticky buns and egg dishes. Lunch brings stuffed focaccia and sandwiches like smoked salmon. Don't miss the eggplant stack, a lasagna-like side dish. Beer and wine are available by the glass for a peaceful lunch in the quiet courtyard.

Fellion's Delicatessen (707-942-6144; 1359 Lincoln Ave., Calistoga) Whenever a place sells Pilsner Urquell by the bottle, it has our respect. This deli stocks more than 100 cold beers in all. Fellion's has tables but a better choice is a grab-and-go winery picnic. Besides the usual offerings of pastrami and the like, Fellion's has quesadillas and even a small salad bar.

Genova Delicatessen (707-253-8686; 1550 Trancas Ave., Napa) You can almost smell Genova from two blocks off, so rich is the bouquet of dried salami, roasting chicken, and simmering pastas. With a history that dates from 1926, Genova is home to marbled cold cuts and glass-case treasures like potato salad, antipasto, and olives. There are a handful of tables.

Napa Valley Olive Oil Manufacturing Co. (707-963-4173; 835 Charter Oak Ave., St. Helena) This faded white barn is a glorious time warp. The shop dates from the 1920s, when Napa Valley was largely populated by Italian farmers. You're as likely to hear Italian inside as English, and the deli counter looks like your (Neapolitan) grandmother's kitchen. Picnic tables outside.

Oakville Grocery (707-944-8802; 7856 St. Helena Hwy., Oakville) What looks like an old country store, with its giant red Coca-Cola sign on the side and wooden screen doors, is actually a gourmet grocery. Goodies include duck pâté, cold cuts, and even caviar. Sandwiches include turkey with pesto and

Oakville Grocery is a gourmet shop in disguise.

Chris Alderman

a glorious lavosh. There's also coffee by the cup, bakery treats, and local wines.

Palisades Market (707-942-9549; 1506 Lincoln Ave., Calistoga) A real find, this modest grocery has an excellent deli — try the roast beef and brie on onion focaccia — plus fresh bread, produce, baked goods, cheese, and wine.

Pometta's Deli (707-944-2365; 7787 St. Helena Hwy., Oakville) This casual stop specializes in barbecued chicken and Italian deli treats. Nice outdoor patio.

V. Sattui Winery (707-963-7774; St. Helena Hwy. at White Ln., St. Helena) Most wineries have a picnic table tucked somewhere, but V. Sattui is Lawn Lunch Central, shaded by tall oaks. The tasting room doubles as a deli shop.

Sonoma County

Basque Boulangerie Café (707-935-7687; 460 1st St. E., Sonoma) More than a bakery, this stylish storefront has sandwiches and a wine bar. It has yet to master a classic croissant, for some reason.

Dry Creek General Store (707-433-4171; 3495 Dry Creek Rd., Healdsburg) A rural gathering spot for more than a century, this is a landmark of Sonoma's rustic heritage. The floors are wooden and warped and under the carport is a tattered upright cola machine. Fancier trappings have been added over the years — a wine rack and a few gourmet goodies. Super deli sandwiches.

East West Café (128 N. Main St., Sebastopol, and 2323 Sonoma Ave., Santa Rosa) These sister cafés specialize in health-minded salads and sandwiches and Mediterranean fare. Try the meza platter, with Middle Eastern treasures like hummus, dolmas, baba ghanoush.

Giovanni's (707-823-1331; Pleasant Hill Ave. N., just off Bodega Hwy., Sebastopol) This Italian-style deli has the usual aromatic delicacies. Good sandwiches, plus local wine. Outdoor seating, but it's in a shopping center.

Healdsburg Charcuterie (707-431-7213; 335 Healdsburg Ave., Healdsburg) A safe bet for sandwiches and salads, plus a good selection of wines by the glass. Roast beef lavosh is a winner. A handful of tables inside, plus the Healdsburg Plaza is nearby.

Jimtown Store (707-433-1212; 6706 Hwy. 128, Healdsburg) An Alexander Valley landmark for a century, this former general store and gas depot was abandoned for years. John Werner and Carrie Brown resuscitated the place in 1991, retaining quaintness while adding a touch of gourmet chic, drawing national attention along the way. Sandwiches are first-rate and the aisles include old-fashioned candy, toys, and memorabilia.

Plaza Street Market is a sophisticated deli and gourmet shop in downtown Healdsburg.

Chris Alderman

Plaza Street Market (707-431-2800; 113 Plaza St., Healdsburg) This sophisticated market on the downtown plaza has an old-fashioned tin ceiling towering high overhead and polished wood highlights. A short menu of sandwiches and salads are offered as well as specialty coffees. Gourmet goodies line the aisle and there's even a modest wine-tasting bar.

Sonoma Cheese Factory (707-996-1931; 2 W. Spain St., Sonoma) This supermarket-sized deli doubles as factory and tourist attraction. The Viviani family has made cheese in Sonoma since 1931 and they produce a fantastic array, all available for samples. In the rear is a large window where you can watch cheese in the making. Sandwiches are fairly standard. There's a covered patio and shady Sonoma Plaza is nearby.

Tote Cuisine (707-578-0898; 710 Village Ct., Santa Rosa) Chef Lisa Hemenway's answer to ho-hum deli food. Eat in this stylish café or take it to go. Try the usual sandwiches or something different like sausage and fennel baguettes or curry coconut drumsticks.

Traverso's (707-542-2530; 3rd & B Sts., Santa Rosa) Traverso's has evolved into the county's best gourmet deli and wine shop, never losing touch with its Italian roots. Dangling from the ceiling are flags of Italy and prosciutto. The deli case is a painting of salads, meats, and other treats, from delicate pastries like a chicken apple yoha to hearty ravioli. Sandwiches are marvelous.

FISH MARKETS

One of the joys of living on the Pacific Ocean is fresh seafood. Most prized locally are Dungeness crab and salmon. Crab season runs from mid-November to the end of May and the local salmon season runs from mid-May to September. There are also a number of oyster farms just south on Tomales Bay and those beefy Pacific oysters are delicious. Below are a handful of specialty fish markets.

Johnson Oyster & Seafood Co. 707-763-4161; 253 N. McDowell Blvd., Petaluma.

Omega 3 Seafood Market 707-257-3474; 1740 Yajome St., Napa.

Lucas Wharf Deli 707-875-3562; 595 Hwy. 1, Bodega Bay.

Tides Wharf Fish Market 707-875-3554; 835 Hwy. 1, Bodega Bay.

The Wharf Fresh Seafood Market 707-433-0515; 1005 Vine St., Healdsburg.

PRODUCE

The bounty of Wine Country goes well beyond grapes, particularly in Sonoma County. *Sonoma County Farm Trails* is an informal collective of farms, ranging from apple orchards to more exotic offerings like insect-eating plant specialist California Carnivores (707-838-1630; 7020 Trenton-Healdsburg Rd., Forestville). For a map and listings, phone Farm Trails (707-996-2154).

Fine produce stands abound in Wine Country. Look for *The Fruit Basket* (707-996-7433; 18474 Hwy. 12, Sonoma). Two farms are particularly worth seeking out. *Kozlowski Farms* (707-887-1587; 5566 Gravenstein Hwy. N., Forestville) is an orchard turned down-home gourmet enterprise. This Sonoma County treasure specializes in jams and jellies, apple butter, raspberry and other vinegars, as well as apples and other fresh produce. Follow the seasons at *Westside Farms* (707-431-1432; 7097 Westside Rd., Healdsburg). This home-spun homestead is open May through November. Find sweet corn, wild berries, herbs, and other treasures in the summer. October brings the pumpkin

Ethnic Food in Wine Country

CHINESE

You'll have more luck in Sonoma County than Napa Valley. We can't recommend **Teng's** (707-963-1161; 1113 Hunt St., St. Helena) for reasons familiar to fans of the genre: cloying sauces, too much filler (i.e. celery), and ingredients that are less than fresh. Better, but still *quite* average, is **Soo Yuan** (707-942-9404; 1354 Lincoln Ave., Calistoga). A standard like Kung Pao Chicken is competently done, hearty and mildly spicy.

In Sonoma County, try **The China Room** (707-539-5570; 500 Mission Blvd., Santa Rosa). The atmosphere is refined; white linen instead of red-tasseled lamps. The food is prepared with great care — no heavy-handed sauces — with a menu of the typical (mu shu pork) and atypical (mariner's love nest). The best Chinese in Wine Country is found at **Gary Chu's** (707-526-5840; 611 5th St. Santa Rosa). The room is an elegant blend of Chinese and Art Deco and the food is stylishly gourmet. Impeccable ingredients are cooked with light sautés instead of oppressive sauces. Try the spicy plum sauce pork.

JAPANESE

This close to San Francisco and the Pacific Ocean, we take our sushi seriously. A good bet in Napa Valley is **Yoshi-Shige** (707-257-3583; 3381 California Blvd., Napa), just off Trancas St. near Hwy. 29. Sonoma County has several fine Japanese restaurants. Our favorites are **Hana** (707-586-0270; Red Lion Plaza, Rohnert Park) and **Tengu** (707-795-9753; 8235 Old Redwood Hwy., Cotati). Next to the Sonoma County Wine and Visitor

The sushi bar at Hana.

Chris Alderman

Center, Hana has a generic Japanese atmosphere and a small sushi bar. A good introduction is the bento box, a light tempura with prawns and vegetables, served with chunks of raw tuna and beautiful California rolls. Tengu is funky café. The salmon teriyaki is dynamite and the octopus sashimi is some of the best we've had.

MEXICAN

In Napa Valley, there's a certain funky appeal to *Ana's Cantina* (707-963-4921; 1205 Main St., St. Helena), a bar with a pool table and lots of character. The food won't win awards but it goes well with a long-neck. Avoid *Armadillo's* (707-963-8082; 1304 Main St. St. Helena), where the atmosphere recalls a colorful village south of the border, but the food is lackluster. A popular spot is *Compadres* (707-944-2406; 6539 Washington St., Yountville) and it looks promising with a lovely outdoor patio and brick walls. But Compadres is an empty piñata. Every dish is a letdown. The atmosphere is lively at *Pacifico* (707-942-4400; 1237 Lincoln Ave., Calistoga) and the margaritas are knockout. The food is hearty but lacks authenticity. If you can overlook its shopping plaza locale, *Zapata* (707-254-8888; Bel Aire Plaza off Trancas St., Napa) has reliable fare and winning margaritas.

In Sonoma County, chains dominate and the results are less than impressive. The *Cantina* (707-523-3663; 500 4th St., Santa Rosa) is a slick brick palace with an active bar and a heated patio, but the food is boring. A better chain experience is at *Chevys* (707-571-1082; 24 4th St., Santa Rosa). The food isn't authentic but it is fresh and nicely done, especially the fajitas. The crowds at *La Casa* (707-996-3406; 121 E. Spain St., Sonoma) might give you the wrong idea. It's a tourist thing. The food is adequate but not worth the fuss.

Rafa's (707-795-7068; 8230 Old Redwood Hwy., Cotati) makes Mexican food a la L.A. It's Americanized Mexican grub at its best. The burritos are as big as footballs and the sauce is mucho tasty. The decor is homey, bordering on tacky. Two inexpensive and low-key shops have the best Mexican in the county. Ignore the atmosphere at *Taqueria El Sombrero* (707-433-3818; 245 Center St., Healdsburg) and *Taqueria Santa Rosa* (1950 Mendocino Ave., Santa Rosa, and 1350 Lincoln Ave., Calistoga) and relish the food. Both use whole beans, not canned refrieds, and grilled meat.

ETC.

Thai anyone? Try *California Thai* (707-573-1441; 522 7th St., Santa Rosa), which ingeniously blends the best of Bangkok and Wine Country cuisine. Thom kha gai, the traditional chicken coconut soup, is sublime. As impressive and more authentic is *Thai House* (707-526-3939; 525 4th St., Santa Rosa). *Rin's* (707-938-1462; 599 Broadway, Sonoma) has some of the freshest Thai around and what a bargain. Likewise *Thai Pot* (707-823-1324; 6961 Sebastopol Ave., Sebastopol). *Tohte* (707-226-7749; 1139 Lincoln Ave., Napa) is new and still polishing its pad Thai.

If you need an Indian fix, Wine Country offers two that will do in a pinch: *Taj Mahal* (707-579-8471; 535 Ross St., Santa Rosa) and *Sizzling Tandoor* (707-579-5999; 409 Mendocino Ave., Santa Rosa). Each are sound dining rooms, with fiery vindaloos and rich curry barani rice dishes. *Russian River Vineyards Restaurant* (707-887-1562; 5700 Gravenstein Hwy., Forestville) is the only Greek food for miles but we can't recommend it.

festival with hay rides, etc. Kids will love the miniature donkeys and other animals in the petting area.

PUBS

Watch out, wine connoisseurs — beer lovers are getting serious, too. Pubs are *the* thing, especially brewpubs, where beer and ale are made on the premises. It's a return to the old days when any city of size had a brewery or two, bottling suds for the local area. It also harks back to England and Germany where beers still have character. The San Francisco Bay area is a leader in brewpubs.

Napa County

The beer is fresh and the beer garden a treat at the Calistoga Inn.

Chris Alderman

The Calistoga Inn (707-942-4101; 1250 Lincoln Ave.) One of our favorite Napa Valley destinations, this micro-brewery and restaurant has a shady beer garden that's so soothing on a scorching day. Try the Calistoga Pale Lager. It's light but still has personality.

Downtown Joe's (707-258-2337; 902 Main St., Napa) This is a stylish and historic downtown Art Deco storefront. There's a comfortable wooden bar and a patio along the Napa River. The copper brew kettles are in plain sight and brewmaster Brian Hunt knows his stuff. Try the cream ale when its available.

Sonoma County

Bear Republic Brewing Co. (707-433-BEER; 345 Healdsburg Ave., Healdsburg) This may be Healdsburg's hottest night spot, featuring food, live music, and some excellent hand-crafted beers. The Red Rocket Ale is a specialty.

Dempsey's (707-765-9694; 50 E. Washington St., Petaluma) Overlooking the Petaluma River, this place is great. Peter Burrell brews superior ales, particularly his Red Rooster, and no pub has better food. Chef Bernadette Burrell worked in the kitchen at Mustards Grill, so expect grilled shark with Indian curry as well as burgers and fries.

Murphy's Irish Pub (707-935-0660; 464 1st St. E., Sonoma) This small but cozy pub is a little bit of Ireland hidden at the end of a cobblestone courtyard off Sonoma Plaza. There's a great selection of imported ales available by the pint.

The Old Vic (707-571-7555; 731 4th St., Santa Rosa) "The Vic" doesn't brew its own beer, but it is a place of many charms, with a comfortable atmosphere and a lively clientele that ranges from pierced grunge rockers to expatriate Brits. There's tasty English food like bangers and pasties and a wide selection of imported and specialty beers on tap.

Pizza & Pizzerias

Pizza may not be the obsession here that it is in cities like Chicago and New York, but folks do like their cheese pies. You know what to expect from Pizza Hut and the rest, so we've rounded up a sampling of the little guys — the independents and small chains.

Some of the best pizza in Napa Valley can be found at *Tomatina* (707-967-9999; 1020 Main St., St. Helena.) The atmosphere is stylish yet relaxed enough for kids, with big tables for large groups. Sonoma County has a similar trattoria in *Mangia Bene* (707-433-2340; 241 Healdsburg Ave., Healdsburg.) The pizza is fresh, the atmosphere is warm, and the price is right.

If you like a bit of panache in your pizza, check out *Checkers* (1414 Lincoln Ave., Calistoga, and 523 4th St., Santa Rosa). Both outlets are festive with abstract art and polished pine and black tile. There are traditional pies of sausage and pepperoni, of course, but there's also Thai pizza, topped with marinated chicken, cilantro, and peanuts.

For those who demand New York-style pizza, there's *La Vera* (707-575-1113; 629 4th St., Santa Rosa). The cheese stretches for a city block and the meats are little explosions of pepperoni and sausage. The crust is that perfect unison of crunchy and chewy. The atmosphere is more formal that most pizza shacks, with polished brass and wood.

Two other pizza parlors are more typically American. Both have several outlets and are family places. The better of the two is *La Prima Pizza* (1010 Adams St., St. Helena, and 1009 Foothill Blvd., Calistoga). It makes a pleasant pie, with a puffy crust that's crisp on the bottom. The toppings are generous and of good quality. *Mary's Pizza Shack* (five locations in Sonoma and one in Napa) is fairly safe American pizza. The crust is a tad salty and the meat toppings rather bland, but the cheeses and veggies are top-rate.

The Powerhouse Brewing Company (707-829-9171; 268 Petaluma Ave., Sebastopol) A former railroad power house, this brewpub is a popular night spot. The food and beer are good, but there's room for improvement.

Santa Rosa Brewing Company (707-544-4677; 458 B St., Santa Rosa) Irishman Tim O'Day is the brewmaster; don't miss his special Irish Ale and Raspberry Ale. Fish and chips are darned tasty here and the hamburgers are fat and juicy.

Third Street Aleworks (707-523-3060; 610 Third St., Santa Rosa) A popular downtown hang-out, this brewpub has a stylish, almost industrial atmosphere, with lots of elbow room, two pool tables, live music, and some excellent ales and lagers.

WINE SHOPS

The specialty wine shops in Napa and Sonoma counties, as you might imagine, are among the finest in the nation, offering a huge variety as well as hard-to-find treasures. You'll be surprised to learn that wine is seldom cheaper at the wineries than local retail shops, unless you catch a sale or buy by the case. You also run the risk, of course, of not being able to find a wine you loved at the winery. It's your gamble.

Napa County

All Season's Café (707-942-6828; 1400 Lincoln Ave., Calistoga) In the rear of this chic café is a cool cellar of wine, with current vintages and a few old treasures. Prices the going rate.

Calistoga Wine Stop (707-942-5556; 1458 Lincoln Ave., Calistoga) Housed in an 1866-vintage Central Pacific railroad car, this shop has a solid line-up of current Napa and Sonoma wines. Prices are average.

St. Helena Wine Center (707-963-1313; 1321 Main St., St. Helena) One of Napa's oldest, dating to 1953, this shop believes in the notion of "only the best," offering few bargains. It has a small but extremely select library of Napa and Sonoma current wines. There's also a tasting bar.

St. Helena Wine Merchants (707-963-7888; 699 St. Helena Hwy., St. Helena) A giant selection of new and older vintages, but no bargains here. There's also a notable assortment of large bottles. Tasting bar.

Vintage 1870 Wine Cellar (707-944-9070; 6525 Washington St., Yountville) This historic building, with polished wood floors and exposed rafters, has a vast stash of wine and micro-brewery beers. No bargains. Tasting bar.

Sweets & Treats

Napa County

Anette's Chocolate & Ice Cream Factory (707-252-4228; 1321 1st St., Napa) This is a dangerous place for weight watchers, offering everything from fresh chocolate turtles and truffles to jelly beans, milkshakes, sundaes.

The Big Dipper (707-963-2616; 1336 Oak Ave., St. Helena) Try this old-fashioned ice cream parlor, which offers the usual delights like sundaes and shaved ice.

The Candy Cellar (707-942-6990; 1367 Lincoln Ave., Calistoga) Relive your childhood as you browse this general store with its wooden barrels stuffed with goodies like taffy, butterscotch, fireballs, candy necklaces, gum, A&W root beer barrels, and the like.

The Chocolate Tree (707-944-2113; Vintage 1870, Yountville) Stop for a treat while you browse the shops of Vintage 1870. Offers homemade candy and Dreyers ice cream.

Good N' Airy Angel (707-942-0714; 1408 Lincoln Ave., Calistoga) A small shop with a potpourri of goodies, from muffins and scones to lemon squares, fresh chocolates, decadent cakes, ice cream, and espresso.

Sonoma County

Sweets From the Heart (707-433-1807; 340 Healdsburg Ave., Healdsburg) An old-fashioned soda fountain, this shop also sells hand-dipped candies, novelty candies, and fresh cookies.

Sonoma County

Bottle Barn (707-528-1161; 3331 Industrial Dr., Santa Rosa) This warehouse has a huge selection, with a few hard-to-find wines and generally bargain prices.

Gaffney's Wine Bar (707-542-8463; 404 Mendocino Ave., Santa Rosa) This bistro is an enjoyable spot. Wine is offered by the bottle or the glass and the selection is super. Comparative tastings are organized regularly and winemakers are frequently on hand to pour their own.

Root & Eastwood Wine & Spirits (707-433-8311; 1123 Vine St., Healdsburg) This small wine shop is packed with some of the top wines in Sonoma and Napa.

Tip Top Liquor Warehouse (707-431-0841; 90 Dry Creek Rd., Healdsburg) This industrial building has an excellent assortment of wine and some of the best prices in Wine Country. Zinfandel and wines from the Healdsburg area are a specialty.

Traverso's (707-542-2530; 3rd & B Sts., Santa Rosa) This Italian deli doesn't carry a huge selection of wine, but offers only the best quality in all price ranges. Bill Traverso knows wine but is so unpretentious about it that you don't have to pretend *you* do. Traverso's has the best stock of Italian wines in the region.

Wine Exchange of Sonoma (707-938-1794; 452 1st St. E., Sonoma) There's an air of restrained refinement to this shop. Few discounts, but look for the best current releases and a few vintage wines. There's also an *enormous* selection of specialty beers. Another plus is the wine and beer tasting bar in the back.

The Vintage 1870 Wine Cellar is one of Napa's wine-tasting centers.

Courtesy The Vintage 1870 Wine Cellar

CHAPTER SIX
On the Vine
WINERIES

Old-timers remember a different, simpler Wine Country. As recently as the 1960s, visitors arrived at local wineries with empty jugs and bottles in hand, ready for a fill-up right from the barrel. But as Napa and Sonoma have gained prominence in the wine world, so has their appeal as vacation meccas. More than eight million tourists come to Napa and Sonoma counties each year. Winery hopping has become an

Robert Nixon/Courtesy Sonoma Valley Visitors Bureau

The vineyards of Wine Country.

avid pastime, and tasting rooms have evolved into bustling centerpieces, sometimes rustic, sometimes chic, but always inviting and fun.

Wineries, like the wines they make, come in different styles and qualities. You can even use the same words to describe them. Is it a sweet or sour experience? Subtle or bold? Is it friendly from the first or does it grow on you? In compiling our list of wineries, we asked ourselves: "What makes a winery worth visiting?" Is it the wine? A pilgrimage to the source of your favorite cabernet sauvignon has great appeal. Is it the fame? "Wow! There's Robert Mondavi — we *have* to stop there." There's also the tour to consider, and is there a fee? Can you picnic? And so on.

Fall is the favorite touring season for many: the vineyards resplendent in rich golds and reds and the wineries and fields hectic with the harvest or "crush" as it's called. Our favorite time is spring, when the mountains and fields are lush and green, the vines budding, trees flowering, and the fields are covered with the yellows of wild mustard.

We've included not only the wineries that regularly offer tours and tastings, but also those that are open by appointment only. The wineries are organized first by region, then alphabetically. Here are a few guidelines to keep in mind when winery touring and wine tasting.

1) Have a designated driver. Those small samples can creep up on you, especially if you're new to wine tasting. Also, you don't have to try *every* wine and wineries are not offended if you pour out a leftover sample.

2) Don't be intimidated by wine's snobbish image. Be yourself. Ask questions. Have fun. A glossary is provided later in this chapter if you need handy details.

3) Bring the right equipment. Take notes. They don't have to be voluminous, just a brief note like "1992 Simi Chardonnay — great" to jog your memory later. While touring, take along crackers and bottled water. It helps to cleanse your palate between wineries.

4) One tour is not much different from the next. One or two is enough. Also, try different kinds. Korbel and Beringer are rich in history, while Mumm and Mondavi are technical wonders.

5) While wine tasting is free at all but a handful of Sonoma County wineries, most Napa Valley wineries charge from $2 to $5. Usually a souvenir glass is thrown in, and the fee may be waived if you buy wine.

6) Don't let "open by appointment only" scare you off. These are often smaller wineries that want to discourage heavy traffic and many are restricted by recent zoning laws. If you're a casual tourist, stick to the big wineries with the big welcome, but if you're serious about wine, these wineries are serious about you.

7) Most wineries have a picnic area. It's good courtesy to buy a bottle beforehand.

NAPA COUNTY WINERIES

Napa & Carneros

ACACIA WINERY
Winemaker: Larry Brooks.
707-226-9991.
2750 Las Amigas Rd.,
   Napa.
Tasting & Tours: 10–4:30
   Mon.–Sat., Noon–4:30
   Sun., by appt.
Tasting Fee: No.

Named after a tree that grows throughout the area, Acacia specializes in chardonnay and pinot noir. Acacia was established in 1979 and sold in 1986 to Chalone Inc., which owns Carmenet and Edna Valley. The winery is a modern California barn that sits on the slopes of the Carneros district, which shoulders the top of the San Pablo Bay. Acacia uses grapes from surrounding vineyards, a region suited to Burgundian grapes.

BOUCHAINE VINE-YARDS

Winemaker: John Montero.
707-252-9065.
1075 Buchli Station Rd.,
Napa.
Tasting & Tours: 10–4
Mon.–Fri. by appt.
Tasting Fee: No.

Built from the vestiges of a winery that dates from the turn of the century, Bouchaine is a grand redwood barn. The winery sits alone on rolling hills that lead to the San Pablo Bay. A fire warms the tasting room on cool Carneros days and a deck offers lovely views when the sun allows. Chardonnay and pinot noir are a specialty but try the crisp and spicy gewürztraminer.

The red and copper stills of Carneros Alambics Distillery look like giant Arabian teapots.

Chris Alderman

CARNEROS ALAMBICS DISTILLERY

Brandy Master: Rob
McNeill.
707-253-9055.
1250 Cuttings Wharf Rd.,
1 mi. S. of Hwy. 12/121,
Napa.
Hours: 10–5 summer,
10:30–4:30 winter.
Tasting: No.
Tours: Yes.
Fee: $2.

If drinking a cognac in front of a glowing fire is your idea of ecstasy, then Carneros Alambics will reveal the secret behind your fantasy. Carneros Alambics' brandy isn't technically cognac — that comes only *from* Cognac in France. Remy Martin of France *does* own Carneros Alambics.

The distillery has eight red and copper stills — imported from France — that look like oversized Arabian teapots. The aging cellar, a large building half-buried in the ground, has an extraordinary perfume — they call it "Angel's Share" — which comes from the alcohol evaporating from the aging brandy. It's like standing in a huge brandy snifter.

Inside, you'll see thousands of Limousin oak barrels in which the brandy ages for at least five years. California law prohibits tasting but they do offer comparative *sniffs*. Don't laugh. It's rather fun.

CARNEROS CREEK WINERY
Winemaker: Melissa Moravec.
707-253-9463.
1285 Dealy Ln., Napa.
Tasting: 10–5 daily.
Tours: By appt.
Tasting Fee: $2.50.
Special Features: Picnic area.

Situated along the stream that lends its name, Carneros Creek was a key player in the revival of Carneros as wine-growing region. It produces a lovely but lean chardonnay and several pinot noirs, including Fleur de Carneros, an easy quaff perfect for picnics. The winery is a modest barn that has been producing wine since the early 1970s. A small tasting room is in the farmhouse nearby.

CODORNIU NAPA
Winemaker: Don Van Staaveren.
707-224-1668.
1345 Henry Rd., Napa.
Old Sonoma Rd. N. from Hwy. 12/121, L. on Dealy Rd.
Hours: 10–5 Mon.–Thurs., 10–3 Fri.–Sun.
Tours: Yes.
Tasting: Sold by the glass.
Fee: $4.
Special Features: Art gallery.

This $23-million winery is a spectacular understatement. Covered with earth and native grasses, Codorniu Napa is an enigma from the road, recalling a buried temple. The mystery begins to unravel as you approach the entrance, a long staircase with a waterfall cascading down the center. Inside is Wine Country's newest and most hi-tech sparkling wine facility.

Codorniu, the Spanish firm that has been making traditional *méthode champenoise* sparkling wine since 1872, opened its Napa bureau in 1991. Inside, it seems anything but a bunker, with elegant decor, a sun-baked atrium, and spectacular views through grand windows. Codorniu non-vintage *brut* has quickly risen to the top of California's sparkling wine. It is creamy and complex, with great finesse.

Domaine Carneros is modeled after an 18th-century French chateau.

Courtesy Domaine Carneros

DOMAINE CARNEROS
Winemaker: Eileen Crane.
707-257-0101.
Off Hwy. 12/121 at Duhig Rd., 5 1/2 mi. W. of Napa.
Hours: 10:30–6 daily.
Tasting: Sold by the glass.
Fee: $4–$5.
Tours: 11, 1, & 3 daily.

The Domaine Carneros winery is an exclamation point along Hwy. 12, towering on a hilltop surrounded by vineyards. Built in the style of an 18th-century French chateau, Domaine Carneros is no everyday winery. But then sparkling wine isn't your everyday libation. Owned by champagne giant Taittinger, Domaine Carneros makes a $14 million statement about its French heritage.

The terrace of this cream and terra cotta chateau overlooks the lovely rolling hills of the Carneros district, which has a climate similar to Champagne. Inside are marble floors and a maple interior crowned with ornate chandeliers. Behind the stylish front is a state-of-the-art winery that released its first wine in the fall of 1990. Domaine Carneros' non-vintage *brut* is a light, elegant sparkler, a melding of French and American tastes.

Wineries are here, there, and everywhere in Sonoma County.

Bob Martin/Courtesy Sonoma Valley Visitors Bureau

HAKUSAN SAKE GARDENS
Brewmaster: Hisato Nishi.
707-258-6160.
Hwy. 12/29 at Jameson Canyon Rd., 4 mi. S. of Napa.
Tasting: 9–6 daily.
Tours: Self-guided.
Tasting Fee: No.
Special Features: Japanese garden.

You're driving along a Napa back road, admiring the scenery: wide skies, stately mountains, eminent wineries, and field upon field of — *rice*? Rice isn't *really* grown in Napa Valley, but grapes aren't the only source of wine. Sake, a rice wine, is the traditional wine of Japan, and Hakusan has been making sake in Napa since 1989.

Kohnan Inc., the firm behind Hakusan, came to Napa because its high-tech plans clashed with certain Japanese traditions. You'll watch a short video on sake while sipping cold and warm sake. (Heat brings out sake's nuttiness.) After tasting, you can follow a self-guided tour along the outside of the brewery, viewing the process through large windows.

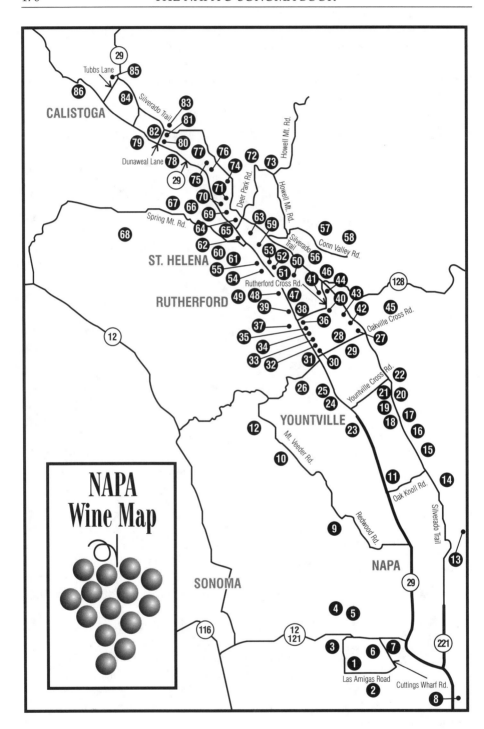

29
Tubbs Lane
85
86
84
CALISTOGA
Silverado Trail
83
81
82
79
80
77 76
Dunaweal Lane 78
29
75
71
67
70
66
69
64
65
62
60
55 61
54
49 48
ST. HELENA
RUTHERFORD
Spring Mt. Rd.
68
72
74
Deer Park Rd.
63
59
53 52
50
51
Rutherford Cross Rd.
47
39
38
37
35
34
33 32
31
36
28
30
29
73
Howell Mt. Rd.
Howell Mt. Rd.
57
58
Conn Valley Rd.
Silverado Trail
56
41 44
46
40 43
42
45
128
Oakville Cross Rd.
27
22
21 20
19
18 17
16
15
Yountville Cross Rd.
26
25
24
YOUNTVILLE
23
12
10
Mt. Veeder Rd.
12
9
Redwood Rd.
Oak Knoll Rd.
11
14
Silverado Trail
13
NAPA
SONOMA
116
12
121
4 5
3
1
Las Amigas Road
6 7
2
Cuttings Wharf Rd.
8
29
221

NAPA Wine Map

NAPA WINERIES

1. Acacia	33. Cakebread	64. Markham
2. Bouchaine	34. Sequoia Grove	65. St. Clement
3. Domaine Carneros	35. St. Supery	66. Philip Togni
4. Codorniu Napa	36. Peju Province	67. Robert Keenan
5. Carneros Creek	37. Niebaum-Coppola	68. Cain
6. Saintsbury	38. Beaulieu	69. Freemark Abbey
7. Carneros Alambic	39. Grgich Hills	70. Folie a Deux
8. Hakusan	40. Caymus	71. Duckhorn
9. Hess Collection	41. Frog's Leap	72. Burgess
10. Mayacamas	42. ZD	73. Viader
11. Trefethen	43. Mumm	74. Rombauer
12. Chateau Potelle	44. Conn Creek	75. Tudal
13. William Hill	45. Chappellet	76. Ehlers Grove
14. Signorello	46. Rutherford Hill	77. Kornell
15. Clos du Val	47. Franciscan	78. Schramsberg
16. Chimney Rock	48. Whitehall Lane	79. von Strasser
17. Stag's Leap	49. Flora Springs	80. Stonegate
18. Pine Ridge	50. Raymond	81. Sterling
19. Silverado	51. V. Sattui	82. Clos Pegase
20. Shafer	52. Heitz	83. Cuvaison
21. S. Anderson	53. Martini	84. Vincent Arroyo
22. Robert Sinskey	54. Sutter Home	85. Chateau Montelena
23. Domaine Chandon	55. Prager	86. Storybrook
24. Cosentino	56. Joseph Phelps	
25. Napa Cellars	57. Anderson's	
26. Vichon	Conn Valley	
27. Girard	58. Buehler	
28. Groth	59. Merryvale	
29. Silver Oak	60. Newton	
30. Opus One	61. Spottswoode	
31. Robert Mondavi	62. Beringer	
32. Turnbull	63. Charles Krug	

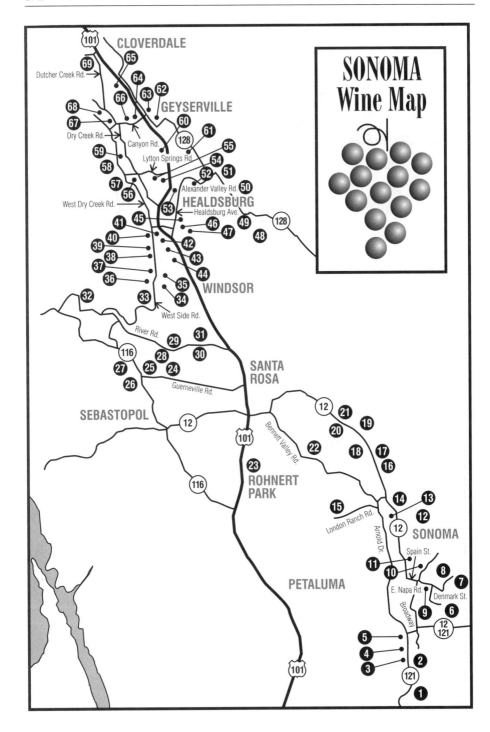

SONOMA
Wine Map

SONOMA WINERIES

1.	Roche	36.	Williams Selyem
2.	Viansa	37.	Belvedere
3.	Cline	38.	Rabbit Ridge
4.	Gloria Ferrer	39.	Armida
5.	Schug	40.	Mill Creek
6.	Gundlach-Bundschu	41.	Alderbrook
7.	Buena Vista	42.	Foppiano
8.	Bartholomew Park	43.	Rodney Strong
9.	Sebastiani	44.	Piper Sonoma
10.	Ravenswood	45.	Kendall-Jackson
11.	Hanzell	46.	Windsor
12.	Carmenet	47.	White Oak
13.	B.R. Cohn	48.	Chalk Hill
14.	Arrowood	49.	Fieldstone
15.	Benziger	50.	Alexander Valley
16.	Kunde	51.	Sausal
17.	Kenwood	52.	Jordan
18.	Remick Ridge	53.	Simi
19.	Chateau St. Jean	54.	Ridge/Lytton Springs
20.	St. Francis	55.	Mazzocco
21.	Landmark	56.	Dry Creek
22.	Matanzas Creek	57.	Lambert Bridge
23.	Sonoma Co. Wine Visitors Ctr.	58.	A. Rafanelli
24.	De Loach	59.	Quivira
25.	Dehlinger	60.	Chateau Souverain
26.	Iron Horse	61.	Murphy-Goode
27.	Topolos	62.	Trentadue
28.	Joseph Swan	63.	Clos du Bois
29.	Sonoma-Cutrer	64.	Geyser Peak
30.	Martinelli	65.	Silver Oak
31.	California Coast Wine Center	66.	J. Pedroncelli
32.	Korbel	67.	Preston
33.	Davis Bynum	68.	Ferrari-Carano
34.	Rochioli	69.	J. Fritz
35.	Hop Kiln		

THE HESS COLLECTION
Winemaker: Randle
  Johnson.
707-255-1144.
4411 Redwood Rd., 10 mi.
  W. of Hwy. 29, Napa.
Tasting: 10–4 daily.
Tours: Self-guided.
Tasting Fee: $2.50.
Special Features: Art
  gallery.

Along the rugged slopes of Mt. Veeder is the most impressive art collection north of San Francisco. The Hess Collection is both a winery and a museum of modern art. Donald Hess, a Swiss mineral magnate, transformed the old Mont La Salle Winery into a showcase for his two passions.

Up a winding road through the thick glades of Mt. Veeder, the ivy-covered winery dates to 1903. It was the first Napa Valley home of Christian Brothers before Hess renovated it and opened it to the public in 1989. Inside, a towering three-story atrium with an elevator and staircase leads to two floors of painting and sculpture by artists such as Francis Bacon and Robert Motherwell. A self-guided tour allows you to view both art and winery. A porthole next to one painting, for example, provides views of the bottling line. Don't miss the Barrel Chai, a dark, cool cellar where wine ages in barrels for up to 22 months. For a more in-depth look at the winery, watch a brief video.

Before leaving, stop in the tasting room. Hess concentrates on two wines: cabernet sauvignon and chardonnay. The chardonnay is stylish and oaky; the cabernet is fabulous and one of Napa Valley's best. There's something about mountain vineyards that make a rich, intense cabernet.

**MAYACAMAS VINE-
  YARDS AND WINERY**
Winemaker: Bob Travers.
707-224-4030.
1155 Lokoya Rd., off Mt.
  Veeder Rd., Napa.
Tasting & Tours: Mon.–Fri.
  by appt.
Tasting Fee: No.

High on the brushy slopes of Mt. Veeder, and literally in the dome of an extinct volcano, this winery traces its origins to 1889, when a San Francisco pickle tycoon built the still-sturdy stone winery. Bob and Elinor Travers have run Mayacamas since 1968. The vineyards are 2,000 feet above sea level and the trek from Hwy. 29 is not for the squeamish. The winery still produces the strapping monster cabernet sauvignons on which it built its reputation in the 1970s.

MONTICELLO CELLARS
Winemaker: John McKay.
707-253-2802.
4242 Big Ranch Rd., off Oak
  Knoll Ave., Napa.
Tasting: 10–4:30 daily.
Tours: 10:30, 12:30, & 2:30
  daily.
Tasting Fee: $3.
Special Features: Picnic
  area.

If the visitor center of this winery looks familiar, check the nickel in your pocket. It's modeled after Thomas Jefferson's home, Monticello. A Jefferson scholar, owner Jay Corley paid tribute to one of America's first wine buffs. Corley began as a grape grower in the early 1970s and started making wine in 1980. Cabernet sauvignon, of late, has superseded chardonnay as the winery's specialty. The cabernet is generally soft and elegant.

SAINTSBURY
Winemaker: Byron Kosuge.
707-252-0592.
1500 Los Carneros Ave.,
  Napa.
Tasting & Tours: 9–5
  Mon.–Fri. by appt.
Tasting Fee: No.

Davbid Graves and Richard Ward came to Carneros in search of Burgundy. Enthused by the district's potential for Burgundian grapes chardonnay and pinot noir, the duo formed Saintsbury — named for the author of the classic *Notes on a Cellar-Book* — in 1981. We have a soft spot for Saintsbury's inexpensive Garnet pinot noir, and its Carneros pinot and chardonnay are typically lush and complex. With its weathered redwood siding and steeply sloped roof, the winery fits snugly amid the grapevines in this rural area.

**SIGNORELLO VINE-
  YARDS**
Winemaker: Steve Devitt.
707-255-5990.
4500 Silverado Trail. Napa.
Tasting & Tours: By appt.
Tasting Fee: No.

This small winery is one of the rising stars in California wine, garnering attention for its vibrant chardonnay and semillon, a cousin of sauvignon blanc. Its stable of red wines includes cabernet sauvignon, merlot, and pinot noir. Ray Signorello's first vintage was 1985 and he prefers a low-tech, natural approach to winemaking. The winery, built in 1990, is a low-key affair — the only way *in* is through a neighbor's gate — and Signorello and Devitt run the whole show.

**TREFETHEN VINE-
  YARDS**
Winemaker: Peter Luthi.
707-255-7700.
1160 Oak Knoll Ave., Napa.
Tasting: 10–4:30 daily.
Tours: By appt.
Tasting Fee: No.

Shaded by a 100-year-old oak, this winery was built in 1886 by Hamden W. McIntyre, the architect behind Inglenook and Greystone Cellars. The Trefethen family bought the winery in 1968 and restored it, painting the redwood beauty a pumpkin orange. Tours highlight the three-level gravity flow system designed by McIntyre, in which grapes are crushed on the third floor, juice fermented on the second and aged in barrels on the ground level. Since its first vintage in 1973, Trefethen has made a name with chardonnay.

WILLIAM HILL WINERY
Winemaker: Jill Davis.
707-224-4477.
1761 Atlas Peak Rd., Napa.
Tasting & Tours: 10–4:30
  daily by appt.
Tasting Fee: No.

William Hill developed high-profile vineyards now harvested by Atlas Peak, the Hess Collection, and Sterling. Hill's first wine was the 1976 vintage but this sleekly modern winery wasn't built until 1990. Hill sold the winery in 1991 but it continues without its namesake, producing consistently good cabernet sauvignons and chardonnays. The tour follows a walkway above the cellar, allowing premium views of the winemaking process.

Yountville & Stag's Leap

S. ANDERSON WINERY
Winemaker: Jac Cole.
707-944-8642.
1473 Yountville Crossroad,
   Yountville.
Tasting: 10–5 daily.
Tours: 10:30 & 2:30 daily.
Tasting Fee: $3.

Afamily-owned winery that offers a personal touch, S. Anderson specializes in sparkling wine and chardonnay, although its limited-release cabernet sauvignon is snatched up quickly. The tasting room is a quaint stone building at the end of a garden path. The aging caves, carved out of a nearby hillside, are the highlight of the tour.

**CHIMNEY ROCK
    WINERY**
Winemaker: Doug Fletcher.
707-257-2641.
5350 Silverado Trail,
   Yountville.
Tasting: 10–5 daily.
Tours: By appt.
Tasting Fee: $3.

Cabernet sauvignon has replaced putting greens at Chimney Rock. Owner Sheldon "Hack" Wilson bought the Chimney Rock golf course in the early 1980s and converted nine of the holes to vineyards. The winery is inspired by the architecture of South Africa, where Wilson was an executive in the soft drink business. Emphasis has recently shifted from white wines to cabernet, which prosper in Stag's Leap.

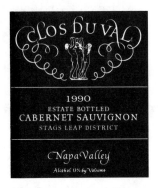

CLOS DU VAL
Winemaker: Bernard
   Portet.
707-259-2200.
5330 Silverado Trail, Napa.
Tasting: 10–5 daily.
Tours: 10:30 daily by appt.
Tasting Fee: $3.
Special Features: Picnic area.

Bernard Portet was raised among the casks and vines of Chateau Lafite-Rothschild, where his father was cellarmaster. The Bordeaux influence is strong here, both in the wines and the winery. An elegant and understated building surrounded by vineyards, Clos du Val evokes a small country winery, with red roses marking the end of each vine row, in typical French fashion. The tasting room has a vaulted ceiling and windows that open into the cellar.

Established in 1972, Clos du Val helped pioneer the notion that cabernet sauvignons need not be muscular monsters to age well. To anyone who has tasted a Lafite-Rothschild, this is no secret, but it wasn't the established thinking in Napa Valley at the time. Clos du Val's cabernets are typically elegant and complex. Clos du Val's roster includes a wonderfully fleshy zinfandel and we're fans of the semillon, but the merlot and pinot noir can be inconsistent.

COSENTINO WINERY
Winemaker: Mitch
  Cosentino.
707-944-1220.
7415 St. Helena Hwy.
  (Hwy. 29), Yountville.
Tasting: 10–5:30 daily.
Tours: By appt.
Tasting Fee: No.

One of Napa Valley's recent additions, Cosentino specializes in blends with romantic names. Cosentino's bordeaux-style blend of cabernet sauvignon, merlot, and cabernet franc is called "The Poet" and it's typically big and tannic. The reserve chardonnay is dubbed "The Sculptor." The merlot and pinot noir lack nom de plumes, but they are excellent. The winery is a modest manor with a friendly tasting room.

DOMAINE CHANDON
Winemaker: Dawnine
  Dyer.
707-944-2280.
California Dr., off Hwy. 29,
  Yountville.
Closed: Mon. & Tues.,
  Nov.–Apr.
Hours: 11–6 daily.
Tours: On the hour, 11–5
  daily.
Tasting Fee: Sold by the
  glass.
Special Features: Restaurant.

The turning point for California sparkling wine came in 1973 when Moet-Hennessy built this ultra-modern winery in the hills west of Yountville. If that famed French champagne house believed in Napa's potential, then California winemaking had come of age. Thus began the rush of European sparkling wine firms to Northern California.

Driving along Hwy. 29, you'd hardly notice the glass and native-stone bunker built into an oak-covered knoll. Inside is a museum with artifacts and explanations of *méthode champenoise*, the classic French process of making bubbly. The tour is thorough, and takes visitors past the mechanized riddling racks, the bottling line, etc.

Domaine Chandon makes a variety of sparkling wines, from a round and refreshing brut, to the expensive and intense Etoile. Most are available by the glass in the stylish tasting salon, where on warm days you can sit on the sun-drenched terrace. The restaurant is considered one of Napa Valley's best (see Chapter Five, *Restaurants & Food Purveyors*).

PINE RIDGE WINERY
Winemaker: Stacy Clark.
707-252-9777.
5901 Silverado Trail,
  Yountville.
Tasting: 11–5 daily.
Tours: By appt.
Tasting Fee: $3.
Special Features: Picnic
  area.

An unassuming winery sequestered among the hills along Silverado Trail. Take your glass onto the patio or explore the shady grounds. There's even a swing. The tour begins in the vineyard and treks through the aging caves, where samples from oak barrels are offered. The winery's cabernet sauvignon has recently recovered from a slump and its chenin blanc is one of the best in Wine Country.

ROBERT SINSKEY VINEYARDS
Winemaker: Jeff Virnig.
707-944-9090.
6320 Silverado Trail, Yountville.
Tasting: 10–4:30 daily.
Tours: By appt.
Tasting Fee: $3.

On a rise overlooking Silverado Trail, this winery blends a modern design with the warmth of stone and redwood. The ceiling of the tasting room stretches 35 feet high and wisteria entwines courtyard columns. Dug into a hillside behind the winery is a cave, which is included on the tour. Pinot noir and merlot are the lead wines and the second label "Aries" offers a remarkable value.

SHAFER VINEYARDS
Winemaker: Elias Fernandez.
707-944-2877.
6154 Silverado Trail, Napa.
Tasting: 9–5 Mon.–Fri. by appt.
Tours: By appt.
Tasting Fee: No.

Dynamite is not often required to plant vineyards, but back in 1972 John Shafer was convinced that hillsides were the best place to grow cabernet sauvignon. Mountain vineyards may be the rage now, but they weren't *then*. The soil is shallow on the hills below the Stag's Leap palisades, so dynamite was required to terrace the vineyards. The vines struggle against the bedrock to find water and nourishment, but these stressed and scrawny vines produce intense wines.

Shafer's winery is a classic California ranch. The tasting room opens through French doors onto a second-floor verandah with an expansive view of lower Napa Valley. Under the vine-covered hill behind the winery is an 8,000-sq.-ft. cave the Shafers completed in 1991. Carved out of solid rock, the cave — cool and immaculately clean — is the high point of the tour.

Shafer's top cabernet sauvignon is the Hillside Select and it is typically brawny. The Stag's Leap District cab is usually blended with merlot, which makes it softer. Merlot is also bottled separately, along with chardonnay and a recent addition dubbed "Firebreak," a blend of cabernet and sangiovese, the chianti grape.

SILVERADO VINEYARDS
Winemaker: Jack Stuart.
707-944-1770.
6121 Silverado Trail, Napa.
Tasting: 11–4:30 daily.
Tours: By appt.
Tasting Fee: No.

Rare is the winery that shines with cabernet sauvignon *and* chardonnay. Add the challenge of merlot and sauvignon blanc and the odds are stacked against it. Somehow, Silverado pulls it off, regularly producing outstanding examples of each. Best of all, its wines remain reasonably priced.

Built by the Walt Disney family in 1981, Silverado offers a dramatic view from its perch atop a Silverado Trail knoll. Look for Mickey Mouse in the stained glass window of the Spanish-style winery. Silverado doesn't pour all its wines in its denlike tasting room, but there's no going wrong. The cabernet is lush and ripe with raspberry fruit; the reserve cabernet is a knock-out, as is the reserve chardonnay.

Chris Alderman

Stag's Leap Wine Cellars is a pilgrimage for many wine lovers.

STAG'S LEAP WINE CELLARS
Winemaker: Warren Winiarski.
707-944-2020.
5766 Silverado Trail, Napa.
Tasting: 10–4 daily.
Tours: By appt.
Tasting Fee: $3; free with tour.

Stag's Leap Wine Cellars falls into the select pilgrimage category. In 1976, it achieved instant fame when its 1973 cabernet won the famous Paris tasting, which changed the way the world looked at California wine. Hidden within an oak grove, Stag's Leap is an ever-growing village of buildings. Founded by the Winiarski family in 1972, the winery has an unassuming charm, despite its fame. The tasting room is merely a table tucked among towering wooden casks in one of the aging cellars.

A handful of wines are offered for tasting every day. Don't expect to sample the winery's premier bottling Cask 23, a cabernet blend with a steep price tag, but the other reserve cabernets are rich with velvety fruit and are often on the list. Be sure to try their lean and crisp chardonnays.

Oakville & Rutherford

BEAULIEU VINEYARDS
Winemaker: Joel Aiken.
707-967-5230.
1960 St. Helena Hwy.
(Hwy. 29), Rutherford.
Tasting: 10–5 daily.
Tours: 11–4 daily.
Tasting Fee: Reserve wines only.
Special Features: Gifts.

If you could sum up Napa Valley winemaking with a single bottle of wine, it would be the Georges de Latour Private Reserve Cabernet Sauvignon by Beaulieu. Though no longer the best cabernet in the valley, it has been the yardstick against which all other cabernets have been measured.

Pronounced *Bowl-You* or called BV for short, Beaulieu is one of Napa's most distinguished wineries, dating back to 1900 when Frenchman Georges de Latour began making wine. In 1938,

Latour hired a young Russian immigrant, Andre Tchelistcheff, who went on to revolutionize California cabernet. Today, though, Beaulieu struggles to maintain that rich tradition.

Built of brick and covered with ivy, the winery isn't particularly impressive, but a tour can be an eye-opener, particularly passing the forest of towering redwood tanks. A video in the visitor center briefs guests on Beaulieu's past and present. Three or four wines are offered; sip as you browse through the museum of old bottles and memorabilia. The crisp sauvignon blanc is good for the price and the chardonnays are much improved. Tastings of the Private Reserve are offered for a fee in a special tasting room.

CAKEBREAD CELLARS
Winemaker: Bruce
  Cakebread.
707-963-5221.
8300 St. Helena Hwy.
  (Hwy. 29), Rutherford.
Tasting: 10–4 daily.
Tours: By appt.
Tasting Fee: No.

The Cakebread clan runs this winery set in prime cabernet sauvignon territory. Jack and Dolores Cakebread began making wine in 1973 and have won a loyal following. In the tasting room of this unpretentious redwood winery, try the melony sauvignon blanc — one of the best. Cakebread's cabernet sauvignons and chardonnay, lean and rigid on release, bloom after a few years. Zinfandel is back on the roster, following a long hiatus.

Tasting the wine at Caymus Vineyards.

Chris Alderman

CAYMUS VINEYARDS
Winemakers: Chuck
  Wagner & John Bolta.
707-967-3010.
8700 Conn Creek Rd.,
  Rutherford.
Tasting: 10–4:30 daily.
Tasting Fee: $2.
Tours: No.

No American wine is more highly regarded than the Caymus Special Selection cabernet sauvignon. OK, you could argue in favor of cabernets by Dunn or Dominus or Diamond Creek, but few wines make the "Best of . . ." lists of critics and wine lovers as often as Caymus SS. At release, people crowd the winery for the honor of paying $75 *a bottle.*

Caymus remains a low-frills family outfit and tampers little with its wines. The main 40-acre vineyard lies east of the Napa River in the heart of Napa Valley's cabernet country, a blessed location. The tasting room is in a modern winery made of sturdy fieldstone, which only recently replaced the original barn. Don't expect to taste the Special Selection, but the regular cabernet and the white blend Conundrum are exceptional.

CHAPPELLET VINEYARD
Winemaker: Phillip Corallo-Titus.
707-963-7136.
1581 Sage Canyon Rd., St. Helena.
Tasting & Tours: Mon.–Fri. by appt.
Tasting Fee: No.

Styled like a pyramid, this winery would make a striking statement along Hwy. 29. Instead, it is hidden among the rustic hills east of the valley. Built in the late 1960s by Donn and Molly Chappellet, the winery was only the second to open in the county after Prohibition. The vineyards are steeply terraced and produce a firm cabernet sauvignon and one of the best chenin blancs in the state.

CHATEAU POTELLE
Winemaker: Marketta Fourmeaux.
707-255-9440.
3875 Mt. Veeder Rd., Oakville.
Tasting & Tours: 12–5 Sat. & Sun., weekdays by appt.
Tasting Fee: No.
Special Features: Picnic area.

High on the crest of Mt. Veeder, Chateau Potelle is a respite from busy Hwy. 29. Bordeaux-born Jean-Noel and Marketta Fourmeaux du Sartel bought Vose vineyards in the early 1980s and renamed it for the family's 900-year-old castle in France. Specialties include cabernet sauvignon and zinfandel. The picnic area has a imposing view. In the winter, call ahead before visiting; hours vary.

CONN CREEK WINERY
Winemaker: Scott Peterson.
707-963-5133.
8711 Silverado Trail, Rutherford.
Tasting: 10–4 daily.
Tours: By appt.
Tasting Fee: No.

This winery made a splash with its early cabernet sauvignons. Its 1974, which ironically it purchased in bulk from a defunct winery, was the star of the vintage, considered one of California's best. It has made solid wines since but never quite lived up to the early promise. Stimson Lane, which owns Columbia Crest in Washington, bought Conn Creek in 1986 and fortunes have improved. Villa Mt. Eden wines are now produced at Conn Creek and offered in the tasting room.

NAPA CELLARS
Winemaker: Don Baker.
707-944-2565.
7481 St. Helena Hwy. (Hwy. 29), Oakville.

Napa Cellars' claim to fame is its geodesic dome. That's the tasting room and its unique shape stops many a car along Napa Valley's main drag. Established as Napa Wine Cellar in 1973, the winery was known as DeMoor Winery for several

Tasting: 10:30–5 daily
(winter), 10:30–5:30 daily
(summer).
Tours: No.
Tasting Fee: $2.
Special Features: Picnic
area, garden.

**FRANCISCAN
VINEYARDS**
Winemaker: Allen
Tenscher.
707-963-7111.
1178 Galleron Rd., at Hwy.
29, Rutherford.
Tasting: 10–5 daily.
Tours: By appt.
Tasting Fee: $3.

years, and it has gone through a number of owners. The focus is cabernet sauvignon, zinfandel, and chardonnay.

Franciscan is the home base of four labels: Estancia, Mt. Veeder, Pinnacles, and of course Franciscan. Each has its niche and combined they are a formidable presence. Franciscan focuses on Oakville grapes, including a delightful zinfandel and a complex reserve chardonnay dubbed "Cuvée Sauvage." Estancia is the bargain label but there's nothing second-rate about its cabernet sauvignon from Alexander Valley. Mt. Veeder specializes in burly mountain-born cabernets and Pinnacles makes fine pinot noir and chardonnay from Monterey grapes. The tasting room is large and dominated by gift items.

FROG'S LEAP WINERY
Winemaker: John Williams.
707-963-4704.
8815 Conn Creek Rd.,
Rutherford.
Tasting & Tours: 9–4
Mon.–Fri. by appt.
Tasting Fee: No.
Special Features: Gifts.

It's rare to find a winery with a sense of humor as well oiled as Frog's Leap. ("Ribbit" is printed on every cork.) The name, a take-off of Stag's Leap Wine Cellars, was inspired by the winery's original site, an old St. Helena frog farm. Founders Larry Turley and John Williams parted ways in 1994 and Williams moved Frog's Leap south and restored a winery that dates from 1884. All five wines — cabernet sauvignon, zinfandel, merlot, chardonnay, and sauvignon blanc — are reliable and often superb.

GIRARD WINERY
Winemaker: Mark Smith.
707-944-8577.
7717 Silverado Trail,
Oakville.
Tasting & Tours: By appt.
Tasting Fee: No.

Hidden in a grove of oaks — thus the acorns on the label — Girard is an unassuming winery that produces noteworthy cabernet sauvignon and chardonnay. Growers since 1974, the Girard family sold their grapes to Mondavi until they built their winery along Silverado Trail in 1980. The tasting room is a friendly spot and a peaceful respite from the harried pace along Hwy. 29.

**GRGICH HILLS
CELLARS**
Winemaker: Mike Grgich.
707-963-2784.

French wine lovers worship the land, but in California, the winemaker is king. Cult followings have a way of developing, as with Mike Grgich, one

Winemaker Mike Grgich enjoys a sip of cabernet sauvignon in the barrel room of his winery.

Chris Alderman

1829 St. Helena Hwy. (Hwy. 29), Rutherford.
Tasting: 9:30–4:30 daily.
Tours: By appt.
Tasting Fee: $2.

of Napa Valley's best-known characters. The scrappy immigrant from the former Yugoslavia became a star in 1976 when as winemaker at Chateau Montelena his 1973 chardonnay beat Burgundy's best whites in the famous Paris tasting. Later, Grgich joined with Austin Hills and opened this winery.

An ivy-covered stucco building with a red-tile roof, Grgich's winery remains a house devoted to chardonnay. Elegant and rich, it's consistently among the finest in California. Grgich also makes a graceful fumé blanc and has considerable luck with zinfandel and cabernet sauvignon. All this can be sampled in Grgich's modest tasting room where the smell of oak and wine float in from the barrel aging room nearby. You might see a feisty little fellow with a black beret — that's Grgich.

GROTH VINEYARDS AND WINERY
Winemaker: Michael Weis.
707-944-0290.
750 Oakville Cross Rd., Oakville.
Tasting: 10–4 Mon.–Sat.
Tours: 11 & 2 daily by appt.
Tasting Fee: $3.

This California Mission-style winery is a grand sight along the Oakville Cross Rd. It's also home to one of California's most sought-after cabernet sauvignons, the Groth Reserve. A former executive with Atari — the hallway near the barrel room is lined with video games — Dennis Groth began making wine in 1982 and his graceful winery was completed in 1990.

The tour is enlightening, beginning on a terrace that overlooks the vineyards, continuing past the bottling line and the cavernous barrel aging room, ending finally at the tasting bar. Groth cabernets typically have a lush elegance married with a firm backbone.

A toast on the terrace of Mumm Napa Valley.

Chris Alderman

MUMM NAPA VALLEY
Winemaker: Greg Fowler.
707-942-3434.
8445 Silverado Trail,
	Rutherford.
Hours: 10:30–6 daily.
Tours: 11–4 daily, on the
	hour.
Tasting Fee: Sold by the
	glass.
Special Features: Patio,
	gifts.

Mumm Napa Valley may have a French parent, but it's a California child through and through. The winery is a long, low ranch barn with redwood siding and a green slate roof. Mumm is one French company that decided to fit in rather than stand out, a philosophy that actually runs deeper than the mere design of a winery. Mumm blends traditional French méthode champenoise with the distinctive fruit of Napa Valley and the result is some of California's best sparkling wines.

The winery tour offers a detailed look at the French way of making sparkling wine. Guides first lead you inside a football field of a room housing giant tanks where the grape juice is fermented. Then they continue through long hallways allowing gallery views of the winemaker's lab, bottling plant, aging cellars, etc.

Brut Prestige is the main release, a snappy blend of pinot noir and chardonnay, and Blanc de Noirs is a zesty rosé. The salon is quaint and country, with sliding glass doors that allow easy views of the Rutherford countryside. There's also an outdoor patio when the day begs a seat in the sun.

**NIEBAUM-COPPOLA
	ESTATE WINERY**
Winemakers: Scott McLeod
	& Tony Soter.
707-967-3495.
1991 St. Helena Hwy.
	(Hwy. 29), Rutherford.
Tasting & Tours: 10–5
	daily.

Francis Ford Coppola, famed director of the *God-father* series and *Apocalypse Now*, rescued the Inglenook chateau from potential oblivion in late 1994. Heublein Inc., a conglomerate with little regard for Napa history, had sold the Inglenook brand name to another firm, and seemed prepared to leave the circa-1888 chateau vacant.

Francis Ford Coppola in the "Captain's Room" at the former Inglenook chateau, now home to the Niebaum-Coppola Estate Winery.

D. Kopol Bonick

Coppola's affections for Inglenook date to the mid-1970s when he bought the former home of Inglenook's founder Gustave Niebaum, which is next to the winery. Coppola released his own wine, "Rubicon," a stout yet elegant bordeaux-style blend, beginning with the 1978 vintage. He has recently added zinfandel and chardonnay and his acquisition of the Inglenook chateau will no doubt expand his horizons.

The chateau itself is the romantic ideal of what a Napa Valley winery should look like: a sturdy stone castle, shrouded in ivy and enveloped by vineyards. Visitors approach the winery through a long tree-lined driveway. Scottish for "cozy corner," Inglenook originated in 1879 when Niebaum, a Finnish sea captain, came to Rutherford and spent some of the fortune he made in the fur trade on building this towering Gothic structure.

OPUS ONE
Winemakers: Tim Mondavi
 & Patrick Leon.
707-963-1979.
7900 St. Helena Hwy.
 (Hwy. 29), Oakville.
Tasting & Tours: By appt.
Tasting Fee: $12.

A joint venture between Robert Mondavi and France's Chateau Mouton-Rothschild, Opus One is an elegant temple, a cross between a Mayan palace and Battlestar Galactica. Designed by the firm that created San Francisco's Transamerica Pyramid, the winery opened in 1991 but was largely inaccessible to the public until 1994. Built of Texas limestone and untreated redwood, the building is partially buried by a berm of earth. The courtyard entrance is a circular colonnade and above is an open-air pavilion that looks out over a sea of vines. The interior blends classic French antiquity with warm California hues.

It's apropos that the winery makes a vivid architectural statement. Opus One has been one of Napa Valley's highest profile wines since its first vintage in 1979. The wine — a blend of cabernet sauvignon, cabernet franc, and merlot — is a classic: rich, oaky, and elegant.

As the tour reveals, few wineries treat their grapes and juice as delicately as Opus One. Arriving in small bins, grapes are sorted by hand — an arduous task — and the juice flows by gravity, not by pump, to the tank room below. The system is advanced in its simplicity. The tasting room fee is extravagant (what do you expect for a $65 bottle of wine?) but the pour is generous. Older vintages are also available for a $12 tasting fee.

PEJU PROVINCE
Winemaker: Anthony Peju.
707-963-3600.
8466 St. Helena Hwy.
    (Hwy. 29), Rutherford.
Tasting: 10–6 daily.
Tours: Guided and self-
    guided.
Tasting Fee: $2.
Special Features: Picnic
    area, garden, sculpture
    collection.

The grounds of this family-owned estate are lovely. Good reason. Tony Peju ran a nursery in Los Angeles before coming north in the early 1980s. A row of beautiful sycamores leads to the French Provincial winery, which is enveloped in white roses and other flowers. There is also a fine collection of marble sculptures. The tour doesn't take long; it's a small place. Cabernet sauvignon and chardonnay are the specialty.

Robert Mondavi Winery is one of Napa Valley's most famous destinations.

**ROBERT MONDAVI
    WINERY**
Winemaker: Patrick
    Mahaney.
800-MONDAVI.
7801 St. Helena Hwy.
    (Hwy. 29), Oakville.
Tasting: 10–4 daily.
Tours: On the hour; reser-
    vations recommended
    weekends & May–Oct.

Robert Mondavi has been such an innovator, such a symbol of the "new" Napa Valley, that it's hard to believe that his winery was founded in 1966. Once too flamboyant for conservative Napa County, his Spanish Mission-style winery now seems as natural as the Mayacamas Mountains. Since first setting out on his own from family-owned Charles Krug, Mondavi has been *the* most outspoken advocate for California and its wines.

Tasting Fee: Free with tour; reserve wines available for a fee.
Special Features: Art gallery, gifts.

Few Napa wineries are busier on a summer day than Mondavi, even though free tastings are available only with a tour, one of the most thorough in the Valley. Guides lead visitors into the vineyards for a lecture on how grapes are grown and harvested; then to the grape presses and a view of all the latest wine wizardry. The tour ends in the tasting room where a selection of wines is offered, along with a mini-course on tasting wine. If a tour seems too much, try the reserve tasting room, where wine is sampled for a fee.

Mondavi bottles one of the most extensive list of wines in the valley. Reds seem to be Mondavi's strong suit. The reserve cabernet sauvignons and pinot noirs become more magnificent every year — and so do the prices. Of course, the regular bottlings are hardly slackers.

Rutherford Hill Winery is a stylish barn.

Courtesy Rutherford Hill Winery

RUTHERFORD HILL WINERY

Winemakers: Kevin Robinson & Kent Barthman.
707-963-7194.
200 Rutherford Hill Rd., off Silverado Trail, Rutherford.
Tasting: 10–4:30 Mon.–Fri., 10–5 Sat. & Sun.
Tours: 11:30, 1:30, & 3:30.
Tasting Fee: $3.
Special Features: Picnic area, gifts, tour includes barrel tasting.

The winery here is a mammoth barn, albeit a stylishly realized barn covered in cedar and perched on the hills overlooking Rutherford. Carved into the hillside behind are the largest manmade aging caves in California, snaking into the rock a half a mile. The titanic cave doors are framed by geometric latticework that recalls Frank Lloyd Wright. Trekking through the cool and humid caves is the tour highlight. Merlot is the star here, and it is typically fleshy with a tannic backbone and it remains reasonably priced.

ST. SUPERY VINEYARD AND WINERY

Winemaker: Michael Scholz.
707-963-4507.
8440 St. Helena Hwy.
(Hwy. 29), Rutherford.
Tours: Self-guided
9:30–4:30 daily; guided
10–3 daily.
Tasting: 9:30–4:30 daily.
Tasting Fee: $2.50.
Special Features: Interactive wine museum, gifts.

Wineries, on the whole, aren't the best place to take kids. St. Supery is the exception. It adds a touch of science museum adventure, with colorful displays, hands-on activities, and modern winery gadgetry.

St. Supery was established in 1982, when French businessman Robert Skalli bought Edward St. Supery's old vineyard and built a state-of-the-art winery next door to St. Supery's original Queen Anne Victorian. A second-floor gallery shows off the day-to-day activities. Windows reveal the bottling line, the barrel aging room, and the like. A highlight is the "smell station," where noses are educated on evaluating cabernet sauvignon and sauvignon blanc. Ever hear cabernet described as cedar or black cherry? Hold your nose to a plastic tube and smell what they mean. Another display gives you a peek under the soil to see the roots of a grapevine. After the tour, St. Supery offers tastings of its cabernet, chardonnay, and sweet moscato.

SEQUOIA GROVE WINERY

Winemaker: James Allen.
707-944-2945.
8338 St. Helena Hwy.
(Hwy. 29), Rutherford.
Tasting 10:30–5 daily.
Tours: By appt.
Tasting Fee: $3.

Dwarfed by century-old sequoia trees, this winery is easy to overlook along Hwy. 29 but the cabernet sauvignons are worth the stop. Wine was made in the redwood barn before Prohibition, but the wine and the winery had been long forgotten when the Allen Family began making wine there again in 1980. Samples are offered from a small table in a corner of the winery. The chardonnay is solid but the regular and reserve cabernets can achieve greatness.

SILVER OAK CELLARS

Winemaker: Dan Baron.
707-944-8808.
915 Oakville Crossroad,
Oakville.
Tasting: 9–4:30 Mon.–Fri.,
10–4:30 Sat.
Tours: 1:30 Mon.–Sat. by
appt.
Tasting Fee: $5.

Not many wineries can live off one wine, but then Silver Oak isn't *just* any winery. Here, cabernet sauvignon has been raised to an art form. Low profile by Napa Valley standards, Silver Oak is known to cabernet lovers around the country, and that's all that matters. The Alexander Valley cabernet is typically more accessible than the Napa Valley bottling but both are velvety and opulent, with tastes that linger.

Silver Oak was established in 1972 on the site of an old Oakville dairy. Some of the dairy buildings are still used, though a Gothic-style masonry winery became home in 1982. Inside is a tasting room paneled with redwood from old wine tanks.

**TURNBULL WINE
  CELLARS**
Winemaker: Kristin Belair.
707-963-5839.
8210 St. Helena Hwy.
  (Hwy. 29), Rutherford.
Tasting: 10–4 daily.
Tours: By appt.
Tasting Fee: No.

Asmall winery in the heart of cabernet sauvignon territory. The redwood winery was
designed by award-winning architect William
Turnbull, a former partner in the winery, which
originated in 1979. The cabernet is known for its
distinct minty quality.

VICHON WINERY
Winemaker: Karen Culler.
707-944-2811.
1595 Oakville Grade,
  Oakville.
Tasting: 10–4:30 Mon.–Fri.,
  10–5 Sat.–Sun.
Tours: By appt.
Tasting Fee: No.
Special Features: Picnic
  area, gifts.

Vichon is a great place for a picnic. Teetering on
the edge of the Oakville Grade, Vichon offers a
stunning view of the valley as well as a shady spot
to relax, nibble on cheese, and sip wine. That
Vichon's wines have considerable charm only
makes a visit more pleasant. Built in 1982 along the
harrowing Oakville Grade, Vichon was bought by
the Mondavi family soon after. The winery has been
tinkering with its line-up in recent years, but cabernet sauvignon and chardonnay remain a focus.

ZD WINES
Winemaker: Robert de
  Leuze.
707-963-5188.
8383 Silverado Trail,
  Rutherford.
Tasting: 10–4:30 daily.
Tours: By appt.
Tasting Fee: $3.

Chardonnay, pinot noir, cabernet sauvignon —
ZD has a way with all three. The winery began
life in 1969 in Sonoma Valley and transplanted to
Napa ten years later. Crowned with a roof of red
tile, the winery was recently expanded by the de
Leuze family. The star is chardonnay, an opulent
beauty, and cabernets are dense and powerful. The
pinots are light but intensely fruity.

St. Helena

**ANDERSON'S CONN
  VALLEY VINEYARDS**
Winemaker: Gus Anderson.
707-963-8600.
680 Rossi Rd., 3 mi. off Sil-
  verado Trail, St. Helena.
Tasting & Tours: By appt.
Tasting Fee: No.

Asmall winery in the foothills east of the valley,
it's well off the beaten path but its cabernet
sauvignon is already one of Napa's rising stars.
The 1987 vintage was the first for the Anderson
family and their cabernet is intense yet elegant. The
Andersons are down-to-earth folks who welcome
serious cab fans, although this isn't an extravagant
venture, and refreshingly so.

BERINGER VINEYARDS
Winemaker: Ed Sbragia.
707-963-4812.

There's something almost regal about the Rhine
House, the circa-1876 mansion that forms the

Chris Alderman

The Rhine House, built in 1876, is the centerpiece of Beringer Vineyards.

2000 Main St. (Hwy. 29), St. Helena.
Tasting: 10–6 summer, 9:30–5 winter.
Tours: 10–5 summer, 10–4 winter.
Tasting Fee: Reserve wines only.
Special Features: Gifts.

centerpiece of Beringer Vineyards. Sitting amid manicured lawns and meticulously restored, the Rhine House suggests that Beringer doesn't take its past or its reputation lightly.

This is one of the few wineries that has it all. A prime tourist attraction with a historical tour, it is also one of Napa's most popular makers of cabernet sauvignon and chardonnay. The oldest continually operated winery in Napa Valley, Beringer was founded by German immigrants, Jacob and Frederick Beringer. The tour offers a few juicy details about the early days.

For a quick taste of wine, go past the Rhine House and up the walk to the Old Bottling Room, where you can take in vino *and* history. The room is decorated with artifacts like a photo of Clark Gable visiting or a dusty bottle of sacramental wine produced during Prohibition. To taste Beringer's top wines, climb the staircase of the Rhine House to the reserve tasting room. The reserve cabernet is stunning.

The tour takes visitors through the original aging cellar, a stone and timber building built by Chinese laborers. If you want to see a working winery, though, you'll be disappointed. The real action takes place across Hwy. 29 and it isn't open to the public.

BUEHLER VINEYARDS
Winemaker: John Buehler, Jr.
707-963-2155.
820 Greenfield Rd., St. Helena.
Tasting & Tours: By appt.
Tasting Fee: No.

"We're not at the end of the world," John Buehler, Jr., likes to say, "but you can see it from here." Buehler is not *that* remote, although it is secluded above the rocky hills that overlook Lake Hennessey. The bread and butter here is zinfandel, both a ripe and tannic red and a dry white.

Buehler, in fact, makes one of Napa's best white zinfandels. The cabernet sauvignon is rather inconsistent.

BURGESS CELLARS
Winemaker: Bill Sorenson.
707-963-4766.
1108 Deer Park Rd., St.
  Helena.
Tasting: 10–4 daily by appt.
Tours: 10:30 & 2:30 daily by
  appt.
Tasting Fee: No.

Built atop the vestiges of a stone winery that dates from the 1880s, Burgess has a low profile and likes it that way. High on the western slopes of Howell Mountain, the two-story stone and redwood winery is not one tourists happen upon. Tom Burgess began in 1972 and built a reputation for chardonnay and a firm and age-worthy zinfandel.

CAIN VINEYARDS & WINERY
Winemaker: Christopher
  Howell.
707-963-1616.
3800 Langtry Rd., off
  Spring Mtn. Rd., St.
  Helena.
Tasting & Tours: 11:30
  Thurs.–Sat. by appt.
Tasting Fee: No.

Asmall but elegant complex of buildings surrounding a courtyard, Cain Cellars sits on a ridge along Spring Mountain. The surrounding vineyards are largely devoted to Bordeaux grapes such as cabernet sauvignon, merlot, and malbec, which are used in red blends. The top wine is the reserve blend "Cain Five," a typically lush and seductive bottling that benefits from age. Cain Cuvée is similar but more modestly scaled and priced.

A tour at Charles Krug Winery includes a close look at the vineyards.

Tim Fish

CHARLES KRUG WINERY
Winemaker: Marc Mondavi.
707-963-5057.
2800 Main St. (Hwy. 29), St.
  Helena.

After working under Agoston Haraszthy in Sonoma, Charles Krug built Napa Valley's first winery in 1861. His massive stone winery was gutted by fire the day after it was finished but he rebuilt. When the Mondavi family bought Krug in 1943, another Napa dynasty began. Robert Mondavi began his own winery in 1966 after a family feud.

Tasting: 10:30–5
  Mon.–Thurs. & 10–6
  Fri.–Sun. (May–Oct.),
  10:30–4:30 Mon.–Thurs.
  & 10–5 Fri.–Sun.
  (Nov.–Apr.).
Tours: Daily except Weds.
Tasting Fee: $3; $6 for
  reserve.
Tour fee: $1.
Special Features: Picnic area.

The historic winery building, in disrepair for many years, has recently regained some of its former glory. Wines are still aged inside in its immense 80-year-old redwood tanks. The rest of the winemaking takes place in a facility just behind. The tour is one of the most thorough and educational in the valley, leading visitors into the vineyards and through the plant. Beginning wine tasters are put at ease here. The winery bottles one of the valley's most exhaustive menus of wines and its cabernet sauvignons have recently regained their former stature.

DUCKHORN VINEYARDS
Winemaker: Thomas
  Rinaldi.
707-963-7108.
3027 Silverado Trail, St.
  Helena.
Tasting & Tours: No.
Sales: 9–5 Mon.–Fri.

Even though tasting and tours are not offered at Duckhorn, fans often stop and have a gander nonetheless. Besides, there is a certain pleasure in buying wine at its source. Since its first release in 1978, Duckhorn has been the leading producer of merlot. All three bottlings are in high demand. Duckhorn makes two cabernet sauvignons and both display intensity and finesse. Its sauvignon blanc is also among the best. Their second label, Decoy, offers good bargains.

**EHLERS GROVE
  WINERY**
Winemaker: Don Spirlock.
707-963-3200.
3222 Ehlers Ln., off Hwy.
  29, St. Helena.
Tasting: 11–5 daily.
Tours: No.
Tasting Fee: No.
Special Features: Picnic
  area.

Once known as a ghost winery, Ehlers Grove is only the latest incarnation inside this grand fieldstone edifice built by Bernard Ehlers in 1886. Often empty over the years, the building has been home to Conn Creek, Saintsbury, and Vichon wineries. After a renovation in 1993, Stratford Winery took over and later adopted its current name. The emphasis is drinkable and fairly priced wines. There's a pleasant picnic area in a grove of olive trees.

**FLORA SPRINGS WINE
  CO.**
Winemaker: Ken Deis.
707-963-5711.
1978 W. Zinfandel Ln., St.
  Helena.
Tasting & Tours: 10–3 daily
  by appt.
Tasting Fee: No.

This handsome stone winery dates from 1888 when Scottish brothers James and William Rennie first made wine here. Later, Louis Martini used the winery to make sherry and age wine. Jerome and Flora Komes arrived in 1977. White wines dominate and the chardonnays display rich fruit. The wines don't always live up to their elaborate names and high prices. The "Soliloquy" sauvignon blanc is often out of balance and the red blend "Trilogy" can lack stuffing, yet the winery is starting to be impressive with its reserve cabernet sauvignon. "Floreal," the second label, offers solid bargains.

FOLIE À DEUX WINERY
Winemaker: Scott Harvey.
800-473-4454.
3070 St. Helena Hwy.
(Hwy. 29), St. Helena.
Tasting: 11–5 daily.
Tours: By appt.
Tasting Fee: No.
Special Features: Picnic
area.

If two psychologists opened a winery, what would they put on the label? An ink blot, of course. No, that's not a joke, that's Folie À Deux. It was conceived by two psychologists with a love of wine and a sense of fun. Its name translates as "Folly for Two," a delusion shared by two people. A yellow cottage sitting on a knoll covered with vines, Folie à Deux was a sheep ranch until grapes took over in 1981. It's a quaint spot with a wood porch and a fireplace in the living room. Try the dry chenin blanc, a fresh and melony boutique of spring flowers. We prefer it over the snobbier, more expensive chardonnays out there.

**FREEMARK ABBEY
WINERY**
Winemaker: Ted Edwards.
707-963-9694.
3022 St. Helena Hwy.
(Hwy. 29), St. Helena.
Tasting: 10–5 daily
(Mar.–Oct.), 10–4:30
Thurs.–Sun. (Nov.–Feb.).
Tours: Daily at 2.
Tasting Fee: $3.
Special Features: Picnic
area; gifts.

Freemark Abbey was a leader in the 1960s and '70s with its Bosche vineyard cabernet sauvignon, but the wine has lost its shine in recent vintages. The chardonnays suffered a similar fate but seem to be improving. An undisputed success is Edelwein Gold, a sweet Johannisberg riesling that's one of California's top dessert wines. Winemaking on the site dates from 1886 when Josephine Tychson built a wood winery, likely the first woman to build a winery in California. The present stone winery was built in 1895 and the tasting room is a lovely space with a wood-beam ceiling.

HEITZ WINE CELLARS
Winemaker: David Heitz.
707-963-3542.
436 St. Helena Hwy. (Hwy.
29), St. Helena.
Tasting: 11–4:30 daily.
Tours: Mon.–Fri. at 2 by
appt.; tours at 500 Taplin
Rd.
Tasting Fee: No.

Driving along Hwy. 29, you'd never know that a redwood shack on the outskirts of St. Helena is home to one of America's most coveted wines. But the wine faithful do and they line up every January to buy Heitz Martha's Vineyard Cabernet Sauvignon.

Curmudgeon and maverick, Joe Heitz worked at Beaulieu before going his own way in 1961. Within a few years, he refurbished a stone winery in the hills of the valley's east side, keeping the old winery on Hwy. 29 as a tasting room. The key to Heitz's success seems to lie in the vineyards. Martha's Vineyard is just west of Oakville and produces some of the valley's most distinctive grapes. (Not everyone cares for its minty quality.)

The modest tasting room features a library of old wines for sale, and typically two or three current wines are poured, seldom the good stuff. Heitz has a chardonnay and pinot noir that garners little notice, but its grignolino, a stout Italian varietal, has considerable charm.

**JOSEPH PHELPS
VINEYARDS**
Winemaker: Craig Williams.
707-963-2745.
200 Taplin Rd., off Silverado Trail, St. Helena.
Tasting & Tours: By appt. 11 & 2:30 Mon.–Fri.; 10, 11:30, 1, & 2:30 Sat.; 11 & 2 Sun.
Tasting Fee: No.

This winery pioneered bordeaux blends in California with its "Insignia" bottling and, except for a brief slump in the late 1980s, it has been among the best of the breed. Bordeaux blends, to explain, use the traditional grapes of that region: cabernet sauvignon, merlot, petit verdot, etc.

Phelps built his large and elegant redwood barn in 1973 and drew immediate attention. The current offerings include a toasty chardonnay and two nicely done cabernets. The Vin du Mistral label is devoted to one of Phelps's passions, Rhone wines, including a superb viognier.

**KORNELL CHAMPAGNE
CELLARS**
Winemaker: Greg Graham.
707-942-0859.
1091 Larkmead Ln., St. Helena.
Tasting: 10–4:30 daily.
Tours: 10–3:30 daily.
Tasting Fee: No.

With so many new extravagant French palaces out there, it might be easy to overlook this old champagne cellar. It would be your loss. To tour and taste wine at Kornell is to sample Napa circa 1960. Son of a Jewish winemaker, Kornell escaped from a German concentration camp and fled to America in 1940. In 1958, he took over the deteriorated Larkmead winery, built in 1906 and now on the National Register of Historic Places. Hanns died recently and the Kornell family no longer runs the place. While Kornell's sparkling wines are hardly our favorite, the winery is a pleasing and offbeat stop along the busy Napa trail.

MARKHAM WINERY
Winemaker: Robert Hunter.
707-963-5292.
2812 St. Helena Hwy.
(Hwy. 29), St. Helena.
Tasting: 10:30–5:30 daily
(summer), 10–4:30 daily
(winter).
Tours: No.
Tasting Fee: $3.

Founded in 1978, Markham quietly went about its business until the Japanese firm Sanraku took over in 1988. The wines were admirable but the winery was largely overlooked along Hwy. 29. Following a multi-million dollar facelift in the early 1990s, the winery and the wines began attracting considerable attention. Beyond large fountains is an expansive and newly affluent tasting room. The house specialties include merlot, cabernet sauvignon, chardonnay, and sauvignon blanc, all done with flair.

LOUIS MARTINI WINERY
Winemaker: Michael Martini.
707-963-2736.
254 St. Helena Hwy. (Hwy. 29), St. Helena.
Tasting & Tours: 10–4:30 daily.
Tasting Fee: No; reserve wines $5.

Run by the third generation of Martinis, this large but unostentatious winery is one of Napa Valley's best known. That's one of the charms of visiting Wine Country. You know the label, why not visit the source? Martini is one of the Valley's great overachievers, producing a voluminous roster that runs from cabernet sauvignon to sherry and other dessert wines. They're all capable and good values. Its top cabernet, Monte Rosso, has recently regained much of its glory.

Originating in Kingsburg, California, in 1922, Martini moved to St. Helena in 1933. Napa's first post-Prohibition success story, Martini flourished under founder Louis M. Martini, one the valley's great characters. Son Louis P. Martini brought the winery into the modern era and today his children, Carolyn and Michael, run it. The winery, like the wine, is a no-frills operation. Industrial outside, the winery's tasting room has a friendly staff and displays that sum up the Martini sense of family.

MERRYVALE VINEYARDS
Winemaker: Robert Levy.
707-963-7777.
1000 Main St., St. Helena.
Tasting: 10–5:30 daily.
Tours: By appt.
Tasting Fee: $3.
Special Features: Gifts, gourmet foods.

As Sunny St. Helena Winery, this historic stone cellar was the first winery built here after Prohibition, and in 1937 it was the Mondavi family's first venture into Napa Valley. It became home to Merryvale in 1985 when the building was renovated, updating its wine technology while retaining much of its historic charm. Done in rich wood, the tasting room feels like a large cabin and behind the iron gates you'll see the cask room with its massive 100-year-old cask. Robert Levy has a gift with many wines, particularly chardonnay and sauvignon blanc.

NEWTON VINEYARD
707-963-9000.
2555 Madrona Ave., St. Helena.
Tasting & Tours: 11 Fri. by appt.
Tasting Fee: No.
Special Features: Garden.

It's fitting that spectacular wines are produced from such a spectacular vantage point. Selling his interest in Sterling Vineyards, Peter Newton and wife Dr. Su Hua Newton carved out a new vineyard and winery on untamed scrub land high on Spring Mountain in 1978. The vineyards surround the winery on steeply terraced hillsides.

Newton has reproduced the lovely English-style gardens of his homeland and Su Hua contributed Chinese red lanterns and gates. There is a tank room at the bottom of a three-story pagoda; because of the building's shape, square tanks were required — highly unusual. Beneath all of this is an extensive cave system that stretches several stories down. As part of the tour, tastings are offered in a barrel aging corridor deep inside one cave. There is not an *average* wine produced at Newton. The merlot is consistently California's best and the cabernet sauvignon and chardonnays are marvelous.

PHILIP TOGNI VINEYARD
Winemaker: Philip Togni.
707-963-3731.
3780 Spring Mtn. Rd., St. Helena.
Tasting & Tours: By appt.
Tasting Fee: No.

Creating a name for himself as winemaker for Mayacamas, Chappellet, Chalone, and Cuvaison, Togni began making his own wine in 1983. His cabernet sauvignon is an assertive beauty that has a legion of fans. His sauvignon blanc is rather unusual, lean and too astringent for our tastes. Togni is a meticulous and hands-on winemaker and the winery is a modest affair.

PRAGER WINERY AND PORT WORKS
Winemaker: James Prager.
707-963-7678.
1281 Lewelling Ln., off Hwy. 29, St. Helena.
Tasting: 10:30–4:30 daily by appt.
Tours: No.
Tasting Fee: No.

Bored with plain chocolate (cabernet sauvignon) and vanilla (chardonnay)? Try this small family winery that produces six styles of port, including two whites. Port, of course, is a slightly sweet wine fortified with brandy. Prager also makes small amounts of cabernet and zinfandel and all the wines are organic. The winery is small and the atmosphere is low-key.

RAYMOND VINEYARD AND CELLARS
Winemakers: Walter Raymond & Kenn Vigoda.
707-963-3141.
849 Zinfandel Ln., St. Helena.
Tasting: 10–4 daily.

Though involved in the Napa Valley wine industry since the year Prohibition ended, the Raymond family didn't start their own winery until 1974. The winery is just off busy Hwy. 29 and has maintained a low profile despite its large production. The Raymonds sold a majority interest in the winery to Japan's Kirin in 1989 but the family

Tours: By appt.
Tasting Fee: No; reserve
wines $1.25.

**ROBERT KEENAN
WINERY**
Winemaker: Nils Venge.
707-963-9177.
3660 Spring Mtn. Rd., St.
Helena.
Tasting & Tours: 9–5
Mon.–Fri. by appt.
Tasting Fee: No.

**ROMBAUER
VINEYARDS**
Winemaker: Greg Graham.
707-963-5170.
3522 Silverado Trail, St.
Helena.
Tasting: 10–5 daily.
Tours: By appt.
Tasting Fee: No.

Headquarters for Napa Valley picnicking is V. Sattui Winery.

V. SATTUI WINERY
Winemaker: Rick
Rosenbrand.
707-963-7774.

remains involved. The cabernet sauvignon and chardonnay are always excellent efforts, and the tasting room is peaceful by Napa standards.

The old Conradi Winery, set in the shady slopes of Spring Mountain, was just a hollow stone shell when Robert Keenan reclaimed it in 1974. The circa 1904 building was reborn as a modern winery. The tasting room is a polished wood loft that runs the length of the building and above the stainless steel tanks and oak barrels. Merlot became Keenan's accidental star when the winery found itself with more merlot than it needed to blend with its cabernet sauvignon. They bottled it separately and it was a huge success.

Sequestered on a shady knoll off Silverado Trail, this family-owned winery is home to more than one wine label. The winery, built into the side of a hill, is one of Napa Valley's busiest custom-crush facilities, leasing most of its space to *homeless* winemakers. The focus is on cabernet sauvignon and chardonnay and they've had success and disappointment with both varieties.

Chris Alderman

Just about every winery has a picnic table tucked somewhere, but V. Sattui is Lawn Lunch Central. The tasting room doubles as a deli shop. The

St. Helena Hwy. (Hwy. 29),
  & White Ln., St. Helena.
Tasting: 9–6 daily.
Tours: By appt.
Tasting Fee: No.
Special Features: Deli, pic-
  nic area, gifts.

front lawn is shaded by tall oaks and filled with frolicking kids. Picnickers won't find a heartier welcome in Napa Valley.

While some wineries prefer simply to make wine and not deal with the public, V. Sattui is just the opposite. Its wines are available *only* at the winery. It's a busy place yet the atmosphere is cordial, not frantic. Though only completed in 1985, the Italian Romanesque winery looks like an old monastery.

V. Sattui is named for Vittorio Sattui, who founded a winery at a different location in 1885. It didn't survive Prohibition, but Vittorio's great-grandson, Daryl, revived the label in 1976. Popular wines here include a light and fruity Johannisberg riesling and a marvelous dry rosé named Gamay Rouge.

**SPOTTSWOODE
WINERY**
Winemaker: Pam Starr.
707-963-0134.
1209 Madrona Ave., St.
  Helena.
Tasting & Tours: Mon.–Fri.
  by appt.
Tasting Fee: No.

The first Spottswoode wines were made in 1982 in the basement of this estate's 1882 Victorian. Ripe and impeccably balanced, Spottswoode's cabernet sauvignon was quickly regarded as among the best in the '80s, a stature it retains today. Spottswoode's success is nearly matched with sauvignon blanc, a wine that's typically intense in citrus and mineral character. Run by the Novak family, Spottswoode is a small enterprise that welcomes devotees of fine cabernet.

**ST. CLEMENT
VINEYARDS**
Winemaker: Dennis Johns.
800-331-8266.
2867 St. Helena Hwy.
  (Hwy. 29), St. Helena.
Tasting: 10–4 daily.
Tours: By appt.
Tasting Fee: $2.

Built in 1878, St. Clement's exquisite Gothic Victorian was one of the earliest bonded wineries in the valley. Wine is no longer produced in the stone cellar. In 1979, a modern winery made of fieldstone was built in the hill behind the mansion, which now serves as a stately visitor center. The wide wood porch offers a soothing view of the valley below and wines are poured in a small parlor. It's so traditional and homespun, it's hard to fathom that St. Clement is owned by Sapporo, Japan's beer giant. The winery has an excellent record with chardonnay, cabernet sauvignon, and merlot. The citrusy sauvignon blanc is nicely done.

SUTTER HOME WINERY
Winemaker: Derek
  Holstein.
707-963-3104.
277 St. Helena Hwy.
  (Hwy. 29), St. Helena.

Who'd have thought back in the '70s that a simple, sweet rosé would become the Grail — some would say *Unholy* Grail — of California wine? Since white zinfandel became one of Wine Country's hottest commodities, Sutter Home has

The home of white zinfandel.

Tim Fish

Tasting: 9–5 daily.
Tours: Garden only.
Tasting Fee: No.

grown from one of Napa Valley's smallest wineries to one of its biggest.

Sutter Home's winery dates from 1874; since 1946, it has been owned and operated by Italian immigrant brothers John and Mario Trinchero. Until 1970, Sutter Home specialized in wine in bulk; its motto was, "If you can carry it or roll it through the front door, we'll fill it with wine." In 1972, winemaker Bob Trinchero began tinkering with a rosé-style zinfandel. Sutter Home called it white zinfandel and it became the best-selling variety in America.

There is no tour — wine is made in a factory up the road — but Sutter Home's tasting room is an expansive space that doubles as a folksy museum of wine and Americana. Visitors should try the *red* zinfandel, as well as the white; it's sturdy and tasty. There's also a line of non-alcoholic wines dubbed *Fre* (Free).

TUDAL WINERY
Winemaker: Arnold Tudal.
707-963-3947.
1015 Big Tree Rd., off Hwy. 29, St. Helena.
Tasting & Tours: By appt.
Tasting Fee: No.

A produce farmer squeezed by the urban sprawl of the East Bay in the early 1970s, Arnold Tudal bought a small walnut grove north of St. Helena and moved the family north. Well, selling walnuts was like working for peanuts, so Louis Martini talked Tudal in planting cabernet sauvignon. The fruit was so impressive that Tudal taught himself to make wine. The winery, a low-lying ranch house with a fieldstone fireplace, produces small amounts of excellent cabernet.

VIADER VINEYARDS
Winemaker: Tony Soter.
707-963-3816.
1120 Deer Park Rd., St. Helena.
Tasting & Tours: By appt.
Tasting Fee: No.

Delia Viader's 18-acre vineyard seems more suited to skiing than grape vines. High above the valley on a rocky 30-degree slope, the vineyard — amazingly — is not terraced. The vines struggle in shallow soil, but these stressed and scrawny vines produce impressive wines. Since her first vintage in 1989, Viader, a native of Argentina, has produced only a single wine, a polished blend of cabernet sauvignon and cabernet franc called "Viader."

WHITEHALL LANE
Winemaker: Gary Galleron.
707-963-9454.
1563 St. Helena Hwy. (Hwy. 29), St. Helena.
Tasting: 11–6 daily.
Tours: 1 & 4 daily.
Tasting Fee: $3.
Special Features: Picnic areas.

This handsomely modern winery, seemingly designed with geometric building blocks, is on its third owners since it opened in 1980. Winemaker Greg Galleron has spent time in the cellars of Chateau Montelena and Grace Family and he prefers elegance over flashy statements. Cabernet sauvignon and merlot are a house specialty. Wine is sampled from barrels during each tour.

Calistoga

CHATEAU MONTELENA
Winemaker: Bo Barrett.
707-942-5105.
1429 Tubbs Ln., Calistoga.
Tasting: 10–4 daily.
Tours: By appt.
Tasting Fee: $5.
Special Features: Picnic grounds.

"Not bad for a kid from the sticks," was all Jim Barrett said when Chateau Montelena jolted the wine world by winning the legendary Paris tasting in 1976. A who's who of French wine cognoscenti selected Chateau Montelena's 1973 chardonnay in a blind tasting over the best of Burgundy. Chateau Montelena's star has been shining brightly ever since.

No serious wine lover would think of leaving Chateau Montelena off the tour list. The wines are stunning and the winery is an elegant and secluded old estate at the foot of Mount St. Helena. Alfred Tubbs founded the original Chateau Montelena in 1882, its French architect using the great chateaux of Bordeaux as inspiration. The approach isn't too impressive, but walk around to the true façade and you'll discover a dramatic stone castle.

During Prohibition, the winery fell into neglect, but in 1958, a Chinese immigrant, Yort Franks, created the Chinese-style Jade Lake and the surrounding garden. Shaded by weeping willows, with swans and geese, walkways, islands,

The façade of Chateau Monte-lena is a classic.

Chris Alderman

and brightly painted pavilions, it is Napa's most coveted picnic spot. Saturdays and Sundays are booked months in advance.

In the handsomely paneled tasting room, three wines are typically poured; the selection varies. Chateau Montelena often pours its older cabernets to give tasters an idea of the wine in its prime. The chardonnays and zinfandels are usually the current vintage, and the chardonnays continue to live up to their reputation as intense, oaky, and lush.

Sharing the fruit of the vine at Clos Pegase.

Chris Alderman

CLOS PEGASE
Winemaker: John
  Quinones.
707-942-4981.
1060 Dunaweal Ln.,
  Calistoga.
Tasting: 10:30–5 daily.
Tours: 11 & 2 daily.

Clos Pegase is architecturally flamboyant, a post-modern throwback to the Babylonian temple; a shrine to the gods of art, wine, and commerce. This commanding structure of tall pillars and archways, in hues of yellow and tan, is the work of noted Princeton architect Michael Graves. It's an eye-catcher; some locals call Clos Pegase "Hollywood's idea of Egypt."

Tasting Fee: $2.
Special Features: Art
   collection.

The name, Clos Pegase, derives from Pegasus, the winged horse that according to the Greeks gave birth to art and wine. Owner Jan Shrem is an avid art collector. The tour offers a glimpse of the collection, including 17th- and 18th-century French statuary artfully displayed in the winery's massive underground cave. Also, a casual browse through the visitor center reveals great treasures.

Clos Pegase's wines include a ripe and complex cabernet sauvignon and a chardonnay that is typically refined but with plenty of forward fruit. A perennial star is the merlot.

CUVAISON WINERY
Winemaker: John Thacher.
707-942-6266.
4550 Silverado Trail,
   Calistoga.
Tours: By appt.
Tasting: 10–5 daily.
Tasting Fee: $3.
Special Features: Picnic
   area, gifts.

Cuvaison has been around since 1970 but has come into its own recently, particularly since the Schmidneiny family of Switzerland boosted quality by wisely investing in Carneros vineyards. Chardonnay is a specialty here but the cabernet sauvignon, merlot, and zinfandel are no wimps.

A white Mission-style building with a red-tiled roof, Cuvaison is bordered by vineyards and a splendid landscaped picnic area. The tasting room is busy but retains a friendly tone. Tasting begins with the chardonnay, usually a remarkable and elegant wine with rich fruit; the cabernet is equally vibrant, intense, and berrylike. Merlot is the current star.

**SCHRAMSBERG
   VINEYARDS**
Winemaker: Mike
   Reynolds.
707-942-4558.
1300 Schramsberg Rd., off
   Hwy. 29, St. Helena.
Tasting & Tours: By appt.
Tasting Fee: No.

No winery symbolizes the rebirth of Napa Valley better than Schramsberg. Jack and Jamie Davies are the quintessential post-Prohibition wine pioneers. When the Davieses bought the old Schramsberg estate in 1965, it was rich in history but near ruin. In 1862 Jacob Schram had established Napa's first hillside vineyard and winery and, with the help of Chinese laborers, built a network of underground cellars. After a few years of sweat equity, the Davieses became the country's premiere producer of *méthode champenoise* sparkling wine, and they remain one of the finest to date.

The grounds of Schramsberg are lovely. The tour offers insight into the winery's history and the art of making bubbly, but it is rather a lecture at times. The highlight is the old cellar caves lined with walls of bottles. In 1994, Schramsberg began offering tastings for the first time with its tour.

The distinctive architecture of Sterling Vineyards.

Chris Alderman

STERLING VINEYARDS
707-942-3344.
1111 Dunaweal Ln.,
 Calistoga.
Tasting: 10:30–4:30 daily.
Tasting: Yes.
Tours: Self-guided.
Tasting Fee: No.
Special Features: Aerial
 tramway to winery; $6
 adults, $3 ages 3–20.

Sterling isn't a just winery, it's an experience. A modern white villa perched atop a tall knoll, it just may be Napa Valley's most dramatic visual statement. Sure, there's a touch of Disneyland — you ascend on an aerial tramway — but that's Sterling's appeal. From the top, the view is unsurpassed.

Sterling retains such a contemporary look that it's hard to believe it was built in 1973. A well-marked self-guided tour allows a leisurely glimpse of the winery's workings and finally leads you to one of Napa's most relaxing tasting rooms. After picking up a glass at the counter — usually a sample of sauvignon blanc — visitors sit at tables inside or on the balcony. Once seated, the wines come to you. A varying selection is poured and most are solid efforts. Sterling can occasionally achieve greatness — particularly with its Reserve Cabernet — but inconsistency is a problem. Reserve wines are available to taste for an additional fee.

STONEGATE WINERY
Winemaker: David
 Spaulding.
707-942-6500.
1183 Dunaweal Ln.,
 Calistoga.
Tasting: 10:30–4:30 daily.
Tours: By appt.
Tasting Fee: None week-
 days; $1.50 Sat., Sun., &
 holidays.

The Spaulding family built this modest winery in 1973, but for more than 20 years there wasn't an actual stone gate to be found. Now the white stone arch is a familiar site along Dunaweal Lane. Stonegate relies heavily on estate-grown grapes; even so, the quality of wines varies from year to year. At its best, the Stonegate merlot is lush and the good cabernet sauvignon is ripe and with medium body.

**STORYBOOK MOUN-
TAIN VINEYARDS**
Winemaker: Jerry Seps.
707-942-5310.
3835 Hwy. 128, Calistoga.
Tasting & Tours: Mon.–Sat.
 by appt.
Tasting Fee: No.

Storybook devotes itself to one wine: zinfandel. The regular and the reserve bottlings are typically powerful and long-lived. Jacob and Adam Grimm — the Grimm Brothers, thus the Storybook name — made wine on the property back in the late 19th century. Jerry Seps restored it in 1976 and this small and unpretentious winery remains his baby. The wines reveal a hands-off attitude; the vineyards are organic and Seps tinkers little with the wine in the cellar.

**VINCENT ARROYO
WINERY**
Winemaker: Vincent
 Arroyo.
707-942-6995.
2361 Greenwood Ave., off
 Hwy. 29, Calistoga.
Tasting: 9–4:30 Mon.–Fri.,
 10–4:30 Sat. & Sun.
Tours: By appt.
Tasting Fee: No.

Talk about a one-man show. Vincent Arroyo does it all, from winemaker to cellar rat; he even built the winery himself in 1989. A visit to this small winery — only 2,000 cases are produced — is a peaceful change from the hectic Napa norm. There's no tasting room per se, but good-natured Arroyo is happy to offer a sample. His favorite is a strapping yet elegant petite sirah.

**VON STRASSER
WINERY**
Winemaker: Rudolf von
 Strasser.
707-942-0930.
1510 Diamond Mtn. Rd., off
 Hwy. 29, Calistoga.
Tasting & Tours: By appt.
Tasting Fee: No.

Its first release arrived in 1993, but von Strasser is already catching the eye of cabernet sauvignon fans. Rudy and Rita von Strasser own prime vineyard space on Diamond Mountain, a stone's throw from the famous Diamond Creek Vineyards. The cab is intensely built and production is minuscule — just under 1,000 cases. The von Strassers are immersed, tending the vineyards and hand-sorting the grapes.

SONOMA COUNTY WINERIES

Sonoma Valley

**ARROWOOD VINE-
YARDS AND WINERY**
Winemaker: Richard
 Arrowood.

When Chateau St. Jean was at its peak, the winemaker was Richard Arrowood, one of the first to make his name in an increasingly

707-938-5170.
14347 Sonoma Hwy. (Hwy. 12), Glen Ellen.
Tasting: 10–4:30 daily.
Tours: By appt.
Tasting Fee: No.

crowded field of celebrity winemakers. In 1986, Arrowood and wife Alis opened this winery and the wines have soared while Chateau St. Jean floundered. A gray and white farmhouse with a wide porch, the winery is built into a knoll and is deceptively small from the outside. A tour includes the usual crushing facilities, bottling line, and barrel room, ending with a tasting, on the porch if weather permits. The king here is chardonnay, round and complex. Cabernet sauvignon and merlot are also first-rate.

BARTHOLOMEW PARK WINERY
Winemaker: Antoine Favero.
707-935-9511.
1000 Vineyard Ln., Sonoma.
Tasting: 10–4:30 daily.
Tours: No.
Tasting Fee: No.
Special Features: Picnic area.

Agoston Haraszthy was the first to plant the classic grapes of France in the state. And this, as tradition holds, is the spot. The winery, a Spanish colonial, was originally a hospital for a women's penitentiary. In 1973, it was restored and became Hacienda Winery. Recently, the Hacienda brand was sold and now Bartholomew Park specializes in Sonoma Valley vineyards and sells the wine exclusively at the winery. The picnic grove is one of the best in Wine Country.

BENZIGER FAMILY WINERY
Winemaker: Joe Benziger.
707-935-3000.
1883 London Ranch Rd., Glen Ellen.
Tasting: 10–5 daily.
Tours: 12:30, 2 and 3:30 daily.
Tasting Fee: No.
Special Features: Picnic area, art gallery.

If this winery seems familiar, there's a reason. Millions know this spot along the gentle slope of Sonoma Mountain as Glen Ellen Winery, the king of the $5 bottle of vino. From a rundown grape ranch purchased from a naked hippie doctor in 1981, the Benziger clan built a multi-million dollar Goliath. Weary, they sold the Glen Ellen brand in 1994, but kept the ranch, which dates from 1860, and now concentrate on their premium Benziger label.

The Benzigers may have downsized but the winery grounds are more beautiful than ever. Past an old farm house and down the hill is the wooden ranch barn that serves as aging cellar and tasting room.

The tour is largely by motorized tram, leading visitors through the vineyards and grape crush facilities, with a final stop at the tasting room. The Benziger cabernet sauvignons can be a knockout in a good vintage and the citrusy sauvignon blanc is a winner. Benziger's Imagery series dabbles in more unusual wines, such as viognier, with intriguing results.

B.R. COHN WINERY
Winemaker: Charlie Tolbert.
707-938-4064.
15140 Sonoma Hwy. (Hwy. 12), Glen Ellen.
Tasting: 10–4:30 daily.
Tours: By appt.
Tasting Fee: No.

Manager for the Doobie Brothers and other rock bands, Bruce Cohn began a second career in wine when he bought Olive Hill Ranch in 1974. Cohn sold his grapes until 1984, when he bottled his first cabernet sauvignon. Ripe and concentrated, it was an immediate hit. Subsequent vintages have faired similarly, but his chardonnay and merlot are more routine. The tasting room, with a wood bar and terra cotta tiles, sits on a knoll covered with olive trees. Olive oil is Cohn's latest passion.

BUENA VISTA WINERY
Winemaker: Judy Matulich-Weitz.
707-938-1266.
18000 Old Winery Rd., Sonoma.
Tasting: 10:30–4:30 daily.
Tours: Daily at 2.
Tasting Fee: No; $3 for reserve wines.
Special Features: Picnic area, art gallery.

This is where it all began — California's oldest premium winery. Buena Vista is where Agoston Haraszthy, known as the father of California wine, began his experiments in 1857. Though others had made wine in Sonoma before this, they had used only the coarse mission variety grapes, brought north by Spanish missionaries for Mass wine. Haraszthy was the first to believe that the noble grapes of Bordeaux and Burgundy could thrive in California.

Visitors to Buena Vista stroll down a gentle quarter-mile path, past thick blackberry bushes and tall eucalyptus trees to the tasting room, set inside the thick stone Press House, built in 1863. Skip the official tour and read the courtyard displays on your own. The wine is made a few miles away.

Buena Vista's reputation has varied widely over the years and the winery rallied in the 1980s with some admirable cabernet sauvignons and chardonnays. While sampling the current releases, don't miss the Lake County sauvignon blanc, a lovely and lemony quaff.

CARMENET WINERY
Winemaker: Jeffrey Baker.
707-996-5870.
1700 Moon Mtn. Rd., Sonoma.
Tasting & Tours: By appt.
Tasting Fee: No.

This estate, high on a rocky and untamed peak of the Mayacamas Mountains, was an "alternative lifestyle community" before the Chalone Wine Group built Carmenet (pronounced *Car-men-ay*) in 1982. The winery is built of dark wood and recalls a modest chateau. The crush takes place under a large wooden pavilion and the surrounding hills are a quilt of vineyards. A tour includes a barrel tasting in the underground cellar, blasted from solid granite. Carmenet makes several bordeaux-style blends, all of fine quality. Try the colombard made from old vines. Delicious.

Chateau St. Jean is a modern version of a medieval French castle.

Chris Alderman

CHATEAU ST. JEAN
707-833-4134.
8555 Hwy. 12, Kenwood.
Tasting: 10–4:30 daily.
Tours: Self-guided.
Tasting Fee: No.
Special Features: Picnic
   area.

Surrounded by thick lawns and tall trees, with Sugarloaf Ridge in the distance, Chateau St. Jean is a visual treat. Opening in 1973, Chateau St. Jean drew immediate acclaim for its white wines, particularly the Robert Young Vineyard chardonnay, a luscious and oaky beauty that helped set the standard for chardonnay.

A slump came in the 1980s and the winery was purchased by Suntory of Japan; star winemaker Dick Arrowood left in 1990. Chateau St. Jean is now part of the corporation that owns Beringer, Chateau Souverain, Napa Ridge, and others. Ironically its red wines are now drawing attention.

The den-like tasting room is in a 1920s-era Mediterranean-style chateau. It's crowded on weekends, and the staff can get a bit harried. Be sure to sample the melony Johannisberg riesling or try a bottle with a picnic; the winery has one of Sonoma's best picnic grounds. The winery is a modern version of a medieval French castle. A self-guided tour offers a complete look at the works and ends in the tower where visitors can look out over Kenwood.

CLINE CELLARS
Winemaker: Matthew
   Cline.
707-935-4310.
24737 Arnold Dr. (Hwy.
   121), Sonoma.
Tasting: 10–6 daily.
Tours: By appt.
Tasting Fee: No.
Special Features: Picnic
   area.

Cline was Rhone before Rhone was popular. Fred Cline got started in the East Bay in 1982, preferring unsung grapes like carignane and mourvedre. Cline's Cotes d'Oakley and Oakley Cuvée — two zestful blends inspired by wines of the Rhone region in France — have been highly praised and rightly so. Cline took up shop in Sonoma's Carneros district in 1991 and the tasting room is inside an 1850s farmhouse with a wraparound porch. The pleasant grounds have duck ponds and rose gardens. Nearby, viognier and syrah, Cline's latest Rhone passions, are newly planted.

GLEN ELLEN WINERY
Winemaker: Peter McCullough.
707-939-6277.
Jack London Village, 14301 Arnold Dr., Glen Ellen.
Tasting: 10–5 daily.
Tours: No.

Someone else may have written the original book on making good, cheap wine, but Glen Ellen has certainly made a fortune on the revised edition. Sonoma County's largest winery, Glen Ellen struck gold in the mid-1980s with its low-priced Proprietor's Reserve wines. The Benziger clan sold the Glen Ellen brand in 1994 to Heublein, but kept its ranch up the road. Glen Ellen wines are made in Sonoma, and this tasting room doubles as a wine history center.

Enjoying a little bubbly at Gloria Ferrer Champagne Caves.

Chris Alderman

GLORIA FERRER CHAMPAGNE CAVES
Winemaker: Bob Iantosca.
707-996-7256.
23555 Arnold Dr. (Hwy. 121), Sonoma.
Hours: 10:30–5:30 daily.
Tours: 11–4 daily on the hour.
Tasting Fee: Sold by the glass.
Special Features: Gourmet food.

If you've had the pleasure of paying a mere $5 for Cordon Negro, the simple but tasty little sparkling wine in the ink-black bottles, then you already know the people behind Gloria Ferrer. Freixenet of Spain is the world's largest producer of sparkling wine and it was drawn to the great promise of California. Gloria Ferrer, named after the wife of Freixenet's president, makes consistently good bubbly at fair prices.

The Carneros location places Gloria Ferrer off the high-traffic areas. Sitting dramatically on a gentle slope of a hill, the winery is a bit of Barcelona done in warm tones of brown and red. The tasting room fireplace glows in the winter, and during the summer the terrace doors are pushed open to the cool breezes from nearby San Pablo Bay.

Gloria Ferrer's tour also has great appeal, particularly the caves carved from the hillside where the sparkling wine ages.

GUNDLACH-
BUNDSCHU WINERY
Winemaker: Linda Trotta.
707-938-5277.
2000 Denmark St., Sonoma.
Tasting: 11–4:30 daily.
Tours: Self-guided.
Tasting Fee: No.
Special Features: Picnic
area.

Passionate about wine and Sonoma Valley, Jim Bundschu does not take *himself* seriously. At a wine auction a few years back, he dressed as Batman and his winery's humorous posters are classic. He even hijacked the Napa Valley Wine Train and — gasp — gave samples of Sonoma Valley wine. Behind all this frivolity is great wine and rich history. Five generations have tended the winery's home vineyard Rhinefarm since 1858, but wine was not bottled from Prohibition until Jim restored the original stone winery in the early 1970s. Down a winding road, it's worth the trek. The zinfandels are luscious and assertive.

HANZELL VINEYARDS
Winemaker: Bob Sessions.
707-996-3860.
18596 Lomita Ave., off
Hwy. 12, Sonoma.
Tasting & Tours: By appt.
Tasting Fee: No.

The original boutique winery, Hanzell has greatly influenced California winemaking. The late Ambassador James Zellerbach, who founded the winery in 1956, patterned it after the chateaux of Burgundy. The winery, with its dark wood and pitched roof, was modeled after Clos de Vougeot and Hanzell was first in California to barrel ferment chardonnay and use French oak barrels for aging. The winery — which makes pinot noir, chardonnay, and cabernet sauvignon — has not always lived up to its old standards.

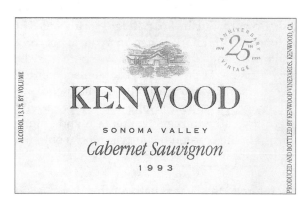

KENWOOD
VINEYARDS
Winemaker: Michael Lee.
707-833-5891.

Don't let Kenwood Vineyards fool you. The tasting room might be in a rustic little barn, but behind the simple charm is a large, savvy winery,

9592 Sonoma Hwy. (Hwy. 12), Kenwood.
Tasting: 10–4:30 daily.
Tours: Weds. 10 & 2:30 by appt.
Tasting Fee: No.
Special Features: Gifts.

one of Sonoma County's largest. Here is a homey and relaxed tasting room with wines that will please everyone in your group. Built by the Pagani Brothers in 1906, the current owners, Marty and Michael Lee and John Sheela, bought the place in 1970.

Kenwood doesn't really have a specialty. White or reds, they have luck with both. There's no better wine with fresh oysters than Kenwood's lemony sauvignon blanc. Try Kenwood's cabernet sauvignons, particularly the expensive but outstanding Artist Series, big wines with great aging potential. On occasional weekends, Kenwood matches a wine with a particular food, seeking to promote food and wine as partners.

KUNDE ESTATE WINERY
Winemaker: David Noyes.
707-833-5501.
10155 Sonoma Hwy. (Hwy. 12), Kenwood.
Tasting: 11–5 daily.
Tours: Sat. & Sun. by appt.
Tasting Fee: No.
Special Features: Picnic area, gifts.

Since 1904, five generations of Kundes have grown grapes, and for the first time since World War II, the clan began making wine again in the late 1980s. The Kundes have 2,000 acres of vineyards; they know the personality of each and put that to use. They also brought in a fine winemaker, David Noyes, who worked at Ridge for 10 years. The strengths so far are chardonnay, typically elegant and creamy, and a muscular zinfandel made from 100-year-old vines. The winery is a stylish white barn; in the hillside beyond, the Kundes have carved out a $5 million cave to age wine.

LANDMARK VINEYARDS
Winemaker: Eric Stern.
707-833-0053.
101 Adobe Canyon Rd., off Hwy. 12, Kenwood.
Tasting: 10–4:30 daily.
Tours: No.
Tasting Fee: No.
Special Features: Gifts.

This attractive Mission-style winery, in the shadow of Sugar Loaf Ridge, is a house of chardonnay. Landmark began in Windsor in 1974 but suburban squeeze forced a move south in 1989, when Damaris Deere Ethridge assumed control. Three chardonnays are currently on the menu and all are impressive. The tasting room is a tasteful space with a cathedral ceiling, fireplace, and granite tasting bar. The cloistered courtyard looks onto the western slopes.

MATANZAS CREEK WINERY
Winemakers: Susan Reed & Bill Parker.
707-528-6464.
6097 Bennett Valley Rd., Santa Rosa.

If you forego the beaten path for this winery, you won't regret it. Matanzas Creek is the only winery in Bennett Valley, a quiet, untouched fold of land west of Kenwood. The first wines were made in 1978 in a converted dairy barn; but these days, if you continue down the long driveway to the foot of

Tasting: 10–4:30 daily.
Tours: By appt.
Tasting Fee: No.
Special Features: Art
gallery.

the Sonoma Mountains, you'll find a state-of-the-art facility with a modest tasting room.

Matanzas Creek makes only three wines, each among the best in California, each inspired by its French counterpart. The chardonnay has the delicate finesse of a white burgundy and the sauvignon blanc is fragrant and flavorful. But the star here is the merlot, a lush, velvety ode to the classic bordeaux of the Pomerol region.

RAVENSWOOD WINERY
Winemaker: Joel Peterson.
707-938-1960.
18701 Gehricke Rd.,
   Sonoma.
Tasting: 10–4:30 daily.
Tours: By appt.
Tasting Fee: No.
Special Features: Picnic
   area, tour includes barrel
   tasting.

Cabernet sauvignon may be a passion, but zinfandel is an obsession. Cursed with a shady reputation by its evil twin, white zinfandel, red zinfandel was once a second-class citizen. Not anymore. At its best, zinfandel is luscious and jammy, equal to cabernet in most ways and at half the price. Zin lovers have long been wise to Ravenswood.

Ravenswood is an unassuming stone winery built into the side of a hill; the location fits the label, a classic image of a circle of ravens. The tasting room is modest in size and is warmed by a fire in cool months. The welcome, unfortunately, is inconsistent; the staff is jovial one trip, reluctantly civil the next. Also, Ravenswood rarely pours its top zinfandels (Cooke, Old Hill, Dickerson), but its regular zins — and its merlots and cabernet sauvignons — are reason enough to visit.

A sure way to sample the good stuff is to visit in the late winter and spring when the zins are still in the barrel. Ravenswood's tour typically includes barrel tasting. Since the winery is small, the tour is brief, but guides are detailed in their discussion of Ravenswood's natural approach to winemaking.

ROCHE WINERY
Winemaker: Steve
  MacRostie.
707-935-7115.
28700 Hwy. 121, Sonoma.
Tasting: 10–6 daily (summer), 10–5 daily (winter).
Tours: No.
Tasting Fee: No.

On the southernmost edge of Sonoma County, in the cool and foggy Carneros district, Roche occupies a lonely spot near San Pablo Bay. The long porch of the white ranch-style winery has an expansive view. Joe and Genevieve Roche planted wines in the early 1980s, even though popular wisdom said the area was too cold. Chardonnay and pinot noir, they discovered, thrive quite nicely and have become the house specialty.

**REMICK RIDGE
  VINEYARD**
707-833-1010.
9575 Sonoma Hwy. (Hwy.
  12), Kenwood.
Tasting: 10–4:30 daily.
Tours: No.
Tasting Fee: No.
Special Features: Gifts,
  gourmet foods.

When his career slowed in the 1970s, comedian Tommy Smothers bought a Kenwood ranch and planted grapes. Smothers Brothers wines soon followed, and over the years the fortunes of the wine have risen and fallen, depending on how distracted Tom was by comedy. Dick Arrowood makes the bulk of the wine now and recent vintages have been impressive. Wines are sampled at this country store, where you'll sometimes find Tom himself. In 1996, Smothers changed the winery's name to Remick Ridge.

**ST. FRANCIS WINERY
  AND VINEYARD**
Winemaker: Tom Mackey.
707-833-4666.
8450 Sonoma Hwy. (Hwy.
  12), Kenwood.
Tours: By appt.
Tasting: 10–4:30 daily.
Tasting Fee: Reserve wines
  only.
Special Features: Picnic
  area, gourmet foods.

Merlot is the current popular flavor, and St. Francis makes two of the best, a regular and a reserve. Both are gorgeous and full-bodied, with enough muscle to age a few years. Critics love them. Another success story for St. Francis is its chardonnay, done in a rich butterscotch style with great fruit. Its old-vines zinfandel packs a punch of brilliant fruit.

Vines have been planted on the property since 1910, though the vineyards date to 1973 and the first crush followed in 1979. The tasting room, in a small house near the winery, is warmed by a fire during the cool Sonoma winters. In the summer, the patio tables beckon with views of Sonoma Mountain.

SCHUG CARNEROS ESTATE
Winemaker: Walter Schug.
707-939-9363.
602 Bonneau Rd., off Hwy. 121, Sonoma.
Tasting: 10–5 daily.
Tours: By appt.
Tasting Fee: No.

Nestled against a windswept hill on the western edge of Carneros is a little bit of Germany. Architecturally, Schug's winery would be more at home along the Rhine, where the winemaker was raised. His wines, too, reflect his European heritage. Schug established his impressive credentials at Joseph Phelps, where he was winemaker from 1973 to 1983. His current wines, poured in a cozy tasting room, are winning, particularly his pinot noirs.

SEBASTIANI VINEYARDS
Winemaker: Mary Sullivan.
707-938-5532.
389 4th St. E., Sonoma.
Tasting: 10–5 daily.
Tours: 10:30–4:30 daily.
Tasting Fee: No.
Special Features: Picnic area, gifts.

For many people, Sebastiani is another way to spell Sonoma. It's the epitome of the county's wine tradition — an unpretentious family winery, big, old, and *Italian*. Sonoma County's largest winery — producing 6 million cases a year — Sebastiani is also one of its most popular tourist attractions.

The winery dates from 1896, when Samuele Sebastiani crushed his first grapes — zinfandel, to be precise — and the press he used is still on display in the tasting room. Samuele's son August, a man with an affinity for bib overalls and stout, simple wines, built the winery's reputation on inexpensive jug wines; since his death in 1980, the family has concentrated on premium wines.

Tours offer a thorough look behind the scenes, from the wine presses to the aging tanks. The highlight is the collection of intricately hand-carved wine casks. The spacious tasting room is partly crafted from old wine tanks. Visitors can taste Sebastiani's wide range of wines. Try the Sonoma County cabernet sauvignon and merlot, delightful wines and excellent bargains.

VIANSA WINERY AND ITALIAN MARKET PLACE
Winemaker: Sam Sebastiani.
707-935-4700.
25200 Arnold Dr. (Hwy. 121), Sonoma.
Tasting: 10–5 daily.
Tours: By appt.
Tasting Fee: No.
Special Features: Gourmet foods, gifts, picnic area.

Sam and Vicki Sebastiani split from the family dynasty a few years back and established this ode to Tuscany high atop a Carneros knoll. Done in warm shades with a terra cotta tile roof and Italian opera music in the background, Viansa is one of Wine Country's most festive spots. Even the stainless steel wine tanks are adorned with colorful faux marble frescoes. The marketplace offers sumptuous Italian picnic fare (see Chapter Five, *Restaurants & Food Purveyors*). Chardonnay and cabernet sauvignon are the backbone of the wine list and Viansa produces sound versions, but the most exciting wines are the Italian varietals. Viansa is having considerable success with nebbiolo, sangiovese, and barbera.

Russian River

ARMIDA WINERY
Winemaker: Frank
 Churchill.
707-433-2222.
2201 Westside Rd.,
 Healdsburg.
Tasting: 11–4 daily.
Tours: By appt.
Tasting Fee: No.

Three unique geodesic domes, this winery occupies the border of Dry Creek and Russian River valleys. After tasting, pause on the wooden deck to relish the view. One of Sonoma County's most recent additions, Armida bottled its first wine in 1990 and opened to the public in 1994, the same year that Steve Cousins, former president of Buena Vista, and his family took ownership. Wines include merlot, chardonnay, and pinot noir, all nicely done and fairly priced.

BELVEDERE WINERY
Winemaker: Kevin Warren.
707-433-8236.
4035 Westside Rd.,
 Healdsburg.
Tasting: 10–4:30 daily.
Tours: No.
Tasting Fee: No.
Special Features: Picnic
 area.

The patio of this winery is shaded by greenery; take your glass of chardonnay outside for a soothing sip. Chardonnay is the pillar at Belvedere, which opened in 1979. The winery's focus has recently shifted to value, offering excellent chardonnay, sound zinfandel, and cabernet sauvignon in the $7 to $10 range. Owner Bill Hambrecht draws from more than 400 acres of his own vineyards.

**CALIFORNIA COAST
WINE CENTER**
5007 Fulton Rd., off Hwy.
 101, Fulton.
Hours: 10–5 daily.
Tasting: Yes.
Special Features: Picnic
 area, gifts.

In 1996, Jess Jackson — the man behind Kendall-Jackson — bought Chateau DeBaun and made it the visitor's center for his California Coast Wine Center line of wines. Each of the 15 brands in California Coast Wine Center has its specialty and its own winemaker. Stonestreet emphasizes Alexander Valley cabernet sauvignon and merlot; Hartford Court's forte is Russian River Valley pinot noir and zinfandel, and Kristone is the most expensive American sparkling wine on the market, to list but a few.

CHALK HILL WINERY
Winemaker: Bill Knuttel
707-838-4306.
10300 Chalk Hill Rd.,
 Healdsburg.
Tasting & Tours: Mon.–Fri.
 by appt.
Tasting Fee: No.

The white soil gives the Chalk Hill area its name, even though it's really volcanic ash, not chalk. Fred and Peggy Furth established this winery well off the beaten path in 1980 and in 1990 hired talented winemaker David Ramey from Matanzas Creek. Ramey was snatched away by Dominus Estate in 1996. White wines thrive in the area and chardonnay is the winery's specialty; it ranges from average to excellent. The sauvignon blanc is consistently a beauty.

DAVIS BYNUM WINERY
Winemaker: Gary Farrell.
707-433-2611.
8075 Westside Rd.,
    Healdsburg.
Tasting: 10–5 daily.
Tours: No.
Tasting Fee: No.
Special Features: Picnic
    area, art gallery.

Davis Bynum has one of the finest winemakers in the business, Gary Farrell, who also bottles under his own name. It's no secret that Farrell's private label outshines Bynum's wine, yet both labels reveal Farrell's gift with just about every wine: pinot noir, zinfandel, chardonnay, you name it. Farrell's private label, unfortunately, is not sampled at the winery.

Set amid tall cool redwoods, Bynum relies on the characteristically restrained grapes of the region. These are subtle wines, not overly oaked, yet strong in varietal character. Bynum began making wine in Albany in 1965, moving to his present home in 1973. The building is rather utilitarian and the tasting room staff could be friendlier.

DEHLINGER WINERY
Winemaker: Tom
    Dehlinger.
707-823-2378.
6300 Guerneville Rd.,
    Sebastopol.
Tours: No.
Tasting: 10–5 daily.
Tasting Fee: No.

This country charmer of a winery is such a low-key affair that you might get the feeling that you're imposing when you visit. Not to worry. Certainly, if it's crush time, you might have to step around a portable grape press or a hose or two to get inside. But that's part of Dehlinger's appeal. Tom Dehlinger emphasizes wine first, to the great pleasure of the winery's devoted following.

As you might expect, Dehlinger has a limited production; it uses only its own grapes, producing about 10,000 cases a year. You will see Dehlinger's unusual octagonal house perched atop a vineyard knoll and just follow the winding gravel road to the low-lying redwood winery. Inside, you'll taste at a wooden bar, surrounded by barrels and aging tanks. Dehlinger has a knack with the grapes of Burgundy: chardonnay and pinot noir, two varieties that thrive in this region. The chardonnays are crisp and buttery and the pinots are snappy and berrylike.

DE LOACH WINERY
Winemaker: Max
    Gasiewicz.
707-526-9111.
1791 Olivet Rd., off River
    Rd., Santa Rosa.
Tasting: 10–4:30 daily.
Tours: 11 & 2 daily.
Tasting Fee: No.
Special Features: Picnic
    area.

Name the wine and De Loach has a knack for it. Its chardonnays, intense and fruity, are among the best. It also produces a masterly collection of zinfandels, made largely from old vines. De Loach's latest success story is sauvignon blanc, typically ripe and grassy. Cecil De Loach began making wine in 1975 while still a San Francisco fireman. Today, the tasting room is in a grand redwood building at the end of a long drive embraced by vineyards.

FOPPIANO VINEYARDS
Winemaker: Bill Regan.
707-433-7272.
12707 Old Redwood Hwy.,
   Healdsburg.
Tasting: 10–4:30 daily.
Tours: By appt.
Tasting Fee: No.

Five generations of Foppianos have tended vines here. John Foppiano arrived from Genoa in 1896 and planted a vineyard. Wine was sold in bulk and later in jug; the family began moving into premium wine in the 1970s. The winery is unabashedly utilitarian and the tasting room is in an unassuming wood cottage. The self-guided vineyard tour is worth a few minutes. Foppiano's stars are zinfandel and a beefy petite sirah made from old vines.

Hops were once dried in the towers of Hop Kiln Winery.

Kris White

HOP KILN WINERY
Winemaker: Steve Strobl.
707-433-6491.
6050 Westside Rd.,
   Healdsburg.
Tasting: 10–5 daily.
Tours: No.
Tasting Fee: Limited-
   release wines only.
Special Features: Picnic
   area, lake.

Hop Kiln began life as an ode to beer, not wine. Hops were a major crop along Sonoma County's Russian River at the turn of the century. This is one of the few remnants from that era. Built in 1905, the unusual stone barn is topped with three pyramid towers. Dr. Martin Griffin bought and restored the barn and began making wine in 1975.

The tasting room inside is rustic but pleasant, warm with wood and history. Tasters can choose from any number of wines. Zinfandel is a specialty and Hop Kiln makes a bold old-style zin that packs in the fruit. Its two generic wines are great bargains: A Thousand Flowers (white) and Marty Griffin's Big Red. Both are delightful, especially for a picnic. Outside, there is a small lake, bordered by a sunny patch of picnic tables — be prepared to share with the ducks.

**IRON HORSE
VINEYARDS**
Winemaker: Forrest Tancer.
707-887-1507.
9786 Ross Station Rd, off
Hwy. 116, Forestville.
Tasting & Tours: By appt.
Tasting Fee: No.

This winery amid the undulating hills of Green Valley is Sonoma County's most respected producer of sparkling wine. Barry and Audrey Sterling bought the estate, a former railroad stop, in 1976. Elegant in its sheer simplicity, the winery stretches through a series of wooden barns and is surrounded by vineyards and gardens. The tour reveals the classic *méthode champenoise* process used in making French-style bubbly. In addition to its line of opulent sparkling wine, Iron Horse produces chardonnay and pinot noir, both fine examples. Its fumé blanc is also a class act.

**JOSEPH SWAN
VINEYARDS**
Winemaker: Rod Berglund.
707-573-3747.
2916 Laguna Rd., off River
Rd., Forestville.
Tasting: 11–4:30 Sat. & Sun.,
weekdays by appt.
Tours: No.
Tasting Fee: No.

Hardly more than a bungalow, this modest structure belies Joseph Swan's near legendary status in Wine Country. Beginning in 1969, Swan was a pioneer of zinfandel, crafting heroically ripe and long-lived wines. Pinot noir became Swan's star in the 1980s. Swan died in 1989 and son-in-law Rod Berglund is now winemaker; although the zins are no longer legendary, they remain grand creations.

**KENDALL-JACKSON
WINE COUNTRY
STORE**
Winemaker: Steve Reeder.
707-433-7102.
337 Healdsburg Ave.,
Healdsburg.
Tasting: 10–5 daily.
Tours: No.
Tasting Fee: No.
Special Features: Gifts.

This storefront tasting room in downtown Healdsburg could be considered an outlet store. Kendall-Jackson is a Wine Country Goliath. What wine lover hasn't tried the eminently sippable Vintner's Reserve chardonnay? K-J wineries dot the countryside and include many labels, from Stonestreet to Cambria. The wine, overall, is reliable and occasionally superb and a varied selection is poured in the tasting room.

**KORBEL CHAMPAGNE
CELLARS**
Winemaker: Greg Gessner.
707-887-2294.
13250 River Rd.,
Guerneville.
Tasting: 9–5 May–Sept.,
9–4:30 Oct.–Apr.
Tours: 10–3 daily, on the
hour.
Tasting Fee: No.
Special Features: Picnic
area, gifts, garden.

As you drive through the gorgeous redwood forests of the Russian River area, you'll see this century-old, ivy-covered stone wine cellar rising nobly from a hillside. Korbel is one of Wine Country's most popular destinations, offering romance, history, and beauty.

In the summer, to avoid the crowds, arrive early in the morning or late in the afternoon. The half-hour tour is great fun. The Korbel brothers from Czechoslovakia came to Guerneville for the trees, which were perfect for cigar boxes. When the trees

The brandy tower at Korbel Champagne Cellars.

Kris White

were cleared, they planted grapes and made wine using *méthode champenoise*, the traditional French method of making champagne. You'll poke your nose in large wood aging tanks and learn the mystery of the riddling room where sediment is slowly tapped from each bottle. The tasting room is one of the friendliest and any or all of its dependable sparklers are offered. In the summer, Korbel's prized antique garden is also available for touring.

MARTINELLI WINERY
Winemaker: Steve Ryan.
707-525-0570.
3360 River Rd., Fulton.
Tasting: 10–5 daily.
Tours: By appt.
Tasting Fee: Limited-release wines only.
Special Features: Picnic area, gifts, art gallery.

This historic hop barn painted a vivid red is home to a prized zinfandel called Jackass Hill. The wine comes from the steepest hillside vineyards in Sonoma County, planted in 1905. Like many old-vine zins, it grabs your taste buds like a two-horse team. Four generations of Martinelli have been farming and the tasting room is a feast of apples, dried fruit, and other goodies.

MILL CREEK VINEYARDS
Winemaker: Hank Skewis.
707-431-2121.
1401 Westside Rd., Healdsburg.
Tasting: 11–4:30 daily.
Tours: No.
Tasting Fee: No.
Special Features: Picnic area.

It's hard to miss this tasting room, a redwood barn with a waterwheel. The Kreck family has been growing grapes since 1965 and bottled their first wine with the 1974 vintage. Mill Creek helped pioneer merlot but is not among the masters. Sauvignon blanc is the winery's best effort and it's a delightful companion for a picnic on the winery's deck.

**PIPER SONOMA
    CELLARS**
Winemaker: Rob McNeill.
707-433-8843.
11447 Old Redwood Hwy.,
    Windsor.
Tasting: 10–5 daily.
Tours: Self-guided.
Tasting Fee: Limited-
    release wines only.
Features: Art gallery.

Don't call it champagne! It's sparkling wine, please. To French vintners like Piper-Heidsieck, owners of Piper Sonoma, champagne can come *only* from the Champagne region of France. Yet even the French see the potential in California or they wouldn't have flocked here.

Housed in a sleek concrete and glass structure, this ultra-modern winery opened in 1982. The tasting room is a stylish café, where visitors are encouraged to sit and sample a sparkler. Visitors tour the winery along a concrete balcony that overlooks the entire plant, where the French technique of making sparkling wine called *méthode champenoise* is detailed.

**RABBIT RIDGE
    VINEYARDS**
Winemaker: Erich Russell.
707-431-7128.
3291 Westside Rd., Healds-
    burg.
Tasting: 11–4:30 daily.
Tours: By appt.
Tasting Fee: $2.
Special Features: Picnic
    area.

There's a sense of passion in the wines of Rabbit Ridge. This modest winery on the northern edge of Russian River Valley makes a vast list of wines, all consistently delightful. Mystique is a fragrant blend of sauvignon blanc, semillon, and Johannisberg riesling. Allure is a hearty yet elegant Rhone blend. The chardonnays are oaky and buttery and the zinfandel is jammy. Erich Russell, the former winemaker at Belvedere, opened his tasting room in a modern wooden barn in 1994.

**ROCHIOLI VINEYARDS
    & WINERY**
Winemaker: Tom Rochioli.
707-433-2305.
6192 Westside Rd., Healds-
    burg.
Tasting: 10–5 daily.
Tours: By appt.
Tasting Fee: No.
Special Features: Picnic
    area, art gallery.

The pinot noir vineyards of Rochioli are the envy of all winemakers. The top pinots in the business — Gary Farrell, Williams Selyem, and of course Rochioli — begin here. Three generations of Rochiolis (pronounced *Row-key-oh-lee*) have been growing grapes along the Russian River. They stay close to the land and because of that, make great wine. In the modest tasting room, which looks out across vineyards toward the river, every wine is a winner. The chardonnay is ripe and buttery and the sauvignon blanc flowery and complex.

**RODNEY STRONG
    VINEYARDS**
Winemaker: Richard Sayre.
707-431-1533.
11455 Old Redwood Hwy.,
    Healdsburg.
Tasting: 10–5 daily.

A dramatic pyramid of concrete and wood, this winery has weathered many incarnations but the constant has been Rodney Strong himself, a former Broadway dancer and a 30-year veteran of wine. The wines are reliable and occasionally superb, with cabernet sauvignon and pinot noir

Tours: 11, 1 & 3 daily.
Tasting Fee: No.
Special Features: Art
  gallery.

among the standouts. Balconies outside the tasting room reveal the winery process, so a tour may be academic. Windsor Vineyards, a sister winery, also makes wine here.

SEGHESIO WINERY
Winemaker: Ted Seghesio.
707-433-3579.
14730 Grove St., Healds-
  burg.
Tasting: By appt.
Tours: No.
Tasting Fee: No.

This no-nonsense winery makes some of the best bargains in Wine Country. Buying vineyards near Geyserville as far back as 1894, the Seghesio family sold wine in bulk until finally bottling their own wine in the early 1980s. Chianti Station, made from sangiovese vines planted early in the century, is Seghesio's masterpiece. The zinfandel, cabernet sauvignon, or chardonnay won't blow you away, but they are nicely done.

SONOMA-CUTRER
  VINEYARDS
Winemaker: Terry Adams.
707-528-1181.
4401 Slusser Rd., Windsor.
Tasting & Tours: By appt.
Tasting Fee: No.

Harvest is called "crush," yet crush is a crude way to describe how Sonoma-Cutrer makes chardonnay. *Pampering* is more like it. Grapes arrive in small boxes and are then chilled to 40 degrees in a specially designed cooling tunnel. Then they are hand-sorted and, left in whole clusters, are put through a gentle membrane press. A tour reveals the entire process, as well as an underground aging cellar.

Once the leader in California chardonnay, Sonoma-Cutrer now has keen competition. Brice Cutrer Jones, a jet fighter pilot in the Vietnam War, founded the winery in 1981 and built an ultra-modern facility that blends into the hills. Sonoma-Cutrer also has two world-class croquet courts.

TOPOLOS AT RUSSIAN
  RIVER VINEYARDS
Winemaker: Jac Jacobs.
800-TOPOLOS.
5700 Gravenstein Hwy. N.
  (Hwy. 116), Forestville.
Tasting: 11–5:30 daily.
Tours: By appt.
Tasting Fee: No.
Special Features: Restau-
  rant.

Hop kiln meets Greek Orthodox in this eccentric wood winery. The wines are equally offbeat, winning an equal number of fans and foes. Mike Topolos prefers hearty reds made from old vines. Zinfandel is the lead wine but Topolos also makes petite sirah and alicante bouschet, a full-bodied workhorse rarely bottled anymore. Sharing the winery building is a restaurant that specializes in Greek food.

WHITE OAK
  VINEYARDS
Winemaker: Ron Bunnell.

This small winery is within walking distance of Healdsburg plaza and the tasting room looks like just another house in the neighborhood. Bill

707-433-8429.
208 Haydon St.,
  Healdsburg.
Tasting: 10–4, Fri.–Sun.
Tours: By appt.
Tasting Fee: No.

Myers, a former Alaskan fisherman, opened the winery in 1981. The tasting room is tiny; turn around and you've taken the tour. The wines, though, are nicely done. Chardonnay and chenin blanc are the backbone, but the ripe zinfandel is garnering more notice.

WILLIAMS SELYEM
Winemaker: Burt Williams.
707-433-6425.
6575 Westside Rd.,
  Healdsburg.
Tasting & Tours: By appt.
Tasting Fee: No.

"**O**ur biggest problem," Burt Williams says, "is allocating the wine and trying to keep the customers happy. That's a good problem to have." Whining about allocations might seem pretentious if Williams Selyem wasn't such an unassuming enterprise. The winery, built in 1989, is a mundane building, basically one long room lit with fluorescents. There is no tasting room and no sign on the road, only a tiny plaque above the door. Yet wine lovers regularly make pilgrimages.

It's the *wine*, not the winery, that does the talking for Williams and Ed Selyem, who consistently produce some of the best pinot noirs in America. It's a hands-on, seat-of-your-pants affair, originating in a Fulton garage in 1981.

WINDSOR VINEYARDS
Winemaker: Carol Skelton.
707-433-2822.
239A Center St.,
  Healdsburg.
Tasting: 10–5 Mon.–Fri.,
  10–6 Sat. & Sun.
Tours: No.
Tasting Fee: No.
Special Features: Gifts.

If you've never heard of Windsor Vineyards, there's good reason. The wine is available only by mail order or at this storefront tasting room just off the Healdsburg plaza. The quality of the wine, however, belies such relative obscurity. Carol Sheraton is an ace winemaker, producing a vast line of wines, all consistently fine. The wine is made down the road at Rodney Strong.

Alexander Valley

**ALEXANDER VALLEY
VINEYARDS**
Winemaker: Hank Wetzel.
707-433-7209.
8644 Hwy. 128,
  Healdsburg.
Tasting: 10–5 daily.
Tours: By appt.
Tasting Fee: No.
Special Features: Picnic
  area.

Cyrus Alexander, who lent his name to this beautiful valley, built his homestead here. His adobe, constructed in the 1840s, remains. The Wetzel family planted vines in the early 1960s, and in 1975 a winery was built with a cool cellar carved into a hill and a gravity flow system that's less stressful to wine. The tasting room is homey, with chairs gathered around a fireplace. The cabernet sauvignons are elegant and easy to drink.

Chris Alderman

Chateau Souverain overlooks Alexander Valley.

CHATEAU SOUVERAIN
Winemaker: Ed Killian.
707-433-3174.
400 Souverain Rd.,
    Independence Ln. exit off
    Hwy. 101, Geyserville.
Tasting: 10–5 daily.
Tours: No.
Tasting Fee: No.
Special Features: Restau-
    rant, gifts.

The dramatic chalet was inspired by the old hop kilns that once spread across the Russian River Valley. As you climb the stairs and look out over the wide courtyard and huge fountain, the view of Alexander Valley is mesmerizing. Adding to the pleasure, the winery has an excellent café (see Chapter Five, *Restaurants*). Souverain's wines have improved dramatically in recent years, particularly the zinfandel and merlot. Prices remain modest.

Built by Pillsbury in 1973, Souverain has gone through a number of owners, with stability finally arriving in 1986 with Wine World Inc., a division of Nestle that also owns Beringer. The tasting room in the lower level of the east tower is a stylish spot with a lofty ceiling.

CLOS DU BOIS
Winemaker: Margaret
    Davenport.
707-857-3100.
19410 Geyserville Rd.,
    Geyserville.
Tasting: 10–4:30 daily.
Tours: By appt.
Tasting Fee: No.
Special Features: Gifts.

Clos du Bois, one of Sonoma's largest and most prominent wineries, seems to do everything well and a few things superbly. They may not produce big flashy wines but they're seldom disappointing, which is surprising considering the roster.

Vineyards are key to this success; the winery has access to some 1,000 prime acres in Alexander and Dry Creek valleys. The reserve chardonnays from the Calcaire and Flintwood vineyards are lush and steely, though we often prefer the straightforward character of the regular chardonnay. Its cabernet sauvignons are increasingly impressive, particularly the Winemaker's Reserve. The pinot noir and merlots are also contenders.

In late 1994, Clos du Bois moved its tasting room from a prefab warehouse in downtown Healdsburg to its winery just south of Geyserville. The tasting room is a friendly spot and the staff is knowledgeable yet they never roll an eye over novice questions.

FIELD STONE WINERY & VINEYARDS
Winemaker: Michael Duffy.
707-433-7266.
10075 Hwy. 128,
 Healdsburg.
Tasting: 10–5 daily.
Tours: By appt.
Tasting Fee: No.
Special Features: Picnic
 area.

Cozy inside an Alexander Valley knoll, this winery takes its name from the rugged stone that decorates the façade. Open the wide wooden door and amble past the oak barrels to the tasting room, and you've pretty much taken the tour. The house specialty is petite sirah from circa 1894 vines. It's a ripe bruiser. Cabernet sauvignon and zinfandel are also recommended. Superb picnic ground.

GEYSER PEAK WINERY
Winemaker: Daryl Groom.
800-255-9463.
22281 Chianti Rd.,
 Geyserville.
Tasting: 10–5 daily.
Tours: No.
Special Features: Picnic
 area, gifts.

The arrival of Australian winemaker Daryl Groom in 1989 put this once-sleepy winery on the map. A former winemaker for Penfolds, he cut his teeth on Grand Hermitage, one of the world's most respected wines. He has the touch, whether the wine is chardonnay or cabernet sauvignon. Groom's sauvignon blanc is one of the best and he is crafting his own little Grand Hermitage with a remarkable new reserve syrah.

Geyser Peak retains much of the rich Sonoma County tradition that Augustus Quitzow originated back in 1880. On the northernmost edge of Wine Country, Geyser Peak is an ivy-covered complex of old and new. The tasting room is constructed of old redwood tanks and the staff pours selections from Geyser Peak's large repertoire. Don't miss the soft Johannisberg riesling, which is ripe with lovely peachy fruit.

JORDAN VINEYARD & WINERY
Winemaker: Rob Davis.
707-431-5250.
1474 Alexander Valley Rd., Healdsburg.
Tasting: No.
Tours: 10 Mon.–Fri. by appt.

This spectacular French-style chateau rose from a former prune orchard in the mid-1970s to become one of Sonoma County's premiere wineries. Covered in ivy, the chateau seems like a grand classic, but inside is a state-of-the-art winery. The forest of towering wood tanks in its aging room are an impressive sight. Jordan's cabernet sauvignon is known for its elegance, and its bubbly "J" and chardonnay are increasingly impressive.

MURPHY-GOODE ESTATE WINERY
Winemaker: Christina Benz.
707-431-7644.
4001 Hwy. 128, Healdsburg.
Tasting: 10:30–4:30 daily.
Tours: No.
Tasting Fee: No.
Special Features: Gifts.

After nearly three decades of growing grapes, Tim Murphy and Dale Goode own some of the best vineyards in Alexander Valley and it shows in their wines. The house specialty is a crisp and complex fumé blanc, but Murphy-Goode manages every wine with finesse, from an elegant cabernet sauvignon to one of the best pinot blancs. Step away from the polished wood bar in the tasting room and peer through the picture window that overlooks the barrel room.

PEDRONCELLI WINERY
Winemaker: John Pedroncelli.
707-857-3531.
1220 Canyon Rd., Geyserville.
Tasting: 10–5 daily.
Tours: No.
Tasting Fee: No.
Special Features: Art gallery.

One of Sonoma County's oldest wineries — its origins date from 1904 — Pedroncelli is an old reliable. The winery and tasting room are agreeable but not elaborate. The wines are solid, though modestly scaled, and the prices are fair. Two generations of Pedroncellis tend the place. Try the cabernet sauvignon, fumé blanc, and zinfandel — all nicely done.

SAUSAL WINERY
Winemaker: David Demostene.
707-433-2285.
7370 Hwy. 128, Healdsburg.

Zinfandel is the top dog at this small winery. The Demostene family bought the ranch back in 1956 and inherited a plot of zinfandel that was planted before 1877. They began bottling in 1974 and the zin is full-bodied yet smooth. If you favor white zin, try Sausal's. The tasting room sits snugly

Tasting: 10–4 daily.
Tours: No.
Tasting Fee: No.
Special Features: Picnic
    area.

SILVER OAK CELLARS
Winemaker: Dan Baron.
707-857-3562.
24625 Chianti Station Rd.,
    Geyserville.
Tasting: 9–4:30 Mon.–Fri.,
    10–4:30 Sat.
Tours: 1:30 Mon.–Sat. by
    appt.
Tasting Fee: $5.

SIMI WINERY
Winemaker: Nick Gold-
    schmidt.
707-433-6981.
16275 Healdsburg Ave.,
    Healdsburg.
Tasting: 10–4:30 daily.
Tours: 11, 1, & 3 daily.
Tasting Fee: Reserve wines
    only.
Special Features: Gifts.

TRENTADUE WINERY
Winemaker: Chris
    Gebhardt.
707-433-3104.
19170 Geyserville Rd.,
    Geyserville.
Tasting: 10–5 daily.
Tours: No.
Tasting Fee: No.

among the vineyards and the vine-covered patio is a soothing spot to sip.

In 1992, cabernet sauvignon specialist Silver Oak turned the former Lyeth Winery into the new home for its Alexander Valley cab. Consider it Silver Oak West. The winery with its steeply pitched roof and flagstone courtyard remains an elegant spot. While only the Alexander Valley bottling is produced here, all of Silver Oaks wines are poured when available. For the full scoop on Silver Oak, see Oakville/Rutherford earlier in this chapter.

If we had to choose only one winery to visit — akin to limiting yourself to one glass of champagne on New Year's Eve — that would be a tough call. We vote for Simi, an alluring combination of history and hi-tech. You never feel as though herded through a factory, even though the winery is hardly small. The staff knows wine but doesn't lord it over you. And best of all — the wines are first rate.

Hidden in a shady grove of trees on the northern outskirts of Healdsburg, Simi has had a history as shaky as it is long. Italian immigrants Pietro and Giuseppe Simi built the original stone winery in 1890 and called the spot Montepulciano. Over the years, changes in ownership brought good times and bad, until French giant Moet-Hennessy bought Simi in 1981 and restored its former glory.

Simi gives one of the best tours, offering peeks at everything from the oak barrel aging room to the bottling line. The tasting room is a cordial spot. Try the sauvignon blanc, always delightful, and the rich and buttery reserve chardonnay. More impressive still are the cabernet sauvignons.

Trentadue makes Arnold Schwarzenegger wines: massive muscular reds that won't be taken lightly. The Trentadue family has been making wine since 1969, favoring hearty classics like carignane and sangiovese. After a spotty history, wine quality took a leap in the 1990s. The tasting room is packed with gifts and picnic supplies, which you

Special Features: Picnic area, gifts, gourmet food.

can put to fine use in the trellis-covered picnic patio.

Dry Creek

White wines are the specialty at Alderbrook Winery

Chris Alderman

ALDERBROOK WINERY
Winemaker: Bob Cabral.
707-433-5987.
2306 Magnolia Dr., Healdsburg.
Tasting: 10–5 daily.
Tours: By appt.
Tasting Fee: No.
Special Features: Picnic area.

With its wraparound porch, bleached pine interior, and fireplace, Alderbrook's tasting room is a touch of New England in Wine Country. Not that Alderbrook specializes in stout reds perfect for cool Vermont nights. White wine is the house forte and the sauvignon blanc and chardonnay are consistently solid, but merlot and pinot noir are increasingly impressive.

A. RAFANELLI WINERY
Winemaker: Dave Rafanelli.
707-433-1385.
4685 W. Dry Creek Rd., Healdsburg.
Tasting & Tours: By appt.
Tasting Fee: No.

If you want to try one of the best zinfandels in Wine Country, a trip to this small folksy redwood barn is a requirement. The wines are nearly impossible to find otherwise. Rafanelli epitomizes old school Sonoma County: good wine, no fuss. Visits are soured only by the uninterested youths who sometimes welcome guests. The Rafanellis have been growing grapes for generations and began making wine in 1974, believing their vineyards, not a winery with hi-tech gadgets, did the talking.

DRY CREEK VINE-YARDS

Winemaker: Larry Levin.
707-433-1000.
3770 Lambert Bridge Rd.,
Healdsburg.
Tasting: 10–4:30 daily.
Tours: No.
Tasting Fee: No.
Special Features: Picnic
area, gifts.

Dry Creek Valley, we've always imagined, is what Napa Valley used to be: small, quiet, unaffected by it all. Driving or pedaling along the peaceful roads, moving from one discovery to the next, is a true pleasure. One of the best stops is this winery that takes its name from the region. Designed after the small country wineries of France, Dry Creek has always reminded us of a simple country chapel, ivy-covered, with a pitched roof, and set amid a lush lawn and shady trees.

It only adds to the pleasure that Dry Creek's wines are consistently fine, often exceptional, as you'll discover in the tasting room. The atmosphere is laid-back and the staff is chatty. Visitors can choose four samples from the winery's impressive list — not an easy task. Dry Creek has made its name with fumé blanc, a marvelous, crisp wine that dominates the winery's production. The chenin blanc is so fruity and distinctive that we prefer it over many chardonnays. As for reds, the zinfandel is always one of the best and the cabernet sauvignon has fine character and can be exceptional in a good vintage.

FERRARI-CARANO VINEYARDS AND WINERY

Winemaker: George
Bursick.
707-433-6700.
8761 Dry Creek Rd.,
Healdsburg.
Tasting 10–5 daily.
Tours: By appt.
Tasting Fee: $2.50.
Special Features: Gifts.

One of the rising stars in California wine, Ferrari-Carano surprised everyone when it entered the scene in the mid-1980s. Chardonnay, of course, is its flagship, a big, lush, complex wine. The fumé blanc is impressive in its own right, while the cabernet sauvignon and merlot are both solid efforts.

Don and Rhonda Carano own the Eldorado Hotel and Casino in Reno so their arrival in Wine Country has been a dramatic one. Situated in northern Dry Creek Valley, Ferrari-Carano is an exclamation point. Villa Fiore, the winery's visitor center, was completed in late 1994 and is an extravagant Mediterranean palace surrounded by brushy lawns, flowers, and vineyards. The tasting room has a faux marble floor and a mahogany and black granite tasting bar. Visitors can descend the limestone staircase to what is possibly the most opulent underground cellar in Wine Country.

J. FRITZ WINERY

Winemaker: David
Hastings.
707-894-3389.
24691 Dutcher Creek Rd.,
Geyserville.

This winery, in the farthest reaches of northern Sonoma Wine Country, is built like a bunker into the side of hill. Well off the road and hidden amid the scrub trees, J. Fritz blends into the countryside. J. Fritz takes zinfandel quite seriously and

Tasting: 10:30–4:30 daily.
Tours: By appt.
Tasting Fee: No.
Special Features: Picnic area, gifts.

it relies on gnarly old vines to make a burly yet graceful zin. Chardonnay and sauvignon blanc are generally fine examples; try the melon, a white that's easy to quaff.

Lambert Bridge Winery is an intimate stop along West Dry Creek Road.

Chris Alderman

LAMBERT BRIDGE WINERY
Winemaker: Julia Iantosca.
707-431-9600.
4085 W. Dry Creek Rd., Healdsburg.
Tasting: 10:30–4:30 daily.
Tours: By appt.
Tasting Fee: No.
Special Features: Picnic area.

Quaint is a woefully overused word, but we can't think of a better way to describe Lambert Bridge. This romantic little winery, with redwood siding and a porch shaded by wisteria, is a comfortable fit among the oaks and vines covering the hillsides that overlook Dry Creek.

Step inside the winery and you're enveloped in darkness and cool air. As your eyes adjust, you find yourself inside a cavernous room, lined with cedar and stacked to its pitched ceiling with oak barrels. An expansive wood tasting bar, added in 1993, subtracts from the former coziness. Open since 1969, Lambert Bridge has maintained a low profile. Chardonnay is a specialty and it's a rich, juicy style with considerable oak. We've never been impressed with its cabernet sauvignon or merlot, finding both rather blunt and harsh.

MAZZOCCO VINEYARDS
Winemaker: Phyllis Zouzounis.

This winery is hardly a visual treat, but it occupies prime zinfandel land. Founded by Tom Mazzocco in 1984, the winery has weathered ups and downs but one constant has remained — great

707-431-8159.
1400 Lytton Springs Rd.,
    Healdsburg.
Tasting: 10–4:30 daily.
Tours: By appt.
Tasting Fee: No.
Special Features: Picnic
    area.

PRESTON VINEYARDS
Winemaker: Kevin Hamel.
707-433-3372.
9282 W. Dry Creek Rd.,
    Healdsburg.
Tasting: 11–4:30 daily.
Tours: By appt.
Tasting Fee: No.
Special Features: Picnic
    area, gifts.

QUIVIRA VINEYARDS
Winemaker: Grady Wann.
707-431-8333.
4900 W. Dry Creek Rd.,
    Healdsburg.
Tasting: 10–4:30 daily.
Tours: By appt.
Tasting Fee: No.
Special Features: Picnic
    area, gifts.

**RIDGE/LYTTON
    SPRINGS WINERY**
Winemaker: Paul Draper.
707-433-7721.
650 Lytton Springs Rd.,
    Healdsburg.
Tasting: 11–4 daily.
Tours: No.
Tasting Fee: No.

zinfandel, big and spicy yet with considerable finesse. Cabernet sauvignon and chardonnay also have charm. The tasting room is a friendly spot.

On the northern edge of Dry Creek Valley, this out-of-the-way winery has been quietly redefining itself in recent years. Lou and Susan Preston began as growers in 1973, specializing in grapes cherished by old Italian farmers: zinfandel, petite sirah, and barbera. A winery followed two years later and Preston made its name with zin and sauvignon blanc. Rhone varietals are the latest emphasis. The viognier is flowery yet dry and complex. The syrah is substantial yet elegant.

The tasting room of this grand California barn was expanded a few years back and it's a comfortable spot, but we miss sipping among the barrels and tanks. There's a plush lawn for picnicking just off the tasting room porch.

Quivira was a wealthy kingdom of legend that explorers believed was hidden in what is now Sonoma County. While the name belongs to antiquity, this Quivira is a modern winery inside and out. Winemaker Doug Nalle, who left in 1989 to concentrate on his own superb zinfandel, set a high standard with zin and sauvignon blanc that Quivira has managed to maintain.

Nervous its cherished supply of Lytton Springs zinfandel grapes would be sold to someone else, Ridge Vineyards purchased this winery in 1991. Lytton Springs still bottles under its own label, but Ridge winemaker Paul Draper oversees production. The corrugated metal winery is not much to see and the tasting bar is tucked behind the stainless steel tanks, but if you like bold and jammy zins made from old vines, it's the place to stop. Selected Ridge wines are sampled. Hours vary in the winter, so call ahead.

Learning the Lingo: A Wine Glossary

No one expects you to be an expert when you're wine tasting, but just in case, here's a cram course in the words of wine, how to say them, and what they mean.

Appellation — A legally defined grape growing region. Alexander Valley, for example, is an appellation.

Blanc de Blanc (*blonc-deh-blonc*) — A sparkling wine made from white grapes, usually chardonnay. Delicate and dry.

Blanc de Noirs (*blonc-deh-nwahr*) — A sparkling wine made from red grapes, usually pinot noir. Sometimes faintly pink. Fruity but dry.

Blush — A pink or salmon-colored wine made from red grapes. Juice from red grapes is actually white. Red wine derives its color from juice left in contact with the grape skin. The longer the contact, the darker the wine.

Brut (*broot*) — The most popular style of sparkling wine. Typically a blend of chardonnay and pinot noir. Dry.

Cabernet Franc (*cab-er-*nay-*fronc*) — Red wine of Bordeaux, similar to cabernet sauvignon but lighter in color and body.

Cabernet Sauvignon (*cab-er-*nay-*so-vin-yon*) — Red, fragrant, and full-bodied grape of Bordeaux. Dry and usually tannic. Can age in the bottle 5 to 10 years.

Chardonnay (*shar-do-*nay) — California's most popular white grape, famed in France as the essence of white burgundy. Produces wine that is fruity, with hints of citrus or butter.

Chenin Blanc (shen-*nin-blonc*) — A white grape that produces a wine that's more delicate and less complex than chardonnay. Slightly sweet.

Crush — Harvesting and pressing of grapes. The beginning of the winemaking process.

Estate bottled — Wines made from vineyards owned or controlled by the winery.

Fermentation — The conversion of grape juice into wine, using yeast to change sugar into alcohol.

Fumé blanc (fu-*may-blonc*) — Same as sauvignon blanc. The name has traditionally been used to describe a dry-style sauvignon blanc.

Futures — Wines sold prior to release and delivered later. Usually at a discount.

Gewürztraminer (*geh-*vurz-*trah-me-ner*) — A white grape that yields a medium-bodied, semi-sweet, and lightly spicy wine.

Johannisberg Riesling (*jo-*hahn-*is-berg-*rees-*ling*) — A white grape that produces a delicate wine, medium-bodied, semi-sweet, with a melony fruit taste.

Late harvest — Sweet dessert wine made from grapes left on the vine longer than usual. *Botrytis cinerea* mold forms, dehydrating the grapes and intensifying the sugar content.

Malolactic fermentation — A second fermentation that converts tart malic acids to softer lactic acids.

Merlot (*mer-*lo) — Increasingly popular red grape from Bordeaux. Similar to cabernet sauvignon, but softer and more opulent.

Méthode champenoise (*meh*-thowd-*sham-pen*-nwas) — Traditional French champagne-making process. Still wine is placed with sugar and yeast into a bottle and then sealed. The yeast devours the sugar, creating bubbles. The wine then "sits on the yeast," or ages in the bottle several years. Finally, the yeast is extracted and the sparkling wine — never once removed from its original bottle — is ready to drink.

Oak — Wine aged in oak barrels picks up some of the smell and taste of the wood. Also contributes to tannins and long aging. Example: "That chardonnay has too much oak for my taste."

Petite Sirah (*peh*-teet-*syr-awh*) — Dark, rich, intense red wine.

Pinot Noir (*pe*-no-*nwahr*) — Silky, fruity, dry red wine that makes the great burgundy of France.

Reserve — A term traditionally used to mean wine held back or reserved for the winery owners, but the meaning has become vague in recent practice. It's now sometimes used to mean better quality grapes, or wine aged longer in oak barrels.

Residual sugar — Unfermented sugar that remains in the wine. Wine is considered sweet if it contains more than half a percent by weight.

Riddling — Process used to extract yeast from sparkling wine. A laborious process that slowly shakes deposits to the neck of the bottle, where they can be removed without disturbing the wine.

Sangiovese (san-jo-*vay*-ze) — The sturdy and often spicy red grape used in chianti.

Sauvignon Blanc (so-*vin-yon-blonc*) A crisp, light white wine with hints of grass and apples.

Semillon (sem-me-*yawn*) A cousin to sauvignon blanc, the two are often blended together.

Sparkling wine — Generic term for champagne. Technically, real champagne can come only from the Champagne region of France.

Syrah (*syr-awh*) — Ruby-colored grape of the Rhone region in France. Smooth, yet with rich and massive fruit.

Tannic — The puckery sensation caused by some wines, particularly young reds. Comes from the skin and stalk of the grapes, as well as oak barrels. It's thought to further a wine's ability to age.

Varietal — A wine named after the grape variety from which it's made. Example: chardonnay is a varietal, bordeaux is not. (Bordeaux is a region in France; bordeaux wine can contain a number of varietals: cabernet sauvignon, merlot, etc.)

Vintage — The year the grapes for a particular wine are harvested. Non-vintage wines can be blends of different years.

Viognier (*vee*-own-*yay*) — This highly perfumed white wine is surprisingly dry on the palate. Native to the Rhone area of France, it is increasingly chic in California.

Viticultural area — A wine-growing region. Russian River Valley, for example, is a viticultural area of Sonoma County.

Zinfandel (*zin-fan-dell*) — A spicy and jamlike red wine. A California specialty. Used also to make a blush wine called white zinfandel.

The Four Ss and a P:
The Unpretentious Art of Wine Tasting

"I know how to taste wine," you say. "Put the glass to your lips and swallow, right?" We can't argue with that method. On the other hand, there is an intricate tasting process that experts use — but there's no need for the casual taster to be *that* correct, either. However, we would like to offer a few tips that will help even novices savor wine more fully. First, understand that palates and preferences are different, but you can distinguish chardonnay from chenin blanc in much the same way you can differentiate pork from beef.

Sight: Hold the glass up and consider the color. Red wines, for example, don't look the same. Pinot noir can be a soft shade of strawberry, while zinfandel is often as dense as blackberry jam.

Swirl: There's a good reason wineries only pour a small amount — aside from the fear of going broke, that is. You can't swirl a full glass without making a puddle. Lightly swirl the glass for a moment and you'll be surprised how the wine changes. When the wine is infused with air it releases its aroma.

Sniff: Take a whiff. Your nose is a key player in wine tasting. First, ask yourself, is the aroma pleasant or not? Some wines have very subtle bouquets, while others will rush your nostrils like linebackers. One is not necessarily better than the other. Wines have characteristic smells. Sauvignon blanc, for example, may smell like freshly mown grass.

Sip: Don't take a big gulp. Swish it around your mouth, adding more air to the wine and exposing it to all your taste buds. Is it sweet or dry? Bitter or sour? A cabernet sauvignon, for example, might make you pucker. Those are tannins which help the wine age. Try to sort out the sensations on your tongue. Chardonnay may have an almost buttery taste and pinot noir may taste lightly of cherry, with a lingering silky sensation.

Pour: We couldn't think of another S-word. Expert tasters always Spit — without it, they'd be passed out on the floor. You don't need to do that, but we would encourage you to take a sip or two and then pour out the rest. Tasting rooms don't mind at all; In fact, they provide buckets especially for it. Also, remember you don't have to try *every* wine, particularly if you're stopping at a lot of wineries.

Sonoma County Wine and Visitor Center

A great idea in a questionable location. Rohnert Park, a place of suburbs and discount shopping, is not exactly the heart of Wine Country. If you're looking for tourist information, however, this is a convenient stop. Part of the Red Lion shopping complex, the visitor center is open 10 to 5 daily and is just off the Golf Course Drive exit of Hwy. 101. The center is home to the Sonoma County Wineries Association and a selection of wines is offered for sale and tasting. There is also a demonstration vineyard and winery, and various displays and maps on the wines, wineries, and history of the county. A similar wine center is in the works for the city of Napa. **Sonoma County Wine and Visitor Center:** 707-586-3795; 5000 Roberts Lake Rd., Rohnert Park.

CHAPTER SEVEN
On the Run
RECREATION

It's so beautiful in Wine Country that a pleasant, leisurely drive is enough activity for most visitors. Rolling hills laced with vineyards, fertile valleys, a breathtaking coastline, and a mild climate — no wonder so many people are drawn to Napa and Sonoma. But there's more than wine and landscapes. If you crave activity, you'll keep busy. From long hikes through a gentle wilderness to rides above it all in hot air balloons, there are recreational activities to fit every style, taste, and budget.

Chris Alderman

Rockhopping at Shell Beach on the Sonoma Coast.

AUTO RACING

Yes, racing in Wine Country. It's our version of Indianapolis 500, where you can experience the thrill of watching the fastest cars in the world. Sears Point Raceway offers speed aplenty in its year-round schedule, which includes races for the hottest factory-backed sports cars, warp speed dragsters, motorcycles, and even vintage cars. **Sears Point International Raceway** (707-938-8448; at the junction of Hwys. 37 & 121, Sonoma).

BALLOONING

Ballooning: ready to ride the sky at dawn.

Ernest Lewin/Courtesy Sonoma County Convention & Visitors Bureau

S oaring silently above the vineyards and rolling hills of the Wine Country in a hot air balloon is an experience you won't quickly forget. Rides start early in the day, before surface winds interfere with the launch, and each ride is unique, depending on the whim of the winds.

Some balloon companies provide pickup at your lodging; most provide continental breakfast and a champagne brunch following the ride. Prices vary, but expect to spend about $155 per person. Reservations are necessary.

For a real balloon extravaganza, take in Sonoma County's Hot Air Balloon Classic each June, when 50 balloons fill the sky over the vineyards in Windsor (see "Seasonal Events" in Chapter Four, *Culture*).

Napa County

Above the West (800-627-2759; Yountville) Pickup from San Francisco and Napa Valley hotels; champagne breakfast; family owned & operated.

Adventures Aloft (707-944-4408; Yountville) Champagne flights daily; Napa Valley's oldest balloon company; seen on TV show "Falcon Crest."

Balloon Aviation of Napa Valley (800-367-6272; Yountville) Flights daily; champagne and brunch flights also available.

Napa Valley Balloons (800-253-2224; Yountville) Launches from Domaine Chandon winery; fleet of 14 balloons; picnic brunch and champagne flights.

Once In a Lifetime (800-659-9915; Calistoga) Flights daily; champagne brunch; walking distance from Calistoga spas.

Up, Up, and Away!

It's 6am. A group of early risers fends off the chilly dawn air with hot coffee, waiting for their ballooning adventure to begin. While the balloon isn't in the air yet, anticipation *is*, as the balloon pilots and helpers unroll expanses of magnificent colored fabrics onto the open field. Before long, giant fans are steadily blowing air into the flat balloons, held open by the pilots. There are signs of life as the balloons grow slowly, like whales rising above the water's surface. But they are still earthbound. Only when the pilot lights his propane burner and begins to heat the trapped air do the balloons rise.

The heated air, lighter than the cold air around it, gradually lifts the weight of the fireproofed nylon fabric, and within 15 minutes one balloon is inflated, standing on the open field — enormous, beautiful. Six or seven passengers hop into the basket with the pilot and the lines are released.

Slowly the balloon heads skyward, changing the perspective of the passengers until they can see the other balloons below them on the field, then buildings around the field, then hills in the distance. There is no sensation of movement since they move with the wind; there is no sound except for the barking of a dog below or an occasional "whoosh" from the pilot's burner to keep the air heated.

The balloon follows the wind effortlessly, drifting over the countryside with the pilot's gentle guidance; he can "find" different currents to ride, like a canoe on a fast-moving stream, but can't change direction at will. He can turn the balloon in a circle, by opening flaps in the balloon with pulleys, but can't choose his landing place.

After about an hour's flight, the pilot allows the air to cool, and the balloon slowly descends. The pilot maneuvers the balloon to avoid trees while finding an open field for landing. The balloon lands gently; there is usually no more than a gentle bump, though occasionally passengers will get tumbled out of the basket — an undignified though not harmful way to return to earth. The company's vans or trucks have followed the trip from below and are immediately on hand to secure and empty the balloon and load everyone in for the ride back.

The disappointment of returning to earth is diminished by a glass or two of champagne and a gourmet brunch designed to complete a memorable experience.

Sonoma County

Air Flamboyant (800-456-4711; Santa Rosa) Operating since 1974; complimentary champagne; brunches.

Wine Country Balloon Safaris (800-759-5638; Santa Rosa) Romance flights for two; champagne; custom videos.

BICYCLING

Exploring Wine Country back roads on two wheels.

Courtesy Sonoma County Convention & Visitors Bureau

Want to slow the pace of your Wine Country tour? Try a bike. With terrain that varies from meandering valleys to steep mountains and a spectacular coastline, there are roads and trails to satisfy everyone from the most leisurely sightseer to ambitious bike fanatics.

Mountain bicycling, which started in Marin County just to the south, is extremely popular in Wine Country. Annadel State Park, at times, has more mountain bikes than runners on its trails, and Austin Creek is also a favorite spot in Sonoma County. Mountain cyclists in Napa County head for Skyline Park (Napa) and Mount St. Helena.

Serious enthusiasts race in a number of annual events, including the *Cherry Pie Race* (a 15-year Napa tradition) and the *Terrible Two* (a grueling 208-mile course in Sonoma County). Charity races are popular in both counties. Most bike shops have information.

Many local parks have extensive bike trails, including *John F. Kennedy Park* (707-257-9529; Napa), *Skyline Wilderness Park* (707-252-0481; Napa), *Ragle Regional Park* (707-527-2041; Sebastopol), and *Spring Lake County Park* (707-539-8092; Santa Rosa).

Bicyclists of every level are welcome to join the *Santa Rosa Cycling Club*'s weekend jaunts. The club meets every Saturday and Sunday (weather permitting) at 9am at the Santa Rosa High School parking lot, and specific ride info can be picked up at local bike shops.

So, rent a bicycle, pack a picnic lunch, and explore a park; or point your wheel toward the nearest country road and enjoy the scenery you would miss from your car. Two excellent guides for specific trails are *Sonoma County Bike Trails* and *Rides In and Around the Napa Valley*.

BIKE RENTALS

Many inns offer bikes for casual day trips and most bike shops rent two-wheelers for the day. Also, **Gateway Adventures and Bike Shop** (800-GO-4-ADVENTURE; 1117 Lincoln Ave., Calistoga, and 20 Healdsbvurg Ave., Healdsburg) delivers bikes to inns in Napa and Sonoma counties and suggests routes and includes helmets, etc.

Napa County

Napa Valley Cyclery: 707-255-3377; 4080 Byway E., Napa
Palisades Mountain Sport: 707-942-9687; 1330B Gerrard, off Washington, Calistoga
St. Helena Cyclery: 707-963-7736; 1156 Main, St. Helena

Sonoma County

Rincon Cyclery: 707-538-0868; 4927 Sonoma Hwy., Santa Rosa
Spoke Folk Cyclery: 707-433-7171; 249 Center St., Healdsburg
Sonoma Valley Cyclery: 707-935-3377; 20079 Broadway, Sonoma

BOATING & WATER SPORTS

The dry summer season may be crucial to growing great grapes, but it also means Napa and Sonoma are anything but wetlands. Man, as usual, devised a way around nature, creating reservoirs for community water supplies and for the delight of water-sport fans.

Napa County

LAKE BERRYESSA

The largest man-made lake in the area, Lake Berryessa is about 15 mi. E. of Rutherford along Hwy. 128. Some 26 mi. long, it's one of northern California's most popular water recreation areas. Berryessa features seven resorts offering complete facilities: full-service marinas, boat rentals for the avid fisherman, sailboats, water ski and jet ski equipment, and overnight accommodations from tent and RV camping to top quality motels. Houseboats are available for rent at Markley Cove for leisurely overnights on the water. Water ski instruction for beginners through competitive-level skiers is available at **Willi's World Class Water Ski Center** (707-966-2441), run by German champion Willi Eller-

Water skiing on Lake
Berryessa; Willi Ellermeier,
champion ski instructor at
Steele Park Resort.

Courtesy World Class Water Ski Center

meier, at the Steele Park Resort. For complete information about the area's offerings, call the **Lake Berryessa Chamber of Commerce,** 800-726-1256.

Lake Berryessa Marina Resort (707-966-2161) Boat launching, campsites, RV hookups, boat rentals, jet skis.

Markley Cove Resort (707-966-2134) Boat launching, boat rentals (including houseboats), water and jet ski rentals; no camping.

Putah Creek Park (707-966-0770) Boat launching, campsites, RV hookups, boat rentals, motel.

Rancho Monticello Resort (707-966-2188) Boat launching, campsites, RV hookups, boat rentals.

Spanish Flat Resort (707-966-7700) Boat launching, campsites, boat rentals, water and jet ski rentals.

Steele Park Resort (800-522-2123) Boat launching, campsites, RV hookups, boat rental, water ski rental, school, motel.

Sonoma County

LAKE SONOMA

Sonoma County's Lake Sonoma, 11 mi. N. of Healdsburg on Dry Creek Rd., offers 3,600 surface acres of scenic recreational waters. There are many secluded coves for the quiet boater or angler, while water and jet skiers are allowed in designated areas. Facilities include a public boat ramp, a full-service marina, campsites, hiking trails, swimming areas, and a visitor center and fish hatchery near the Warm Springs Dam. For information, try the *Lake Sonoma Visitor Center* (707-433-9483) or *Lake Sonoma Marina* (707-433-2200), which offers boat rentals, including fishing, paddle, sail, ski, canoes, and jet skis.

Canoeing on Spring Lake, Santa Rosa.

Kris White

RUSSIAN RIVER

Since the Pacific Ocean is chilly and the surf a bit rugged (See "The Coast" in this chapter), the Russian River is a good alternative for a leisure day on the water. Canoes and kayaks can be rented near Healdsburg or Guerneville for a leisurely trip, stopping to relax or swim along the way. Don't be surprised if you spot a few nude sunbathers. The county doesn't condone it, but the freewheeling '60s still live in West County.

Burke's Russian River Canoe Trips (707-887-1222; River Road at Mirabel, 1 mi. N. of Forestville) Leisurely 10 mi. trip to Guerneville; $28 per canoe, shuttle included. Closed mid-Oct. to April.

California Rivers and Kiwi Kayak Company (707-838-8919; 10070 Old Redwood Hwy., Windsor) One-person Kiwi kayaks are rented by the day ($20 weekdays, $22 weekends). These kayaks are more stable and easier to handle than many; they're very portable and can be driven to any river or lake in Wine Country.

W.C. Trowbridge Canoe Trips (800-640-1386; 20 Healdsburg Ave., Healdsburg) Choice of 7 routes, from 5 to 11 miles; $34 per canoe; shuttle available. Also offers overnight trips.

OTHER SITES

Lake Ralphine (707-543-3292; Howarth Park, Santa Rosa) A popular spot for water activities, from sailboating to feeding ducks. Stocked with fish, this small man-made lake has a city-run boat rental, where rowboats, canoes, paddleboats, and sailboats (experienced sailors only) are available for a minimal fee. Sailing classes are held during the summer. Power boats are not permitted.

Reeling one in from the shore at Spring Lake.

Kris White

Spring Lake (707-539-8092, off Montgomery Dr. in Santa Rosa) A lovely 75-acre lake open only to canoes, rowboats, and sailboats, all of which can be rented during the summer. Windsurfing and rafting are also allowed. There is a separate lagoon for swimming.

CAMPING

Wine Country campgrounds and RV parks are plentiful for the adventurous who like to "rough it." Camping may be a low-key affair, but don't be laid-back about reserving a spot. Camp sites fill up quickly in the summer months. Reservations, in fact, are mandatory at most California state parks and

Stoking the morning campfire in Wine Country.

Kris White

beaches, and are accepted up to eight weeks in advance or as late as 48 hours prior to the first day of the reservation, if space is available. State campgrounds are noted with an asterisk (*) in the listing.

Camping fees in Wine Country state parks vary with the season and the park. (Fees in late 1994 ranged from $12 to $21 per night per campsite.) As a rule, campgrounds described as "developed" have flush toilets, hot showers, drinking water, improved roads, and campsites with a table and stove or fire ring. Primitive campsites usually have chemical or pit toilets, tables, and a central water supply. Environmental campsites are primitive sites in undisturbed natural settings. En-route campsites are day-use parking areas where self-contained trailers, campers, and motor homes may park overnight.

To make reservations in state campgrounds, call **MISTIX** at 800-444-7275. Discover, Master Card, Visa, or American Express will hold your campsite; there is a $6.75 service fee for making reservations.

Fees at privately operated parks and resorts are generally $12 to 20 per night for tent camping, and from $27 to $30 per night for RV sites with hookups.

Napa Valley

*Bothe–Napa Valley State Park (707-942-4575; 3801 St. Helena Hwy. N., Calistoga 94515; midway bet. St. Helena & Calistoga off Hwy. 29) This 1,920-acre state park has 48 developed campsites. Campers up to 31 ft. and trailers to 24 ft. can be accommodated; a sanitation station is provided. Horseback riding trails, hiking, swimming pool, picnic area, and exhibits. Handicap-accessible in all areas.

Calistoga Ranch Campground (707-942-6565; 580 Lommel Rd., Calistoga 94515; SE. of Calistoga off Silverado Trail on Lommel Rd.) A 167-acre park with 150 campsites for tents, RVs (full hookups), and trailers. Olympic-size swimming pool, fishing lake, hiking trails, picnic areas, restrooms with showers, laundry, and snack bar.

Napa County Fairgrounds (707-942-5111; 1435 Oak St., Calistoga 94515) Camping, showers, RV hookups, dump station.

Napa Town & Country Fairgrounds (707-253-4900; 575 3rd St., Napa 94558) RV parking with full hookups and dump station.

Napa Valley RV Resort (707-252-7777; 500 Lincoln Ave., Napa 94558; 1.4 mi. E. of Hwy. 29 on Lincoln Ave. in Napa) Dubbed "a luxurious RV park," this paved resort open year-round has 145 pull-through and back-in spaces, all with full hookups. Laundromat, mini-mart, snack bar, jogging paths.

Putah Creek Resort (707-966-2116; 7600 Knoxville Rd., Napa 94558; Hwy. 128 to Knoxville Rd. at Lake Berryessa.) A full-service resort with 200 campsites, 55 RV sites, and 26-unit motel. Grocery store, restaurant and lounge, delicatessen, snack bar. Also a marina with fishing supplies, bait shop, and rentals.

Rancho Monticello Resort (707-966-2188; 6590 Knoxville Rd., Napa 94558; on Knoxville Rd. about 4 1/2 mi. off Hwy. 128) Travel trailer and camping sites with RV hookups. Restaurant, beer garden, fishing boat rentals, grocery, snack bar.

Spanish Flat Resort (707-966-7700; PO Box 9116, Napa 94558; Hwy. 128 to Knoxville Rd., Lake Berryessa) 120 lakeside tent and RV sites, sanitation station, restroom with showers, convenience store, and snack bar.

Sonoma County

*Austin Creek State Recreation Area (707-869-2015; Armstrong Woods Rd., Guerneville 95446; 3 mi. N. of Guerneville) A rugged, natural setting of 4,230 acres with just 24 primitive hike-in campsites. Trailers and campers over 20 ft. prohibited.

Bridgehaven Campground (707-865-2473; PO Box 56, Jenner 95450; S. of Jenner on Hwy. 1) On the Russian River near the coast. 41 tent, trailer, and RV sites in a quiet setting. Just off River Rd., with easy access to both wineries and coastal attractions.

Casini Ranch Family Campground (707-865-2255; PO Box 22, Duncans Mills 95430; 22855 Moscow Rd., off Hwy. 116 at Duncans Mills, 1/2 mi. E. on Moscow Rd.) A family campground on the Russian River with 225 pull-through spaces, many riverfront sites. Boat and canoe rentals, fishing, swimming, playground, general store, laundry.

KOA San Francisco North (707-763-1492; 20 Rainsville Rd., Petaluma 94952; Old Redwood Hwy. exit off Hwy. 101, W. to Stony Point Rd., N. to Rainsville Rd.) A 60-acre rural farm setting with 312 tent and RV sites with full hookups. Swimming pool, hot tub, convenience store, laundromats, playground, camping cabins.

River Bend RV & Campground (707-887-7662; 11820 River Rd., Forestville 95436; about 10 mi. W. of Hwy. 101 on River Road) Full-service with hookups, general store, canoe rentals; 24-hour on-site security.

The ***Sonoma Coast State Beach** encompasses 5,000 acres, with two developed campgrounds — Bodega Dunes and Wrights Beach — and two primitive sites: Willowcreek and Pomo. *Bodega Dunes Campground* (707-875-3483 or 707-865-2391; Bodega Bay 94923; 1/2 mi. N. of Bodega Bay on Hwy. 1) The larger of the two state beach campgrounds with 98 developed campsites. Trailers and campers up to 31 ft.; a sanitation station is provided. Picnicking, hiking, fishing, horseback riding, and exhibits. Most facilities wheelchair-accessible. *Wrights Beach Campground* (707-875-3483 or 707-865-2391; Bodega Bay 94923; 6 mi. N. of Bodega Bay on Hwy. 1) 30 developed campsites; 11 environmental campsites; trailers to 24 ft. and campers to 27 ft. allowed. Picnicking, hiking, fishing, horseback riding, and exhibits. No showers. Some facilities wheelchair-accessible. ***Willowcreek Campground*** (707-875-3483 or 707-865-2391; Bodega Bay 94923; Willowcreek Rd., 1 ¹/₂ mi. off Hwy. 1) 12 undeveloped camping sites, a small hike from your car. Picnic tables and fire rings. No showers. Chemical toilets. ***Pomo Environmental Campground*** (707-875-3483 or 707-865-2391; Bodega Bay 94923; Willowcreek Rd., 3 mi. off Hwy. 1) 20 undeveloped camping sites, a small hike from your car. Picnic tables and fire rings. No showers. Chemical toilets. First-come, first-served — no reservations.

Hiking a coastal trail in Salt Point State Park.

Richard Hensley/Courtesy Sonoma County Convention & Visitors Bureau

*Salt Point State Park (707-865-2391 or 707-847-3221; 25050 Coast Hwy. 1, Jenner 95450; 20 mi. N. of Jenner on Hwy. 1) 130 developed campsites (no showers); 10 hike-in tent sites, and 30 en-route sites on 5,970 acres. Trailers and campers over 31 ft. prohibited.

Sonoma County Fairgrounds (707-545-4200; 1350 Bennett Valley Rd., Santa Rosa 95401; at intersection of Hwy. 101 & Hwy. 12 E.) Full hookups for RVs; tent campers welcome. Restrooms, showers, picnic areas. In the heart of town near freeway; traffic noise could be disruptive.

*Sugarloaf Ridge State Park (707-833-5712; 2605 Adobe Canyon Rd., Kenwood 95452; 7 mi. E. of Santa Rosa on Hwy. 12, N. on Adobe Canyon Rd.) A 2,500-acre park with 50 developed campsites, nature trail, hiking, horseback riding trails, and exhibits. Trailers and campers to 22 ft.

THE COAST

Sonoma County's 62-mile coastline has a rustic beauty which is scarcely changed from the days when the Miwok and Pomo Indians were the only inhabitants. Not that the white man hasn't left his mark. Early Russians settlers

The Sonoma coastline is one of the most stunning in California.

Courtesy Sonoma County Convention & Visitors Bureau

in the 1800s decimated the sea otter population for the highly prized pelts. Now under government protection, the sea otter is slowly making a comeback — although much to the distress of abalone divers who compete for the otters' favorite food. The Americanization of California, along with the population surge after the Gold Rush, created a need for timber, so the giant redwoods near the coast were heavily harvested. Lush forests, thankfully, remain.

Visitors flock to the Sonoma Coast to enjoy some of the most spectacular views in all of California. The rugged cliffs, continually battered by the wild Pacific Ocean, afford a setting of breathtaking beauty. Thanks to the foresight of those who fought to preserve public access to the coast, there are many outlets from which to view the ocean along Hwy. 1. Particularly popular is the stretch between Bodega Bay and Jenner, where several beaches offer a variety of topography and vistas for hiking, picnicking, wetsuit diving, surfing, or just relaxing.

Whatever your activities, it is always important to remember that the Pacific Ocean can be dangerous. Every year there are deaths caused by unpredictable waves and the strong undertow. Be cautious.

Bodega Bay Harbor offers protection from the rough Pacific surf and is the home port for many commercial fishing boats. Gaining fame as the setting of Alfred Hitchcock's *The Birds,* the town of Bodega Bay has now become a well-known stopover and destination spot for residents and visitors alike. Sport-fishing, harbor cruises, and whale-watching trips can be arranged from Porto Bodega Marina, off Hwy. 1 on Bay Flat Rd. The gentle beaches on the west side of the harbor afford a perfect spot for windsurfing or sea kayaking.

BEACHES

Here are some of the beaches along the coast, listed from north to south. For detailed information, call the **Sonoma County Convention Visitors Bureau** (707-586-8100). Some of the beaches have a day-use fee.

The Bodega Headlands (707-875-3483; at the end of Bay Flat Rd., off Hwy. 1, Bodega Bay) Originally part of the Sierra Nevadas, it stretches like a curved arm out to sea. For 40 million years it has ridden the Pacific Plate northward, out of step with land on the other side of the San Andreas fault. The cliffs of the Headlands provide a spectacular vista of the Pacific and the coast and is a favorite spot to watch for whales in the winter and early spring. Not a bad idea to bring binoculars and a jacket. Also of interest at the Headlands is the *Bodega Marine Lab* (707-875-2211), open to the public on Fridays from 2 to 4pm. Very educational and kids will love it.

Doran Regional Park (707-875-3540; Doran Beach Rd., off Hwy. 1, S. of Bodega Bay) A popular family spot because of its level sandy beach and overnight camping facilities. An annual sand castle competition is held every August. Day-use fee.

Salt Point State Park (707-847-3221; 25050 Hwy. 1, N. of Timber Cove) 4,114 acres along five mi. of shore, offering picnicking, fishing, skin diving, hiking, and horseback riding. More than 14 mi. of trails wind through tall forests, windswept headlands, a stunted Pygmy Forest, and grassy valleys along the San Andreas fault. Camping is available. Adjacent to the park is Kruse Rhododendron State Reserve. In May and June, the brilliant pink blossoms of native rhododendrons brighten the forest along the path.

Goat Rock Beach (707-875-3483; Off Hwy. 1, So. of Jenner) Named for the huge beach rock that bears a resemblance to the hunched back of a grazing goat. The beach extends from the sand bars along the mouth of the Russian River, where sea lions and their young haul out along the river at certain times of the year. They're fun to watch, but please don't disturb them.

Sonoma Coast State Beach (707-875-3483; Salmon Creek, Bodega Bay) This is actually a chain of many beaches along 18 mi. of coastline, from Goat Rock to Bodega Head. Each has its own personality and invites different activities, whether it's tide pooling or a serious game of volleyball. Wildflowers brighten the cliffs in the spring. The coast is always cool in the summer, supplying an escape from inland heat.

SCUBA DIVING

Scuba diving is a popular water sport along the Sonoma Coast. The water temperatures, ranging from 40 to 55 degrees, make a full wetsuit a minimum requirement, with many divers preferring dry suits for added comfort. Diving is a year-long activity, as long as the sea is calm. Divers must respect the power of the ocean.

Abalone can be harvested from April to December (excluding July). Scuba equipment is not allowed while hunting these succulent creatures, and there is a limit of four per person.

Diving Center of Santa Rosa (707-527-8527; 2696 Santa Rosa Ave.) Diving courses, rentals, equipment sales, diving trips.

The Pinnacles Dive Center (800-439-3483; 2112 Armory Dr., Santa Rosa) Diving courses, rentals, equipment sales, diving trips.

Rohnert Park Dive Center (584-2323; 5665B Redwood Dr.) Instruction, rentals, sales, trips.

TIDE POOLING

The Sonoma coastline has its own wildlife preserve — the tide pool. Here the rocky coast is as productive as a tropical rain forest. As the tide goes out, twice daily, small oases are left behind among the rocks, shelters for starfish, snails, sea anemone, and a multitude of other visible and almost invisible life forms.

There is little movement at first glance, but with a little patience you'll find there's much to discover. Follow a hermit crab as it creeps out of its turban shell and maneuvers over a rock. Watch the sea anemone's green tentacles entwine a mussel. Track the crayola green fish or sculpins as they dart in and out of the rocks. And search out the starfish playing dead. Tide pools are full of old-timers. Snails may be 20 to 30 years old and a starfish may be 10 years old.

Please do not remove anything from the pools; even an empty shell might be a hermit crab's mobile home. Tide-poolers are advised to wear waterproof boots for the best exploration. Be cautious. Crabs pinch, octopuses bite, and sea urchin spines are prickly. Also, beware of sleeper waves — those unexpectedly large waves that sneak up and sweep away beachcombers. For additional insight into the world of the tide pool, visit the *Bodega Marine Lab* (707-875-2211), open to the public on Fridays from 2 to 4pm.

Where are the best places to tide pool? Nearly any rocky place along the *Sonoma Coast State Beach*, which stretches between Bodega Bay and Jenner. The Bodega Bay Marine Lab recommends two. Try the north end of *Salmon Beach*, which is accessible from any Hwy. 1 pull-off north of the Salmon Creek bridge. *Shell Beach*, a few miles south of Jenner on Hwy. 1, is more remote, requiring a trip down steep stairs, but it's worth it.

CROQUET

The difference between your casual backyard croquet game and a world-class croquet tournament is the difference between a quick game of checkers and tournament-level chess. Each year *Sonoma-Cutrer Winery* (707-528-1181; 4401 Slusser Rd., Windsor) is the host of the *Wine Country International*

Croquet Championship, where contestants come to decide who is the world champion. The tournament raises thousands of dollars for charities, and the entrance fee includes a courtside gourmet luncheon with the winery's finest offerings. Croquet in Napa County takes place at **Meadowood Resort** (707-963-3646; 900 Meadowood Ln., St. Helena), where two tournament courts are available for guests and members. A charity tournament takes place each summer, with pros and semi-pros dazzling the crowd with their finesse.

FAMILY FUN

The Wine Country isn't just a playground for adults. Kids and kids at heart can find all sorts of fun, from pony rides and water slides to a planetarium show guaranteed to stretch the imagination. Also see "Swimming" and "Boating & Water Sports" in this chapter for other family activity suggestions.

Napa County

Napa Valley Riverboat Company (707-226-2628; Main Street Landing, Napa) The "City of Napa" is a modestly scaled sternwheeler that treks up and down the Napa River; Saturday dinner and Sunday brunch cruises available; price range: $30–$50.

Chris Alderman

Old Faithful Geyser near Calistoga erupts and draws tourists like clockwork.

Old Faithful Geyser (707-942-6463; 1299 Tubbs Ln., 1 mi. N. of Calistoga) One of just three regularly erupting geysers in the world, it shoots steam and vapor 60 feet into the air for 3 minutes; repeats every 40 minutes. Since seismic activity influences the frequency of the eruptions, many believe Old Faithful predicts earthquakes. Open daily; picnic grounds. Admission: $5 adult, $2 children 6–12, children under 6 free.

Petrified Forest (942-6667; Petrified Forest Rd., 5 mi. W. of Calistoga) Remains of a redwood forest turned to stone by molten lava from the eruption of Mount St. Helena 3 million years ago. The Petrified Forest was discovered in 1870 and immortalized by Robert Louis Stevenson in "The Silverado Squatters"; picnic grounds; museum; open daily. Admission: $3 adults, $1 children 4–11, children under 4 free.

Sonoma County

The Club House Family Fun Center (707-996-3616; 19171 Sonoma Hwy., Sonoma) Game arcade and miniature golf course that features scale models of historic Sonoma landmarks.

Howarth Park (707-528-5115; Montgomery & Summerfield Rds., Santa Rosa) Popular city-run park offers merry-go-round, pony rides, small railroad; play and picnic areas; paddleboats, canoes, rowboats to rent and ducks to feed on Lake Ralphine. Some activities summer only.

J's Amusements (707-869-3102; Off Hwy. 116, Guerneville) Go-carts, waterslide, rollercoaster, carnival rides, arcade.

Pet-A-Llama Ranch (707-823-9395; 5505 Lone Pine Rd., Sebastopol) Feed and pet llamas. See wool spinning demonstrations and hand-woven goods. Open 10am–4pm Sat. & Sun. Free.

Petaluma Queen (800-750-7501; 255 Weller St., Petaluma) Ride an authentic 101-foot-long paddlewheel boat along the Petaluma River; lunch and dinner cruises available. Price range: $15 to $49.

Planetarium (707-527-4371; Santa Rosa Junior College, 1501 Mendocino Ave., Santa Rosa) This excellent planetarium is open to the public on weekends during the school year. Shows at 7 and 8:30pm. Fri. & Sat.; no reservations, so arrive early. No children under 5.

Safari West (707-579-2551; 3115 Porter Creek Rd., Santa Rosa) A 240-acre park featuring 150 species, including 400 rare and endangered animals. Not a drive-through animal park, but a 2 $1/2$-hour tour that is comparable to a real African safari. Admission: $48 adults, $24 children.

Scandia Family Fun Center (707-584-1361; 5301 Redwood Drive, Rohnert Park) Little Indy Racers, miniature golf, baseball batting cages, game arcade. A favorite recreation center for kids and families. Packed on summer weekends. Separate fees for each activity.

Traintown (707-938-3912; 20264 Broadway, 1 mi. S. of Sonoma Plaza) Ride a scale-model steam train through 10 acres of beautifully landscaped park, through a 140-foot tunnel, across bridges, passing historic replica structures.

Made for kids and kids at heart: Traintown in Sonoma.

Courtesy Traintown

Open daily June–Sept.; weekends the rest of the year. Admission: $3.50 adults, $2.50 children.

FISHING

For the expert or the novice, Wine Country offers a fine variety of fishing opportunities. Where else could you hook a giant salmon in the Pacific one morning, then snag a trophy bass in one of California's largest man-made lakes that afternoon?

Remember to pick up a fishing license through a local sporting supply or department store. See "Boating & Water Sports" in this chapter for additional information.

Napa County

Lake Berryessa is a designated trophy lake, boasting trout, bass (both large mouth and black), crappie, bluegill, and catfish. With seven resorts, camping, and full-service marinas, there are unlimited facilities for every type of fishing. For more information, see "Boating & Water Sports" in this chapter or call the *Lake Berryessa Chamber of Commerce* (800-726-1256).

Lake Hennessey (4 mi. E. of Rutherford on Hwy. 128) A water source for the city of Napa; fishing and boating are allowed, though the only facilities are a car-top launch ramp and picnic grounds.

Sportfishing keeps Bodega Bay a busy port.

Kris White

Napa River can be fished for stripers or sturgeon year-round. *J. F. Kennedy Park* (707-257-9529; Streblow Dr., off Hwy. 121, Napa) provides a boat launch ramp and is a good spot for fishing off the river bank. The *Napa Sea Ranch* (707-252-2799; 3333 Cuttings Wharf, Napa) also offers a boat launch ramp as well as a bait & tackle store, and 1,800 feet of river frontage.

Sonoma County

Lake Sonoma (11 mi. N. of Healdsburg on Dry Creek Rd.) 53 mi. of shoreline and secluded coves for the quiet angler as well as a boat launch ramp and a full-service marina for boat rentals. Fish include bass, Sacramento perch, channel catfish, red ear perch, and blue catfish. Of interest is the Fish Hatchery, where visitors can watch tankfuls of lively young salmon and steelhead, which are released into Dry Creek when they reach 6 to 7 inches long. *Visitor Center & Hatchery* (707-433-9483) and *Marina* (707-433-2200).

Lake Ralphine and **Spring Lake** in Santa Rosa are popular destinations with families for low-key fishing expeditions. Both lakes are stocked with catfish, black bass, trout, and bluegill, and practically guarantee beginners a catch. Both lakes offer boat rentals.

The Russian River offers smallish runs of steelhead trout and salmon fishing Nov. through March. The Russian River can be fished from its banks or from canoes and other non-powered boats.

Bodega Bay is home port for sportfishing boats, offering all-day trips on the Pacific Ocean. Leaving daily (weather permitting), 55- and 65-ft. boats search out 200 species of rock and bottom fish and, between Apr. and Nov., the prized salmon. The cost is about $45 a person, with equipment rental extra. Or you can take the ride just for fun.

Bodega Bay Sport Fishing Center (707-875-3344; 1500 Bay Flat Road, Bodega Bay) Daily charter boats; equipment rentals; four 65-ft. boats available; sportfishing for many species of rock and bottom fish and salmon; whale-watching tours.

New Sea Angler & Jaws Sport Fishing (707-875-3495; The Boathouse, 1445 Hwy. 1, Bodega Bay) 55- and 65-ft. boats; daily trips for salmon and rock fish; trips to Cordell Banks and Farrallon Islands.

Fly-fishing enthusiasts will appreciate the fly-casting practice pond constructed in Galvin Park (Bennett Valley, Santa Rosa) by the city of Santa Rosa and the Russian River Flyfishers Club. Clinics are held the third Sunday of each month, with free lessons and equipment supplied. Call *Lyle's Tackle & Travel* (707-527-9887; 2690 Santa Rosa Ave., Santa Rosa) to reserve a place. For local fishing information call Lyle's or *King's Western Angler* (707-542-4432; 532 College Ave., Santa Rosa).

FLYING

You won't need a pilot's license to zoom low over Wine Country. Take a scenic flying tour above vineyards and mountains or try aerobatics in a 1940 biplane, or soar on thermal lifts in a motorless glider. For those whose psyches crave an extra thrill, there's hang-gliding and para-gliding by the cliffs near Jenner or Mount St. Helena; rentals can be arranged with *Airtime of San*

Off to ride the thermals above Napa Valley.

Penn/Courtesy Calistoga Chamber of Commerce

Francisco (415-759-1177). Skydiving is about as close to being airborne on your own as it comes. *Skydance Skydiving* (800-752-3262; Yolo County Airport, Davis) has what you need, whether you're a first-time or a world-class jumper.

Napa County

Bridgeford Flying Service (707-224-0887; Napa County Airport, Napa) Specializes in scenic tours and charter flights. Their Napa Valley tour lasts about an hour and costs $95 for up to three people. The coastal tour ($200) lasts about two hours.

Calistoga Gliders Inc. (707-942-5000; 1546 Lincoln Ave., Calistoga) Ride the thermals like an eagle, when the tow-plane releases the glider at 3,000 feet. Twenty-minute flight for one person, $79; for two, $110; open year-round; call ahead for reservations on weekends. Biplane rides also available: $95 for one, $120 for two.

Sonoma County

Aero-Schellville (707-938-2444; Schellville Airport, 23982 Arnold Dr., Sonoma) Red Baron, move over. These scenic tours of Sonoma Valley are in vintage biplanes, meticulously restored. Aerobatic flights are also available, offering loops, rolls, and 'kamikaze' flights — not for the faint of heart.

Aeroventure (707-778-6767; Petaluma Airport) Scenic tours; $87 per hour (up to 560 lb. weight); $97 per hour (up to 700 lb.)

Dragonfly Aviation (707-575-8750; Sonoma County Airport, Santa Rosa) Scenic tours and charters; $76 per hour with up to three passengers; $410 per hour with up to six passengers; luxury twin-engine planes.

Peregrine Helicopters (707-575-7670; 2244 Airport Blvd., Santa Rosa) Scenic tours of Wine Country, the coast, and the Golden Gate Bridge; $500 per hour with maximum of 4 people.

GOLF

Golf courses cover the rich valleys and rolling hills of Wine Country as eagerly as vineyards. One of the region's favorite recreational activities, golf can be played year-round in this mild climate. Where to play? The visitor can stay at a premier resort with its own course, such as Silverado or Meadowood, or at accommodations with courses close at hand, such as Red Lion Inn and Sonoma Mission Inn. Other visitors and residents are free to sample a variety of public and semi-private courses (private clubs that also allow the public to play). Many private clubs allow members of other clubs to enjoy the benefits of their own members.

Walking the greens in Napa Valley.

Penn/Courtesy Meadowood

GOLF COURSES

Greens Fees Price Code   Inexpensive: Under $15
Moderate: $15 to $25
Expensive: Over $25

Napa County

Aetna Springs (800-675-2115; 1600 Aetna Springs Rd., Pope Valley) 9 holes; par 36; public course established in the 1890s; driving range; pro; lessons; snack bar. Price: Inexpensive.

Chardonnay Club (707-257-8950; 2555 Jameson Canyon Rd., Napa) Two 18-hole championship courses; par 72; Scottish links-style; semi-private course; driving range; 5 pros; shop; club house. Price: Expensive.

Chimney Rock Golf Course (707-255-3363; 5320 Silverado Trail, Napa) 9 holes; par 36; semi-private course; pro; shop; restaurant. Price: Moderate.

Napa Municipal Golf Course (707-255-4333; Napa-Vallejo Hwy., Napa) 18 holes; par 72; public course; driving range; instruction; cocktail lounge; reserve tee time 7 days in advance. Price: Moderate.

Meadowood Resort (707-963-3646; 900 Meadowood Ln., St. Helena) Private to members and guests; 9 holes; par 31; tree-lined narrow course. Price: Expensive.

Mount St. Helena Golf Course (707-942-9966; Napa County Fairground, Calistoga) 9 holes; par 34; public course; shop; snack bar. Price: Inexpensive.

Napa Valley Country Club (707-252-1111; 3385 Hagen Rd., Napa) Private; 18 holes; par 72; shop; pro; lessons open to public (252-1114). Price: Expensive.

Silverado Country Club and Resort (707-257-0200; 1600 Atlas Peak Rd., Napa) Private to members and guests; 18 holes; par 72; pro; shop; host to annual Senior PGA tournament in Oct.; considered by many the best course in Northern California. Price: Expensive.

Sonoma County

Bennett Valley Golf Course (707-528-3673; 3330 Yulupa Ave., Santa Rosa) 18 holes; par 72; municipal course; 3 pros; shop; driving range; restaurant; bar; reserve a week ahead. Price: Inexpensive.

Bodega Harbour Golf Links (707-875-3538; 21301 Heron Dr., Bodega Bay) 18 championship holes; par 70; designed by Robert Trent Jones; semi-private course; 2 pros; shop; lessons; restaurant and lounge; spectacular ocean view from all holes. Price: Expensive.

Fountaingrove Country Club (707-579-4653; 1525 Fountaingrove Pkwy., Santa Rosa) 18 championship holes; par 72; designed by Ted Robinson. Semi-private course; pro; shop; restaurant; tennis courts. Price: Expensive.

Healdsburg Municipal Golf Course (707-433-4275; 927 S. Fitch Mountain Rd., Healdsburg) 9 holes; par 35; public course; pro; shop; putting green; restaurant and lounge. Price: Inexpensive.

Mountain Shadows Golf Resort (707-584-7766; 100 Golf Course Dr., Rohnert Park) Two 18-hole championship courses; par 72; public course; pro; shop; practice range; restaurant and lounge. Price: Moderate to Expensive.

Oakmont Golf Club (707-539-0415; 7025 Oakmont Dr., Santa Rosa) Two 18-hole championship courses; par 72 and 63; designed by Ted Robinson; public course; 4 pros; 2 shops; driving range; lessons; reservations suggested. Price: Moderate to Expensive.

Sea Ranch Golf Links (707-785-2468; Sea Ranch) 9 holes; par 36; links-style course designed by Robert Muir Graves; public course; pro; shop; driving range; lessons; snack bar; ocean view from every hole. Price: Moderate to Expensive.

Sebastopol Golf Course (707-823-9852; 2881 Scott's Right-Of-Way, Sebastopol) 9 holes; par 31; public course; pro; shop; snack bar; picnic facilities. Price: Inexpensive.

Sonoma Golf Club (707-996-0300; 17700 Arnold Dr., Sonoma) 18 championship holes; par 72; public course; just completed $8.5-million renovation; driving range; putting green; restaurant. Price: Expensive.

HIKING & PARKS

The rolling hills of Wine Country invite a brisk walk.

Chris Alderman

Whether you choose a trail through sand dunes or redwoods, grassy valleys or mountain forests, there is no better way to appreciate the natural beauty of Wine Country than to pack a snack and leave the roads behind you. Each season has its own personality: brilliant wildflowers in the spring, dry heat and golden grass in summer, colored foliage in the fall, cool breezes and green hills in winter. A number of state and county parks await you, whether you are toting a baby for his first hike or ready for serious backpacking. For help with the details of your trip, see Bob Lorentzen's *The Hiker's Hip Pocket Guide to Sonoma County* (includes some hikes in Napa County).

Remember, though you are not likely to find bears, mountain lions are seen occasionally and rattlesnakes and ticks are common in the back country. Stay away from poison oak, and don't forget to take your own water on summer hikes.

Napa County

Bothe-Napa State Park (707-942-4575; 3801 Hwy. 29, 4 mi. N. of St. Helena) Originally home to the Wappo Indians, this land became a country retreat for the wealthy San Francisco Hitchcock family in the 1870s. The History Trail passes a pioneer cemetery to Bale Grist Mill, a partially restored 1846 flour mill; 1,917 acres; day-use fee; 6 miles of hiking trails.

John F. Kennedy Park (707-257-9529; 2291 Streblow Dr. off Hwy. 121, Napa) This 340-acre park features hiking trails along the Napa River and plenty of undeveloped open space, as well as softball fields, playgrounds, and boat launch ramps.

Watch out! Poison oak is plentiful in Napa and Sonoma counties.

Margaret Warriner Buck

Robert Louis Stevenson State Park (707-942-4575; 7 mi. N. of Calistoga on Hwy. 29) Composed of ancient lava, Mount St. Helena rises 4343 ft. to provide the highest landmark in Wine Country. In 1841, Russian settlers from Fort Ross scaled the peak, naming it for their commandant's wife Elena. In 1880, Robert Louis Stevenson spent two months near the mountain, recovering from tuberculosis. It made a lasting impression on him, and he renamed it Spyglass Hill in his most famous work *Treasure Island;* 3,300 acres; 10-mi. round trip to summit, past the once-prosperous Silverado Mine; undeveloped except for trails; open daily during daylight hours.

Skyline Wilderness Park (707-252-0481; 2201 W. Imola Ave., Napa) Wilderness close to downtown Napa, with 35 mi. of hiking, mountain bike, and horse trails. Its oak-wooded hills are ideal for hiking. On a clear day, there are spectacular views of San Francisco from the park's ridges. A small lake offers bass fishing; 850 acres; open daily year-round; day-use fee.

Westwood Hills Wilderness Park (707-257-9529; Browns Valley Road at Laurel Street, Napa) City-owned park with hiking trails, native flora and fauna; 111 acres.

White Sulphur Springs (707-963-8588; 3100 White Sulphur Springs Rd., St. Helena) Secluded countryside 3 mi. W. of St. Helena, with hiking trails throughout; year-round creek and waterfalls. Day-use fee.

Sonoma County

Annadel State Park (707-539-3911; 6201 Channel Dr., off Montgomery Dr., Santa Rosa) Surrounded by an increasingly developed Santa Rosa, Annadel offers 5,000 acres of hills, creeks, woodlands, and meadows reached by 40 miles of trails used by hikers, horseback riders, and mountain bikers.

Courtesy Sonoma County Convention & Visitors Bureau

Redwoods tower like skyscrapers in western Sonoma County.

Annadel visitors enjoy a small central lake created by the last owner Joe Coney and named after himself and his wife Ilsa as Lake Ilsanjo; day-use fee.

Armstrong Redwoods State Reserve (707-869-2015; 17000 Armstrong Woods Rd., Guerneville) In the late 1800s, Col. James Armstrong sought to preserve this ancient grove of redwoods he had come to love. Because of his efforts and those of his family, Sonoma is fortunate to be able to enjoy this virgin stand of 1,000-year-old trees stretching 300 ft. high — one of the largest of which is named after the Colonel. Walk among these giants, where, even on the hottest day, you will feel their cool serenity; 750 acres; day-use fee; hiking trails, picnic sites, outdoor theater; open year-round until sunset.

Austin Creek State Recreation Area (707-869-2015; 17000 Armstrong Woods Rd., Guerneville) Adjacent to Armstrong Grove, this undeveloped park offers miles of trails for hikers and equestrians through canyons, enormous glades, and dark, cool forests; 4,200 acres; day-use fee; camping available.

Hood Mountain Regional Park (707-527-2041; Santa Rosa) Accessible by car from Alamos Road or by a 4-hour hike from Sugarloaf Ridge State Park, Hood Mountain (elevation 2,730 ft.) commands an imposing view of the Mayacamas Range; day-use fee.

Lake Sonoma (707-433-9483; 3333 Skaggs Spring Rd. near Dry Creek Road, Healdsburg) 40 miles of trails wind through the redwood groves and oak woodlands surrounding Sonoma's newest man-made lake. Visitor Center is at the base of the dam; 3,600 acres; camping, boating, swimming, fish hatchery.

Jack London State Historic Park (707-938-5216; 2400 London Ranch Rd., off Arnold Dr., Glen Ellen) Writer Jack London fell in love with the Valley of the Moon, and began buying land there in 1905. By the time he died in 1916, he was immersed in the innovative projects of his "Beauty Ranch." Visitors can see the remains of the London's Wolf House mansion; 7 miles of trails as well as a scenic 3 $^{1}/_{2}$ mi. climb with breathtaking views of the Valley of the Moon; 800 acres; day-use fee; open daily.

Ragle Ranch Regional Park (707-527-2041; Ragle Rd., off Bodega Hwy., Sebastopol) This former ranch offers trails through a rugged wilderness of oak woodlands and creeks; baseball fields, playgrounds, picnic areas; 156 acres.

Sugarloaf Ridge State Park (707-833-5712; 2605 Adobe Canyon Rd. off Hwy. 12, Santa Rosa) The Wappo Indians lived in this beautiful area before being decimated by European diseases in the 1830s. Purchased by the state in 1920 as a site for a dam which was never built, Sugarloaf Ridge now offers 25 mi. of trails through a varied landscape, including ridges surrounding Bald Mountain and meadows along Sonoma Creek. 2,700 acres; day-use fee; camping.

HORSEBACK RIDING

You might call this a sea horse. Sea Horse Stables in Bodega Bay offers beach rides.

Edmond Bridant/Courtesy Sonoma County Convention & Visitors Bureau

The Wine Country adamantly maintains its rural flavor, despite its growing population and worldwide tourist appeal. With an estimated 26,000 horses in Sonoma County alone, there is plenty of interest in horse breeding, competition, and riding. Some 50 horse events take place annually at the Sonoma County Fairgrounds, including top shows such as the California State Horse Show which attracts visitors from all over the West.

Like Jack London, who was described by one biographer as the "sailor on horseback," many Wine Country residents and visitors take to the hills on horseback to explore the countryside as the early California settlers did before them. Bridle paths and trails can be found at *Annadel, Armstrong Redwoods, Austin Creek, Bothe–Napa Valley, Jack London, Salt Point, Skyline,* and *Sug-*

Horseback riding is a peaceful way to explore Wine Country.

Courtesy Sonoma Cattle Co.

arloaf Ridge parks. For those without their own steeds, the following stables rent horses for the day. Two-hour trail rides average $35.

Napa County

Wild Horse Valley Ranch (707-224-0727; Wild Horse Valley Rd., Napa) Riding trips offered, with 3,600 acres of trails for every kind of rider, or bring your own horse to ride. The ranch also offers a race track, indoor arenas, polo, cross-country courses, riding school, tack shop, and horse boarding.

Sonoma County

Armstrong Woods Pack Station (707-579-1520; Armstrong Redwoods State Park, 17000 Armstrong Woods Rd., Guerneville) Rentals for trail rides through Armstrong Redwoods and Austin Creek parks; half day or full day with gourmet lunch available.

Sea Horse Stables (707-875-2721; 2660 Hwy. 1, Bodega Bay) Scenic guided trail rides for riders of all levels; one- or two-hour treks on the ranch and dunes. Open year-round.

Sonoma Cattle Company (707-996-8566; Jack London State Park, 2400 London Ranch Rd., Glen Ellen) Rentals for Jack London and Sugarloaf Ridge state parks; guided tours for one- or two-hour tours (Apr. through Oct.); barbecue rides and day trips available.

HORSE RACING

Horse racing fans converge each summer at the *Sonoma County Fair* (707-545-4200; 1350 Bennett Valley Rd., Santa Rosa) to watch California's fastest horses vying for a purse of nearly $2 million. During the rest of the year, the fairgrounds offer *The Jockey Club* (800-454-RACE), with simultaneous broadcasting of races at Golden Gate Fields, Bay Meadows, and Hollywood Park.

RACQUETBALL

For the executive who needs stress relief or the athlete who loves fast action on an indoor court, racquetball is a lively game that demands focus and coordination. It is increasingly popular among the health-conscious in Napa and Sonoma, especially during the rainy winter months when tennis is iffy. Private clubs with courts charge an annual or monthly fee; public courts charge by the hour. Most require advance registration.

Napa County

La Cancha Racquetball Health Center (707-252-8033; 1850 Soscol Ave., Napa) Private club; 6 courts; holds tournaments with other clubs.

Pay 'N Play Racquetball of America (707-257-2226; 875 Sousa Ln., Napa) Public automated 24-hour racquetball and handball courts; equipment rental; 4 courts; leagues and tournaments; no reservations necessary.

Sonoma County

The Parkpoint Club (707-578-1640; 1200 N. Dutton Ave., Santa Rosa) Private; full health club; 6 courts; tournaments.

Rohnert Park Sports Center (707-584-4800; 5405 Snyder Ln., Rohnert Park) Public, with yearly membership available; 2 courts; tournaments; equipment rental.

ROCK CLIMBING

For those who like to live on the edge, rock climbing has become a sport with built-in adventure, but it's important to do it right. *Sonoma Outfitters* (707-528-1920; 145 3rd St., Santa Rosa) offers a complete selection of shoes and equipment plus a climbing wall (open weekend afternoons) for practice. Classes are also offered.

When you're ready for the real thing, favorite climbing spots in the area are *Sunset Boulder* at Goat Rock on the Sonoma Coast and *Mount St. Helena* in Napa. Check out the book *Bouldering in the Bay Area* for other possible challenges.

RUNNING

Runners find that Napa and Sonoma counties can be a pleasant challenge.

Kris White

Joggers of all ages, sizes, and shapes can be seen on park trails and roadsides in Sonoma and Napa Counties. The fresh air and rural countryside of the Wine Country, along with its mild climate, have made running an extremely popular year-round activity for the health conscious.

For those serious runners looking for competition, several take place each year, including the *Napa Valley Marathon,* which is run from Calistoga to Napa on the second Sunday in March. Another demanding event is the *International Vineman Triathlon,* combining running, bicycling, and swimming competitions. Many races in both counties benefit local causes, such as Sonoma County's "Human Race." Get specific schedules from the *Sonoma County Convention and Visitors Bureau* (707-586-8100) or the *Napa Valley Conference and Visitors Bureau* (707-963-7395).

SKATING

ICE SKATING

Famed cartoonist and ice-skating buff Charles Schulz built the ***Redwood Empire Ice Arena*** (707-546-7147; 1667 W. Steel Ln., Santa Rosa) in 1969, and it has become one of Sonoma County's most popular spots. The rink, surrounded by walls painted with Alpine scenes, is the site for recreational and would-be Olympic skaters, birthday parties (more than 8,000 to date), and holiday ice shows with professional figure skaters. Next door is ***Snoopy's Gallery & Gift Shop*** (707-546-3385), filled with every conceivable item relating to Snoopy and the "Peanuts" gang, as well as skating gear including hi-tech in-line skates.

ROLLER SKATING

It's still a fun-time favorite with kids, teens, and adults. After all, they say it's the best aerobic exercise around.

Cal Skate: 707-585-0500; 6100 Commerce Blvd., Rohnert Park
Star Skate World: 707-544-7000; 2075 Occidental Rd., Santa Rosa

SPAS

Long before pioneers came to settle Northern California, Indians knew the locations of hot springs and used the steamy pools, volcanic mud, and

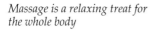
Massage is a relaxing treat for the whole body

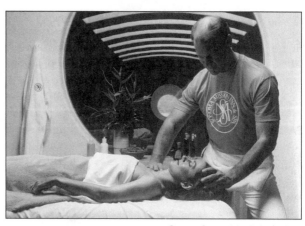

Courtesy Sonoma Mission Inn and Spa

Playing with Mud

Wine Country, along with all its other striking features, is blessed with a little extra something: geothermal activity from down under. The most popular signs of hot steam and bubbling mineral water are the "Spa" signs along Lincoln Avenue in downtown Calistoga, where salvation is offered to the body and soul in the form of mud and mineral baths.

What exactly is a mud bath treatment? First, you immerse yourself in a thick, warm, black mass of volcanic ash and/or peat moss, mixed with naturally heated mineral water. It's like a warm cocoon enveloping you, but just relax and go with it. The benefits? Relaxed muscles and joints and soft renewed skin. There are drawbacks, of course. Some may find the mud too warm, and others may feel claustrophobic being engulfed in so much earth. Also, the mud sticks like glue as you wash it off in a lukewarm shower.

Afterward, you soak in warm mineral water, then open your pores in a eucalyptus-scented, geyser-heated steam room. Finish up with a cooling blanket wrap. Ahhhh. If you can handle additional pleasure, expert masseuses will work your body into a silly-putty state.

---

mineral waters to heal and soak away pains. Calistoga remains the most popular destination for mud, mineral baths, and professional massage, but health spas are beginning to dot the entire Wine Countryside. Many spas are part of resorts or other places to stay; check Chapter Three, *Lodging*, for more information.

Napa County

CALISTOGA MASSAGE CENTER
707-942-6193.
1219 Washington St.,
  Calistoga.
Hours: Noon–8pm, with
  extended weekend
  hours.
Credit Cards: AE, MC, V.

As the name suggests, this spa concentrates on massage. There are no whirlpools or mineral baths, but they do offer facials. One unique feature is a massage for two, a nice touch when couples are pampering themselves. One-hour massage: $48.

CALISTOGA SPA HOT SPRINGS
707-942-6269.
1006 Washington St.,
  Calistoga.
Open: 8:30am–4:30pm
  daily.
Credit Cards: MC, V.

Stylishly designed, with hi-tech masonry, polished metal accents, and glass-block walls, this is one of Calistoga's most pleasant spa experiences. Massage rooms are equipped with skylights, a nice touch. Mud baths use a traditional blend of volcanic ash, peat moss, and hot-spring water. Large steam rooms. Staff is extremely attentive. Massage is generally Swedish technique. One of the best pool destinations in Napa, with four naturally heated outside pools, varying from a 83-degree lap pool to a huge 105-degree covered whirlpool. The wading pool signals that kids are welcome here. Pools are open to the public for day use and surrounded by pleasant and private landscaping. Also, large exercise room. Mud bath, mineral whirlpool, and half-hour massage: $62.

CALISTOGA VILLAGE INN AND SPA
707-942-0991.
1880 Lincoln Ave.,
  Calistoga.
Credit Cards: AE, MC, V.

A small facility removed from the bustle of the downtown strip, this was once known as the French Spa. The name has changed but the French-style spa equipment remains. Changing rooms are makeshift but the spa rooms are pleasantly adorned with blue and white tiles. Mud treatment is one of best in town, using a pleasant mix of peat moss and white clay, mildly heated by mineral water before you enter. French steam cabinets — contraptions that cover everything except your head — substitute for steam rooms, an enjoyable change. Specialties include herbal wraps and an invigorating salt scrub. Outside mineral pools have a magnificent view of surrounding mountains. There is a wading pool for kids and the pool house has a whirlpool and sauna. Mud bath, mineral whirlpool, and half-hour massage: $65.

DR. WILKINSON'S HOT SPRINGS
707-942-4102.
1507 Lincoln Ave.,
  Calistoga.
Open: 8:30am–4:30pm
  daily.
Credit Cards: AE, MC, V.

John "Doc" Wilkinson was a young chiropractor when he gave his first spa treatment in 1946. One of the most popular spas on Calistoga's main drag, Dr. Wilkinson's remains a no-frills outfit. The concrete block walls of the spa area create a utilitarian atmosphere, the steam room is closet-size, and the mineral baths are simple claw-foot tubs. But the staff is first-rate. Mud baths use a traditional blend of volcanic ash, peat moss, and hot-spring water. One of the best massages in Calistoga is found here, with both Swedish and Shiatsu technique. The salon offers facials and acupressure face lifts, etc. Outdoor pools are *not* open for day use. Mud bath, mineral whirlpool, and half-hour massage: $69.

EUROSPA
707-942-6829.
1202 Pine St., Calistoga.
Hours: 10am–6pm, with
  extended weekend
  hours.
Credit Cards: D, MC, V.

Eurospa takes its lead from the continent, as its name suggests. If the century-old traditions of Calistoga and its thick and hot mud baths lack appeal, Eurospa is a change of pace. In the Pine Street Inn, the spa sets an intimate yet airy mood. Spa rooms have pleasant views of the grounds, and after treatments guests are free to roam outside to use the pool and Jacuzzi. The specialty here is the fango mud bath, a light warm chocolate-milk-like blend of mineral water and powdered mud from Germany. Other treatments include milk-whey baths, aromatherapy facials, body wraps, and Swedish and Shiatsu massage. Mud bath and half-hour massage: $59.

GOLDEN HAVEN SPA HOT SPRINGS
707-942-6793
1713 Lake St., Calistoga.
Open: 9am–9pm daily.
Credit Cards: AE, MC, V.

In a residential neighborhood three blocks from Calistoga's downtown, the Golden Haven is not fancy but has been drawing a following since the 1950s. Service is pleasant and the atmosphere low-key. One of the few spas that offers mud baths and mineral baths for couples — a cozy touch. Mud baths use a mix of peat moss, clay, and mineral water. Specialties include an inch-reducing European body wrap and oatmeal facial scrubs. Massage is Swedish, with Esalen, acupressure, and deep tissue. Spa guests have access to outside Jacuzzi and a large 80-degree pool. Mud bath, mineral whirlpool, and half-hour massage: $64.

INDIAN HOT SPRINGS SPA
707-942-4913.
1712 Lincoln Ave.,
   Calistoga.
Hours: 9am–8pm daily.
Credit Cards: MC, V.

Wappo Indians built sweat lodges on this site and later it was home to Calistoga's original resort. Its huge mineral pool — an Olympic-size beauty originally built in 1913 — has bright blue green water that remains at 80 degrees in the summer. It's even hotter in the winter, when steam rolls off the water and into the sky above Calistoga. The pool is open for day use and draws thousands of summer visitors. Children are welcome. Three active geysers supply water as warm as 212 degrees. The facility is old but well maintained. Mud baths use only volcanic ash, taken from the resort's 16-acre site. Facial treatments are also available. Mud bath, mineral whirlpool, and half-hour massage: $85.

CALISTOGA OASIS SPA
707-942-2122.
1300 Washington St.,
   Calistoga.
Open: 9am–5pm Tues. &
   Wed., 9am–9pm
   Thurs.–Mon.
Credit Cards: MC, V.

A bungalow next to the Roman Spa Motel, the International Spa offers a variety of treatments, from traditional mud and massage to herbal facials, foot reflexology, and seaweed baths and wraps. All treatments are for singles or couples. Massage is Swedish and Esalen. Roman Spa's outdoor pool and Finnish sauna are open to International Spa guests. Mud bath, mineral whirlpool, and half-hour massage: $69.

LAVENDER HILL SPA
707-942-4495.

This relative newcomer, a charming yellow house that was once a bed and breakfast, caters

1015 Foothill Blvd. (Hwy. 29), Calistoga.
Hours: 9am–9pm daily.
Credit Cards: MC, V.

to couples. It has private, cushioned tubs built for two and double massage tables. One massage room even has a fireplace. Mud baths are fango-style, a light warm chocolate-milk-like blend of mineral water and powdered volcanic ash. If you're turned off by the thick traditional mud baths, this may be for you. Other treatments include seaweed baths, mineral salt baths, facials, herbal blanket wraps, personal perfume blending, and massage. There is no pool, but afterward, gather your thoughts in the graceful garden. Mud bath and half-hour massage: $72.

LINCOLN AVENUE SPA
707-942-5296.
1339 Lincoln Ave., Calistoga.
Open: 9am–9pm.
Credit Cards: AE, MC, V.

Housed in a sturdy rock building — originally Calistoga's first bank — this relatively new spa is in the heart of downtown. Although you won't find any ink pens on chains, the spa has preserved the interior well, even retaining the vault. Lincoln Avenue offers a few unusual treatments. If being buried in mud is not your cup of tea, try the body mud, in which a balm of warm herbs is applied to your skin, followed by a towel wrap and soothing steam treatment. The mud comes in different "flavors" as well, including seaweed and mint. Other treatments include facials and acupressure face lifts. Treatments for singles or couples. No pools or whirlpools. Body mud and half-hour massage: $62.

MEADOWOOD
707-963-3646.
900 Meadowood Lane, St. Helena.
Hours: 7am–8pm daily.
Credit Cards: AE, DC, MC, V.

Want to be pampered? The health spa at Meadowood resort is the place. Napa Valley's newest and perhaps best spa, it comes at a price, yet a basic massage is priced competitively. Also, if you're addicted to mud, this is not your place. Meadowood specializes in face and body treatments as well as fitness programs. The setting alone soothes the soul. The spa is set in the lush foothills of Howell Mountain and the outside pool and Jacuzzi are surrounded by towering trees . A Meadowood specialty is the chardonnay massage, which uses a pleasant wine-based gel that's invigorating, not oily. Other treatments include something called a "salt glow," as well as facials, waxing, and various therapeutic combinations of all. Massage rooms are darkly lit and light jazz is piped in. Fifty-minute massage with use of steam room, sauna, and pools: $60 (resort guests) and $75 (public).

MOUNT VIEW SPA
707-942-5789.
1457 Lincoln Ave., Calistoga.

If you're turned off by the communal locker room atmosphere of many Calistoga spas, this spa has the solitude you crave. Private treatment rooms

Hours: 9am–9pm daily.
Credit Cards: AE, MC, V.

have steam rooms, and two-person Jacuzzi tubs, for both singles and couples. Part of the newly restored Mount View Hotel, the spa is elegant yet unpretentiously appointed. Mud treatments come in two forms: fango bath, a light warm chocolate-milk-like blend of mineral water, herbs, and powdered volcanic ash, as well as mud wraps, in which the body is painted with a glaze of Dead Sea mud, honey, and glycerin, then wrapped in warm blankets. Other treatments include seaweed wraps and baths, waxing, facials, and milk baths. Massages include Swedish, sports-style therapeutic, and Shiatsu. Mud bath with half-hour massage: $65.

NANCE'S HOT SPRINGS
707-942-6211.
1614 Lincoln Ave.,
  Calistoga.
Open: 9am–5pm Mon–Fri.,
  9am–7pm Sat. & Sun.
Credit Cards: AE, MC, V.

One of oldest spas, this is a popular spot with folks who relish a simple, old-fashioned Calistoga atmosphere. Co-owner Frank Hughes, in his 70s, is still giving massages after more than 45 years. Spa rooms are low on ambiance, with claw-foot tubs and tiled mud baths. Massage is Swedish. Indoor pool heated with 102-degree mineral water. Mud bath, mineral whirlpool, and half-hour massage: $62.

**WHITE SULPHUR
SPRINGS RESORT
AND SPA**
707-963-4361.
3100 White Sulphur
  Springs Rd., St. Helena.
Credit Cards: MC, V.

The first resort built in California, White Sulphur Springs dates from 1852. Its first owners were physicians who believed the sulphur springs helped relieve arthritis and rheumatism and by the turn of the century it was a fashionable watering hole. The grounds cover 330 spectacular acres of redwood, madrone, and fir, explored easily through hiking trails. The lodge and spa were recently updated but retain a sense of history and rustic charm. Spa rooms view the outdoors through high windows. Treatments include massage, facials, and herbal and mud wraps. Visitors soothe themselves in a free-flowing, rock-lined mineral pool that stays between 85 and 92 degrees. Mud wrap with half-hour massage: $55.

Sonoma County

OSMOSIS
707-823-8231.
209 Bohemian Hwy.,
  Freestone.
Hours: 9:30am–8pm daily.
Credit Cards: MC, V.

A truly unique experience, Osmosis is the only place in the Western World to experience Japanese-style enzyme baths. The baths are similar to mud baths in only one way — you're covered from neck to toe. In this case it's not mud but a sawdust-like mix of fragrant cedar, rice bran, and

The enzyme baths at Osmosis in Sonoma County are an invigorating alternative to mud.

Courtesy Osmosis

more than 600 active enzymes. The concoction ferments and generates gentle and natural heat. Guests don kimonos and begin their treatment in a Japanese sitting room, sipping enzyme tea as they gaze through shoji doors into the Japanese garden. Baths can be taken solo or with a friend. The treatment concludes with a shower and a 30-minute blanket wrap or Swedish or Shiatsu massage. Enzyme bath with 75-minute massage: $105.

A SIMPLE TOUCH
707-433-6856.
239C Center St.,
 Healdsburg.
Open: 10am–6pm Thurs.,
 Sun., & Mon.; 10am–9pm
 Fri. & Sat.
Credit Cards: MC, V.

An intimate spot just off the Healdsburg Square, this spa is a welcome addition to northern Sonoma County. With a single bath and two treatment rooms, Simple Touch offers individualized care. The lobby welcomes you with soft peach tones and a warm atmosphere. Mud baths are fango-style, a light warm chocolate-milk-like blend of mineral water and powdered mud. There are also seaweed and sea salt baths, as well as rose petal wraps, herbal facials, and Swedish, Shiatsu, and sports massage. Mud bath with half hour massage: $52.

**SONOMA MISSION INN
AND SPA**
707-938-9000.
18140 Sonoma Hwy. (Hwy.
 12), Boyes Hot Springs.
Open: 6am–9pm
 Sun.–Thurs., 6am–10pm
 Fri.–Sat.
Credit Cards: AE, DC, MC,
 V.

Who's that lounging in the mineral pool? Billy Crystal? A Wine Country favorite for the rich and famous, the waters here have made this site a destination since Native Americans first considered it a healing ground. It's also Wine Country's most expensive spa. The inn has recently tapped into a new source of mineral water and the soft and lightly green liquid warms the pool and Jacuzzi. The spa house is a stylish combo of Mission and

Art Deco and the pool area is in a peaceful grove of trees. The array of treatments is boggling, from Swedish and sports massage to mud and seaweed body wraps, hair and foot care, waxing, color analysis, and nearly a dozen different facials. There is also a fitness center. Pools are open to the public for day use during the week. Mud wrap with 45-minute massage: $151.

SONOMA SPA
707-939-8770.
457 1st St. W., Sonoma.
Hours: 9am–9pm daily.
Credit Cards: AE, MC, V.

Opening up shop a few years ago, this spa brought a much-needed dose of indulgence to downtown Sonoma. The Greek Revival storefront looks out onto historic Sonoma Plaza. No traditional mud baths here, but treatments are available for singles and couples and include Swedish and Esalen massage, as well as rose petal body masques, cooling body mud, herbal wraps, facials, and foot reflexology. Mud and wraps treatments include an herbal sauna. Mud wrap with half-hour massage: $68.

SWIMMING

Swimming at Lake Ilsanjo in Annadel Park is a fine way to cool off.

Chris Alderman

Summer in the Wine Country brings day after day of blue skies — that is, after the sun breaks through the morning fog. It does get hot in the summer and a dip in cool water is luscious relief. Remember, the Pacific Ocean — with year-round temperatures around 50 degrees and dangerous undercurrents — is not a good choice. For those whose swimming is more for exercise than for fun, indoor pools with lap lanes are also available year-round. In Calistoga, many spas open their pools to the public for day use for a nominal fee.

Napa County

Bothe–Napa Valley State Park (707-942-4575; Hwy. 29, 4 mi. N. of St. Helena) Swimming pool open mid-June through Labor Day; day-use fee.

Lake Berryessa (800-726-1256; W. of Rutherford on Hwy. 128) Miles of clear blue water, with temperatures up to 75 degrees, make this an ideal destination in the summer. Several resorts, including Putah Creek, Spanish Flat, and Steele Park, offer swimming areas. (See "Boating" in this chapter for specific information on resorts.)

St. Helena Community Pool (707-963-7946; 1401 Grayson Ave.) Open all summer.

Sonoma County

Agua Caliente Springs (707-996-6822; 17350 Vailetti Dr., Sonoma) Originally opened in 1888. Offers outdoor large warm mineral pool, cold water diving pool, wading pool, indoor pool with whirlpool, picnic and barbecue, open daily in summer; weekends summer and fall.

Lake Sonoma (707-433-2200; 11 mi. N. of Healdsburg on Dry Creek Rd.) Beaches at Lake Sonoma Marina and at Yorty Creek, along with picnic, hiking, and boating facilities.

Morton's Warm Springs (707-833-5511; 1651 Warm Springs Rd., Kenwood) Two large pools, one wading pool; picnic grounds, volleyball and baseball. Open summer only. Perfect for group outings.

Russian River residents and visitors alike enjoy swimming in the slow-flowing, deep green Russian River. Swimming areas are at *Veterans Memorial Beach* in Healdsburg (707-433-1625; Healdsburg Ave.), *Monte Rio Beach,* and at *Johnson's Beach* in Guerneville (707-869-2022), both just off River Road, where inner tubes and paddleboats can also be rented.

Spring Lake (707-539-8092; off Summerfield Rd., Santa Rosa) The 72-acre swimming lagoon — separated from the lake's boating and fishing areas — is filled with kids and their families every hot day of summer. A gentle sandy shoreline, water floats to mark depth, rafts and tubes to rent, and lifeguards help make this a great swimming experience for beginners.

Windsor Waterworks and Slide (707-838-7760; 8225 Conde Ln., Windsor) Outdoor pool, wading pool, picnic sites, and four rollercoaster waterslides make this a cool spot to be on a scorching summer day. One ride down the slide and you're hooked.

YMCA (707-545-9622; 1111 College Ave., Santa Rosa) The Y's indoor heated pool is open daily year-round for laps, exercise, instruction, and family fun; day and evening hours.

TENNIS

Tennis courts abound in Wine Country.

Janeen Belsardi

In an area where the climate is mild and it rains only 6 months out of the year, you would expect tennis to be an avid sport — is it ever. With a variety of both public and private tennis courts offering instruction and competition, Wine Country gives the tennis enthusiast plenty of action.

The *Sonoma County Tennis Association* (707-585-3155), active since 1982, has been instrumental in organizing tournaments throughout the year for all levels of players from youth to A-division, singles and doubles. With 1100 members from Sonoma, Napa, and Marin counties, the SCTA sponsors matches mainly at Sonoma State University in Rohnert Park and Galvin Park in Santa Rosa. The public is invited to watch.

Napa County

Calistoga Public Courts (707-942-2838) are available year-round at Stevenson and Grant Sts.; 4 courts; lighted; city-run instruction in summer.

Meadowood Resort (707-963-3646; 900 Meadowood Ln., St. Helena) Courts open to members and guests; pro.

Napa Public Courts (707-257-9529) Available during the summer at Napa Valley College (Vallejo Hwy., Napa), Vintage High School (1375 Trower Ave.),

Napa High School (2475 Jefferson St.), Silverado Middle School (1133 Coombsville Rd.); city-run instruction.

Napa Valley Country Club (707-252-1111; 3385 Hagen Rd., Napa) Private; pro; lessons open to public; active spot.

St. Helena Public Courts (707-963-5706) are available at Robert Louis Stevenson School (1316 Hill View Pl.) and St. Helena High School (1401 Grayson Ave.); city-operated courts at Crane Park (off Crane Ave.); active. women's city league program for A and B players.

Silverado Country Club and Resort (707-257-0200; 1600 Atlas Peak Rd., Napa) Open to members and guests; pro.

Sonoma County

Countryside Racquet Club (707-527-9948; 3950 Sebastopol Rd., Santa Rosa) Courts open to members and guests; pro; 8 lighted courts; leagues and tournaments; very active.

La Cantera Racquet and Swim Club (707-544-9494; 3737 Montgomery Dr., Santa Rosa) Courts open to members and guests; pro; 12 courts, 4 lighted; leagues and tournaments.

Montecito Heights Health and Racquet Club (707-526-0529; 2777 4th St., Santa Rosa) Courts open to members and guests; pro; 5 courts, none lighted; leagues and tournaments.

Rancho Arroyo Racquet Club (707-795-5461; 85 Corona Rd., Petaluma) Courts open to members and guests; pro; 7 courts, 2 lighted; leagues and tournaments.

Rohnert Park Public Courts (707-584-7357) At seven parks: Alicia (300 Arlen Dr.), Ladybug (8517 Liman Wy.), Dorotea, Eagle, Sunrise, Honeybee (1170 Golf Course Dr.), and Golis. The Recreation Department offers instruction and sponsors the Rohnert Park Tennis Club, a group that draws players from Sonoma, Napa, and Marin counties.

Santa Rosa Public Courts (707-543-3282) are available at Howarth and Galvin parks, Burbank Playground, Santa Rosa Junior College, and Santa Rosa and Montgomery high schools.

WHALE WATCHING

One of the great attractions in California is the opportunity to watch gray whales in their annual round-trip migration between summer feeding grounds in the Bering Sea and their breeding and birthing waters off Baja Cali-

Illustration by Jacqueline Schonewald

Whale watching, from land or by boat, is a grand experience.

fornia. From late May through Oct., the gray whales feed in the cold waters to build up fat for their 12,000-mile pilgrimage. Then, beginning in late Nov., they head south, passing close enough to shore to navigate by sight, as well as to avoid killer whales in the deeper waters. Their return usually starts in late Feb. and lasts until early June.

The Point Reyes Lighthouse (415-663-1092) At the tip of the Point Reyes National Seashore in Marin County, about a 1 $^1/_2$ hour drive from Santa Rosa; offers one of the best vantage points in the state for whale watching. The Lighthouse is open from 10 to 4:30 daily except Tues. and Weds., but parking is limited and extremely crowded on weekends. Call ahead to find out if there is any visibility, since the Lighthouse sits on the windiest and rainiest spot on the entire Pacific Coast.

Sonoma County offers other good whale-watching sites, including *Gualala Point, Stillwater Cove, Fort Ross,* and *Bodega Head.* On a clear day you will have plenty of company to share sightings — all bundled against the sea breezes, toting binoculars and picnic lunches, and ready to spend several hours watching for the telltale white spouts shooting above the blue Pacific waters.

For a close-up view, reserve a place on a whale-watching boat out of Bodega Bay. Remember that it's typically 15 degrees colder on the water, so wear plenty of warm clothes. Law prohibits boaters from harassing whales, but the large mammals have little fear of man and often approach boats at sea. All boats leave from Porto Bodega Marina on Bay Flat Rd., off Hwy. 1. Season is Jan. through April and boats run weather permitting. Cost is about $25 per person.

Bodega Bay Sport Fishing Center: 707-875-3344; 1500 Bay Flat Road, Bodega Bay

New Sea Angler & Jaws Sport Fishing: 707-875-3495; The Boathouse, 1445 Hwy. 1, Bodega Bay

NEIGHBORS

Marine World & Africa USA is just a short drive south of Napa.

Courtesy Marine World/Africa USA

Marine World & Africa USA (707-643-ORCA; Marine World Pkwy. off I-80, Vallejo) Only a short drive away. This 160-acre facility includes whale and seal shows, elephant rides, and the usual wild creatures. Walk through a glass tunnel surrounded by sharks or see robotic dinosaurs in action. Open daily. Admission: $24.95 adults, $16.95 children 4–12, children under 4 free.

CHAPTER EIGHT
For the Sport of It
SHOPPING

Chris Alderman

Lost in a book at the cozy Book Cellar.

Shopping is sporting, an exercise in endurance, an exhausting workout, a test of willpower and pure capitalistic fun. Just start off your day with a shot of espresso, slip on your Pro-Walkers, catalog your credit cards, and set off for your marathon through Wine Country.

This chapter is your compass. It will guide you to traditional and offbeat stores. Some will be within easy reach, others will be off the beaten path. Some antique stores listed will make you feel as though you're prowling an attic. There are *Life* magazines, carousel horses, and fine pine furniture that dates from the 1870s.

The section on furniture will show you a new breed of artist/designers who create both comfort and style in one sitting. Bale Mill Designs and Palladio carve their designs out of pine, while R.S. Basso designs custom-made sofas and chairs. (You have to admire the entrepreneur in these artists.)

You could lose a day or two wandering through the bookstores listed here. All are user-friendly, equipped with beautiful books, classical music, and — for the most part — helpful clerks.

As for clothing, we list shops both conservative and chic. Indeed: if you take our tour of clothing stores, you will come across — *perhaps for the first time in your life* — a pair of silk boxer shorts priced at $58. We were naturally befuddled. Just when did it begin costing more to *undress* than to dress?

You'll find in our gift listings that artists are celebrated in stores like Legends and Options. Legends sells paintings, clothes, and gifts handcrafted by artists throughout the country. Options pays tribute to artists as well with a museumlike menagerie of unique gift items.

For those who don't have anything in particular on the shopping list, check out the shopping areas listed. Most are burgeoning meccas of retail sales, growing fast and furiously, thanks to the affluent, latte-drinking tourists and locals with expensive tastes.

So, hit an automated teller machine, harvest some cash, and pick a city, any city: Calistoga, St. Helena, Yountville, Napa, Healdsburg, Sonoma, Santa Rosa, or Sebastopol. They all have a special charm. You'll find that Sonoma County stores tend to be funkier than their Napa counterparts as a rule. Artifax in Sonoma, for one, is a sensory experience not to be missed. And you don't even have to pay a cover charge.

ANTIQUES

Napa County

Antique Fair (707-944-8440; 6512 Washington St., Yountville; open 10–5 daily) When you step through these doors, you feel as though you're walking into an estate. If you fancy large, stately French walnut pieces, the Antique Fair is for you. There are huge armoires, tables, bookcases, carved bed frames, and more.

Erika Hills Antiques, The Painted Illusions (707-963-0919; 115 Main St., St. Helena; open 10–5:30 Weds.–Mon.) The emphasis here is on painted furniture, old and new. The store has its own line, as well as furniture from

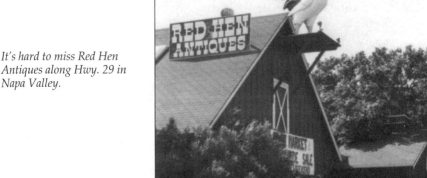

It's hard to miss Red Hen Antiques along Hwy. 29 in Napa Valley.

Chris Alderman

Europe and Mexico. You'll also find marble fountains and fireplaces and lots of painted porcelain.

The Irish Pedlar Antiques (707-253-9091; 1988 Wise Dr., Napa; open 10–5 Tues.–Sun.) The shop specializes in primitive pine with its oldest piece dating back to the 1840s. There is German and English pine as well, but about 75 percent of its stock is Irish. Plenty of linens, cookware, knickknacks, and quilts.

Red Hen Antiques (707-257-0822; 5091 Hwy. 29, Napa, open 10–5 daily) More like a museum than an attic. Attics aren't usually 18,000 sq. ft., after all. The Red Hen is the largest antique store in Napa Valley with rare finds ranging from porcelain dishes, *Life* and *Post* magazines, player pianos, and grandfather clocks. Look for the big white chicken along Hwy. 29.

Wexford and Woods (707-942-9729; 1347 Lincoln Ave., Calistoga; open 10–6 Sun.–Thurs., 10–9 Fri. & Sat.) The sweet scent of this shop beckons and shoppers who answer the call will find a curious match inside: skin care products from around the world and antique pine furniture imported from Ireland. Of course this attractive shop has other items in stock as well, such as baskets, paintings, pottery, and candles.

Sonoma County

Antique shops are booming in Sonoma County, encouraged by both tourists and locals who have reverence for furniture with a history. The pockets of the greatest growth are in Sonoma, Healdsburg, and naturally Sebastopol's Antique Row. We offer an expanded list of shops listed by city.

Finding just the right item at the Irish Cottage in Healdsburg.

Chris Alderman

HEALDSBURG

The Irish Cottage (707-433-4850; 112 Matheson St.; open 10:30–5 daily) A quaint and cozy shop on the square with plenty to peruse: pine dressers and tables, 19th-century cabinets and chests, as well as Irish imported woolens.

Healdsburg Classic Antiques (707-433-4315; 226 Healdsburg Ave.; open 11–5 daily) An enormous shop that spans two Quonset huts and includes about 20 dealers. You'll find a line of oversized furniture here as well as Indian baskets, pottery, and musical instruments.

Antique Harvest and Robert's Relics (707-433-0223; 225 Healdsburg Ave.; open 10–5 Mon.–Sat., 11–5 Sun.) Items range from country pine to Victorian, with lamps, brass, and Art Deco furnishings to boot. Meander through the wares of more than 10 dealers.

Angel Studio (707-433-6056; 226 Healdsburg Ave., Healdsburg; open 11–5 daily) The store sells estate art, jewelry, and antiques, as well as handcrafted pine furniture. It's fun to visit this store/studio because the Churchills are often busy with a pine table or chair.

SANTA ROSA

Marianne's Third Street Antiques (707-579-5749; 111 3rd St.; open 10–5:30 Mon.–Sat., 11–5 Sun.) This store is for the serious antique shopper. There are carefully chosen European armoires, tables, chairs, and desks. Nothing low-grade here.

Whistlestop Antiques (707-542-9474; 130 4th St.; open 10–5:30 Mon.–Sat., 11–4:30 Sun.) Browse through the collectibles of some 35 dealers and sift through estate and costume jewelry, jade, china, used books, and a general line of country furniture. Note the handy section devoted to supplies for refurbishing furniture.

The Silver Shop (707-546-7515; 107 3rd St.; open 10–5 Mon.–Fri., Sat. by appointment) This store offers a good selection of vintage silverware and also does silver appraisals.

SEBASTOPOL

Antique Society (707-829-1733; 2661 Gravenstein Hwy. S.; open 10–5 daily) This is Sonoma County's largest antique collective with more than 100 dealers. Naturally you'll find a wide assortment of antiques and collectibles from estate jewelry to furniture, including oak , country, and primitive.

Lone Pine Antiques (707-823-6768; 3598 Gravenstein Hwy. S.; open 10–5 daily, closed Tues. & Thurs.) If you were to build a pub in your own home, this would be the place to shop for accessories. The store's specialties are old advertising and toys. Coca-Cola memorabilia collectors will find old grocery display cases, and beer buffs can buy brewers' neon signs.

Ray's Trading Co. (707-829-9726; 3570 Gravenstein Hwy. S.; open 10–5 Tues.–Sat.) This is a salvage company recognized as an important resource for Bay Area people restoring Victorian homes. Ray's stocks bins full of antique doorknobs, drawer pulls, even whole windows and doors.

Sebastopol Antique Mall (707-823-1936; 755 Petaluma Ave.; open 10–6 daily) Sip a little vino and peruse upscale antiques in this unique setting. Yes, there is a wine bar and even a restaurant that serves lunches for marathon shoppers. Look for antiques and accessories such as Japanese tansu (chests), old clocks (including baroque), jewelry, desks, and dining room tables.

SONOMA

The Buffy (707-996-5626; 414 First St. E.; open 12–5 daily) Collectors of Staffordshire porcelain animals can come here for more finds. The focus is on genteel European antique furniture with many fine china cabinets and tables. Look for delicate china tea sets here, as well.

Country Pine English Antiques (707-938-8315; 23999 Arnold Dr.; open 10–5:30 Mon.–Sat., 11–5 Sun.) The emphasis here is on antiques from England and northern Ireland. But the shop also designs and sells pine beds and tables to order. Look for accessories as well such as candles, table linens, and bedding.

Tenenbaum Antiques (707-935-7147; 128 W. Napa St.; open 10–5 Tues.–Sat.) Formerly named Possessions, Tenenbaum Antiques has a wide variety of estate furnishings and fine accessories, including paintings. Look for lovely oak and mahogany furniture, bronze sculptures, and Asian artifacts.

BOOKS

Napa County

Bookends Book Store (707-224-1077; 1014 Coombs St., Napa; open 9:30–6 Mon.–Sat., 9:30–9 Thurs., 10–5 Sun.) A bookstore with a serious, smart feel to it. The store's varied inventory appeals to a general audience. Clerks do a great deal of special ordering for customers.

The Book Cellar (707-963-3901; 1354 Main St., St. Helena; open 10–5:30 Mon.–Sat., 11–5 Sun.) Wine lovers will relish the wine section of this charming bookstore because it has more than 100 titles of wine-related books. Easily one of the finest bookstores in Wine Country, the Book Cellar feels like a cozy home library. The store also features expanded sections on travel, fiction, and art. Note its extraordinary collection of classical music and jazz on CD.

Calistoga Bookstore (707-942-4123; 1343 Lincoln Ave., Calistoga; open 10–6 daily) It's always a good sign when you see a tabby napping in the front window of a bookstore. Calistoga Bookstore appeals to the general readers but specialties include Native Americans, history, mythology.

Copperfield's (707-252-8002; 1301 1st St., Napa; open 10–9 Mon.–Sat., 12–6 Sun.) Seventy percent of its stock is used books. See Sonoma County for details.

Main Street Books (707-963-1338; 1371 Main St., St. Helena; open 10–5:30 Mon.–Sat.) A small, quaint bookstore with a few comfortable chairs for the weary. There is a children's corner and a used book room, but otherwise it has a relatively modest selection of books.

Kids are king at Napa Book Company.

Chris Alderman

Napa Book Co. (707-224-3893; 1239 1st St., Napa; open 10:30–5:30 Mon.–Sat.) This bookstore definitely caters to children and moms and pops. There are plenty of parenting books and books for teachers, but 80% of the books are for kids. And manager Susan Turbin apparently knows how to reach them — she's been a teacher for more than 20 years.

Sonoma County

Apex Books (707-996-4769; 526 Broadway, Sonoma; open 11–6 Thurs.–Tues.) Hollywood memorabilia abounds in this bookstore. The owner was a former art director in Hollywood and is quite the film buff. The shop offers mostly used books as well as collectibles.

Barnes and Noble (707-576-7494; 700 4th St., Santa Rosa; open 9–11 daily) Nine shiny cash registers are lined up signifying the biggest bookstore in all Wine County: 20,000 square feet. Barnes and Noble is certainly giving the local, independent booksellers a run for their money. The bookstore has expanded sections on local authors, local travel, and local wineries. It also has an array of books on African Americans, Native Americans, gays, lesbians, and women. Coffee lovers will no doubt take a coffee break in Starbucks Cafe.

Books Inc. (707-546-9695; Coddingtown Center, Santa Rosa; open 9:30–9 Mon.–Sat., 11–6 Sun.) This bookstore has a fine selection of Napa and Sonoma books in its extensive travel section. The store also has expanded sections on cooking, children's books, child care, fiction, and metaphysics. Remaindered books are its forte and many books are 50% to 90% off the original price.

Finding a good read is easy at Copperfield's

Chris Alderman

Copperfield's (707-829-1286; 138 N. Main St., Sebastopol) This small chain also has outlets in Petaluma, Rohnert Park, and two stores in Santa Rosa. Copperfield's has built its business on customer service. The Sebastopol store is mainly general interest, but this being Northern California, there are several shelves devoted to holistic health, massage, and yoga.

North Light Books (707-579-9000; 95 5th St., Santa Rosa; open 9–9 Mon.–Thurs., 9–10 Fri. & Sat., 11–5 Sun.) This cozy, 800-square-foot bookstore boasts that it is "not mainstream." Its strengths lie in literary fiction, spirituality, and kids' books. This small shop always has an owner on duty, so expect good service from literary folk who have a passion for books.

Plaza Books (707-996-8474; 40 W. Spain St., Sonoma; open 11–6 daily) Shopping here is like browsing through your grandfather's library. The stock includes rare, collectible, and general used books, and some are museum-quality tomes more than 100 years old. You'll come across some first editions, while others are merely used books.

Readers' Books (707-939-1779; 127 E. Napa St., Sonoma; open 10–6 Sun.–Thurs., 10–9 Fri. & Sat.) While this bookstore is not the City Lights of Sonoma County, the store does have a reputation for being urban-like and very literary. The rocking chairs encourage people to linger. Expect great classics and fiction, an expansive cookbook section, and a myriad of books for children.

Sonoma Bookends Bookstore (707-938-5926; 201 W. Napa St., Suite #18, Sonoma; open 9:30–6 Mon.–Sat., 9:30–8 Thurs., 10–5:30 Sun.) This general bookstore caters to the tourist with expanded travel and wine sections. It also features local authors. The store's travel section focuses on California, the Bay Area, and Wine Country, and there's also a fine selection of United States Geological Survey maps.

Toyon Books (707-433-9270; 104 Matheson St., Healdsburg; open 9–10 Mon.–Sat., 10–6 Sun.) Sightseers looking for more information about the Sonoma Valley's wineries will find a large "Wines and Vineyards" section at the front of this general interest bookstore. Also prominently displayed are many titles on self-help and spiritual awareness, as well as a good selection of new fiction for the literary traveler.

CLOTHING

Napa County

Amelia Claire (707-963-8502; 1230 Main St., St. Helena; open 10–6 daily) This upscale shoe store carries everything from Cole Hahn to Nine West, from casual to elegant. It is the only shoe store in St. Helena, so the locals are loyal. The accessories include unique sweaters, hats, hosiery, bags, and belts.

Mario's Great Clothes for Men (707-963-1603; 1223 Main St., St. Helena; open 10–6 daily) It seems people shop here to make a statement — an expensive statement. Charmeuse silk boxer shorts are priced at $58. Charmeuse silk pajamas will run about $325. The shop carries designer clothes by Nicole Miller, Jhane Barnes, Xanella, and Cole Haan with clothes from casual to elegant.

Modern Eve (707-257-2824; 1222 1st St., Napa; open 10–5:30 Mon.–Sat., closed Sun.) Conservative women's clothing for the most part, with just a few racks of high-styled evening gowns that glitter with gold. Customers range from thirtysomething to 80. And small women will be pleased to see the Missy and Petite clothing sections.

Chris Alderman

Getting the right fit at Amelia Claire in St. Helena.

Overland Sheepskin Co. (707-944-0778; 6505 Washington St., Yountville; open 10–8 Fri.–Sat., 10–6 Sun.) Overland is in what was once a watering hole — The Old Whistle Stop Bar — from 1958 until 1989. And before that it was the Yountville Railroad Depot. The shop is devoted to fighting mother nature's cool winters in Wine Country, as well frigid climates elsewhere. There are leather wallets and luggage, fur coats, rustic rain gear, and fur hats. It caters to the locals with gloves and slippers and Merino Spanish lamb coats which feel like sweaters.

Splash (707-254-0767; 1416 2nd St., Napa; open 8–8 Mon.–Fri., 9–5 Sat., 9–3 Sun.) Cowabunga! This nifty shop is for beach fanatics. You may sport a tan after shopping here because there are five tanning rooms. Look for a line of Jag & DeWeese swimwear as well as Speedos for men and women. Accessories include sunglasses, towels, goggles, and swim caps. A smaller, second store is in St. Helena (707-967-1012).

Sonoma County

Dramatica (707-939-1413; 103 W. Napa St., Sonoma; open 10–6 daily) Look for funky and fun contemporary women's apparel with dresses ranging from $50 to $300. This store takes the edge off the business suit for women. Dramatica carries suits made of floral patterns, as well as delicate chiffon and rayon dresses. Nifty accessories include antique-looking buttons to dress up a dull shirt.

Fabrications (707-433-6243; 118 Matheson St., Healdsburg; open 10–5 Mon.–Sat.) Adventurous home sewers will be inspired by this store's exotic collection of natural fabrics from Guatemala, Bali, Africa, and other international locales. Dark batik fabrics and unusual silks are specialties. The store also caters to experienced quilt makers with quilting books and accessories. Don't miss the collection of antique buttons, especially fun to peruse.

Hot Couture (707-528-7247; 101 3rd St., Santa Rosa; open 10–6 Mon.–Sat., 11–5 Sun.) If you always wanted to dress like Jackie Kennedy before she became Jackie O. or Elvis before he got fat, you can find the required duds at this vintage clothing store. Owners John and Marta Koehne stock clothing from the 1900s to the '60s, as well as a collection of turn-of-the-century Victorian clothes for serious buyers. (Hot Couture also has costume rentals.)

Las Manos (707-578-1649; 129 4th St., Santa Rosa; open 10–6, Mon.–Sat., 11–4:30 Sun.) Somehow you don't expect to find Central American clothing and jewelry at Railroad Square, but it's a pleasure nonetheless. Las Manos owners Bruce and Diana Barkley make periodic forays to Guatemala where they own a clothing factory, and they tote home chunky knit sweaters and flowing rayon blouses and skirts in bright, primary colors. There are a few bright men's shirts here to choose from. Just right for a beach party!

Romaro's of Sonoma (707-939-1371; 403 1st St. W., Sonoma; open 10–6 Mon.–Thurs., 10–8 Fri. & Sat., 10–7 Sun.) This shop is in the lovely lobby of the El Dorado Hotel in downtown Sonoma. The store caters to women who relish Wine Country living and dressing up for wine tastings and fine dining. The store carries sportswear, suits, and elegant dresses; lines of clothing include Zanella, Joan Bass, Mondi, and Adrienne Vittadini.

Tzabaco (707-433-5265; 320 Center St., Healdsburg; open 11–5 Sat., 11–5 Sun.) A shop for those who really appreciate designer-wear. Lines of clothing include Diesel, International News, Ike Behar, and Gene Meyer ties. But don't let this designer lingo scare you off. Clothes range from $40 to $600-plus and are just the thing for a relaxed, country-casual style.

FURNITURE

Napa County

Bale Mill Designs (707-963-4595; 3431 Hwy. 29, St. Helena; open 10–5 daily) The store builds pine furniture in an 18th-century style. The owners are partial to French, English, and American traditional styles and create many big farm tables and tasting tables for wineries, as well as chests, armoires, etc.

R.S. Basso (707-963-0391; 1219 Main, St. Helena; open 10–6 daily) This unique store offers custom-designed upholstery with rows of fabric ranging from vibrant florals to elegant chintz. All you need is a hip idea and some measurements. The owners say "the client is the designer." The shop also sells high-end accessories and country furnishings.

Sonoma County

Palladio (707-433-4343; 324 Healdsburg Ave., Healdsburg; open 10–5 daily) Perhaps the most elegant store in all of Wine Country, Palladio ushers you into the Mediterranean-style shop with a landscaped courtyard and fountains. Sister to Bale Mill Designs in St. Helena, Palladio carves most of its designs from pine and has a line of furniture that includes tables, cupboards, and armoires.

R.S. Basso has both a Sebastopol and a Healdsburg store in Sonoma County. The Sebastopol store is at 186 N. Main St.; 707-829-1373; open 10–5:30 Mon.–Sat., 11–5 Sun. The Healdsburg store is at 115 Plaza; 707-431-1925; open 10:30–6 Mon.–Sat., 11–5 Sun. See Napa County for details.

Randolph Johnson Designs (707-577-8196; 608 5th Street, Santa Rosa; open 9–5 Mon.–Fri.) Keep your eye on Junior because items in this studio/shop may cost $15,000. Peruse the handcrafted pottery, glassware, electrical fixtures, and furniture, and admire the artistry.

GIFTS

Napa County

Hurd Beeswax Candles & Hurd Gift & Gourmet (707-963-7211; 3020 St. Helena Hwy. N., St. Helena; open 8:30–5 Mon.–Fri., 10–5:30 Sat. & Sun.) Hurd is a tourist trap to be sure, but it's fun all the same. All the candles are

Manager Mary Sue Frediani lights a spiral candle at Hurd Beeswax Candles in St. Helena.

handcrafted from sheets of pure beeswax and there are more than 200 designs. In the gift and gourmet section, you'll find kitchenware, cookbooks, wine-tasting guides, corkscrews, champagne stoppers, and more festive ware.

Flying Carpets & Art Decor (707-252-8757; 1238 1st St., Napa; open 10–5 Tues.–Sat.) Slipping into this interesting shop is like visiting a traveling art exhibit. On occasion you'll find a display of masks, pottery, and art, aside from rugs from 14 different countries. The store also has Oriental and ethnic jewelry. (The owners have a second store at 1152 Main St., St. Helena; 707-967-9192; open 10–5 Weds.–Sun.)

N.V. Traditions (707-226-2044; 1202 Main St., Napa; open 7–5:30 Mon.–Fri., 9–5 Sat., 11–4 Sun.) This quaint store is a gift shop, a coffee café, and a tasting room for Bayview Cellars. Look for lines of fine dishware such as Lindt-Styneist, Essex, and Denby. You'll also find wine paraphernalia such as glassware, carafes, and racks amid the general line of gifts: lotions, hand therapies, etc.

Stillwaters (707-963-1782; 1228 Main St.. St. Helena; open 10–6 daily) This store appeals to the unisex shopper who loves the outdoors. Stillwaters has woodsy and casual yet upscale lines of clothing by Columbia and Ex Officio. There are also plenty of leather jackets and vests, belts, ties, and yes, even Joe Boxer boxer shorts. Accessories include fly-fishing boxes, binoculars, and books for the well-dressed adventurer.

T's 'n Tops (707-253-7177; 1319 1st St., Napa; open 10–5:30 Mon.–Sat., 10–8 Thurs., 12–4 Sun.) "How can I cope with Life when I can't even program my VCR?" This is the kind of philosophical, soul-searching question we found emblazoned on one T's 'n Tops T-shirt. The shop is Napa Valley's largest store

Vanderbilt & Co. offers classic and contemporary home accessories.

Chris Alderman

for custom T-shirts and sweatshirts. Tourists will naturally gravitate to the festive T-shirts celebrating Wine Country.

Vanderbilt & Company (707-963-1010; 1429 Main St.; St. Helena; open 9:30–5:30 daily) This store is brimming with the smart and artsy accessorizing you might find while flipping through a glossy home and garden catalog. From bedding to kitchenware to patio suits — V&C has everything you need to warm up your home with a little country mirth or cool it off with contemporary savvy. Peruse the 5,000 square feet of home accessories which range from $1 cards to $10,000 paintings, with furniture, candles, and books somewhere in between.

Sonoma County

Artifax delights all the senses.

Chris Alderman

Artifax International Gallery & Gifts (707-996-9494; 450 1st St. E., Sonoma; open 10–6 Mon.–Sat., 11–5 Sun.) A true sensory experience. You'll see exotic textiles and carved masks here, smell burning incense, and hear tapes of evocative African drums and other world music. Artifax's owners import eastern ritual art and crafts, mostly from the Third World. Carved masks and woven fabrics make up much of the stock. There are also authentic musical instruments and earrings crafted from beads or coins. Artifax sells a big selection of beads — to create your own jewelry — from Africa, China, Tibet, and other countries.

Hearth Song (707*829*0944; 156 N. Main St., Sebastopol; open 10–6 Mon.–Sat., 12–5 Sun.) Children who dream of knights and princesses and castles can feed their fantasies at this store specializing in creative toys largely imported from Europe. The emphasis is on toys to stimulate a child's imagination, such as magic wands, crowns, and elf caps. There are many easy craft sets for children. Parents will like the unbreakable doll houses and castles. Hearth Song is a retail and mail-order catalog company.

Legends (707-939-8100, 483 1st Street W., Sonoma; open 10–6 daily, 11–6 Sun.) This is really a neat place. Inspired by the movie *Dead Poets Society*, the Michlig family migrated west from Melborne, Florida, to create this unique shop which celebrates artists. Legends debuts the work of 300-plus artists from across the U.S. and it ranges from paintings, wood sculptures, chimes, lamps, ties — everything handmade. Many items come with a background sheet telling more about the art and artist.

Main Street Traditions (707-829-3667; 145 N. Main St., Sebastopol; open 10–5:30 Mon.–Sat., 11–4:30 Sun.) This is superb one-stop shopping. Stock includes hand-colored photographs, greeting cards, copper pans, gourmet oils and vinegar, and yes, even antique furniture such as a pine harvest table from England, a mahogany cabinet, and a Mission-style desk. You may need a truck to haul your purchases home.

Options has a sense of whimsy and sophistication.

Chris Alderman

Options (707-431-8861; 126 Plaza St., Healdsburg; open 10–6 Mon.–Sat., 11–6 Sun.) This shop has a clear sense of fun and style. It's stocked with whimsi-cal one-of-a-kind items as well as sophisticated collectibles. Look for jew-elry, furniture, lighting, baskets, pottery, and ceramics. Seventy percent of its inventory is imported. Nifty kimonos and Kilim rugs. Rusinow also offers a custom buying service and has catalogs in her shop for customers to peruse.

Wine Country Gifts (707-996-3453; 407 1st St. W., Sonoma; open 10–6 daily) Here's the place to find unusual Wine Country gifts for friends back home (especially if you've already loaded them down with bottles of vino). Terra cotta wine coolers (a variation on the ice bucket) with cherub figures make easy gifts. The shop also sells champagne flutes, Bluestone wine glasses, serving pieces, and grape-related jewelry.

Zambezi Trading Co. (707-939-1333; 107 W. Napa St., Sonoma; open 10–6 daily) This interesting store celebrates the African tribes of the Zambezi River and their wares. There are huge metal sculptures, woven baskets, wall hangings, hand-painted fabrics, wood tables, and cabinets made from recycled railroad ties. You'll easily lose an hour just browsing.

JEWELRY

Napa County

Indulge your exotic tastes at the Artful Eye in Calistoga.

Chris Alderman

The Artful Eye (707-942-4743; 1333A Lincoln Ave., Calistoga; open 10–6 daily) Walking through the Artful Eye is like meandering through a museum. The jewelry is all handcrafted by some 300 local artists and many of the pieces seem inspired by ancient cultures. Materials run the gamut: glass, feathers, sterling silver, rope, fine gemstones, and even diamonds. The jewelry ranges in price from $8 to $3,000, but the majority of pieces are lower-end sterling silver. There's now a second Artful Eye at 316 Center St., Healdsburg, 707-433-9190, open 10–6 daily.

The Beaded Nomad (707-258-8004; 1122 1st St., Napa; open 11–6 Mon.–Sat., 12–5 Sun.) You don't have to be a child of the '60s to relish this jewelry shop which features beads, beads, and more beads. The store caters to those who like to use their hands. Not to worry. Design assistance is available.

David's (707-963-0239; 1339 Main St., St. Helena; open 10–5:30 Tues.–Sat., closed Sun. & Mon.) Essentially a designer's showcase for jewelry, this shop has a smart, contemporary feel — much like the style of the jewelry itself. David, the owner, is one of several designers whose work is displayed. Virtually every piece is handcrafted. The style is contemporary. There are clean, straight lines and unusual shapes playing up classic gemstones and diamonds.

The William Pacific Co. (707-963-6000; 1269 Main St., St. Helena; open 10–5:30 daily) This store sells fine jewelry, gemstones, and jade. Aside from fashion jewelry, you'll also find an eclectic collection of gifts from China. The selection changes constantly.

Sonoma County

Classic Copies (707-996-7956; 491 1st St. W., Sonoma) Do you dream of having Tiffany jewels on a dime-store budget? Classic Copies sells fake necklaces, earrings, and rings with synthetic stones that look like the real thing. While most of the metal is gold tone, there are some 14 karat gold pieces. Ray Stanz says the store attracts wealthy women afraid their real jewels will be stolen, as well as dreamers who want to look like a million. Which are you?

Mary Stage (707-938-1818; 126 W. Napa St., Sonoma; open 10–5 Tues.–Sat.) Mary Stage concentrates on estate-purchased jewelry and silver, with a heavy emphasis on 1920s items for women. Some of the prettiest finds are delicate women's watches with bands. Men's pocket watches are also featured. There's a good selection of jewelry with stones such as jade, coral, and onyx.

Tribal Beginnings (707-829-2174; 6914 Sebastopol Ave., Sebastopol; open 11–5:30 Tues.–Sat., or by appointment) This is one of the few places in Napa and Sonoma offering authentic Native American antique jewelry, and textiles from Southwestern Indian tribes such as the Navaho and Zuni as well as the local tribes of Pomo and Hupa. Some of the most beautiful pieces are antique silver and turquoise jewelry. Expect to pay big bucks for the authentic goods. If you're looking for something for a smaller budget, the store has a few porcupine quill and bead earrings. (They're prettier than they sound.)

OUTLETS

Tired of boutique shopping? If you still have the stamina, amble on over to these factory outlet malls. But beware. People have been known to lose themselves for days in outlet villages. Shopping madness they call it.

Napa Factory Stores (707-226-9876; 999 Freeway Dr., Napa, open 10–8 daily) The maze of stores include Liz Claiborne, Book Warehouse, Timberland, Jones New York, Bass, Van Heusen, Windsor Shirt Co., Geoffrey Beene, Nautica, and Harry & David.

Petaluma Village Factory Outlets (707-778-9300; 2200 Petaluma Blvd. N., Petaluma; 10–8 daily) Stores are continually evolving and the roster to date includes Levi's Outlet, Brooks Brothers, Van Heusen, Bass Shoes, Corning Revere, Geoffrey Beene, Le Gourmet Chef, and Harry & David.

SHOPPING AREAS

Downtown shopping in Wine Country is not a lost art. In fact, it's booming. Colorful shops are springing up like a vibrant crop of mustard. What follows is a listing of the most clever stores clustered in shopping areas — ones you won't want to miss. More information about these shops is usually given above in this chapter. Most of the stores are right on the strip or on the square, but some are tucked a block or two back. There's no doubt — there are great finds in the nooks and crannies of Wine Country.

Downtown Calistoga is just one shopping area brimming with stores.

Chris Alderman

Napa County

CALISTOGA

When a mud treatment and a massage renders you al dente, you're ready to hit the Lincoln Avenue strip of stores, the main drag in town. Be sure to check out the following stores: **The Calistoga Bookstore, The Artful Eye,** and **Evans Design Studio Outlet.**

ST. HELENA

You better schedule a good 12-hour day of shopping in this quaint yet cosmopolitan Main St. U.S.A. St. Helena has some of the best shopping in all of Wine Country. Look for **David's, Vanderbilt & Co., Stillwaters, Amelia Claire, The Book Cellar,** and **Erika Hills Antiques.**

YOUNTVILLE

The predominant shopping area is Vintage 1870 and it plays to tourists. The historic complex was once the Groezinger Winery and it has stone flooring, brick walls, and wooden rafters. You'll find some interesting shops such as **Hansel & Gretel Clothes Loft, Wee Bit O' Wool,** and **A Little Romance.** But the most original shopping in Yountville is off the beaten path. Check out **Overland Sheepskin Co.** and **Antique Fair.**

NAPA

Napa's downtown is a mix of old and new architecture, but the homes in the area are definitely historic Napa with plenty of "Painted Ladies." It's a fun backdrop to a town that is gaining stature as a shopping destination. Look for **N.V. Traditions, Modern Eve, Splash, T's 'N Tops, The Beaded Nomad, Copperfield's,** and the **Napa Book Co.**

Sonoma County

HEALDSBURG

Taking a stroll at Healdsburg's town plaza is like stepping into a Norman Rockwell print. Healdsburg may just be the town that time forgot. Its plaza is lined with inviting, upscale shop such as **Palladio, R.H. Basso, Options, Tzabaco, The Irish Cottage,** and **Toyon Books.**

SANTA ROSA

Santa Rosa's downtown may be on the cusp of a revival, thanks to the Barnes and Noble bookstore which made its home in the old Rosenberg department store. But for now the downtown is mostly a cozy blend of bookstores and coffee houses. Be sure to check out **Copperfield's Annex.**

SEBASTOPOL

Downtown Sebastopol has a folksy, old-time feel to it. People here never seem to be in a hurry, as though it's perpetually a lazy Sunday morning, and it makes shopping a relaxing treat. Look for **Main St. Traditions, Hearth Song, Copperfield's,** and **Tribal Beginnings.** If antiques are your pleasure, just a few blocks down the road on Gravenstein Highway is "Antique Row," a cluster of homey shops. **Peruse Sebastopol Antique Mall, Ray's Trading Co., Lone Pine Antiques,** and **Antique Society.**

SONOMA

This little winery town with its Old World-style plaza is quickly being gentrified. A few years ago the downtown square was home to some country shops and mundane food purveyors. Today it has high-styled clothing stores, gourmet food shops, and ethnic stores with African masks and textiles. Look for **Zambezi Trading Co., Legends, Artifax,** and **Readers' Books.**

CHAPTER NINE
Just the Facts, Ma'am
INFORMATION

Dairy farming is second only to grape growing as the largest agricultural concern in Wine Country.

Courtesy Sonoma County Convention & Visitors Bureau

This chapter will prove to be as comforting as Linus's blanket. The information compiled covers emergencies as well as everyday practical matters. A little peace of mind goes a long way when you want to savor Wine Country. This chapter caters to both the tourist and newcomer, with information running the gamut from weather reports and visitors bureaus to real estate matters and school listings. So acquaint yourself with Napa and Sonoma. You may decide to stretch your two-week stay into a lifetime.

AMBULANCE, FIRE, POLICE, COAST GUARD

Simply dial 911 in both Napa and Sonoma counties. You will reach an operator who will swiftly put you through to the right agency: Fire and rescue, ambulance, local police, sheriff, California Highway Patrol, or Coast Guard Search and Rescue.

To report rape and sexual assault: Napa Emergency Woman's Services at 707-255-6397 or Sonoma County's Rape Crisis at 707-545-7273.

For the Poison Control Center call 800-523-2222.

AREA CODES, ZIP CODES, CITY HALLS

AREA CODES

Napa and Sonoma counties:	707
San Francisco:	415
Oakland and Berkeley:	510

Area codes for adjacent counties:	
Marin	415
Mendocino	707
Alameda and Contra Costa	510
Lake County	707
Solano	707
Yolo	916

ZIP CODES & CITY HALLS

	Zip Code	City Hall
Napa County		
Calistoga	94515	707-942-2800
St. Helena	94574	707-963-2741

	Zip Code	City Hall
Yountville	94599	707-944-8851
Napa	94558	707-257-9503
	94559	
	94581	

Sonoma County

	Zip Code	City Hall
Bodega Bay	94923	
Healdsburg	95448	707-431-3317
Sebastopol	95472	707-823-7863
Santa Rosa	95401	707-524-5361
	95402	
	95403	
	95404	
	95405	
	95406	
	95407	
Sonoma	95476	707-938-3681
Petaluma	94952	707-778-4345
	94953	
	94954	

BANKS

If you have a bank card, you're the king of cash in the age of the automated teller. Hungry for a few more traveler's checks? Listed below are a sampling of regional and national banks. Each branch office is equipped with at least one automated teller machine. Note the systems to which each bank is electronically linked.

Bank of America (707-542-4433 or 800-441-6437) Linked to Plus, Star, Interlink, Cirrus, and ATM systems.
Locations: 1429 Lincoln Ave., Calistoga
2 Financial Plaza, Napa
1700 1st St., Napa
1001 Adams, St. Helena
35 W. Napa St., Sonoma
502 Healdsburg Ave., Healdsburg
1155 W. Steele Lane, Santa Rosa
2420 Sonoma Ave., Santa Rosa
6580 Oakmont Dr., Santa Rosa
7185 Healdsburg Ave., Sebastopol

Wells Fargo Bank (707-996-2262 or 707-579-4248) Linked to Star, Plus, and Interlink systems.
Locations: 1115 Vine St., Healdsburg
  2960 Cleveland Ave., Santa Rosa
  200 B St., Santa Rosa
  2405 4th St., Santa Rosa
  1799 Marlowe Rd., Santa Rosa
  480 W. Napa St., Sonoma

West America Bank (707-226-9932 or 800-660-2265) Linked to Star, Cirrus, Plus, Explore, and Maestro systems.
Locations: 1 Financial Plaza, Napa
  1400 Clay St., Napa
  1221 Imola Ave., Napa
  6470 Washington St., Yountville
  1000 Adams, St., Helena
  1110 Washington St., Calistoga

BIBLIOGRAPHY

Browse through our bookshelves. Wine Country can be a curious place, what with the specter of ghost wineries and the mystique of winemaking. Consider, if you will, the two lists compiled: Books You Can Buy and Books You Can Borrow.

Books You Can Buy lists titles generally available in Sonoma and Napa bookstores, nationally or from the publishers. For more information on Napa and Sonoma booksellers, see "Books" in Chapter Eight, *Shopping*.

Oak trees dot the hillsides of Wine Country.

Chris Alderman

Books You Can Borrow are generally found in Napa and Sonoma local libraries and in most public libraries elsewhere. They are typically no longer for sale.

For wine books, two helpful — and free — sources are the *Napa Valley Wine Library* (707-963-5244; St. Helena Public Library, 1492 Library Ln.) and the *Sonoma County Wine Library* (707-433-3772; Healdsburg Public Library, 139 Piper St.) For more information, see "Libraries" in Chapter Four, *Culture.*

BOOKS YOU CAN BUY

WINE AND FOOD

Ash, John and Sid Goldstein. *American Game Cooking.* New York: Addison-Wesley, 1991. 288 pp., photos, $16.95.

Bailey, Lee. *California Wine Country Cooking.* New York: Potter, 1991. 176 pp., photos, $30.

Berger, Dan. *Beyond the Grape, An Inside Look at Napa Valley.* Wilmington, Del.: Atomium Books, 1992. Photos, $34.95.

Berger, Dan and Richard Hinkle. *Beyond the Grape, An Inside Look at Sonoma County.* Wilmington, Del.: Atomium Books, 1991. 256 pp., photos, $34.95.

Bernstein, Leonard S. *The Official Guide to Wine Snobbery.* New York: Quill Press, 1982. 160 pp., illus., $4.95.

Chappellet, Molly. *A Vineyard Garden.* New York: Viking Studio Books, 1991. 291 pp., photos, $40.

Cox, Jeff. *From Vines to Wines.* Pownal, Vermont: Storey Books for Country Living, 1989. 281 pp., $12.95.

Johnson, Hugh. Vintage: *The Story of Wine.* New York: Simon & Schuster, 1989. 464 pp., photos, illus., bibliog., index, $39.95.

Jordan, Michele Anna. *A Cook's Tour of Sonoma.* New York: Addison-Wesley, 1990. 296 pp., illus., $16.95.

Kramer, Matt. *Making Sense of Wine.* New York: William Morrow, 1989. 190 pp., bibliog., index, $16.95.

Parker, Robert M. Jr. *Parker's Wine Buyer's Guide.* New York: Simon & Schuster, 3rd ed., 1993. 160 pp., charts, appendix, index, $21.00

Thompson, Bob. *The Wine Atlas of California.* New York: Simon & Schuster, 1993. 239 pp., maps, illus., $45.

Steiman, Harvey. *California Kitchen.* San Francisco: Chronicle Books, 1990. 304 pp., photos, $12.95.

Sterling, Joy. *A Cultivated Life.* New York: Villard Books, 1993. 239 pp., illus., $22.

Wine Spectator Magazine. *Ultimate Guide to Buying Wine.* New York: Wine Spectator Press, annual. 750 pp., photos, illus., $22.95.

LITERARY WORKS

London, Jack. *Call of the Wild and Selected Stories*. New York: Penguin Books, 1960. 176 pp., $2.50.

Author Robert Louis Stevenson loved Napa Valley.

Courtesy Silverado Museum

Stevenson, Robert Louis. *The Works of Robert Louis Stevenson*. London: Octopus Pub. Group, 1989. 687 pp., $7.98.

BIOGRAPHIES

Dreyer, Peter. *A Gardener Touched With Genius, The Life of Luther Burbank*. Berkeley, CA: Univ. of California Press, 1985. 230 pp., photos, index, $12.95.
London, Joan. *Jack London and His Daughters*. Berkeley, CA: Heyday Books, 1990. 179 pp., photos, $10.95.

LOCAL HISTORIES

Conaway, James. *Napa, The Story of an American Eden*. Boston, MA: Houghton Mifflin, 1990. 506 pp., photos, $24.95.
Heintz, William F. *Wine Country: A History of Napa Valley, The Early Years 1838 to 1920*. Santa Barbara, CA.: Capra Press, 1990. 326 pp., photos, illus., $29.95.
LeBaron, Gaye, Dee Blackman, Joann Mitchell, and Harvey Hansen. *Santa Rosa: A Nineteenth Century Town*. Historia Ltd. 210 pp., photos, sources and notes, index.
LeBaron, Gaye and Joann Mitchell. *Santa Rosa: A Twentieth Century Town*. Santa Rosa, CA: Historia Ltd. ,1993. 350 pp., photos, $59.95.
Wilson, Simone. *Sonoma County: The River of Time*. Chatsworth, CA.: Windsor Publications, 1990. 121 pp., photos, illus., index, $25.95.

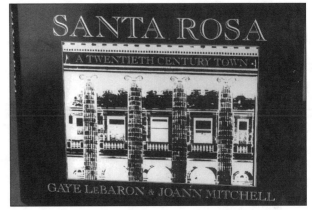

Gaye LeBaron and Joann Mitchell have chronicled the history of Santa Rosa in two books.

Courtesy Gaye LeBaron

RECREATION

Emmery, Lena & Sally Taylor. *Grape Expeditions in California.* San Francisco, CA: Sally Taylor & Friends, 1987. 74 pp., illus., maps, $7.50.

Lorentzen, Bob. *The Hiker's Hip Pocket Guide to Sonoma County.* Mendocino, CA: Bored Feet Publications, 1990. 201 pp., illus., maps, bibliog., index, $11.95.

Powers, Peter. *Touring California's Wine Country by Bicycle.* Eugene, OR: Terra-graphics, 1990. 171 pp., maps, illus., $10.95.

TRAVEL

Matson, Robert W. *Sonoma Coast, North of San Francisco, The Untamable Coast.* Santa Rosa, CA: Sea Wolf Publishing, 1991. 73 pp., photos, illus., maps, $4.95.

Sangwan, B. *The Complete Wine Country Guidebook, Discovering California's Napa and Sonoma Valleys.* Tahoe City, CA: Indian Chief Publishing House, 1990. 135 pp., wine glossary, index, $7.95.

BOOKS YOU CAN BORROW

Dutton, Joan Parry. *They Left Their Mark: Famous Passages through the Wine Country.* Illuminations Press., 1983. 180 pp., photos, bibliog., index. A historical look at the famous people who traveled through Wine Country and the influence they had on the region.

Haynes, Irene W. *Ghost Wineries of Napa Valley.* Sally Taylor & Friends Publishing, 1980. 73 pp., photos, index. Take an eerie tour of old and abandoned wineries, if you dare.

Heintz, William F. *Wine Country: A History of Napa Valley, The Early Years 1838 to 1920.* Capra Press, 1990. 326 pp., photos, illus. A study of winemakers through Napa history.

Issler, Anne Roller. *Stevenson at Silverado.* Caxton Printers, Ltd. 1939. 247 pp., photos. Follows Stevenson as he roams through Napa Valley. The book gives insight into his work "The Silverado Squatters."

Johnson, Rheta Grimsley. *Good Grief: The Story of Charles M. Schulz.* Pharos Books, 1989. 254 pp., drawings, cartoons, bibliography. An intimate portrait of Charles Schulz, the Santa Rosan behind the comic strip "Peanuts."

King, Norton L. *Napa County: A Historical Overview.* Self published, 1967. 98 pp., photos, bibliog., index. Geographic, topographic, and geologic origins of Wine Country.

Kraft, Ken and Pat. *Luther Burbank: The Wizard and the Man.* Meredith Press, 1967. 261 pp., bibliog., index. Burbank was as famous as Henry Ford in 1915 and this book chronicles his life in Santa Rosa.

Lundquist, James. *Jack London: Adventures, Ideas & Fiction.* Ungar, 1987. 188 pp. bibliog., index. A biography of the man who wrote *The Sea Wolf* and *The Call of the Wild.*

CHILD CARE

Child care spells relief for some parents who want to roam Wine Country without their teetotaling tots. For travelers and newcomers alike, here's a sampling of licensed child care centers. Parents can find out more about licensed day care providers by studying their files at Community Care Licensing in the California State Building, 50 D. St., in Santa Rosa. The following organizations make free child care referrals:

Community Child Care Council of Sonoma County: 707-544-3077
Community Resources For Children: Napa, 707-253-0366

Here are a few specific options:

Napa County

La Petite Academy: Napa,, 707-257-7796
Little Friends: Napa, 707-252-8899
Silver Lining Child Care Center Preschool: Napa, 707-226-KIDS

Sonoma County

Alphabet Soup Pre-School and Day Care Center: Sebastopol, 707-829-9460
Happy Time Christian Pre-School & Day Care: Santa Rosa, 707-527-9135
Healdsburg Montessori Children's House: Healdsburg, 707-431-1727

CLIMATE & WEATHER REPORTS

CLIMATE

The late Luther Burbank, known as the plant wizard, called Napa and Sonoma counties "The chosen spot of all the earth as far as nature is concerned."

The moderate weather is a blessing for those who have suffered Midwestern blizzards. In Napa and Sonoma, the winter is cool, with temperatures dipping down to the 40s. Rainy season begins in late December and lingers until April. Of course, the droughts in recent years have made the season somewhat unpredictable and the locals count raindrops with good cheer. Rain makes for a lush countryside and hillsides ribbed with vineyards.

TEMPERATURE AND PRECIPITATION

Average Temperatures

	Napa	Sonoma
October	63.5	64.1
January	46.8	47.8
April	60.4	61.0
July	69.2	71.7

Average Annual Total Precipitation (1993)

	Napa	Sonoma
rain	16.07	19.82
snow	0	0

WEATHER REPORTS

Napa County

Calistoga	707-942-2800
St. Helena	707-963-3601

Sonoma County

Cloverdale	707-894-3545
Healdsburg	707-431-3362
Sonoma	707-938-1519

GUIDED TOURS

L ooking for some packaged fun? Consider our list of tours. They will take you on a Wine Country adventure via a stretch limo, horse-drawn wagon, or even a cable car.

California Wine Tours (707-586-1568; 22455 Broadway, Sonoma) This tour is a treat for the pampered. Guests board a stretch limo for up to six hours of touring and wine tasting. The custom-designed tours include complimentary champagne and a beverage bar. Price per person is $39.00.

Getaway Wine Country Bicycle Tours and Rentals (707-942-0332; 1117 Lincoln Ave., Calistoga) Day trips priced at $79 per person have bikers pedaling to six or seven wineries with a gourmet lunch to boot. The company also books two- and five-day bike trips and delivers rentals to bed and breakfasts. Adventurers will find the Pedal and Paddle Tour invigorating. It features a half day of canoeing and a half day of bicycling.

Wine Country Wagons (707-833-2724; PO Box 1069, Kenwood) A rustic tour of wineries in the Kenwood area of northern Sonoma Valley is offered on a wagon drawn by Belgian draft horses. A gourmet lunch is included. By reservation only from May to October.

Wine & Dine Tours (707-963-8930; 1250 Church St., Suite E, St. Helena) This tour is for the discriminating traveler who would like to stop in at small boutique wineries in Napa Valley and Sonoma Valley. Most of the wineries are private or by appointment only. Guests will be treated to lunch and bubbly on every tour. The guides also encourage wedding planners to give a call so the company can set up custom tours for out-of-towners.

HANDICAPPED SERVICES

W ine Country is accessible — even in a wheelchair. Napa and Sonoma offer a number of easy solutions to help anyone with a handicap get to-and-fro.

Dial-A-Ride-Services, Inter City Van-Go (707-252-2600, Greater Napa Area; 707-963-4222, Upper Valley) All vans are wheelchair-accessible.

Handyvan-Calistoga (707-963-4229) The vans are wheelchair-accessible.

The Vine (707-255-7631) The Valley Intracity Neighborhood Express has five routes in the city of Napa. All buses are wheelchair-accessible.

U-Drive Wheelchair Access Vans (707-258-0800) Vans can accommodate two wheelchairs.

Volunteer Wheels of Sonoma County (707-573-3377) Transportation for senior citizens and disabled riders.

The Hiker's Hip Pocket Guide to Sonoma County, Bored Feet Pub., includes a special section for the handicapped indicating which scenic trails are accessible.

HOSPITALS

Community Hospital (707-576-4000; 3325 Chanate Rd. Santa Rosa) 24-hour emergency care. Emergency Room, 707-576-4040.

Healdsburg General Hospital (707-431-6500; 1375 University Ave., Healdsburg) 24-hour emergency care. Physician on duty. Call the general number and ask for the Emergency Room.

Petaluma Valley Hospital (707-778-1111; 400 N. McDowell Blvd., Petaluma) 24-hour emergency care. Emergency Room, 707-778-2634).

Santa Rosa Memorial Hospital (707-546-3210; 1165 Montgomery Dr., Santa Rosa) 24-hour emergency services. Physician on duty.

Sonoma Valley Hospital (707-935-5000; 347 Andrieux St., Sonoma) 24-hour emergency care. Emergency Room, 707-935-5100.

The Sonoma County Museum, a former post office.

Chris Alderman

LATE NIGHT FOOD AND FUEL

Insomnia after too much gourmet food or wine? Or perhaps you're just a weary traveler looking for a place to gas up. Whatever the case, here are some options for nightbirds.

Napa County

Bel Aire Shell Service: 707-226-1720; 1491 Trancas St., Napa

Lucky: 707-255-7767; 1312 Trancas St., Napa

Safeway: 707-963-3833; 1026 Hunt Ave., St. Helena

Sonoma County

Lucky: 707-545-8906; 390 Coddingtown Mall, Santa Rosa

Safeway: 707-996-0633; 477 W. Napa St., Sonoma

Santa Rosa Exxon: 707-546-9493; Coddington Mall, Santa Rosa

MEDIA: MAGAZINES, NEWSPAPERS, RADIO STATIONS, TELEVISION

MAGAZINES AND NEWSPAPERS

Appellation (800-799-3393; PO Box 516, Napa; quarterly) A nationally recognized magazine with a true sense of style and intelligence, with insight into what life in Napa Valley is all about.

The Business Journal (707-579-2900; 5510 Skylane Blvd., Suite 201, Santa Rosa; twice-monthly Sonoma and Marin counties, monthly Napa and Solano counties) The region's rendition of the *Wall Street Journal,* with news on the deals and the players and profiles on key business leaders.

California Visitors Review (707-938-0780; PO Box 92, El Verano; weekly) A good magazine for tourists, with articles on winemakers, inns, and restaurants. Helpful maps included in each issue. Free.

Healdsburg Tribune (707-433-4451; 706 Healdsburg Ave., Healdsburg; Weds. & Fri.) This Sonoma County paper, born in 1953, still has the flavor of the 50s.

Napa Valley Register (707-226-3711; 1615 2nd St., Napa; daily) The paper made its first run in 1865 and has proven over the years to give a good local account of Napa County.

Press Democrat (707-546-2020; 427 Mendocino Ave., Santa Rosa; daily) Purchased by the *New York Times* in the 1980s, the *Press Democrat* is the largest newspaper in the North Bay. It emphasizes Sonoma County, with newly expanded coverage of the Napa food and wine scene.

San Francisco Chronicle (415-777-7000; 901 Mission St., San Francisco; daily) This metro is not impressive to look at but it's a good source for national and international news. There are often good Wine Country articles in the food and people sections.

San Francisco Examiner (415-777-7800; 110 5th St.; San Francisco; daily) This metro has a much cleaner look and wittier style than the *Chronicle*. Unfortunately too few Bay Area readers make it a daily habit, since it's an afternoon paper.

Sonoma Business (707-575-8282; 50 Courthouse Square, Suite 105, Santa Rosa; monthly) Covers business and industry in Sonoma County well. It delves into the "politics" of business.

Sonoma County Independent (707-527-1200; 540 Mendocino Ave., Santa Rosa; weekly) Edgy alternative weekly with strong — and liberal — views on politics in Northern California.

Sonoma Index-Tribune (707-938-2111; 117 W. Napa St., Sonoma; twice weekly) A community paper that focuses exclusively on life in Sonoma Valley.

St. Helena Star (707-963-2731; 1328 Main St.; St. Helena; weekly) A folksy weekly that covers this town in the heart of Napa Valley.

RADIO STATIONS

KHBG 95.9 FM (Healdsburg, 707-433-9599) Adult album alternative.

KJZY 93.7 FM (Sebastopol, 707-528-4434) Light jazz.

KLCQ 92.9 FM (Santa Rosa, 707-543-0100) Pop-rock from the '70s.

KRPQ 105 FM (Rohnert Park, 707-584-1058) Country music.

KSRO 1350 AM (Santa Rosa, 707-543-0100) News and talk.

KVON 1440 AM (Napa, 707-252-1440) General news and talk.

KVYN 99.3 FM (Napa, 707-252-1440) Adult contemporary.

KXFX 101.7 FM (Santa Rosa, 707-543-0100) Rock.

KZST 100 FM (Santa Rosa, 707-528-2424) Adult contemporary.

KRSH 98.7 FM (Middletown/Santa Rosa, 707-270-5774) Adult album alternative.

KRCB 91.1 FM (Santa Rosa, 707-585-8522) National Public Radio and classical music.

TELEVISION

There's only one local station in all of Wine Country. **KFTY, Channel 50,** broadcasts from 533 Mendocino Ave., Santa Rosa (707-526-5050). Depending on your location, San Francisco and Oakland stations are often within range as well.

Both counties have access to cable television that offers most Bay Area and Sacramento TV channels, as well as the usual cable fare such as CNN, HBO, USA Network. **Viacom** services both the city of Napa (707-255-0300) and Petaluma (707-763-9800). **Post-Newsweek** supplies cable to Santa Rosa (707-544-7337) and **Multivision** services the city of Sonoma (707-996-8482) and Sebastopol (707-584-4617). **ML Media** hooks into St. Helena (707-963-7121).

REAL ESTATE

Buying a piece of the American Dream — real estate — is downright costly for Californians. In fact, for some it is a nightmare. But if you come to Wine Country and decide to stay, here is information that may help you.

Housing costs in Sonoma and Napa are among the highest in the country. The median price for a house in Napa County, for instance, is $182,500. Following the 1990-1991 recession, prices have remained fairly stable. Whatever the case, most natives won't dicker over price endlessly. They know they're not just purchasing real estate — they're also buying rights to the nearby ocean, the steep mountains, and a tapestry of vineyards in the countryside: a rare combination.

For information on real estate matters, consult the yellow pages of Napa and Sonoma phone books under Real Estate Agents. For insight into the real estate market, call the **Napa Chamber of Commerce** (707-226-7455), the **Napa County Association of Realtors** (707-255-1040), and the **Sonoma County Realtors Association** (707-542-1579). The latter two organizations compile statistics on area real estate. You can also follow the local newspapers. The *Press Democrat*, for instance, has a complete Real Estate section published every Sunday (see "Media" in this chapter).

RELIGIOUS SERVICES & ORGANIZATIONS

The best sources for information about church and synagogue services are the Saturday editions of the *Napa Register* and the *Press Democrat*. The Napa and Sonoma County phone books have comprehensive lists of all mainstream religious organizations along with specific church and synagogue numbers. You can also consult pamphlets put out by the Napa and Sonoma visitors bureaus. For nontraditional groups, keep an eye on community bulletin boards at colleges such as Sonoma State University and Napa Valley College.

ROAD SERVICE

Puncture your tire on a broken bottle of 1986 Jordan Cabernet? Stranger things are known to have happened. For emergency road service from AAA, anywhere in Napa or Sonoma Counties, call (800)-222-4357. Listed below are other 24-hour emergency road services.

Napa County

Calistoga Towing: 707-942-4445
Napa Vintage Towing: 707-226-3780
St. Helena Towing: 707-963-1869

Sonoma County

Pellegrini's Towing: Healdsburg; 707-433-1760
Sebastopol Towing: 707-823-1061
Santa Rosa Towing: 707-542-1600

SCHOOLS

PUBLIC SCHOOL DISTRICTS

Napa County

Calistoga Joint Unified School District: Calistoga; 707-942-4703
Napa County School District: Napa; 707-253-6800
St. Helena Unified School District: St. Helena; 707-967-2708

Sonoma County

Cotati-Rohnert Park Unified School District: Cotati; 707-792-4700
Healdsburg School District: Healdsburg; 707-431-3435
Piner-Olivet Union School District: Santa Rosa; 707-522-3000
Roseland School District: Santa Rosa; 707-545-0102
Santa Rosa School District: Santa Rosa; 707-528-5373
Sonoma Valley Unified School District: Sonoma; 707-935-6000

PRIVATE AND RELIGIOUS SCHOOLS

Napa County

Highlands Christian Preschool: Calistoga; 707-942-5557
Kolbe Academy: Napa; 707-255-6412
St. Helena Montessori School: St. Helena; 707-963-1527
St. John The Baptist Catholic School: Napa; 707-255-3533

Sonoma County

Montessori Pre-School & Elementary School of Santa Rosa: Santa Rosa; 707-539-7980
Open Bible Christian Academy: Santa Rosa; 707-528-0546
Sebastopol Christian School: Sebastopol; 707-823-2754
St. Luke Lutheran Preschool & Day Care Center: Santa Rosa; 707-545-0526
Ursuline High School: Santa Rosa; 707-524-1130

COLLEGES

Napa County

Napa Valley College: Napa; 707-253-3000

Sonoma County

Santa Rosa Junior College: Santa Rosa; 707-527-4011
Empire College, Business School and Law School: Santa Rosa; 707-546-4000
Sonoma State University: Rohnert Park; 707-664-2394

The shady campus of Santa Rosa Junior College.

Courtesy SRJC

TOURIST INFORMATION

Napa County

Calistoga Chamber of Commerce: 707-942-6333; 1458 Lincoln Ave.
Napa Valley Conference and Visitors Bureau: 707-226-7459; 1310 Napa Town
  Center, Napa
St. Helena Chamber of Commerce: 707-963-4456; 1010A Main St.
Yountville Chamber of Commerce: 707-944-0904; 6515 Yount St.

Sonoma County

Healdsburg Chamber of Commerce: 707-433-6935; 217 Healdsburg Ave.
Petaluma Area Chamber of Commerce: 707-762-2785; 799 Baywood Dr.,
  Petaluma
Russian River Region Visitor Information Centers: 707-869-9212; Guerneville
  office, 14034 Armstrong Woods Rd.
Santa Rosa Chamber of Commerce: 707-545-1414; 637 1st St.
Sebastopol Chamber of Commerce: 707-823-3032; 265 S. Main St.
  Sonoma Coast Visitor Information: 707-875-2868; 850 Hwy. 1, Bodega Bay
Sonoma County Convention & Visitors Bureau: 707-586-8100; 5000 Roberts
  Lake Rd., Rohnert Park, Suite A
Sonoma Valley Visitors Bureau: 707-996-1090; 453 1st St. E., Sonoma. A second
  office is now open below Viansa Winery, 25200 Arnold Dr., 707-935-4747

IF TIME IS SHORT

Ideally your visit to the Wine Country should be long enough to include visits to several of the attractions in each category. But if time is of the essence and you find yourself forced to choose just *one* restaurant for dining, or one winery to visit, then perhaps we can help. Here are our personal favorites — with emphasis on the personal. Not everyone might pick these particular spots, but we feel confident you will enjoy them as much as we do.

INNS

Oak Knoll Inn (707-255-2200; 2200 E. Oak Knoll Ave., Napa) An intimate and luxurious inn just north of the city of Napa. The hospitality is exceptional and the breakfasts are among the best in Wine Country.

Inn at Occidental (707-874-1047; 3657 Church St., Occidental) Well off the beaten path but worth it. Perched on a hill overlooking the quiet village of Occidental, this Victorian inn is a jewel.

CULTURAL ATTRACTIONS

The Hess Collection (707-255-1144; 4411 Redwood Dr., Napa) This stylish winery has one of the most impressive art collections north of San Francisco. Plus the wine is superb.

Mission San Francisco Solano (707-938-1519; corner of Spain St. & 1st St. E., Sonoma Plaza, Sonoma) Wine Country history doesn't get any richer than this. Built before 1841, the white adobe with a red-tile roof was the last mission built in California.

RESTAURANTS

Terra (707-963-8931; 1345 Railroad Ave., St. Helena) Chef Hioryoshi Sone is brilliant, pairing the best of Western and Eastern cuisine. The restaurant, with tall arched windows and stone walls, draws locals in-the-know, rather than tourists.

Willowside (707-523-4814; 3535 Guerneville Rd., Santa Rosa) This red roundhouse has a funky atmosphere and great food — hearty fare prepared with flair.

WINERIES

For beginners: **Korbel Champagne Cellars** (707-887-2294; 13250 River Rd., Guerneville) No mystery why visitors flock here. It has everything: rich history, a beautiful locale, a great tour, and lots of bubbly.

For wine buffs: **Opus One** (707-963-1979; 7900 St. Helena Hwy., Oakville) This distinctive winery was largely inaccessible to the public until 1994. You'll still need an appointment. It makes one wine — a block-buster red.

RECREATION

Lazy fun: A *spa treatment* is a must. A one-hour massage with whirlpool bath is Nirvana. (Mud baths, though, aren't for everyone.) Our favorites include **Calistoga Spa Hot Springs, Meadowood Resort** outside St. Helena, and the unique Japanese-style spa **Osmosis** in Occidental.

Real adventure: A *hot air balloon ride* over Wine Country is beautiful and exhilarating. See "Ballooning" in Chapter Seven, *Recreation,* for details and suggested companies. For high adventure, try Calistoga Gliders Inc. (707-942-5000; 1546 Lincoln Ave., Calistoga) for a *glider ride* that floats on thermals like an eagle. Don't worry, a pilot is included.

Index

LODGING BY PRICE: INNS, B&Bs

Price Codes
Inexpensive: Up to $75
Moderate: $75 to $125
Expensive: $125 to $175
Very Expensive: Over $175

Napa County

INEXPENSIVE
Calistoga Inn
Nance's Hot Springs
Silverado Motel

INEXPENSIVE–MODERATE
Calistoga Spa Hot Springs
Dr. Wilkinson's Hot Springs
Golden Haven Hot Springs and Resort
Hideaway Cottages
The Webber Place
White Sulphur Springs Resort

INEXPENSIVE–EXPENSIVE
Calistoga Village Inn and Spa
El Bonita Motel
John Muir Inn
La Residence Country Inn

MODERATE
Brookside Vineyard
Burgundy House
Culver's Country Inn
Larkmead Country Inn
Napa Valley Railway Inn
Pine Street Inn and Eurospa
Rose Garden Inn
Quail Mountain B&B

MODERATE–EXPENSIVE
Ambrose Bierce House
Arbor Guest House
Beazley House
Bordeaux House

MODERATE–EXPENSIVE
Camellia Inn
Campbell Ranch Inn
Doubletree Hotel
El Dorado Hotel
The Farmhouse Inn
The Gables
George Alexander House
Glenelly Inn
Haydon Street Inn
Hidden Oak
Ridenhour Ranch House Inn
River's End
Sonoma Valley Inn, Best Western
Thistle Dew Inn
Trojan Horse Inn
Victorian Garden Inn

MODERATE–VERY EXPENSIVE
Applewood
Bodega Bay Lodge

Gaige House Inn
Holiday Inn (Bodega Bay)
Inn at Occidental
Inn at the Tides
Raford House Inn
Red Lion Hotel
Vintners Inn

EXPENSIVE
Healdsburg Inn on the Plaza
Sea Ranch Lodge

EXPENSIVE–VERY EXPENSIVE
Belle de Jour Inn
Madrona Manor
Timber Cove Inn

VERY EXPENSIVE
Kenwood Inn and Spa
Sonoma Mission Inn and Spa
Timberhill Ranch

RESTAURANTS BY PRICE

Price Codes
Inexpensive	up to $10
Moderate	$10 to $22
Expensive	$22 to $35
Very Expensive	$35 or more

Napa County

MODERATE
All Season's Café
Boskos Ristorante
The Diner
The Grill at Meadowood
Frankie, Johnnie and Luigi Too
Mustards Grill
Pairs Parkside Café
Rutherford Grill
Spring Street Restaurant

MODERATE–EXPENSIVE
Bistro Don Giovanni
Catahoula Restaurant and Saloon
Ristorante Piatti
Wappo Bar and Bistro

EXPENSIVE
Brava Terrace
Brix
Calistoga Inn
Napa Valley Grille
Pinot Blanc
Showley's at Miramonte
Terra
Tra Vigne
Trilogy
Wine Spectator Greystone Restaurant

PRIX-FIXE
The French Laundry

RESTAURANTS BY CUISINE

For your convenience, we list here restaurants serving specific cuisines. Those places serving more than one type of cuisine are listed under more than one category.

About the Authors

Chad Surmick

Forsaking corn for grapes, Tim Fish and Peg Melnik moved from the Midwest to Sonoma County in 1989. Fish is Food and Wine Editor for the Santa Rosa *Press Democrat* and was previously the Arts and Entertainment critic for the *New York Times*-owned daily. Melnik is the editor of *MelnikNotes*, a parenting newsletter.

Fish was raised in Indiana and while earning his journalism degree at Western Kentucky University, he won *Rolling Stone* magazine's college journalism award and was an intern at *Forbes* magazine in New York City. He has worked at daily newspapers in Kentucky, Illinois, and Ohio.

Melnik earned a degree in English education at the University of Illinois and followed that with a masters degree in public affairs reporting. Melnik has worked for daily newspapers in Iowa and Ohio and her freelance credits include the *Los Angeles Times, San Francisco Chronicle*, and the *Boston Herald*.

Married since 1986, Fish and Melnik have a daughter, Sophie, born in June 1991, a week before the deadline of the first edition.